MANAGING
TEENS
with ADHD

GRAD L. FLICK, Ph.D.

D1566898

**THE CENTER FOR APPLIED
RESEARCH IN EDUCATION**
West Nyack, New York 10994

Library of Congress Cataloging-in-Publication Data

Flick, Grad L.
    Managing teens with ADHD : practical tools & strategies for dealing with
difficult behaviors / Grad L. Flick.
            p. cm.
    Includes bibliographical references and index.
    ISBN 0–13–014809–1
        1. Attention-deficit disorder in adolescence—Patients—Care. 2. Attention-deficit
hyperactivity disorder—Patients—Care. 3. Behavior therapy for teenagers. I. Title.

RJ506.H9 F624 2000
616.85'00835—dc21

                                                                                    99-052693

© 2000 *by* The Center for Applied Research in Education

Acquisitions Editor: *Susan Kolwicz*
Production Editor: *Mariann Hutlak*
Interior Design & Composition: *Dee Coroneos*

Printed in the United States of America

10 9 8 7 6 5 4 3 2 1

ISBN 0-13-014809-1

**THE CENTER FOR APPLIED RESEARCH
IN EDUCATION**
West Nyack, NY 10994

www.phdirect.com

DEDICATION

This book is dedicated to our grandson, Jordan—
may his challenges of life be filled with wonderment and joy.

ACKNOWLEDGMENTS

I wish to recognize the contributions of many special individuals for their assistance and influence in the production of this book. First, my wife and partner in business, Alma Flick, Ph.D., who contributed to the writing of Chapter Four on parenting styles. Alma, who has an MSW Degree in Social Work and a Doctor of Philosophy degree in clinical counseling, has collaborated on behavioral counseling in private practice, and who not only shared her expertise in workshop presentations, but also shared experiences in raising our son, Marcus (who grew up with ADHD). Her enduring love and support over the past 35 years of marriage has been a true source of inspiration.

I am indebted to my long-time friend, Nina Roland, who served as reader, critic, and consultant. I have called upon her assistance many times in years past; she has always been a great help contributing to clarity and focus in these projects.

Many thanks go out to my primary typist, Angela Johnson. Despite her many projects she has always shown great efficiency in her work. Thanks also go to secondary typists Paula Trawick, Danette Roberts, Tina Koval, Carla Sirmon, and Elise Everette. Much appreciation goes to Leah Triplett for help with scheduling appointments and to her 16-year-old daughter, Sara Triplett, who offered clerical assistance as well as comments from a teenager's perspective. I am also grateful to Cindy King, R.N., who not only assists with patient care, but also offers many helpful comments.

Special thanks go to Kevin Passer, M.D., and David Dugger, M.D., who read and offered critical and constructive comments on the medication section. Deepest thanks and appreciation also go to Vincent Lancon who serves as programmer for several special computer training programs, and to Jerry Maddux for help with computer operations. Appreciation is noted for our newly appointed office manager, Kristy Holston.

Last, I express my deepest appreciation and recognition to my editor, Susan Kolwicz, for her pertinent technical advice and support throughout this project. She has always responded to requests and has given relevant feedback when needed. I also would like to give recognition to my publisher, Win Huppuch, who has been a pleasure to meet and work with.

ABOUT THE AUTHOR

Grad L. Flick received his Ph.D. in Clinical Psychology from the University of Miami in 1969 with APA-approved internship at the University of Florida Medical Center. A licensed psychologist since 1971, Dr. Flick has specializations in neuropsychology and applied psychophysiology. He has been certified in stress management and employee assistance, and he has Fellow and Diplomatic status from the American Board of Medical Psychotherapists. He has also held positions in psychology at the University of New Orleans and Louisiana State University School of Medicine, and has served as consultant to several hospitals in the New Orleans and Mississippi Gulf Coast area. Since 1971, he has been in private practice and is currently director of Seacoast Psychological Associates, Inc. Dr. Flick and his wife, Alma L. Flick, Ph.D., specialize in the evaluation and treatment of children, adolescents, and adults with Attention Deficit Disorder, and other learning and behavioral problems. Dr. Grad Flick is also director of the ADD Clinic, which offers year-round programs for children, adolescents, and adults, as well as behavioral and cognitive therapies, and traditional and group therapies. A Summer Camp and summer program for children with ADD/ADHD are also offered.

Dr. Flick, who is currently Adjunct Professor at the University of Southern Mississippi Regional Gulf Park Campus in Long Beach has numerous publication credits, has conducted many workshops for both parents and teachers on ADD, and has given lectures to various parent and teacher organizations on ADD and Child Management. He is the author of *Power Parenting for Children with ADD/ADHD: A Practical Parent's Guide for Managing Difficult Behaviors* (The Center for Applied Research in Education, 1996), *ADD/ADHD Behavior-Change Resource Kit* (The Center for Applied Research in Education, 1997), and *Managing Difficult Behavior in the Classroom: A Pocket Guide for Teachers* (Seacoast Publications, 1999). He has over 28 years' experience in both research and clinical practice with children who present attentional, learning, and/or behavioral disorders. Drs. Grad and Alma Flick have also parented a child with learning disability and Attention Deficit Hyperactivity Disorder.

ABOUT THIS BOOK

Over the past twenty years, numerous books and articles have been written about Attention Deficit Disorders in children. However, there has been a dearth of materials addressing the needs of adolescents with ADHD. This book will provide a resource for teachers and parents bringing together information on the current state of knowledge regarding attention deficit disorders in adolescents, along with established techniques to deal with their problematic behaviors. This book will be of interest to teachers who must cope with problems of the teen with ADHD in the classroom, as well as for parents of teens with ADHD who are faced with their behaviors at home. This book will also be of interest to those professionals who deal with teenagers with ADHD in clinical situations. Physicians, psychiatrists, psychologists, social workers, counselors, and other mental health workers will be given a better general understanding of the behaviors of teens with ADHD and how they develop; they will learn how to promote strategies and techniques for dealing with those behaviors in their respective situations. Given the relative paucity of books addressing this developmental segment of ADHD behaviors, the current work will represent a pioneering effort on which to build and extrapolate future assessment and treatment programs. Here you will find information about positive interventions; about family issues, social problems, educational challenges, strategies and training; about preparation for adulthood; and resources and support networks.

Chapter One presents a general review of current facts and concepts regarding ADHD, beginning with a description of the basic criteria used to document the ADHD diagnosis. It is important to emphasize that while a simple descriptive term will be used throughout this book (i.e., ADHD), there are subtypes of ADHD—some with hyperactivity and some without. This chapter elaborates on various associated ADHD characteristics and the biological basis for the behaviors. There is a discussion of the developmental characteristics of ADHD behaviors, which are perhaps first exhibited in childhood, and how these behaviors evolve to their usual manifestations during adolescence. Many changes occur over this growth period and the symptomatic pattern described in DSM-IV must be modified to account for these developmental changes with age. Finally, this chapter addresses the specific needs of adolescents with ADHD. These needs result from specific characteristics of ADHD problem behaviors which are seen in addition to the usual problems of adolescents.

Chapter Two focuses on the assessment of ADHD in adolescents. As with children, family history and developmental information are critical factors in the assessment of ADHD in teens. In addition, rating scales are also completed by both parents and teachers during the typical assessment process; there are also some specific rating scales which provide information about ADHD for certain developmental stages. Some common psychological and neuropsychological tests will focus primarily on those issues involved in "ruling out" or "ruling in" various co-morbid or mimic conditions. Basic ability and achievement tests, as well as other tests assessing visual–motor, visual–spatial, and fine motor coordination are covered. In addition, self-report inventories are available and allow the adolescent to contribute to a greater degree to the diagnostic process. Adolescents can offer a great deal of information, not only with regard to their own self assessment, but also may influence decisions on treatment options which offer the greatest potential for success. By early adolescence, most teens have command over a number of specific skills which have been developed over the years; but teens with ADHD, who are generally immature, may exhibit obvious deficiencies in such skill areas as organization and time management, to name just two. Consequently, an analysis of skill deficits is quite helpful in preparing future prescriptive recommendations for the young adult in question. Appropriate diagnosis and effective treatment planning depend also on a clear understanding of numerous co-morbid and mimic conditions which occur alongside ADHD throughout the developmental life cycle. Such various disorders appear to surface in conjunction with ADHD or may evolve from it. Consideration of these important conditions is critical for treatment planning for the ADHD teen. Most treatment programs are based more on assessment of problematic behavior than on specific diagnostic categories.

The third chapter discusses various medical and clinical interventions used with ADHD adolescents, stressing the importance of a symptomatic or problem-oriented approach to treatment. Consequently, if the ADHD adolescent also exhibits co-morbid condition(s), the severity of each such condition must be assessed so treatment can be directed towards dealing with each component in order of its impact. Quite often, besides ADHD behavior, there are several other conditions which may need to be treated, including depression (which is fairly common for ADHD teens), anxiety, oppositional disorders, conduct disorders, obsessive–compulsive disorders, or bipolar disorders. Thus, the concept of multiple impact therapies is presented, discussing how each component of the overall clinical picture can be addressed by specific problem-oriented treatment approaches. The overall clinical picture of the ADHD adolescent is generally complex and more severe; high impact therapy involving several components is therefore most beneficial. Axillary issues, such as the difficulty teens often present in taking medications, are addressed. Fairly comprehensive information is presented, although it is not meant to supplement personal medication consultation with the teen's physician. Specific medication issues for teens are discussed, since there is often a need for adjusted doses of medication and even different medications as the child with ADHD grows up. Those ADHD teens who exhibit less severe behavioral characteristics of ADHD may benefit greatly from "coaching." Coaching strategies can be used to address problems centering around organizational behavior, time management, long- and short-range planning, and general coping skills. Since many teens have much difficulty accepting the idea of "therapy" for their problems, there appears to be a greater general acceptance of the idea of coaching; the "coaching" concept is generally well understood with regard to its use in sporting activities. Many teens with ADHD may also greatly profit from a small group-oriented processing format to learn strategies and techniques for dealing with their problematic behaviors. Within such a small group setting, there is obviously less threat and better acceptance of this classroom format educational orientation program. Additionally, the use of an intense summer camp experience is discussed. The camp focuses on a strong behavioral component with follow-up sessions year round. This type of experience has proven quite beneficial in modifying some resistant and difficult to manage behavior. Research reports on such camps have been quite positive and their application for teens with ADHD appears to be beneficial. The use of skill training for attentional and other problems of the ADHD teen is discussed. Such programs appear to help in addressing problems of skill generalization and these skills are obviously critical for the teen with ADHD. Other therapeutic interventions are explored, including parent and teacher behavioral training, direct training of compulsive behavior, family therapy approaches, and the use of therapeutic prosthetics or assistive devices that help the teen with ADHD deal with problematic behavior.

Chapter Four presents family issues regarding the ADHD teen. Specific needs assessment regarding family issues provides the basic structure on which problematic behaviors may be modified. Various parenting styles are noted with regard to their impact on the developmental characteristics of ADHD. General parenting strategies are presented, which consider the teenager's need to be involved in decisions on discipline, as well as his or her need for greater independence in functioning. This discussion also includes a detailed focus on problem solving and conflict resolution techniques.

Educational issues for teens with ADHD are discussed in Chapter Five; this begins with a survey of various problems and concepts regarding educational issues. There is a summary of the current state of the Individuals with Disabilities Education Act (IDEA) and 504 regulations and their implications for Individualized Education Plans (IEP). School discipline is also covered. Accommodations in and out of the classroom are considered with focus on parents, teachers, and the teen. Since many adolescents with ADHD are deficient in school-related skills, there is focus on study strategies, organizational skills, test taking, and mnemonics. Various strategies and techniques are offered for the teachers to assist in the development of skills in these various areas; homework difficulties are given considerable emphasis. Self-esteem issues are especially critical during this adolescent period of development and techniques for promoting and maintaining adequate self-esteem are discussed. As an option to regular school placement, home-schooling is explored for specific pros and cons. In addition, since many adolescents with ADHD have encountered failure in their academic endeavors, the impact of these failures and grade retention is discussed, along with their impact on self-concept and self-esteem.

Beyond these educational issues, Chapter Six reviews classroom and home behavior management for ADHD teens. Consistent with treatment at earlier developmental levels, a generally positive behavioral orientation is adopted. For parents, home behavioral interventions are discussed, focusing on basic behavior management: behavior contracts, behavior penalty, grounding, positive practice, point systems, behavioral momentum, and positive response programs. For classroom teachers in both regular and special classes, specific strategies for dealing with inappropriate ADHD teen behavior are discussed. In addition, there is a review of special management techniques focusing on the typical ADHD symptoms, including hyperactivity, restlessness or excess talking, distractibility, impulsivity, and others. General classroom behavior management may be made even more effective by collaborating with parents and other persons significant to the teenager in question. Innovative use of student-mediated conflict resolution outside of the classroom is also explored, primarily for those disruptive behaviors outside of the classroom.

Chapter Seven discusses specific social problems of teens with ADHD, focusing first on peer relations and the teen's concerns about peer acceptance and rejection—issues which are magnified for the adolescent with ADHD. Another significant area of adolescent development involves the heterosexual relations or dating behavior. Then, issues concerning acceptance and rejection in heterosexual relations (or dating) are discussed, including how the characteristics of ADHD affect developing relationships. Other typical problem areas during adolescence involve such things as gang behavior and violence, which are explored with regard to ADHD and other co-morbid disorders. Delinquent antisocial teen behavior is analyzed with these diagnostic entities in mind. Various types of criminal activities are discussed and the relationship between ADHD and such delinquent antisocial behaviors noted. Since such behavior involving delinquent or antisocial acts have sometimes been found to be associated with ADHD, the frequencies of such behaviors are reported along with their etiologies. The use of alcohol, drugs, and other addictive substances is also discussed as potential problems for teens with ADHD. Last, the contribution of self-esteem issues is noted with regard to the social skills or lack thereof in the adolescent years.

Preparing for adulthood with ADHD is discussed in Chapter Eight with focus on vocational/occupational issues. Likewise, the influence of ADHD on adolescents' potential level of abilities, achievements, and behavior are also discussed with an orientation towards future involvement in either job, military, or school activities. Many problematic ADHD behaviors of childhood may actually evolve into behaviors that become assets for the adolescent or adult with ADHD. However, continuing problems around self-concept and self-esteem may affect adult vocational and occupational status. An interview is presented with a resilient adult who has ADHD and recalls some of the issues encountered during the teenage years, along with the pain, suffering, frustration, anger, and depression that were experienced. A report of a successful adult entertainer provides some added support for ADHD characteristics becoming an asset for some occupations.

Chapter Nine's primary focus is on sources of support for the adolescent with ADHD. Many significant people in the adolescent's life can be quite helpful during this difficult period of development, and can help the adolescent specifically with his symptomatic ADHD behavior. Many adolescents who make the necessary adjustments and who go on to become successful adults often pay significant tribute to a teacher, a parent, or a friend who showed special understanding and guidance with their problems and who helped them in some way to manage those behaviors.

In Chapter Ten, various resources are discussed which the adolescent may utilize to cope with ADHD behavior. Obviously these resources include books, magazines, tapes, and videos about ADHD. In addition, some unique applications involving computers and other electronic assist devices are explored. There are also personal resources as noted in a segment on "inner-personal support." In contrast, inter-personal support involves utilization of assistance from various other significant persons in the adolescent's life, like peer groups and activities involving peers, as well as advisors and coaches. Last, much benefit may be obtained from direct learning with the so-called "hands-on" activities. This type of "apprenticeship training" may certainly obviate the need for extensive reading or writing as such activities would be closely supervised during an "apprenticeship" with direct feedback from a supervisor or a significant other. In short, there are many opportunities for "on–the–job" training for those with ADHD. It is perhaps encouraging and motivating to learn about others who have encountered such difficulties in their lives, yet have succeeded in overcoming various obstacles. Biographies of significant adults with ADHD are therefore listed as an additional resource for the adolescent with ADHD.

At the end of the book are appendices which include: (a) a handout for teens on questions about ADHD, (b) a handout for parents and teachers on understanding and managing ADHD in the teen years, and (c) information on legal rights for persons with ADHD. A 12-step program is outlined for parents and teachers. Complete diagnostic criteria for ADHD and frequent co-morbid conditions of conduct disorder and oppositional defiant disorder are included. A personal guide for teens with ADHD is provided. For clinicians there is an overview of clinical procedures and a protocol for an intake interview. Permission to copy and distribute handouts is noted for each section. Resources for parents, teachers, clinicians, and teens are also listed. These include books, videos, support groups, and internet resources that may be of assistance in coping with ADHD in teens.

Grad L. Flick

CONTENTS

Chapter 3
MEDICAL AND CLINICAL INTERVENTIONS
FOR ADOLESCENT ADHD • 63

Chapter 4
FAMILY ISSUES FOR TEENS WITH ADHD • 117

Chapter 5
EDUCATIONAL ISSUES FOR ADHD TEENS • 147

Chapter 6
BEHAVIOR MANAGEMENT FOR ADHD TEENS
AT HOME AND IN SCHOOL • 191

Chapter 7
SOCIAL PROBLEMS OF TEENS WITH ADHD • 263

Chapter 8
PREPARING FOR ADULTHOOD WITH ADHD • 277

Chapter 9
NETWORK OF SUPPORT • 287

Chapter 10
RESOURCES FOR TEENS WITH ADHD • 295

APPENDICES • 303

RESOURCES • 389

INDEX • 411

Chapter 1

WHAT IS ADD/ADHD?

Before addressing some of the basic characteristics of ADHD, it will be helpful to look at a few relevant statistics regarding ADD/ADHD. For this introductory section, the terms ADD and ADHD will be used. ADD has generally referred to a milder expression of one of the Attention Deficit Disorders, i.e., without hyperactivity. Thereafter, the simple term ADHD will be used throughout the remainder of the book.

DESCRIPTIVE STATISTICAL OVERVIEW OF ADD/ADHD

⮕ These disorders affect roughly 3% to 5% of all school-age children. Range 1–10%. Roughly 3.5 million youngsters have ADHD.

⮕ Most reports indicate a ratio of 3 or 4 boys to each girl affected. Range of sex ratio from 3:1 to 9:1.

⮕ Rates of ADHD in other cultures have been estimated. In New Zealand (2–6.7%); Germany (8.7%); Japan (7.7%); and in China (8.9%).

⮕ According to a study by Dr. Biederman and colleagues, the ADHD group had co-morbid CD (22%), ODD (65%), Major Depressive Disorder (29%), Bipolar Disorder (11%), various Anxiety Disorders (27%), Tic Disorders (17%), and Enuresis (30%).

⮕ There is a 25% to 35% chance that if one member in a family has ADHD, other family members may have it.

⮕ About 25% of the students with ADHD are retained a grade.

⮕ About 33% of the students with ADHD may fail to graduate from high school.

⮕ About 25% to 30% of older adolescents and adults develop problems with substance abuse and drugs.

➠ Roughly 75% to 80% of all those with ADHD respond to stimulant medication.

➠ Up to 40% of all referrals to mental health centers involve ADHD (from Barkley, 1995).

➠ Many with ADHD have serious problems:

about 20% have set fires

about 30% have engaged in theft

about 40% tried tobacco and alcohol at an early age

about 25% have been expelled from high school for misconduct

➠ Teens with ADHD are four times more likely to have serious auto accidents, and three times more likely to be cited for speeding.

➠ General outcomes (Flick, 1998) suggest that about 20% manifest no problems as adults, about 60% of adults show mild to moderate problems, and about 20% of adults manifest serious emotional or conduct problems.

BASIC CHARACTERISTICS OF ADHD

ADHD represents a variety of attention deficit disorders, ranging from the milder condition without hyperactivity (ADD or ADHD without hyperactivity—primarily inattentive type) to the more severe condition with hyperactivity (ADHD). Again, for brevity, a single term "ADHD" will be used as a general description of all attention deficit disorders. Three subtypes are now (in DSM–IV) defined by three basic characteristics: (1) Inattention, (2) Hyperactivity, and (3) Impulsivity. In addition, a cluster of associated characteristics may include disorganization, poor peer/sibling relations, aggressive behavior, poor self-concept/self-esteem, sensation-seeking behavior, daydreaming, poor coordination, memory problems, persistent obsessive thinking, and inconsistency, the hallmark characteristic.

The basic combinations of the three essential characteristics, along with other associated characteristics, give the attention deficit disorders their almost infinite variation in appearance. ADHD is used to cover both attention deficit disorders and attention deficit/hyperactivity disorders. ADHD is also used interchangeably to represent the complex pattern of all attention deficit disorders. A brief review of the core characteristics of ADHD, along with associated characteristics, follows.

INATTENTION

The most basic trait is a lack of focused attention. It is not that children with ADHD do not attend; *they attend to everything*. All stimuli impinge on their senses with equal potency. Such students appear to satiate quickly on tasks, but because they are easily distracted by all stimuli, they often get off task. There are various factors that can manipulate attention, such as the complexity and potency of external stimuli and/or intrinsic internal factors related to physiological fluctuations in the nervous system. In fact, Zentall (1985) described this trait as an "attentional bias towards novelty" when discussing the tendency of those with ADHD to seek out or be attracted by novel stimuli. Many students have little difficulty focusing in a one-to-one situation; but in a complex environment or noisy classroom, they may have numerous problems with compliance and task performance. Conversely, some children and adolescents may even become distracted by their own internal thoughts and sensations, rather than by external stimuli.

IMPULSIVITY

This core characteristic reflects a general lack of control. Many of these children and adolescents may be aware of right and wrong and may even be able to cite a rule at home or in the classroom; *they simply don't think until after they act.* Because of the impulsive style, children and adolescents in particular, have a higher incidence of accident proneness. This characteristic is also manifested when these children and adolescents so often interrupt and talk over others or blurt out answers in class; they may also have a characteristically short fuse, explosively venting anger. These are the children and adolescents who begin work on projects before getting all the directions, and rush through their work making many careless errors. Socially, they may have much difficulty taking turns and trouble with rule-governed behavior that games often require. These children and adolescents also learn very slowly from their mistakes. Since their behavior is primarily reflexive, they are generally unaware of how they get into trouble. Dr. Robin (1998) has divided impulsivity into three separate components: (1) Behavioral Impulsivity—where the teen must have things right now; (2) Cognitive Impulsivity—where the teen might rush through school work; and (3) Emotional Impulsivity—where the teen might become easily frustrated, agitated, moody, and/or emotionally overactive.

HYPERACTIVITY

This core characteristic is perhaps the most salient one. Some mothers have even noted that hyperactivity was present before birth. Although most young children are active, the truly hyperactive behavior may not be recognized until the child is placed in a situation that requires some self-control of movement, typically when the child enters preschool or kindergarten. Children with ADHD are likely to be described as restless, finding it hard to settle down into a quiet activity, and thus having much difficulty with quiet reading or nap time. Their behavior is described as "driven" as they go from one thing to another, becoming easily bored and satiated on one task and moving to other tasks for increased stimulation. Enhanced self-stimulation includes such things as humming or making noise, lots of talking, and more overt motor activity such as running around the classroom (more characteristic of young children with ADHD).

Compared with the behaviors of a normal child, many of these behaviors cannot be ignored. Fortunately, during adolescence there is usually a significant decrease in overt activity; many teens do, however, continue to show restlessness (e.g., a swinging foot or tapping a pencil) or excess talking.

ADDITIONAL CHARACTERISTICS

While the triad of characteristics (inattention, impulsivity, and hyperactivity) is often used to describe the basic ADHD symptom picture and defines the three basic sub-types, there are a number of associated characteristics that contribute to the individuality and almost infinite variation of clinical patterns of ADHD.

DISORGANIZATION

This characteristic may be manifested either in the child's physical appearance or in the way he keeps track of important things or both. Lack of organization and planning are often seen in those children and adolescents who wait until the last minute (i.e., procrastinate) to prepare for projects and tests. Some children may later overcompensate for this disorganization, developing an obsessive–compulsive routine to promote order in later childhood or during adolescence.

POOR PEER/SIBLING RELATIONS

Many children and adolescents with ADHD often misread social cues and impulsively exhibit socially inappropriate behaviors, for example, blurting out something insulting to others, or blatantly intruding on others' games or activities. Then these children and adolescents may be perceived as bossy and intrusive. While some of these children with ADHD adapt and change their behaviors somewhat over the years, these interactive difficulties in relationships may resurface as new social adjustments are required during adolescence.

AGGRESSIVE BEHAVIOR

This characteristic generally contributes to a long-term negative outcome for the child with ADHD. When aggressive behavior is associated with ADHD, there is a poorer prognosis for outcome. When aggressiveness is combined with ADHD, it is more difficult to deal with this condition and to manage the child's behavior. Aggressive behavior often signifies the presence of a co-morbid condition, such as oppositional–defiant disorder or conduct disorder.

POOR SELF-CONCEPT AND SELF-ESTEEM

Children with ADHD are very sensitive emotionally as well as neurologically to their difficulties and failures. Besides their personal frustration and awareness of failure, these children often experience harsh criticism and considerable negative feedback from peers, siblings, and, unfortunately, at times, from adults as well. Self-perceptions are poor and over time these children may become increasingly more doubtful about their ability to cope with academic and social situations during adolescence. They often feel vulnerable, inadequate, and, at times, even quite depressed.

SENSATION-SEEKING BEHAVIOR

Most children with ADHD are in a state of low arousal and seek out more stimulation than would be forthcoming from typical hyperactive behavior. Especially true during the teenage years, they will seek out forms of excitement that can be dangerous. Sensation-seeking behaviors can range from quite dangerous activities to those that simply stimulate the child or adolescent to allow him to deal more adequately with a situation that is perceived as "boring" (e.g., the classroom).

DAYDREAMING

This characteristic, too, is associated with an underlying low level of arousal. Basically in a sleepy state, in class or in some other "boring" situation, the child or adolescent slips easily into a dreamlike activity or daydreaming. This state is quite consistent with the degree of activation in the brain, and when many of these ADHD students are unmedicated, there is a tendency to fall asleep in class. Creating some type of excitement by getting out of the seat, disturbing the class, or engaging in clowning behavior may thus represent the child's or adolescent's attempt to adapt to such an underlying "sleepy state."

POOR COORDINATION

Many children have difficulty with fine-motor tasks, especially handwriting. As written assignments become more frequent, the child's attempts at control often break down and the child may characteristically show a progressive deterioration of handwriting. These children and adolescents with ADHD often show a number of "battle scars" from various accidents associated with poor coordination combined with impulsivity. While many of these children and adolescents may have trouble with fine-motor coordination, many others excel in gross-motor coordination and may become quite competent in some sport.

MEMORY PROBLEMS

This characteristic reflects a particular difficulty with working memory, i.e., the one that is active and relevant for short periods of time when one has to remember to bring the right key to unlock a door or to remember a statement when it is his turn to speak. Other examples might include forgetting things in daily routines, such as books or needed tools for a project.

PERSISTENT OBSESSIVE THINKING

This characteristic implies that the child and younger adolescent may get an idea in his mind and have difficulty letting it drop. For example, after being told "no," he may continue to request that his parents buy him something in a store. This problem seems to be intimately associated with difficulty in reading or misreading social cues. Essentially, he simply does not get the message from the parent, even after numerous repetitions of saying "no" or providing answers.

INCONSISTENCY

This is, perhaps, the hallmark characteristic of ADHD. Basically, the child or adolescent is described by his parents and teachers as having "good" or "bad" days. On some days, he may complete all of his assigned work; on others, none. At times he may be cooperative; at other times, angry and defiant. He is most always moody. Many of these problems are also associated with transitions. Significant changes in the family, such as separation or divorce, a significant move, changing schools, or even minor changes, such as resetting the clock forward or backward, may bring about some problematic behavior. The teen with ADHD will adapt best when activities are structured, when he is given immediate feedback on his performance, and when motivation is maximized utilizing effective manipulation of consequences.

POSSIBLE CAUSES OF ADHD

Although inattentive types of ADHD may not be noticed during the teenage years, the hyperactive component is typically first noticed at an early age when the child begins school. Difficulty adjusting to the demands in the school setting is often the characteristic trigger. Most children and adolescents with ADHD have inherited this condition from his or her parents. It is now generally accepted that ADHD is a genetic disorder, which has some definite neurobiological correlates. While all of the neurophysiological and neuroanatomical components are not fully known, there is increasing evidence for involvement of neurotransmitters in the brain and some subcortical neural structures. In short, many professionals now consider this disorder as a neurobiological condition with complex behavioral correlates. It is also generally agreed that this condition is a lifelong one that presents varying challenges from infancy through adulthood. It is also generally agreed that there is almost an infinite variety of clinical manifestations of the ADHD patterns with combinations of basic and associated characteristics that vary in their presence and in their degree.

BIOLOGICAL BASIS FOR ADHD

Over the past 25 years, much has been learned about the neurobiological basis for ADHD, beginning with the early work of Satterfield and Dawson on psychophysiological parameters, up to the current work on Brain Imaging. Integration of research from several disciplines, including genetic studies, neuroanatomical evidence, and neuropsychological findings all point to strong biological bases for ADHD that has a genetic cause.

GENETIC EVIDENCE

A comprehensive review by Lily Hechtman, M.D., suggested a genetic component for ADHD based on studies of twins, adopted children, and children in families where there is a history of ADHD. Adoption studies support a genetic linkage. Likewise, family studies suggest that confounding of ADHD with conduct disorder may be associated with greater related pathology in parents. Faraone and associates showed that the risk of a child having an antisocial disorder is much higher if the first-degree relative has conduct or oppositional disorders.

However, there have been numerous criticisms and obvious limitations of these studies. Specifically, family studies must often depend upon reliable recall by participants and most of these cases may be biased with regard to selectivity factors. For example, more severe cases of ADHD may come to medical centers where these studies are conducted. Twin studies are limited in that results are difficult to generalize to non-twins. In addition, twins have increased prenatal risk and the shared fetal environment. Adoption studies also reflect a selectivity bias in that adoptive parents are often screened out for psychopathology, but with adopted children there may be unknown factors associated with poor prenatal care, low birth weight, diet, and so on.

In molecular genetic approaches, an excellent candidate gene has been discovered. Irwin Wallman and others found preferential transmission of the Dopamine transporter 10-copy allele in ADHD combined type, which was not found with the basically inattentive type (ADD). In summary, genetic tests (when developed) may still not replace the behavioral criteria that are now used to diagnose ADHD. However, these genetic tests may help to clarify and subtype ADHD patterns, and may eventually lead to novel and more specific treatments.

NEUROANATOMICAL EVIDENCE

In 1987, Mirky noted that attention has distinct and separate aspects including: focusing, executing, sustaining, and shifting. He indicated that each of these aspects of attention may involve different but interconnected regions of the brain that form a system. Problems with different aspects of attention may thus depend on where in this system of brain the damage or dysfunction occurs.

Likewise, Flick, using the model of attentional processes formulated by Sohlberg and Mateer, states that "a child may have one or more of these difficulties (in focused, sustained, selective, alternating, and divided attention), and there may be different complex neurobiological correlates for each condition." Numerous areas of the brain have been implicated as noted in a review of the literature. In recent years, technological advances have spawned a new wave of investigations.

In a classic work, Zametkin studied glucose metabolism using positive emission tomography (PET) scans of 25 biological parents of hyperactive children, who gave retrospective histories of childhood hyperactivity. No medications were known to be given to this group in childhood. After normalization of glucose metabolic rates (to minimize individual variation of global glucose metabolism affecting regional metabolism), the premotor and prefrontal cortex (left hemisphere only) showed significantly reduced glucose metabolism. Clearly, this study had methodological difficulties as diagnosis of ADHD in adults was based only on retrospective reports.

As noted by Colby, damage anywhere in the system that provides direct or indirect cortical control over eye movements could produce the oculomotor symptoms found in ADHD. He further points out that "'visual hemi-neglect' is associated with deficits in eye movements." Recent studies indicate that children with ADHD without hyperactivity also show evidence of neglect.

Recent reports by Rapaport on brain-imaging studies at the National Institutes of Mental Health indicate a smaller anterior frontal area and a lack of asymmetry in parts of the basal ganglia (caudate and globus pallidus). In normal children, the right side appears larger than the left; in hyperactive children, there is a lack of this asymmetry. Hyperactives also reportedly have a smaller total cerebral volume.

Predictive studies using these instruments alone have correctly identified, solely by the computer, with about 78-percent accuracy, correct group classification as normal or hyperactive. While these data may not be useful clinically, they are reliable and have been replicated. Dr. Rapaport has postulated that something may happen during early development of the brain of the ADHD child. Subsequent studies looking at those children who were on stimulant medication versus those who were not on stimulant medication revealed similar findings. This indicated that the use of stimulant medication did not affect the asymmetry of the basal ganglia and that this neuroanatomical difference appears to be generally characteristic of the ADHD pattern in males. Similar findings have been reported in females with ADHD.

Additional studies have also revealed more space in the posterior fossa in hyperactive versus normal controls, and MRI studies of brain function while engaged in a reverse Continuous Performance Test (CPT) reveals activation in the prefrontal brain regions that occur during this behavioral inhibition task (i.e., asking the child to refrain from pressing a button only when the target stimulus, the letter X, appears).

Castellanos and colleagues, using the MRI, discovered that normal boys showed a significant asymmetry of the caudate with the right side 3 percent larger than the left, on average. In contrast, ADHD boys showed no asymmetry. Researchers also reported that the right prefrontal brain region was significantly smaller in ADHD boys compared with normals, while the left side was not different from normals. In addition, the globus pallidus was found to be significantly smaller, especially on the right side.

There have also been a number of reports of abnormalities in the corpus callosum. These studies reportedly support Heilman and colleagues' (1991) prediction of right-sided abnormalities of the prefrontal basal ganglia circuit in cases of ADHD. In general, there is apparently a greater degree of dysfunction within the right hemisphere of the brain in ADHD. It is proffered that prior studies showing left-sided differences may have reflected a higher percentage of co-morbid Learning Disability (LD) problems in those cases used.

NEUROPSYCHOLOGICAL EVIDENCE

Chelune noted that the prefrontal regions have reciprocal pathways with the reticular formation and diencephalic structures that mediate arousal and behavioral inhibition to irrelevant stimuli. Comparison of normal controls with children who manifest ADHD symptoms on the Wisconsin Card Sorting Test supported frontal lobe dysfunction in ADHD children. A battery of tests was used that not only looked at frontal lobe functions, but also included a variety of other measures of IQ, reading skills, and verbal memory, as well as an assessment of attentional and impulsivity factors. The postulate, that disturbances in frontal lobe functions may be related to impulse control and responsible for the kind of cognitive impairments typically found with ADHD, was supported. The conclusion was that inability to control, direct, and sustain attention appears as a core deficiency of ADHD and not impulsivity. Additional studies have also revealed deficits in children with ADHD that are compatible with frontal lobe dysfunction.

NEUROCHEMICAL EVIDENCE

Shaywitz and associates were first to propose a dopamine hypothesis for ADHD in 1977. A number of more recent studies support the involvement of dopamine in ADHD.

The noradrenergic system has also been implicated in ADHD. McCraken suggested that stimulant medication increases dopamine release and results in an increase in adrenergic-mediated inhibition of the noradrenergic locus coeruleus. This interpretation allows for combined reaction of both dopamine and norepinephrine systems. There is little evidence for the involvement of serotonin in ADHD. In addition to dopamine and norepinephrine, other neurotransmitters may be involved in ADHD, but may be less important.

Castellanos (1997) has proposed a pathophysiological model of ADHD that is based on central dopaminergic systems and their regulation of prefrontal circuits. He and his colleagues believe that ADHD symptoms, such as hyperactivity and impulsivity, are associated with the relative overactivity of the dopamine circuit (extending from the substantia nigra to the striatum). "This nigral–striatal circuit is tightly regulated by inhibitory auto-receptors as well as by long-distance feedback from the cortex, and slow diffusion of therapeutic doses of stimulants via oral administration is hypothesized to produce a net inhibition of dopaminergic neurotransmission."

Offering an interesting conclusion, Castellanos (1997) notes that the attention paid in this review to pharmacologic effects on neuronal circuits should not be interpreted as implying that ADHD is exclusively treatable with medications. He notes that, "Behavior Modification schedules increase the salience of socially sanctioned responses, thus increasing the likelihood that specific midbrain dopaminergic neurons will be activated, leading to better control of hyperactivity/impulsivity. At the cortical level, coaching cognitive strategies (Graham and Harris, 1996) can assist in the amelioration of executive dysfunction associated with the symptoms of inattention."

In summary, it is clear that ADHD is a complex disorder involving three basic areas of brain functions. First, there is clear frontal lobe influence in the characteristic ADHD symptomology. Within the frontal lobe, the orbitofrontal circuit mediates appropriate emotional responses and control, impulse control, planning, organization, and judgment. There is also difficulty with the modulation of emotions as the person may show rapid mood swings (i.e., emotionally labile). This same area also appears to mediate obsessive–compulsive behaviors.

Second, there is involvement of the posterior parietal lobe, projecting to both frontal and premotor areas, and responsible for intersensory integration. The associated visual–spatial problems affecting reading, math, spelling, writing, right–left orientation problems, drawing difficulty, motor coordination, and some evidence of hemi-neglect may all be linked to the parietal lobe connection.

Third, there is the involvement of the Reticular Activating System (RAS). This appears to be the underlying (subcortical) activation system that drives the cortical areas of the brain so that information may be appropriately processed and stored. Without sufficient activation, the brain would remain in a sleepy under-aroused state. Should the RAS be in an over-aroused state, there would likewise be difficulty in processing information or in functioning. The key factor appears to be one of difficulty with *appropriate activation* at the *appropriate time*. Furthermore, without adequate filtering in the RAS, the person will be distracted by stimuli from both outside (e.g., noise) as well as inside the person (e.g., thoughts).

The limbic system appears to be closely linked to other subcortical centers, as well as to the higher cortical areas of the brain. It is part of the "emotional brain." When dysfunctional, it may be associated with aberrant emotional reactions, disturbed sleep patterns, and impaired stress coping.

In general, there are excitatory and inhibitory mechanisms in the brain. While there is adequate inhibitory control in most persons, when such areas of the brain are deficient, damaged, or poorly developed, this may lead to impulsive acting-out behaviors. There are also clear indications of neurophysiological components as well, since deficits in neurotransmitters have been found. The overall variation in patterns of ADHD behaviors may therefore be related to the complex neuroanatomical and neurophysiological interrelationships. The total biological picture is certainly not complete, but it is becoming increasingly clearer as brain–behavior research continues to focus on this area.

DEVELOPMENTAL CHARACTERISTICS FROM CHILDHOOD TO ADOLESCENCE

Dr. Russell Barkley has stated that up to 80% of school-age children with the diagnosis of ADHD will continue to present symptoms in adolescence and between 30% and 65% will continue to present symptoms into adulthood. Other experts project that up to 80% of children with ADHD will continue to manifest some problems in the future.

THE PRESCHOOL CHILD

Sometimes mothers have reported that they noticed their children were more active before birth. During infancy, the early ADHD pattern may be characterized by unpredictable behavior, shrill crying, irritability, and overactivity. Sleep problems have also been noted as these infants may show only brief periods of quiet sleep. Later on in the preschool years, such children begin to exhibit greater motoric restless behavior, rapid changes in mood, temper tantrums, continued poor sleep, a low tolerance for frustration, and a short attention span. Many of these children also show speech and language problems and are described as more clumsy. They generally experience more difficulty, especially with aggressive behavior, in group settings. As a result, many of these children have problems adapting to the preschool situation.

THE SCHOOL-AGE CHILD

At school age the behavior pattern appears to become worse as these youngsters enter the classroom and are expected to sit quietly, focus on their assigned tasks, and get along with others in the class. Problems are now likely to occur at home and at school. Homework routinely assigned to the children at an early age becomes another potential battlefield. Additionally, these children, who have much difficulty with rule-governed behavior, find both handling chores at home and completing assignments at school difficult. They experience either tolerance or outright rejection from others as social problems tend to increase. Late childhood social conflicts are well established.

Dr. Barkley points out that at between 7 and 10 years of age at least 30% to 50% of the children with ADHD are likely to develop, as well, symptoms of conduct disorder and antisocial behavior, such as lying, petty thievery, and resistance to authority. Twenty-five percent or more may have problems with fighting with other children.

THE ADOLESCENT

During this period of development, it is usual for the ADHD symptom pattern to change, manifested by a noticeable decrease in hyperactivity, yet other problems with attention and impulsivity remain. By adolescence the child may have a history of failures in academic performance (about 58% according to Barkley) as well as marked difficulties in his or her social relations (20% to 30% displaying antisocial behavior according to Barkley). Many of these teenagers in search of acceptance may tend to associate with peers who have similar problems; this often results in the escalation of risk-taking behavior. Teens with ADHD are certainly more subject to peer pressure regarding the use of alcohol or other addictive substances (as many as 30% experimenting with or abusing alcohol and marijuana). Sadly, an estimated 35% of ADHD children quit school. Depression also appears to be more common for ADHD adolescents, along with poor self-concept, low self-esteem, and poor self-confidence, making future success seem unlikely, all of which contribute to their diminished motivation to complete school and to their deep concern about social acceptance.

ADDRESSING THE NEEDS OF ADHD ADOLESCENTS

Before looking specifically at the needs of adolescents with ADHD, let's first consider general adolescent development so as to provide an overall background on which to interpret ADHD characteristics.

GENERAL ADOLESCENCE

Each stage of development presents special tasks and problems. Adolescence is a period of great change, marking a transition from childhood to adult life. During this time, both boys and girls must establish identities as more mature individuals, deciding what kind of role they wish to play in life, and separating from the primary family unit to become independent perhaps with a goal to establish their own family.

Roughly, between 12 to 14 years of age, all children begin to experience physical changes, and some as early as 10 years of age. There is a general increase in awareness of sexual differentiation. Each young adolescent may experience a great deal of self-consciousness about his or her body and/or appearance, and all may become preoccupied with establishing individual sexual identity. During this phase there is much experimentation with different behaviors, including dress, actions, and speech.

There is increasing identity with other young adolescents, increasing competition, and increasing emphasis on peer acceptance. During this early period of adolescence, there is relatively little interest in heterosexual relations. When sexual interest is present, it may simply reflect the young adolescent's power to attract or support his or her own concept of adequacy. During this period, there is a great deal of self-doubt and preoccupation with self, making self-esteem quite precarious. There is also a reluctance to admit to any problems during this period of development. Physical activity often correlates with experienced pain or discomfort.

During this period, the young adolescent experiences an increased intensity of wanting to be both dependent and independent, reflecting the conflicting need for autonomy versus the need for security—being able to seek out and depend on adults when life's problems become overwhelming. There is general difficulty accepting responsibility during this stage. The thought of becoming an adult and the change in perception of the young adolescent by both him- or herself and the adults in his or her life may arouse much confusion and anxiety. Boys may suddenly become sensitive to being male in relation to their female teachers; girls may become provocative with their male teachers and many experience the typical adolescent "crush." Both boys and girls are typically restless, yet boys more so. Conversation is often confused and fragmented. During this time, it is difficult to have conversations without much giggling, touching, horseplay, or acting up. Attention is brief, and the adolescent shows limited ability to handle any anxiety-provoking topic.

Somewhere between 15 and 17 years of age, the adolescent generally is facing decisions that are more adult and have to do with vocational and occupational choices. There is, by this time, increasing independence and generally more intimate relations with the opposite sex. More decisions also tend to center around the management of sexual relations. General interest in members of the same sex, which was more typical of an early phase of adolescence, may become more refined into relationships based on comradeship or competition.

Although the problems surrounding identity are still considerable, these issues are expressed more specifically with regard to what kind of an adult the person is most closely identified with and what role the adolescent is going to play, specifically regarding sexual identity. It is somewhat easier for adolescents during this stage of development to admit to problems and concerns they have about themselves. They are also generally more willing to accept help and are able to sustain focused discussions for longer periods of time. Furthermore, there is less tendency to fluctuate between dependency and independency issues, greater acceptance of responsibility for planning life goals, along with a greater capacity to maintain functioning as an independent adult person.

Adolescents with ADHD will undergo the same physical changes in development as with normal teens. They will also face similar challenges throughout their development. Specifically, teens with ADHD have the same desire for independence, establishing their own identity, learning how to relate to both same and opposite sexes, understanding and coping with their emerging sexuality, and completing their education and/or training for their future vocation, occupation, or job. However, they may, in general, lag behind other teens especially with regard to the assumption of responsibilities that lead toward greater independence and also with regard to their social–emotional development.

The three steps of normal adolescence may be summarized as follows:

1. *Early Adolescence (12–14 years).* During this period, growth and development is rapid. Parental authority and rules are challenged. There is worry about being different from one's peers. "But my friends do it" is often used to justify clothing, dating practices, attending functions, engagement in activities, and grooming. School appears more challenging, both academically and socially. At this time the teen struggles with identity issues and movement toward greater independence.

2. *Middle Adolescence (15–17 years).* Teens now generally spend more time with peers than with family. There is some thinking about the future regarding college, work, or technical training. While teens are most influenced by peers on most issues, parents still retain major influence over their teen about career and educational goals. This period is also marked by increased dating and experimentation—mostly of the risk-taking variety. Complaints about interference with independence also increases during this stage. It is also a time that intellectual interest becomes more important and concerns about sexual attraction, sexual identity, and love interest intensify.

3. *Late Adolescence (18–21 years).* Teens begin college, work, or military life. Parents become accepted more readily and some sharing with them generally returns. More intimate love relationships develop, and more definitive plans for school, work, military, and family life are made. Self-identity strengthens, and problem solving, delay of gratification, verbal experiences, and decision making all improve, while stabilization occurs in social–emotional and vocational interest areas. The teen becomes more outer directed and shows a more mature sense of independence and self-reliance. The capacity to self-regulate self-esteem, to resolve conflicts, to establish and realize goals all appear during this stage.

The typical adolescent is faced with five basic developmental demands. Achieving independence is the primary one, followed by establishing an identity, developing close interpersonal ties, coping with their sexuality, and completing their education/training to decide on a vocation or occupation. Most ADHD teens feel generally inferior to their peers and may actually be deficient or delayed in meeting these five basic developmental demands.

ADOLESCENT ADHD DEVELOPMENT

During early adolescence, between the ages of 12 to 14 years, many teens with ADHD feel quite different from and perhaps already have a lower self-image than other youngsters. Although some teens with ADHD are socially adept, others have personalities that make it difficult for them to relate to others, to listen appropriately, and even to make eye contact. Peer groups allow most teens to look at others their own age for comparative purposes, but the teen with ADHD may look at the peer group from the point of immaturity, exhibiting an inability to relate because of poor social skills and low self-esteem.

Compared with other teens, the teenager with ADHD may be extremely influenced to participate in activities that are age inappropriate (for example, smoking, drinking, sexual activity), especially if these activities seem to enhance their appearance of maturity. When the ADHD student enters middle school, there are often overwhelming challenges. Demands associated with problems in dealing with multiple teachers, and increased requirements for memorization and organization often appear to overwhelm the adolescent with ADHD. Consequently, considerable stress is experienced. Grades are often affected as increased stress and frequent behavioral and emotional difficulties add to the adolescent's problems. While teens with ADHD may outwardly exhibit anger, those without hyperactivity may experience confusion internally.

In general, the teen's ADHD symptoms tend to be exacerbated by stress, appear more pronounced in unstructured situations, and may also be affected by the demands and expectation in various situations. For example, when confronted by a crisis, the teen with ADHD may show a greater overreaction emotionally than the non-ADHD teen, sometimes displaying temporary panic symptom characteristics. During this early adolescent period, it is not atypical for these young teens to show denial, resentment, and mostly an indifferent attitude toward their ADHD diagnosis and/or problems.

During middle adolescence for teens 15 to 17 years of age, there is a growing ability to express thoughts and feelings. However, teens with ADHD are delayed in both cognitive and conceptual skills. While most teenagers are under considerable stress to engage in somewhat risky behavior by their peers, these risks and temptations are further magnified for those teens with ADHD. According to Dr. Joseph Biederman, teens with ADHD are also at increased risk for the development of Bipolar Disorder (BD), where there are highs and lows in mood. In his studies, he found that 11% of the children had BD at the beginning, but four years later 23% had manifested this disorder.

During this middle adolescence period, many teens with ADHD are able to better accept and process information and feedback about their ADHD behavior and diagnosis. However, it is during this period that such awareness results in sadness, grief, and finally relief. The end process of this progressive evolution in coping with ADHD may not have complete closure until the teen reaches near adulthood.

By late adolescence, covering ages 18 to 21, older teens with ADHD may still be struggling with identity issues, trying to manage their environments and to assume more responsibilities. During this period, it is essential that the teen develop the ability to handle responsibility. In general, even older adolescents with ADHD may experience continuing difficulty with sustained attention, poor self-esteem, lack of acceptance by others, and difficulty managing frustration. There is considerable doubt regarding whether their efforts will pay off in terms of better academic performance along with the perception that their school work is difficult and sometimes even impossible. Many doubts abound regarding whether they can handle the material, which at times seems endless. Immaturity continues to plague the student with ADHD well into adulthood.

Sometimes it is quite difficult to identify the student with ADHD because many of the same behaviors and attitudes are also shown by adolescents who do not have ADHD. While it has often been noted that, in children, more males than females have ADHD (ratio of 4:1), according to Dr. Thomas Phelan, the two groups may be equally diagnosed. He believes that females are more likely to be diagnosed at a later age as their symptoms may be more subtle. When they reach adulthood, the numbers of males and females are equal. However, Gordon (1996) has noted that the preponderance of males to females with regard to ADHD characteristics may reflect a kind of "vestigial function" needed by primitive man for survival (i.e., the broad open focus and quick reactions were adaptive behaviors). Thus, he has described ADHD as a "male thing."

Some of the characteristic problems for the adolescent are compared to how these same issues appear for adolescents with ADHD:

1. *Impulsivity.* In general, most adolescents have trouble with this issue. The adolescent with ADHD experiences greater difficulty and has more frequent problems with impulsive behavior.

2. *Daydreaming.* Again, many teenagers experience this difficulty but the frequency and intensity of this problem is certainly greater in the adolescent with ADHD.

3. *Disorganization.* During early adolescence, students have many adjustments to make; over time this improves. However, for the adolescent with ADHD, there is constant and continuing difficulty keeping track of books and papers, arranging complicated schedules, dealing with multiple teacher expectations, and planning long-term projects and assignments. Teachers often comment that this is one of the major problems for students.

4. *Poor motivation.* In general, there is little motivation to achieve in areas that are perceived as boring. For the adolescent with ADHD, this becomes a problem of even greater magnitude.

5. *Distractibility.* There are many distractions for all adolescents primarily involving socialization and sexual issues. For the adolescent with ADHD, there is increased concern regarding peer acceptance with the tendency to "pay attention" to distracting comments or gestures made by other adolescents in order to gain acceptance. Clearly, sexuality is also a major distraction for all adolescents, but for the immature adolescent with ADHD, there is often greater difficulty showing appropriate responses and interactions with members of the opposite sex.

All of these issues, significant for adolescents in general, are exacerbated for adolescents with ADHD. Their inability to regulate their behavior, coupled with inadequate self-monitoring skills, put such teens at elevated risks for school failure, poor social interpersonal relationships, and perhaps to some degree future delinquent or antisocial behavior.

Teachers should be aware of ADHD characteristics, looking for those students who appear restless, fidget, and who tend to chronically respond in ways that reflect a lack of thought process. These students may also be quite disorganized, turning in papers that are sloppy with scribbling and handwriting that is almost unreadable. Furthermore, these students may appear bored, have difficulty listening and following directions, and seem to be generally in a state of "fog." Although seemingly bright, their academic performance may show considerable variability. Grades may also be affected by carelessness and chronic lateness in turning in papers. These students appear to have much difficulty profiting from feedback on unacceptable behavior and may continue to engage in inappropriate behaviors (for example, talking in class), regardless of how often they are reprimanded.

Some of these students with ADHD appear to constantly socialize. Incessant talking and writing notes to other classmates occupy the majority of their time, such that they may have little awareness of what is going on in class. Some youngsters with ADHD may engage in behavior that is silly or ridiculous, getting the attention of their classmates as the "class clown." Other adolescents with ADHD appear to be "lost in space" with their disorganization and forgetfulness. Still others may exhibit awkward coordination (sometimes described as a "klutz") and may be especially disruptive in social situations.

Some other adolescents with ADHD may have more serious conduct problems or oppositional–defiant disorders and may exhibit aggressive and sometimes violent behavior, in addition to the basic characteristics of ADHD. This is the adolescent who is clearly disrespectful to authority, has little motivation to engage in academic work, and may primarily associate with others who have similar problems. This is also the ADHD adolescent who is always "in trouble." Numerous detentions and suspensions have been accumulated for this adolescent who seems headed toward delinquent, antisocial, or criminal behavior.

In summary, the most important factor that seems to save the adolescent from developing either delinquent behavior or more serious behavioral/emotional problems is the availability of a person who cares for them and has faith in them. This factor alone can make a difference. In addition, there is a general need for parents especially to have some positive time each week with their teen. This can serve as a buffer against the stress of having to deal with the student's having a greater number of teachers, changing from one class to another, and more homework assignments, together with less personal attention from teachers.

One of the most significant predictors of later delinquent behavior is the manifestation of conduct-disordered behavior or antisocial behavior in the teen's parents.

Such teens with ADHD may receive frequent and sometimes severe criticism of their behavior, resulting in frustration, resentment, and feelings of inadequacy, which often accumulate over time.

BEING POSITIVE ABOUT ADOLESCENT ADHD BEHAVIOR

While there is often much emphasis on the problematic behavior, negative feelings, and perceptions, it must be stressed that adolescents with ADHD have many strengths and "good points." Many of these points are adopted from those noted by Colleen Alexander-Roberts. Some of these are briefly enumerated here: (1) They often see the "big picture," as theirs is an "open focus." (2) They are bright and creative, seeing different aspects of a situation that may result in the creation of new products or inventions. (3) There is risk-taking that may have personal referents, yet may provide exploration and discovery. (4) Since they are likely to process more information than is needed in a situation, there may be a broad range of observations that are made. (5) Because of this increased information processing, they are able to react quickly when under threat. Sometimes their impulsive style—coupled with broad range information processing—can be an advantage. (6) Many with ADHD are able to exert a "hyper focused" state when dealing with certain projects. (7) Such individuals may also be described as insightful and very perceptive about other people and situations. (8) Many with ADHD have a high energy level and are able to accomplish many tasks. (9) Those individuals may also make "great negotiators" as they have had a lot of practice. (10) Those with ADHD who develop good survival skills for adapting to varying situations are seen as "highly persistent," as they go through a series of "approaches" to deal with problems or crisis situations. (11) Because they have had to deal with many problem situations, such individuals with ADHD are often seen as being very intuitive thinkers. (12) Many reports have also stressed that such individuals are also quite intelligent. As will be noted in a future section, many of our most talented persons, and even those who were eccentric geniuses, were thought to have had ADHD. Having ADHD may therefore not be the "curse" that many see it as; rather, it may actually be a "blessing in disguise."

Chapter 2

ASSESSMENT OF ADHD IN ADOLESCENCE

HISTORY AND BACKGROUND INFORMATION

Like most evaluations of ADHD, the assessment of ADHD in teens is quite similar to that of younger children. However, there are some important differences to note. First, the symptomatic pattern of ADHD characteristics may be somewhat different for the older child and teen, as compared with the younger child. The patterns are more complex and there are some developmental changes that have evolved over time. Specifically, there is generally less hyperactivity; the teen may show restless or agitated behavior, but overt activity has usually diminished.

Second, in many cases there is a prior evaluation to compare with current findings. There is also a greater amount of background data, including prior school records, grades, behavior reports, and accumulated behavior observations by parents and teachers. However, there are some cases where the teen is evaluated for ADHD for the first time. Teachers, parents, and perhaps even clinicians may have misdiagnosed the teen at an earlier age. Some of the more subtle forms of ADHD (i.e., Inattentive Type) may go unnoticed by teachers, parents, and clinicians. However, more is known about these more subtle forms of ADHD and more information is being disseminated to teachers and health-care professionals.

Third, in the evaluation of teens, many self-report measures may be included as the adolescent is capable of providing much information that may be helpful in diagnosis and assessment. Whether prior background information or a history was obtained, it is a good idea to repeat this component of the assessment. Not all clinicians are aware of some of the critical information needed so that certain essential pieces of information may have been omitted.

It is first necessary to obtain the basic presenting complaints; this is typically gotten from the parents, although adolescents may provide much relevant self-report information. This information from the parent(s) provides a brief summary of the current problems that prompted the parent to bring in the teen for evaluation. It is then essential to obtain information about the family medical history, including medical and psychiatric conditions on both sides of the family, along with the teen's medical history. The birth history may include indicators of neonatal distress, anoxia, maternal smoking, and/or alcohol/drug use during pregnancy, as well as other risk factors. Clinicians may refer to the overview of clinical procedures and the protocol for ADHD Intake Interview found in Appendix 15.

DIAGNOSTIC INTERVIEW FOR CHILDREN AND ADOLESCENTS (DICA–IV)

DICA–IV provides a computerized diagnostic interview based on the DSM–IV classification system. It is appropriate for children and adolescents ages 6 through 17 years. This self-report instrument (DICA–IV Child/Adolescent version) provides an effective screening for a broad range of behavioral problems and requires only a fourth-grade reading level.

The DICA Parent version contains the same categories plus two additional ones focusing on (a) pregnancy and birth, and (b) on the early development of the youth. This additional information may allow for the identification of some of the factors that may have contributed to the youth's current behavioral pattern. The focus on some specific problem areas may indicate at-risk behaviors that will require intervention. The DICA–IV may be especially helpful when there is limited time for a comprehensive intake. However, it may also be administered in addition to a comprehensive intake interview.

One interesting feature of the DICA–IV is the Stein–Reich Critical Items. These flags indicate responses that might reflect a potentially dangerous behavior; for example, suicidal thoughts, violent acting-out tendencies, or substance abuse. Some items may indicate specific risk factors. In 1996, Barkley reported that "nicotine from cigarette smoking and alcohol from drinking during pregnancy have been shown to cause significant abnormalities in the development of the caudate nucleus in the frontal region of the brain in children." It has also been noted that the greater the number of complications during pregnancy, the greater the risk of ADHD. A history of ear infections, especially with high fevers, may also be a contributing factor. Other possible significant medical conditions in the teen's history include asthma, thyroid dysfunction, hypoglycemia, hearing defects, sleep apnea, encephalitis (brain infection), mild brain damage (head trauma), and seizure disorders to name just a few.

In addition to this background medical information, reports of laboratory tests (e.g., EEG, MRI, etc.) when available may be requested. Review of old report cards, work samples from earlier grades, and any additional psychological and educational test results, behavior ratings by teachers, parent conferences, IEPs, etc., would all be helpful in the assessment of the adolescent. It may also be helpful to obtain actual records to back up reports by parents that may have been based on unintentionally inaccurate misperceptions of prior school problems.

During the intake interview with parents, information is obtained on the parents' thoughts, perceptions, and expectations about family life. Queries are also made regarding the parents' hopes for their teen in life, and how they see the teen achieving set goals with the burden of ADHD.

Information is also needed regarding how the adolescent functions within the family and what that family is like. Although ADHD is a neurobiological disorder, its expression is clearly affected by outside factors, the most critical ones involving family dynamics. This requires exploring not only how the teen gets along with his or her parents, but also the relationship between the parents, as well as each individual parent's possible psychopathology. A screening for family relationship problems may begin with administration of the Conflict Behavior Questionnaire and Issues Checklist (see Appendix 6).

Information is also obtained from the parents' ratings of the teen's present behavior, in general, using *The ADHD Behavior Checklist* from Robin. An examination of school problems must not only consider the nature and severity of these problems, but also their range and persistence over the school years up to the present time. Robin's *School Symptom History Grid* is used for this purpose. Copies of these two instruments may also be found in Appendix 6.

BEHAVIOR OBSERVATIONS AND RATING SCALES FOR TEENS

In addition to the background and developmental history, four sets of observations are obtained (from parents, teachers, the psychological examiner, and the teen him/herself) on the teen undergoing assessment for ADHD. First, parents present their observation regarding the teen's major problems and behavioral difficulties. Second, teachers may provide a general behavioral description of the adolescent from their viewpoint; at the same time behavior ratings are obtained. In addition to narrative descriptions of problem behaviors by parents and teachers, both complete more formal rating scales that provide norm-referenced comparisons to other children of similar age and sex. This breakdown has been essential as there are developmental differences with increasing age as well as sex differences with regard to ADHD in teens. Samples of the rating scales such as the ACTeRS, Conners, ADHD test, BASC Scales, and others are found in Appendix 6.

Information from these rating scales may be most helpful, especially those ratings from the teen's teacher. Behaviors may be rated in school with reference to behaviors of other teens of similar age and sex. These ratings may not only help in the diagnosis and assessment, but may also serve as baseline observations with which the teen's progress can be compared. These initial ratings may be repeated periodically to monitor behavior changes as a function of medical and behavioral interventions.

On occasions, it may be helpful to observe the teen's behavior in or out of the classroom. *The ADHD School Observation Code Kit* by Drs. Ken Gadow, Joyce Sprafkin, and Edith Nolan may be helpful in quantifying and organizing behavioral observations in different settings. Other direct observation methods include: *The Classroom Observation of Conduct in ADD* (Atkins, 1985); *The ADHD Behavior Coding System* (Barkley, 1990); and *The Child Behavior Direct Observation Form* (Ackenback, 1986).

A third set of observations is obtained from the psychological examiner. These observations serve as a context for the interpretation of test results, and provide basic information about how the teen dealt with the "assigned tasks" and his or her behavioral/emotional state during the process of responding to these tasks. Many of these tasks are similar to some of the cognitive activities inherent in school subjects, so comments made while working on these tasks may be quite revealing.

This "micro classroom" context is created so that the teen's adaptive skills can be assessed. Clearly, the way the teen feels during the test session will affect test scores. Illness, lack of sleep, fear, depression, resentment, and lack of clear understandings of the purpose of the evaluation all affect the results. Behavioral observation during the assessment may reveal considerable information about how the teen approached each task, what strategies were used, and how the teen felt about the performance. Awkward pencil grip, blocking on verbal responses, long pauses, word-finding difficulty, restless behavior, excessive talking, looking around at each noise and distraction are just some of the many observations that the examiner may record.

Some of the behaviors may be of no surprise to the experienced examiner; however, some observations may be quite unique and highly individual, relating to something very specific about this particular teen. Much of this individuality in clinical presentation is quite helpful in planning a program of treatment. Since the teen with ADHD often does well in a one-to-one situation, this performance on psychological tests with the examiner may be viewed as one that would be manifested in an ideal situation. Thus, the assessment reveals more about how the teen might function in an ideal situation with maximum academic performance and assessment of abilities within the context of the teen's natural physiological tendencies.

Sᴇʟꜰ-ʀᴇᴘᴏʀᴛ Rᴀᴛɪɴɢ Sᴄᴀʟᴇꜱ ꜰᴏʀ Tᴇᴇɴꜱ

A fourth set of observations is obtained from the teen. Three rating scales for adolescents with ADHD include the Conners–Wells, the BASC, and the Brown Scales:

1. The *Conners–Wells Adolescent Self-Report Scale* contains 84 items on subscales of Family Problems, Anger Control Problems, DSM–IV Symptoms, Emotional Problems, Conduct Problems, Cognitive Problems, the Hyperactive–Impulsive, and the ADHD Index. A 27-item short form contains only the last four scales. This scale is very useful as symptoms clearly change with age and self-report becomes more accurate as the teen gets older. Also, co-morbid problems develop and

become more consistent with increasing age. Often, this scale may be given along with the Brown Scales (described below) since they each seem to cover somewhat different aspects of ADHD in adolescents.

2. *The Behavioral Assessment System for Children (BASC) Self-Report of Personality* has two age levels: child (8–11 years) and adolescent (12–18 years). Four composite scores include: (a) School Maladjustment, (b) Clinical Maladjustment, (c) Personal Adjustment, and (d) an overall composite—The Emotional Symptoms Index. This form requires about 30 minutes to complete. There is also a Student Observation System, a form to be used to observe and record classroom behavior directly. Both positive and negative behaviors are noted by the observer.

3. *The Brown Scales.* These self-report measures are generally recorded by the examiner. They tap salient and clinically useful dimensions of ADHD not typically covered by other scales or tests. It consists of 40 items grouped into five clusters: (a) Activating and organizing to work—nine items relating to getting started on tasks, (b) sustaining attention and concentration—nine items related to maintaining attention to tasks, (c) sustaining energy and effort—nine items related to energy and effort on tasks, (d) managing affective interference—seven items related to mood, and (e) utilizing working memory and accessing recall—six items related to forgetfulness. However, none of these components address the Behavior Inhibition concept proposed by Dr. Barkley.

There is an adolescent and an adult version of these scales. The adolescent version was normed on 12- to 18-year-olds. This task is often administered in the presence of a parent; following the teen's rating on each item, the parent is asked to rate that item, but only the teen's self-report ratings are used to obtain normative scores. This scale supports a multifaceted conceptualization of ADHD and may often be administered along with the BASC or Conners–Wells self-report scales.

In screening for ADHD, a cutoff score of 50 (raw score) has reportedly resulted in a false negative rate of 10% and a false positive rate of 22% for teens. Several classifications are possible. If rated scores are less than 45, this suggests ADHD possible but not likely. When scores range from 45 to 59, ADHD is probable but not certain. Scores greater than 60 suggest ADHD highly probable. Any cluster T-Score above 65 is clinically significant.

4. *Learning Styles Inventory.* The LSI is a self-report inventory that purports to measure learning preferences. It was designed for junior high, high school, and college students. Comprised of 30 items, it provides information in four areas: (1) *preferred conditions for learning*—focusing on issues such as independent versus group learning, the effect of discipline, type of teacher, etc.; (2) *areas of interest*—reflecting preference for working with numbers, language, inanimate objects, or people; (3) *mode of learning*—indicating the most efficient and effective way that information is processed (i.e., does the student prefer to process new information

by listening [auditory], reading [visual], or hands-on activity [kinesthetic]; (4) *expectation for course grade*—focusing on how well the student expects to perform in class.

Standardized on 2,500 students, the LSI requires a seventh-grade reading level. With regard to an inspection of the technical characteristics of its psychometric properties, this test ranks low in all basic test requirements. However, it may still provide some useful information and may be worthy of further clinical analysis.

PSYCHOLOGICAL AND NEUROPSYCHOLOGICAL TESTS

There is no one specific test for diagnosing ADHD. Recently, however, a test entitled "Attention Deficit/Hyperactivity Disorder Test" has been published. This test is helpful in gathering and organizing background information from the parents and is based solely on DSM–IV Criteria; it does not, however, consider the teen's performance on various tasks. It should not be assumed, because of its title, that this test alone is sufficient to diagnose ADHD. Clinical observation—combined with the results of the teen's performance on specific psychological and neuropsychological tests measuring verbal, nonverbal, visual–motor, fine-motor, gross-motor, memory, executive control, and attentional skills—are all essential for the psychologist and/or neuropsychologist to describe the pattern of behaviors that the teen presents and to formulate a diagnosis. Because of the complexities of the evaluation, a neuropsychological rationale will be proposed.

RATIONALE FOR NEUROPSYCHOLOGICAL ASSESSMENT

The underlying assumption in the field of neuropsychology is that the brain mediates behavior. First, the behaviors that are part of the typical clinical picture of ADHD are quite complex. It is highly unusual for the teen being evaluated for ADHD to have only ADHD. In most cases, the pattern may consist of secondary and even tertiary problem areas, in addition to the primary disorder of ADHD. The usual approach of a neuropsychologist is to orchestrate a complex battery of tests to measure a complex array of symptoms. Then, through a process of ruling in specific conditions and ruling out others, the initial symptom picture becomes clearer.

Since the teen's behavior in her natural environment is of prime concern, the goal is to present neuropsychological tasks similar to those in which the teen must ultimately function. In the case of the ADHD teen, measures of attention—both simple and complex—are essential. As noted by Barkley, "Attention plays a critical role in the neuropsychological assessment of children with developmental, learning, or other neuropsychological problems because it underlies the very capacity of children to undergo any form of psychological testing." Additionally, measures of behavioral response inhibition would also be needed to document the teen's impulsive style.

Furthermore, estimates of activity level, organizational skills, cognitive flexibility, social–emotional development, visual–motor skills, and a general capacity to adapt to situational changes are all important.

Second, in the history of working with ADHD, it has been noted that some of the first cases identified as having "ADHD" were those early post-encephalitic cases. Thus, a direct connection was made between some of the typical "ADHD characteristics" and a brain disorder. While the type of organic involvement in such cases was nonspecific, there was a clear parallel of varied post-encephalitic symptoms with the current ADD symptoms such that a multivariate (i.e., many variables or symptomatic behaviors) approach to the assessment of neurophysiologically driven behaviors is warranted. Other forms of organic dysfunction may also involve attentional and behavioral response systems so that one may see ADHD-like behavior in neuropsychological cases of epilepsy, head injury, structural brain lesions, and others.

Third, several research reports have been written on the use of specific neuropsychological test batteries to evaluate children with ADHD. These studies have focused on assessment of frontal lobe functions and other neuropsychological skills using measures such as the Wisconsin Card Sorting Test, verbal fluency tests, reading tests, and attentional (continuous performance, or CPT) tests. In one study, a battery of tests was used that not only looked at frontal lobe functions, but included a variety of other measures of IQ, reading skill, and verbal memory, as well as an assessment of attentional and impulsivity factors. The idea that disturbances in frontal lobe functions may be related to impulse control and responsible for the kind of cognitive impairments noted with ADHD is supported. The conclusion was that inability to control, direct, and sustain attention appears as a core deficiency of ADHD and not impulsivity. However, others believe that behavioral inhibition reflects the core difficulty and not attention problems. In a recently proposed theory, Barkley (1995) suggests that the problem of self-control may warrant renaming ADHD as a "Development Disorder of Self-Control."

SPECIFIC TESTS VS. TEST BATTERIES

As Barkley notes, "Over the past 50 years, the view of attention as a single, unitary construct has given way to theories of attention as being multidimensional." However, much of the early work in neuropsychology focused on finding a simple test that would detect organic brain disorders. Tests such as the Bender–Gestalt quickly became accepted as diagnostic instruments for "organacity," but with an abundance of research studies, it became clear that a single test such as the Bender–Gestalt should not be used as a screening instrument of organic dysfunction. It was, however, found to be a useful addition to a battery of tests where each test would assess a specific brain–behavior relationship. In the evaluation of complex organic problems, test batteries such as Reitan–Indiana Neuropsychological Test Battery and a later developed test battery, the Luria–Nebraska Neuropsychological Test Battery, may be more useful than single tests alone. Many variations of these batteries, as well as a number of other very specific batteries, have been developed. Other batteries have been proposed to evaluate patients exposed to toxic materials. To date, however, no specific battery has been developed for the assessment of ADHD.

Various tests to measure attention have been discussed by Barkley. Fennell has suggested basic domains of function that are typically assessed in a child neuropsychological examination. She has then listed commonly used neuropsychological tests in the evaluation of attention deficit disorder within a broader context of learning disability. Many problems have been discussed with regard to the traditional static test batteries, which may be lacking in theory-based constructs, as well as being poorly referenced to real-life criteria. Consequently, neuropsychological test batteries that cover a broad range of functions and have sufficient flexibility to include assessment of the many varied co-morbid conditions are preferred.

A MULTIDISCIPLINARY EVALUATION

It is clear that any neuropsychological evaluation that attempts to assess ADHD characteristics must take into consideration the following factors:

1. ADHD is a complex disorder that has, in itself, many facets or variations.

2. ADHD has more basic subtypes than those described in DSM–IV.

3. The concept of attention has several subcategories; the concept of behavioral–inhibition may likewise be subdivided.

4. ADHD is a developmental disorder that changes over the life span. Thus, for comparative purposes and to utilize the deficit approach to neuropsychological assessment, one must be familiar with normal neuropsychological and general behavioral development.

5. ADHD also involves situational components in which some of the variations are manifested, such as when behavior problems appear only in school or just the reverse.

6. Knowledge of co-morbid conditions and adjunctive problems frequently associated with ADHD is essential.

A typical evaluation for ADHD may first focus on:

1. *The History.* A good developmental history that is provided by the mother or caretaker familiar with the child may be able to provide some of the pathognomonic signs of ADHD from background information.

2. *Rating Forms.* Information from both the teen's teacher and the parent may be useful in detecting some of the behavioral signs exhibited either in school or at home. Adolescent self-report measures are also quite helpful.

3. *Specific Objective Measures of Attention.* There are several fairly well-developed instruments (usually computer based) that have good and, in some cases, extensive, normative data where a person's performance may be compared to one or more norms. The author's Test of Attentional Deficits (TOAD) has norms for three age groups: (1) 5–7, (2) 8–12, and (3) 13 and up; a research version is available.

4. *Cognitive Measures.* Involving the assessment of abilities, achievements, memory, visual–motor, language, visual–spatial, sensory, motor, executive control, and social–emotional skills may all be needed to answer some of the questions regarding possible co-morbid conditions or additional facets that tend to make each ADHD pattern somewhat unique. A basic subset of these may be used for screening purposes.

5. *Behavioral and Emotional Characteristics.* Involving the assessment of problematic behaviors as well as some of the more significant co-morbid characteristics of Oppositional Defiant Disorder or Conduct Disorder. While the Millon Adolescent Clinical Inventory and the Jessness Inventory have been used most frequently at the ADD Clinic in Biloxi, the Adolescent Psychopathology Scale appears to be a promising and useful addition.

As Rourke has so eloquently pointed out, the current emphasis on neuropsychological evaluations (for the LD teen) is not concerned with localization issues or even that there is demonstrable brain dysfunction. The primary concern in the evaluation of the LD child, as it would be for the teen with ADHD, is on documenting strengths and weaknesses as they relate to the real-life issues of learning or adapting to one's environment. The pattern thus obtained on neuropsychological testing would shed some light on the direction and overall thrust of treatment and/or habitation for the adolescent.

In the following sections, many of the currently accepted neuropsychological tests are discussed.

COMPONENTS OF THE NEUROPSYCHOLOGICAL ASSESSMENT

The various tests that make up the neuropsych battery to assess children and adolescents with ADHD may depend upon each clinician's choice. However, various categories of functions will be emphasized in the test battery. These specific functions relate to the various deficits and problems associated not only with ADHD, but also with the often found co-morbid disorders. Thus, a wide range of functions is assessed to assist the psychologist to not only rule in ADHD, but also rule out associated co-morbid disorders and mimic syndromes.

The following categories of functions are addressed: (1) Ability; (2) Achievement; (3) Executive Control (frontal lobe) Functions; (4) Visual–Motor Skills; (5) Motor

Skills; (6) Memory; (7) Attentional Skills; (8) Self-concept/Self-esteem; (9) Social Skills; (10) Visual–Spatial Skills; (11) Language Skills; and (12) Behavioral–Emotional Assessment. Each of these areas is briefly discussed here. For a more in-depth discussion of the majority of these tests, see other references in testing such as the *Practitioner's Guide to Developmental and Psychological Testing* by Dr. Glen P. Aylward (New York: Plenum, 1994) or specific test manuals for additional technical information. Dr. Aylward's information on several of the tests listed is included in this section. Also consult the *Special Educator's Complete Guide to 109 Diagnostic Tests* by Drs. Roger Pierangelo and George Guiliani (Paramus, NJ: Prentice Hall, 1998).

ASSESSMENT OF ABILITY

The "gold standard" for assessment of abilities is the Wechsler Intelligence Scale for Children–III (ages 6 to 16 years, 11 months). It provides Verbal Performance (basically nonverbal/visual–spatial assessment) and Full Scale IQ Scores. The verbal subtests include information, similarities, arithmetic, vocabulary, comprehension, and digit span. The performance subtests include picture completion, picture arrangement, block design, object assembly, coding, mazes, and symbol search. Factor scores are: (1) Verbal Comprehension, (2) Perceptual Organization, (3) Freedom from Distractibility, and (4) Processing Speed. While some clinicians do look at the factor scores for problems with attention and concentration on the Freedom from Distractibility Factor score, others find much inconsistency and do not believe that this score provides a reliable and valid measure of attentional processes. Most clinicians do look for consistent patterns across various tests, and will include this factor score as one measure to look at. For older adolescents 17–19 years, the WAIS–III may be used.

For clinicians who want a quick measure of the child's ability in short screening evaluations, the Kaufman Brief Intelligence Test (KBIT) is available. With estimates of verbal and nonverbal functions, as well as a composite score, these test scores correlate fairly well with other established measures of ability. There are some indications that WISC–III scores may be accurately estimated by KBIT scores in a sample of children and adolescents with ADHD (Flick, unpublished data), and especially for children and teens with average or above WISC–III scores. Other data show that in other populations, the KBIT fairly accurately predicts (i.e., estimates) WISC–III scores.

ASSESSMENT OF ACHIEVEMENT

The Wechsler Individual Achievement Test (WIAT) was co-normed with the WISC–III, thus allowing for meaningful analysis of ability–achievement discrepancies important in the diagnosis of learning disabilities. It consists of subtests on (a) Basic Reading, (b) Math Reasoning, (c) Spelling, (d) Reading Comprehension, (e) Numerical Operations, (f) Listening Comprehension, (g) Oral Expression, and (h) Written Expression. There is a brief screener comprised of three subtests (a), (b), and (c).

A very popular brief screen for academic achievement is the WRAT–3. It consists of Reading (word recognition), Spelling (written), and Arithmetic (calculations written). However, no measures of Reading Comprehension or Math Reasoning are obtained.

ASSESSMENT OF EXECUTIVE CONTROL

While there are many available neuropsychological measures of frontal lobe functions, these three are helpful for use with ADHD children and adolescents: the Trail Making Test, the Stroop Color Word Test, and the Wisconsin Card Sorting Test.

The Trail Making Test primarily assesses motor speed and mental flexibility. Sequencing is an obvious component of Part A where the teen connects a series of numbered circles. In Part B, the task is more complex and requires the teen to connect alternating numbers and letters in sequence. Thus, not only is motor speed involved, but also the teen's ability to shift and to hold in working memory specific elements of two sequences.

The Stroop Color Word Test requires that the teen inhibit competing information before making a response. An example would be to read names of colors printed in a different color (e.g., the word "red" printed in green). Vocal–motor speed and holding information in working memory are both needed to accurately inhibit competing information and respond appropriately on this test.

The Wisconsin Card Sorting Test requires again mental flexibility and conceptual problem solving. The teen must be able to use feedback on her responses to formulate a concept of the correct response pattern based on color, form, or number. This test has been one of the most useful in assessing frontal lobe functions and is used in most neuropsych batteries as well.

ASSESSMENT OF VISUAL–MOTOR SKILLS

While the Bender–Gestalt Test has been the choice of clinicians for many years, it has limitations in use with teens. For example, most children are able to complete the task by age 8 years. Older children and teens may thus not be identified when their visual–motor problems are more subtle and therefore not detected by this test.

The Developmental Test of Visual–Motor Integration (fourth edition) has been normed on children and teens 3 years to 18 years of age. It provides 24 drawing tasks that are developmentally sequenced in order of increasing complexity. A developmental age is computed as well as the visual–motor standard scores and percentile ranks. Useful supplemental tests allow the clinician to evaluate the relative contributions of visual perception and motor coordination. An overall profile of visual, motor, and visual–motor performance allows the clinician to sort out the relevant contributions of visual and motor functions.

Another useful test is the Minnesota Percepto Diagnostic Test that measures both visual perception and visual–motor skills. It was normed on over 4,000 subjects and can be used with children and young teens in the age range of 5–14 years. It can also be used with adults (over 16 years).

ASSESSMENT OF MOTOR SKILLS

In most neuropsychological test batteries, motor speed is assessed by the Finger Tapping or the Finger Oscillation Test. However, there are some other measures of fine-motor coordination that may also be useful in evaluating adolescents with ADHD. Another motor test typically used in neuropsych batteries is the Strength of Grip Test. This measure provides an estimate of motor strength that may reflect more significant problems than an ADHD pattern.

ASSESSMENT OF MEMORY FUNCTIONS

The Wide Range Assessment of Memory and Learning (WRAML) is a very useful test in the evaluation of a teen with ADHD. The WRAML incorporates measures of both visual and verbal memory, some of which are very sensitive to attentional problems, and is appropriate for children and teens ages 5 to 17 years. The Sentence Memory and Number/Letter Memory, along with Design Memory and the Fingers Windows visual memory subtests, are especially sensitive. Another is the Test of Memory and Learning (TOMAL) used to evaluate children ages 5 through 19 years. It features verbal and non-verbal memory scores, as well as supplemental composite scores of an Attention and Concentration Index and a Learning Index.

ASSESSMENT OF ATTENTIONAL SKILLS

The use of a continuous performance test (CPT) dates back to the late 1950s when Rosvold and colleagues used the CPT to evaluate attentional processes in epileptic patients. The original CPT was a noncomputerized version. Since then, several variations of the CPT have been developed; there are now an even dozen instruments, including one under development by the author (i.e., the Test of Attentional Deficits, or TOAD).

One of the earliest computerized versions is the *Gordon Diagnostic System* (1987) or *GDS*, normed on over 1,300 children preschool age through age 16 years. Developed by Dr. Michael Gordon, this system consists of three distinctive tasks in a self-contained computerized unit. The first task measures self-control and is entitled the Delay Task; this procedure is unique to the GDS among all computerized attentional assessment instruments. For this task, the teen is told that he can press a large blue button as quickly or as slowly as he wishes. He is informed that if he presses too fast, he will not earn points; but, at the right pace, he earns a point and a light comes on each time he presses the button with the appropriate delay. This provides a description, over a timed interval, of how the teen is able to pace himself when *he* is in control of the task.

The second GDS task is entitled Vigilance and measures the teen's ability to pick out a sequence of two numbers that are repeated periodically during the timed interval. On this task, the clinician is able to determine how well the teen is able to accurately pick out the sequences and thus assess any attentional lapses. The clinician is also able to determine how impulsive the teen may be by the number of errors she makes during the task. Impulsivity is reflected by the teen's rapid pressing of the button when she sees the first number in the sequence without waiting to see if it is followed by the second number.

A third and similar GDS task is labeled the Distractibility Task. On this task, the adolescent again must pick out the identified sequence (e.g., a five followed by a three), but now there are numbers flashing randomly on either side of the center screen. This is a very complex task that seemingly generates a state of high arousal. It is quite difficult even for adults and may provide important information about distractibility, primarily for older children and teens with ADHD. Recently, an auditory module has been added to the GDS. The auditory vigilance task is identical to the visual vigilance task, except that the numbers are heard via headphones while the screen is covered.

A second computerized assessment procedure is called the *Test of Variables of Attention*, or *TOVA* (ages 4 years to over 80 years of age); it utilizes software for the IBM PC-compatible computers and the Apple IIe. On this 22.5-minute visual CPT assessment, the child presses a firing button whenever a correct target stimulus is presented. There is a considerable body of research on this instrument that is purported to be useful in predicting appropriate medication, titrating the dose, and monitoring medication patterns in ADD and other neurological conditions for children, adolescents, and adults. Developed by Dr. Lawrence Greenberg, this procedure is nonlanguage-based (to differentiate ADHD from learning disorders), requires no right–left discrimination, and has negligible practice effects.

The Intermediate Visual and Auditory Continuous Performance Test (IVA)—age 5 through adult—was developed by Dr. Joseph Sandford and Ann Turner. All test instructions and test stimuli are presented visually and auditorily by the computer. This procedure takes 13 minutes and provides a computer report with measures of various parameters reflecting dimensions of inattention, impulsivity, and hyperactivity.

A unique form of computerized assessment of attention is the *Conners Continuous Performance Test* (6 years to adult) introduced by Dr. C. Keith Conners, originally developed in the mid 1970s. This procedure differs from others in that the child must press a key for any letter presented except the letter "X." Thus, the focus of this CPT is on "behavioral inhibition." The Conners CPT takes about 14 minutes to administer. However, only visual attention is measured. A computer report provides for interpretation of scores and the overall summary compares scores with the general population norms (preferable) or to ADHD norms.

The Conners CPT has been shown to be sensitive to medication (i.e., Ritalin®). On medication, children's Reaction Times were faster, Standard Error measures smaller, and the percentage of hits higher compared with times when they were off medication.

Reaction Times averaging over 900 msec were deemed slow. Attentional difficulties on the Conners CPT are indicated by:

a. errors of omission

b. reaction times for hits

c. changes over time (i.e., atypical response speed)

Impulsivity is reflected by:

a. errors of commission

b. reaction time on hits

Other measures include:

1. d'—reflecting an individual's "perceptual sensitivity" or ability to discriminate targets from non-targets

2. b—a measure of the person's frequency of responding (Conners notes that "risk takers" respond more readily than they should)

Any T-Score = or > 60 or any percentile = or > 90 would be significant; the more measures that reach significance, the stronger the evidence for attentional difficulty. One of the most important features of the Conners CPT is the variation of interstimulus interval; some persons with ADHD may often lose their attention on the longer interstimulus interval presentations and these intervals appear to be more dose sensitive, subject to deterioration in performance at too high a dose level.

Last, the Conners CPT allows the clinician to compare a person's scores with either general norms or with ADHD norms. (Conners recommends the former for most clinical purposes.)

A comparative study of the diagnostic accuracy of the Gordon, TOVA, and IVA by Dr. Joseph Sandford using 57 children generally between 7 to 12 years of age revealed that IVA showed a 7.7% false negative rate, while the TOVA was 12.5% and the Gordon was 36.0%. The IVA identified 90% of the 30 children without ADHD, and 89% of the 27 with ADHD.

While not included in the study, independently determined false negative rates for the Conners CPT was reported to be 26.1% for children ages 6 to 17 in a cross-validation study. Identification of ADHD was at the rate of 86.5% for the Conners CPT. From clinical use, the Conners CPT has been noted to provide a somewhat more challenging task, especially for ADHD adolescents. However, future research will need to be conducted using all CPT instruments and well-defined diagnostic criterion groups to assess the comparative efficacy of each procedure.

The *Test of Attentional Deficits* or *TOAD* (Attend-O™ Volume 1) is a comprehensive computerized assessment of hierarchically arranged components of attention, utilizing the basic format of a continuous performance test or CPT. Developed by Dr. Grad Flick, TOAD (1999) is based on a model of attention training proposed by Sohlberg and Mateer in 1987. Their clinical model suggests five subtypes or variables of attention: (1) focused, (2) sustained, (3) selective, (4) alternating, and (5) divided attention.

A complete discussion of this breakdown is discussed in Chapter 3 in the section on training attention skills with *Attend-O™ Volume 2: Attention Training Games (ATG)*. The training and test components are essentially identical. The TOAD does add two new assessments on visual and auditory behavioral inhibition tasks, which are not included in ATG. Behavioral inhibition training procedures are currently under development so that the assessment with TOAD will provide a format for training on simple and complex attentional tasks, including Behavioral Inhibition. TOAD has been published as a research instrument. Preliminary norms have been developed for three age levels: I (ages 5–7 years); II (ages 8–12 years); and III (ages 13 years and up). The maximum age for normative data at this point is 16 years.

For the initial study there were 88 subjects ranging in age from 5 to 16 years. There were three criterion groups: Group 1—with a primary diagnosis of ADD/ADHD and some secondary behavioral/emotional problems; Group 2—with a primary diagnosis of CD, ODD, or LD and some secondary characteristics of ADD/ADHD; and Group 3—a relatively normal group that may have had some mild stress problems or minor medical problems that did not affect their school or home life.

Correct classification using TOAD test variables predicated from about 70% to a maximum of 100% with better predictive accuracy obtained with older adolescents. Overall correct classification was: for Age Level I (69.2%); for Age Level II (80.4%); and Age Level III (100%). The false negative (FN) rates were: Age Level I (30.8%); Age Level II (14.3%); and Age Level III (0%). When criterion groups 1 and 2 were combined into a simple clinical group, the classification results were: Age Level I (correct 78.6%; FN 21.4%); Level II (correct 80.4%; FN 14.3%); Level III (correct 93.8%; FN 8.3%).

Using the clinical versus normal groups comparison, a total of 82.95% of all cases were correctly classified into clinical and normal groups. The overall false negative rate was 17.01%. These initial results suggest: (a) a glaring need for a larger sample of cases and cross-validation studies, (b) the initial results at this stage of test development is encouraging, (c) age clearly matters (perhaps it is greater stability or more accurate diagnostic classification that may account for the increase in predictive accuracy with age), and (d) an attempt was made in this predictive study to emulate the typical decision process that is used in clinical practice.

Most cases involving ADHD, and especially teens with ADHD, are complex and typically qualify for more than one diagnostic classification category. It is clear that no single test, including any CPT, should be used to arrive at a diagnosis. Notwithstanding, such tests as the TOAD may not only aid the clinician in the diagnostic process, but may also delineate specific patterns of attentional deficits that should be included in the overall treatment program. In general, training or treatment may be linked to assessment.

The Attend-O™ Volume 2 (ATG) may thus be used to focus on deficits that exceed the cut-off for significance as measured by the TOAD. Use of both of these research instruments may provide a logical and meaningful assessment with the basis of a treatment program for adolescents as well as younger children with ADHD. Much research needs to be completed before this may be used on a wide scale. However, the initial research investigation is encouraging to explore further research applications in both school and clinical settings.

ASSESSMENT OF SELF-CONCEPT/SELF-ESTEEM

A teen's perception of him- or herself is an especially important component in the evaluation of adolescents with ADHD. Much of the information obtained in this area of assessment comes from clinical observation and report, as well as projective test data; for example, figure drawings, kinetic family drawing, sentence completion, and other similar projective test measures. However, there are some test instruments that may provide helpful information that is more objective.

The Multidimensional Self-Concept Scale (MSCS) assesses global self-concept and provides information on six areas of psychosocial functioning, including social competence, affect, academic, family, and physical domains. It is administered in about 20 minutes for children ages 9 through 19 (grades 5 through 12). Results reflect overall classifications with percentile ranks and a profile of normative scale strengths and weaknesses. This instrument appears to have good psychometric characteristics and provides a clear definition of self-concept that employs a behavioral rationale for the construct.

A second instrument, called the Self-Esteem Index (SEI), is a normative-based measure reflecting how children perceive and value themselves and is thus closely related to the self-concept. It can be administered in about 30 minutes and is appropriate for children ages 7 through 18 years. In addition to the four basic scales reflecting Academic Competence, Family Acceptance, Peer Popularity, and Personal Security, there is an overall Self-Esteem Quotient. The perceptions of Academic Competence, Family Acceptance, and Peer Popularity are especially important measures to consider in the evaluation of the teen with ADHD.

ASSESSMENT OF SOCIAL SKILLS

In addition to information obtained clinically and from direct observation (e.g., BASC Direct Behavioral Observations or the ADHD School Observation Code), there are two instruments that may be helpful in assessing social skills.

The Social Skills Rating System (ages 3 to 18 years) utilizes ratings from parents, teachers, and the child (self-reports can be used in grades 3–12) to assess behaviors that affect the teacher–student relationship, peer acceptance, and academic performance. It also detects problems such as shyness, difficulty initiating conversations, and problems in making friends. Five positive social behaviors are measured, including Cooperation,

Assertion, Responsibility, Empathy, and Self-Control on the Social Skills Scale. The Problem Behaviors Scale assesses behaviors that may interfere with the development of positive social skills, including Externalizing Problems, Internalizing Problems, and Hyperactivity. The Academic Competence Scale gives a quick estimate of academic functioning, motivation, and parental support. A separate computerized program, the Assessment Intervention Record (AIR), allows the clinician to plan appropriate interventions.

A relatively new rating scale called the Walker–McConnell Scale of Social Competence and School Adjustment appears to target specific social skills on which the student needs instruction and practice. Completed by the classroom teacher, this scale is appropriate for children in kindergarten through grade 6 (elementary version), and grades 7 through 12 (adolescent version). The adolescent version contains four factor scales: Self-Control, Peer Relations, School Adjustment, and Empathy. In general, this instrument is useful in obtaining information in two primary areas of adjustments in school: (1) adaptive classroom behavior and (2) interpersonal social competence. Both of these adjustments are seemingly critical to ultimate success in school, as well as to the child's overall social development.

ASSESSMENT OF VISUAL–SPATIAL SKILLS

The Minnesota Percepto Diagnostic Test (ages 5 to 14 years) may be used for assessment of both visual–perception and visual–motor skills in young teens. Scores are corrected for both age and IQ. A "testing the limits" procedure is used and information is obtained to infer visual–motor, visual–perceptual, or more complex integrative difficulties. However, while utilization of this one test may be efficient, it lacks some critical information on complex visual–perceptual processes.

ASSESSMENT OF LANGUAGE SKILLS

A comprehensive language evaluation may be provided by a new edition of the Peabody Picture Vocabulary Test–III, Third Edition (PPVT–III), co-normed with the Expressive Vocabulary Test (EVT). Both tests are suitable for patients 2.5 to over 85 years of age, and both can generally be individually administered within about 30 minutes. These tests are, however, limited to receptive and expressive vocabulary, along with word retrieval.

BEHAVIORAL–EMOTIONAL ASSESSMENT

As noted by Aylward, "the *Child Behavior Checklist (CBCL)* often is considered the 'gold standard' in the assessment of children's behavior problems." This instrument is appropriate for ages 4 through 18 years. The parent form may be completed in about 20 minutes by any parent with a minimum fifth-grade reading level. A teacher form to rate children ages 6 through 18 and a Youth Self-Report Form (for ages 11–18 years) are also available. The Social Competence Scale is categorized by activities, social, and school-related items. The Behavior Problems Scale yields eight problem scales that are grouped into (1) Internalizing Behaviors, (2) Externalizing Behaviors, and (3) neither (1) or (2). On the Teacher's Scale, an adaptive functions profile replaces social competence with factors including unpopular, inattentive, nervous–overactive, anxious, social withdrawal, self-distraction, obsessive–compulsive, and aggressive. On the Self-Report Form, there are only two basic scales: Competence and Behavior Problems. As Aylward points out, "The inattention scale also reportedly differentiates ADHD with and without hyperactivity."

The *Personality Inventory for Children (PIC),* completed by parents, provides a description of personality characteristics applicable to children 6 to 16 years of age. It is developed along the same format as the Minnesota Multiphasic Personality Inventory (MMPI). The original version of the PIC contained 600 items, making it difficult for some parents to complete it within two hours. In its present form, 280 items allow for scoring of the 12 clinical scales, a general adjustment scale, and four factors, including: (1) Undisciplined/Poor Self-Control, (2) Social Incompetence, (3) Internalization, Somatic Symptoms, and (4) Cognitive Development. According to Aylward, "the PIC is useful in differentiating hyperactive, learning disabled, and normal children, as well as learning disabled versus behaviorally disordered students."

The *Minnesota Multiphasic Personality Inventory–Adolescent (MMPI–A)* is an empirically-based measure of adolescent psychopathology appropriate for teens 14–18 years old. It requires a sixth-grade education. This true–false test consists of 478 items and preserves many of the features of the original MMPI. There are Basic Validity Scales (8 in number), 10 Basic Clinical Scales, and numerous Supplementary Scales, Content Scales, Harris–Lingos Subscales, and Social Introversion Subscales. Special indices involving Welsh Codes, Percent True/False, and Response Percentages are also provided. In addition to the teen's test-taking attitude, there are four areas of focus in a comprehensive interpretive report: (1) Symptomatic Patterns, (2) Interpersonal Relationships, (3) Behavioral Stability, and (4) Diagnostic and Treatment Considerations. A specialized report is available for correctional settings as well as substance-abuse treatment settings. The primary focus is on treatment strategies for these delinquent behavior patterns.

The *Millon Adolescent Clinical Inventory (MACI)* is a brief self-report personality inventory that is appropriate for use with adolescents ages 13–19 years old. It requires only a sixth-grade reading level and consists of 160 true–false items. Many of the items have been modified or added to be consistent with the DSM–IV. Furthermore, diagnostic suggestions are aligned with DSM–IV classifications. The test was normed on 1,017 adolescents involved in inpatient or residential treatment programs. The MACI contains 27 scales in three categories: (1) Personality Patterns, (2) Expressed Concerns, and (3) Clinical Syndromes. There is also a section (Modifying Indices) that helps to identify test-taking attitudes or confused/random responding, which may invalidate the profile.

The *Jessness Inventory* is a 155-item questionnaire (answered true–false) that is appropriate for children, adolescents, and adults as a measure of antisocial behavior tendencies. It is a self-report instrument that yields ten trait scores, an index of asocial tendencies, and nine personality subtype scales. The ten trait/attitude scales include: (1) Social Maladjustment, (2) Value Orientation, (3) Immaturity, (4) Autism, (5) Alienation, (6) Manifest Aggression, (7) Withdrawal–Depression, (8) Social Anxiety, (9) Repression, and (10) Denial.

There is an additional Asocial Index. The nine subtypes are: (1) Undersocialized/ Active, (2) Undersocialized/Passive, (3) Conformist, (4) Group-oriented, (5) Pragmatist, (6) Autonomy-oriented, (7) Introspective, (8) Inhibited, and (9) Adaptive. Combined with the *Jessness Behavior Checklist,* where norms are available on a large delinquent sample aged 13 to 20 years, interpretations and treatment suggestions may focus on areas of family relations, self-esteem, interpersonal relations, and school/achievement. A post-release risk may be estimated for young delinquents.

The *Adolescent Psychopathology Scale (APS)* is a broad bandwidth measure of adolescent psychopathology, personality, social–emotional problems, and competencies that may be used with teens 12 to 19 years of age. It consists of 40 scales that measure four domains of psychological functioning: Clinical Disorders (20 scales), Personality Disorders (5 scales), Psychosocial Problem Content areas (11 scales), and Response Style Indicator scales (4 scales).

The APS is based on the conceptual distinction between internalizing and externalizing expression of symptoms. This instrument is designed to empirically assess the severity of symptoms associated with specific DSM–IV clinical and personality disorders, and does not provide formal diagnoses of these disorders. This approach is therefore consistent with the conceptualization of "assessment" of the adolescent's problem behaviors (compared with a diagnosis).

The unique multiple-response format allows for more precise description of these problematic behaviors. For example, some symptoms might best be evaluated as either present or absent (i.e., true–false), while others might best be described by their general frequency or duration format (e.g., substance-abuse items rated on a 5-point scale related to frequency of use).

Another departure from the typical response format is that symptoms are evaluated across different time periods with the duration interval determined to a large extent by DSM–IV criteria. Those items related to Personality Disorders do not have a specific time period, but are evaluated to describe the long-term pervasive trait nature of the symptoms. Using multiple cut-off scores to designate clinically relevant levels of symptoms, high scores on the APS reflect severity of a DSM–IV disorder, but does not provide a formal diagnosis for that disorder. Norms were developed for the total standardization sample of 1,827 school-based adolescents and separately based on gender, age groups, and gender by age group. There was also a clinical sample of 506 teens from a wide cross-section of clinical, treatment, and referral settings.

Items on the APS were written to require a third-grade reading level. Extensive data are reported to support the psychometric integrity of the APS. Based upon DSM–IV criteria, the APS appears to have adequate content validity. Construct validity was shown by the strong similarity between the factor structure of the APS and criteria for corresponding DSM–IV disorders.

While clinicians may certainly be interested in specific scales that focus on ADHD, CD, ODD, substance abuse, and mood and anxiety disorder scales, the broad content covered by the test may be useful in identifying some problems that might not be covered during the clinical interview or by other psychological tests. The APS has just been published; to date, there are no known studies with ADHD or other co-morbid conditions. Additional research and clinical use will determine the overall utility of this instrument. Based on its unique assessment procedure and excellent psychometric properties, this instrument may become the new "gold standard" for the assessment of adolescents and especially for the assessment of teens with ADHD and various co-morbid conditions.

ADDITIONAL ASSESSMENT PROCEDURES

The Dyslexia Screening Instrument is a useful addition to the clinician's test battery, especially when a reading disability is suspected. This 33-item scale is rated by the child's teacher on characteristics that may be typically observed in the classroom. Appropriate for use with children ages 6 through 21 years, it is scored by computer using a discriminate function prediction of Pass, Fail (i.e., consistent with dyslexia), or Inconclusive Classifications.

THE REYNOLD'S ADOLESCENT DEPRESSION SCALE (RADS)

This scale may be a useful addition to a battery of tests for adolescents, especially when depression is suggested. The RADS is a screening instrument that may be administered to adolescents in grades 7–12 to assess depressive symptomology. The 30 items rated on a 4-point scale can be administered in about five to ten minutes. The RADS has excellent psychometric properties and has been standardized on 2,460 adolescents. With over six years of extensive research, the RADS is the first specific depression scale developed for use with adolescents. Since depression may often be masked by other problems, RADS may be helpful, especially in the assessment of teens with ADHD and other co-morbid problems, including LD (poor academic performance), CD and ODD (behavior/conduct disorders), and substance-abuse problems, as well as alleged anxiety or mood problems. Clinical studies have revealed that many youngsters will honestly and openly describe their depressive symptomology; the RADS may be an excellent screening device for use in schools, especially where there is a high incidence of learning, emotional–behavioral, or pure conduct problems.

THE EYBERG CHILD BEHAVIOR INVENTORY (ECBI) AND THE SUTTER–EYBERG STUDENT BEHAVIOR INVENTORY–REVISED (SESBI–R)

These may also be useful additions to a battery of procedures for adolescents who may not exhibit severe levels of behavior disturbances. Both of these brief rating scales assess the current frequency and severity of disruptive behaviors in home and school settings, as well as the extent to which parents and/or teachers find the behavior troublesome. On both the 36-item ECBI and the 38-item SESBI–R, the parent or teacher indicates how often each behavior occurs on a 7-point scale, and whether or not the behavior is a problem (Yes/No Problem Scale). These procedures require only about 5 minutes to administer and about 5 minutes to score; a sixth-grade reading level is required. Psychometric strength appears good for both rating scales to provide adequate and efficient screening and tracking of disruptive behaviors in children and adolescents from ages 2 to 16 years. The primary limitation would be the lack of full coverage for the late adolescent (17–19 years) age group. Test items are, however, of a nonpathological nature and may therefore measure behaviors that are common to all children. The authors state, "By recognizing and rating normal behavior problems, parents and teachers may be less reluctant to endorse problem behaviors of the children they care for."

RATING SCALES

There are many rating scales for ADHD. (This rationale was previously discussed in the section on behavioral observations.) Some of the more frequently used rating scales that appear most helpful in comprehensive assessments are briefly reviewed here. However, it should be pointed out that there is generally poor agreement between either parent or teacher ratings and performance on a CPT; specifically, there may be agreement in about one quarter of cases. (For more in-depth information, the clinician is referred to the section on Behavioral Assessment in Dr. Glen Aylward's *Practitioner's Guide to Developmental and Psychological Testing.*) The following rating scales can be completed by parents, teachers, and the adolescent.

PARENT RATING SCALES

The most comprehensive is the Conners Parent Rating Scales–Revised (CPRS–R) for persons ages 3 to 17 years. The CPRS–R represents 30 years of research and development. Its reliability and validity stats exceed the original version. It includes eight scales and two indices: (1) Oppositional, (2) Cognitive Problems, (3) Hyperactive–Impulsive, (4) Anxious–Shy, (5) Perfectionism, (6) Social Problems, (7) Psychosomatic, and (8) DSM–IV Symptom subscales, plus the ADHD Index (to distinguish ADHD from non-ADHD children and adolescents) and the Global Index (formerly the Hyperactivity

Index), the latter of which has ten of the best items from the original CRS and is especially sensitive to medication effects. The 80-item version is preferred, but when there are time constraints, a 27-item CPRS–RS that includes the first four scales along with the ADHD Index is useful. In addition to rating their teen's behavior, some parents may be asked to rate their own behavior as a child or teen, especially if there is other evidence suggesting the presence of ADHD in one or both parents.

Parents are also asked to complete the *ADHD Test* (Gilliam, 1995). Normed on more than 1,200 persons ages 3 to 23, this 36-item rating scale takes into consideration some of the developmental changes from childhood through adolescence by providing separate norms for males and females of different age groups. Based on DSM–IV criteria, it provides an overall ADHD Quotient, as well as scaled scores for Hyperactivity, Impulsivity, and Inattention.

TEACHER RATING SCALES

The Conners Teacher Rating Scale–Revised (CTRS–R) contains 59 items that parallel the Parent Rating Scale, except for the Psychosomatic Scale, and was normed from ratings of over 2,000 teachers on persons ages 3 to 17 years. The shorter 28-item CTRS–RS covers the first three scales of the parallel parent form along with the Global Index. The 10-item Conners Abbreviated Teacher Questionnaire is reportedly "diagnostically" sensitive not only to hyperactivity, but also to conduct disorder. Since most teens have several teachers, the short form of this scale may be more useful. Specifically, it may be best to integrate rating scale data from several teachers to assess how the teen manifests ADHD behavior in different contexts.

The recently published Spadafore–ADHD–Rating Scale, standardized on 760 students, is designed for use by teachers for children ages 5 to 19. It was reportedly intended not only to detect ADHD, but also to indicate the severity of problem behaviors. It consists of a 50-item behavior questionnaire (rating impulsivity, hyperactivity/attention, and social adjustment) and a 9-item ADHD Index. The latter ADHD Index includes criteria used to quantify on-task/off-task behaviors. The Behavior Scale is described as an effective screener that may be used to satisfy the assessment requirements of a 504 referral. However, this scale is also described as a "comprehensive evaluation" by the author of the scale (Spadafore), allegedly since the items cover a wide range of symptoms. There is no available companion instrument for parents. An ADHD Observation Form is included to report results in five different categories and requires about ten minutes to complete. The Medication Monitor is comprehensive and may be useful by itself as a stand-alone measure that can be repeated over many weeks of treatment monitoring.

The ADD–H Comprehensive Teacher Rating Scale (ACTeRS) employs 24 items and 4 scales: Attention, Hyperactivity, Social Skills, and Oppositional Behavior. This rating scale provides separate norms for females and males (equivalent to ages 5 through 13). This scale is medication sensitive and appears helpful in distinguishing between ADHD with and without hyperactivity. A recently developed parent form is now available with similar scales, as well as an additional scale focusing on early childhood behavior.

Since teacher ratings may be prone to halo and/or practice effects, some have recommended that two questionnaires be completed for a baseline measure as ratings often improve between the first and second administration without any intervention. However, Dr. Arnold Goldstein has also noted that some "teacher ratings of aggressive, disruptive, or acting-out behaviors are very often erroneously high." A small number of disruptive behaviors may lead to a global impression of the teen as a troublemaker or chronically aggressive.

COMBINED RATING SCALES

The Behavioral Assessment System for Children (BASC) is a newly developed comprehensive assessment of behavior and self-perception. It represents multi-raters with co-normed data from teachers and parents, as well as children and adolescents. About 10,000 children and adolescents were rated by more than 2,000 teachers and more than 3,000 parents. It covers behavior, cognitive, and emotional data that are not only descriptive, but are also a diagnostic aid. The BASC reportedly measures "dimensions of behavior and emotions that are easily linked to the criteria in DSM–IV and the Individuals with Disabilities Act (IDEA)."

The BASC Teacher Rating Scale is subdivided by age with preschool (4–5 years), child (6–11 years), and adolescent (12–18 years) forms. It takes about 10 to 20 minutes to complete and provides four composites: Externalizing Problems, Internalizing Problems, School Problems, and Adaptive Skills. There is also an F Index, a validity check on "Faking."

The BASC Parent Rating Scale also has forms with three age levels using the same domains as those on the teacher scale, with the exception of the Learning Problems Scale on the School Problems Composite and the Study Skills Scale on the Adaptive Skills Composite. An F Index (to estimate Faking) is also included.

The BASC Self Report of Personality has two age levels: child (8–11 years) and adolescent (12–18 years). Four composite scores include: (1) School Maladjustment, (2) Clinical Maladjustment, (3) Personal Adjustment, and (4) Emotional Symptoms Index (an overall composite). This form requires about 30 minutes to complete. In addition to these rating scales, there is a Structured Developmental History that can be given in interview format by the clinician or may even be completed by the parent. There is also a Student Observation System, a form that can be used to observe and record classroom behavior directly for the identified child or adolescent. This form allows for recording of both positive and negative behaviors. The BASC Monitor for ADHD Rating Scales is a recent addition that allows the clinician to monitor and track both parent and teacher ratings. With the BASC Monitor, software trends may be plotted and treatment outcome documented. Overall, the BASC system is quite comprehensive and might even replace several instruments that may typically be used by the clinician. Its development and presentation appears to reflect good psychometric construction and appealing clinical utility.

School-Based Rating Forms

There are a few rating forms that are psychometrically sound and were developed specifically and primarily for use by educators and school psychologists. However, these scales may also be useful in evaluation screening conducted independently of the school's assessment.

The Attention Deficit Disorders Evaluation Scale–Secondary-Age Student (ADDES–S)

The ADDES–S was developed according to DSM–IV criteria for ADHD for ages 11 through 18 years, with separate norms for males and females. The ADDES–S was specifically designed to document behavioral observations made by teachers in secondary school environments. This rating scale was standardized on 1,280 students including those with ADHD.

The ADDES–S categorizes behavior patterns in areas of (a) Inattention and (b) Hyperactivity–Impulsivity. The scale has a *school* version (60 items) for educators and a *home* version (46 items) for parent reports. The ADDES–S provides information relevant for decision making on IEP goals, behavioral objectives, and intervention strategies. A computerized scoring program and intervention manual will facilitate the decision-making process, especially regarding goals and objectives as well as specific intervention for each student's unique pattern of ADHD problems.

The Learning Disability Evaluation Scale (LDES)

The LDES provides educators a vehicle for the identification of performance behaviors most characteristic of LD. The LDES provides a profile based on the currently accepted definition of LD. The 88 items are scored to provide a profile of subscales to classify the student's difficulty in areas of listening, thinking, speaking, reading, writing, spelling, or mathematical calculations. The sum of standard scores on these subscales generates an overall learning quotient. The LDES was standardized on 6,160 students from 19 states and 71 school districts. This sample included those students previously identified with LD. Norms are available for students in kindergarten through grade 12. A computerized program facilitates scoring and interpretation; a companion computerized *LD Intervention Manual* contains goals, objectives, and intervention strategies for the 88 specific learning difficulties identified by the LDES. These intervention strategies may be used in special education classes, but may also be employed by regular education teachers working with the LD student in a regular classroom. The intervention manual is especially useful in IEP development and to create a truly individualized educational program, especially when combined with other recommended accommodations.

THE BEHAVIOR DISORDERS IDENTIFICATION SCALE (BDIS)

This scale focuses on both overt indicators of behavior disorders, as well as more subtle signs of withdrawal, depression, and suicidal tendencies. The BDIS was designed to meet all state and federal guidelines for the identification of behaviorally disordered/emotionally disturbed students from 4 1/2 to 21 years of age. A *school* version (83 items) and a *home* version (73 items) are available.

The BDIS was standardized on 4,957 students from 23 states and 71 school districts, with separate norms for males and females. Computerized scoring and manual for behavioral interventions are available. IEP goals and objectives may therefore be matched to specific behavior problems. The BDIS may also be invaluable for referral and testing by independent practitioners.

Each one of the three rating scales may provide information that is useful directly in educational planning and behavioral treatment interventions. In addition, the information gleaned from these scales may be used by clinicians who provide independent psychological/neuropsychological evaluations; many of the direct behavior observations made by the classroom teacher may compliment test data or other parent/clinician observations.

THE DIAGNOSTIC PROCESS

The accompanying chart (Figure 2.1) on the next page depicts the complex process used to make a complete and accurate evaluation of a teen's presenting problems (at school and/or at home) and then to formulate a comprehensive individualized program for management of the teen's behavior. There may be one or more presenting problems that significantly affect the teen's performance and behavior in school and, perhaps, his behavior at home. While an important objective of this process is formulation of the primary, secondary, and tertiary diagnoses, the evaluation process also gives the clinician an overall picture of the child's strengths and weaknesses that are incorporated into the individualized treatment program of behavior management and other clinical procedures. Based on the assessment, the treatment program will have behavioral modification components; it may or may not include a medication regimen; and it will include mechanisms to monitor and evaluate progress. Specific problem areas and symptomatic behaviors become targets for change.

To begin this process, it is essential for the clinician to obtain information from several sources, including at least the teen's parents and teachers (at school, at music lessons, in Sunday School, from coaches for sports activities, etc.) and, of course, from the teen him- or herself. Observations during a direct interview and rating forms completed by the parents provide parental input. This information will include the teen's medical history (e.g., seizures, head traumas, medications), developmental milestones,

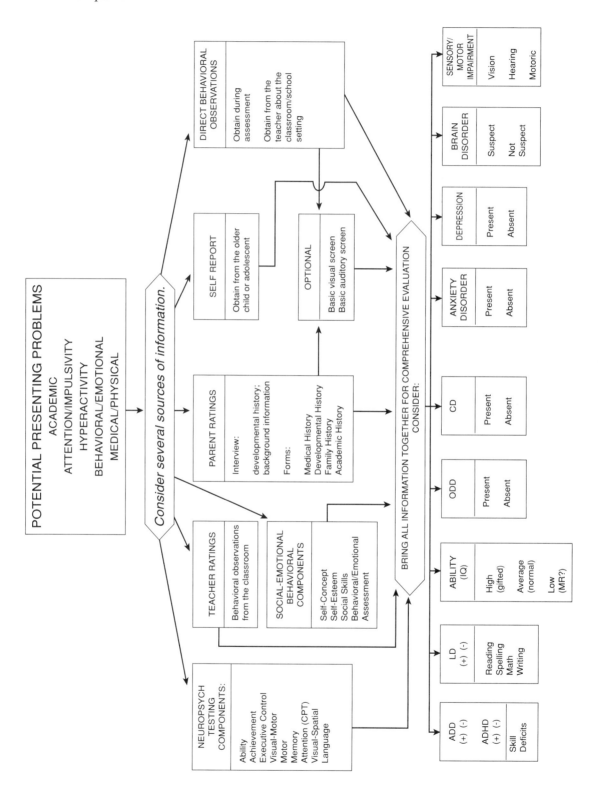

Figure 2.1   DIAGNOSTIC PROCESS FLOW CHART

family medical history (e.g., regarding possible familial genetic disorders), and the teen's academic history; all this information can be invaluable in raising suspicions about certain diagnoses or in making hypotheses to be considered and ruled in or ruled out with test procedures. Then, combining this information with results from a wide range of test procedures, the clinician is able to formulate a pattern of strengths and weaknesses, assets and deficits that either support or negate "suspected" diagnoses. Independent observations in the classroom (or other school-like settings) would certainly help to diagnose and document the ADHD disorders since those settings tend to elicit many ADHD-like behavioral symptoms.

Note that the self-reporting data and interview of the teen one-on-one are especially critical when evaluating an older child or adolescent. As they get older, adolescents can provide more valid and reliable information about their behavior, especially about externalizing (acting-out) problems. Direct behavioral observations during the testing session provide a wealth of information about how the teen copes with easy or difficult material, whether a basic visual or hearing problem may exist, and information about many other issues related to general maturation, self-concept, attitudes toward academic tasks, coordination problems, arousal level, and potential neurological problems.

Assessment of behavioral and emotional characteristics provides the last component; such assessment reflects whether the teen presents evidence of externalizing problems (e.g., aggression, defiance, conduct disorders) or internalizing problems (e.g., anxiety, obsessive–compulsive tendencies, depression).

Once all data and evidence have been gathered, a number of diagnostic conditions may be considered based on: the general background information; the parent, teacher, and self ratings; behavioral observations at home, school, and in assessment situations; and, of course, considering the neuropsychological test data. Typically, more than one diagnostic condition is present; it is the exception for an adolescent to manifest only one condition. Thus, the implication for treatment is almost always that a multi-modal program will be needed to deal with a complex pattern of symptoms and problems.

The position assumed at the ADD Clinic in Biloxi, Mississippi is that each separate component of the behavior/problem pattern must be addressed. While medications are often very helpful, they are sometimes ineffective with aggression problems of ODD (oppositional deficit disorder) and CD (conduct disorder) during adolescence. Likewise, medications may have little effect on learning disabilities. Furthermore, "pills do not teach skills" and ADHD teens almost always need basic skills development through training. Specific behavioral training procedures (for parents and sometimes teachers as well as for the teen) will be used to address some of these skill deficits.

Thus, an individualized, multi-modal treatment program can be developed to address the teen's deficits (perhaps including organizational skills, learning strategies, training in following directions, and development of social skills and study skills) and periodically to evaluate progress; this program will include use of appropriate and targeted *medications,* when needed, as well as appropriate targeted *behavioral interventions.*

INTERPRETATION OF TEST DATA

Much information is often collected in the evaluation of a teenager with ADHD. The first step in the interpretation of this data is to list all of the tests given with their respective standard scores or percentile ranks. This will allow for a direct comparison of the strengths and weaknesses across a variety of dimensions assessed and the development of a profile for this teen. An example of this process of test data integration follows, with the entire list of tests used and the neuropsychological report that are presented in Appendix 11.

Typically, a feedback session is held with parents and the teen. For younger teens (<16 years old), primary feedback is given to parents and a short feedback is provided to the teen. For older teens (16 years and up), feedback is given to both parents and teens together. In addition to test results, information about treatment planning is discussed. If the evaluation and assessment was conducted during an unstable or crisis period for the adolescent, additional time may be needed (up to 6 months) before any definitive diagnostic impressions may be rendered. This would not, however, preclude treatment planning and implementation since most treatments will target specific behaviors or problem areas for the adolescent, regardless of the diagnostic labels employed. Some of these treatment approaches may include the teens' teachers or other school staff. While many schools are quite willing to cooperate in treatment programs, some confrontational situations may develop that will require more persuasive recommendations that may entail formal legal advocacy.

SKILL-DEFICIT ASSESSMENT

As noted earlier in this chapter, a distinction was made between diagnosis and assessment. While a diagnosis may be necessary for statistical purposes, insurance claims, and legal documentation for services, it says very little, if anything, about what treatment program might be beneficial for the teen with ADHD. There is a great variation in the pattern of test results with many possible co-morbid conditions. How then is it possible to provide a treatment program? The answer lies in the assessment of strengths and weaknesses for any individual teen. Various treatment modules may be described with their component "skill deficits." Alternately, of course, those components that represent strengths for an individual teen could be labeled "skill assets." While skill assets may be periodically reinforced to "shore up" the teen's self-concept and enhance self-esteem, the primary focus may be on the skill-deficit components. It is primarily through the development of these skills that the teen will be better able to cope.

There are four basic modules and altogether 23 skill components. These are as follows:

Basic Skills	Academic Skills	Personal Skills	Interpersonal Skills
Organizational	Study	Relaxation/Stress management	Communication
Problem solving	Memory	Anger management	Social
Time management	Note taking	Physical (exercise)	Conflict resolution
Impulse control	Homework	Sports	
Self-monitoring	Test taking	Coping (emotional)	
Attentional	Reading		
	Math		
	Spelling		
	Handwriting		

While there is some overlap among categories, these components may describe and define problem areas for most all teens with ADHD. There is no simple test or procedure that will provide an indicator of the teen's development across these components. The pattern of deficits must now be culled from test data, background information, behavioral reports, and observations. Many of these skills will be discussed in more detail in Chapter 3 under skill development and in Chapter 5 under skill training.

CO-MORBIDITY/MIMIC SYNDROMES

Numerous psychological and medical/neurological conditions are often associated with ADHD in about 85% of all cases, and must be considered in making a differential diagnosis. Often these other conditions may share symptoms with ADHD or may involve ADHD-like behaviors. Some of the potential overlaps with other diagnostic conditions are shown in Figure 2.2. This list of overlapping symptoms demonstrates that quite often the clinician is presented with a very complex symptom picture. The clinician must be able to determine the primary condition and sort out what may be secondary or tertiary (i.e., co-morbid) conditions. The clinician must also be able to distinguish between ADHD symptomology and other conditions that mimic ADHD behavioral symptoms. Following are two lists—one of medical conditions and the other of psychological conditions that may be co-morbid with ADHD or that may be considered in differential diagnosis. These lists are followed by in-depth discussions of ADHD associated with medical conditions and ADHD associated with psychological conditions.

Figure 2.2
OVERLAPS WITH OTHER CONDITIONS

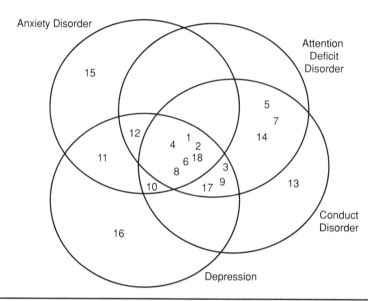

	Symptomatic Behavioral Characteristic	Attention Deficit Disorder	Anxiety Disorder	Depression	Conduct Disorder
1	Poor Concentration	X	X	X	X
2	Restless	X	X	?	X
3	Fails to Complete Tasks	X		X	X
4	Daydreams	X	X	X	X
5	Impulsive	X			X
6	Poor Sleep	X	X	X	X
7	Aggressive	?		?	X
8	Mood Disturbance	X	X	X	X
9	Poor Self-Concept	X		X	X
10	Quiet and Withdrawn	?		X	
11	Guilt Over Transgressions		X	X	
12	Memory Problems	X	X	X	
13	Stealing/Lying				X
14	Poor Social Skills	X			X
15	Fearful/Avoidance	?	X	?	
16	Crying	?	?	X	
17	Sensation Seeking (High Risk)	X		?	X
18	Difficulty Focusing on Task	X	?	?	?

Key: X = Symptom Usually Present
? = Symptom Possible
Blank = Symptom Not Usually Present

MIMIC SYNDROMES AND *MEDICAL* CONDITIONS
CO-MORBID WITH ADHD

Reaction to Anticonvulsants
    (phenobarbital/Dilantin)

Reaction to Theophylline
    (for Asthma)

Tourette's Syndrome

Movement Disorder—
    Sydenham's Chorea

Epilepsy

Narcolepsy

Structural Brain Lesion

Sleep Apnea

Head Trauma

Otitis Media

Anemia

Fragile-X Syndrome

Sinusitis

Pinworms

Thyroid Disorder

Isoniazid

Lead

MIMIC SYNDROMES AND *PSYCHOLOGICAL* CONDITIONS
CO-MORBID WITH ADHD

Adjustment Disorder

Anxiety Disorder

Depression/Dysthymia

Bipolar Disorder

Mental Retardation

Learning Disability

Conduct Disorder

Oppositional Defiant Disorder

Obsessive Compulsive Disorder

Pervasive Developmental Disorder

ADHD ASSOCIATED WITH MEDICAL CONDITIONS

Numerous medical conditions and certain medications used to treat some medical conditions may cause impairment of attention (resulting in changes in one's degree of alertness) and movement functions (resulting in increased motor activity), or may compromise one's judgment (so as to make one's responses appear impulsive).

Some medications quite effectively treat a medical problem for a child without ADHD, but exacerbate the behavior in the teen with ADHD. *Anticonvulsants* may cause even more problems for the ADHD adolescent who also suffers from seizures. Phenobarbital and other anticonvulsants like clonazepam, phenytoin, and dilantin may further depress Reticular Activating System (RAS) activity and may generate more severe ADHD behaviors.

Conversely, some drugs may cause ADHD-like behaviors in a teen without ADHD. In particular, Isoniazid, an *anti-tuberculosis drug,* may cause a form of anemia and has effects upon the nervous system similar to lead toxins. In addition to dizziness, weakness, headaches, and nausea, its use may result in cerebral dysfunction, causing some ADHD-like behaviors.

Allergy and asthma medications (e.g., Theophylline and Atarax) have been shown to sometimes cause or worsen attentional problems, hyperactivity, and some behavior problems regardless of the presence or absence of ADHD. These medications may also make behavior worse in ADHD children and may generate ADHD-like behavior in teens who do not have ADHD.

The Centers for Disease Control and Prevention have indicated that *lead* is the number one environmental health threat in the United States. However, in Conners's Risk Model, protective factors may counteract some toxic effects. Specifically, Conners points out that diets rich in calcium and iron may block the absorption of lead and thus prevent the typical hyperactivity that may result from ingestion of lead. The concept of the "risk model" may thus explain why some persons exposed to toxic substances may not get sick or show a "typical" or expected response.

Medical conditions associated with ADHD include the following.

TOURETTE'S SYNDROME

This is one of the "tic" disorders that usually occurs prior to 18 years of age and is characterized by sudden, involuntary, and recurrent specific movements and vocalizations. These tic movements and vocal emissions may change over time and typically include such things as grunting, hissing, barking, whistling, sniffing, snorting, and clearing of the throat. Blatant cursing occurs in about half of these cases. ADHD occurs in about half of those persons with Tourette's. Symptoms of Tourette's are sometimes brought on by the administration of stimulant medications used to treat ADHD symptoms. In other cases, Tourette's Syndrome would have appeared whether or not stimulant medications were used.

EAR INFECTIONS

Clinically, many adolescents with ADHD appear to have a history of ear infections with high fevers. When such ear infections occur within the first two years of life, there may be an interruption of development in the brain and nervous system for specific functions that relate to symptomatic ADHD behavior; motoric and attentional control problems may thus develop.

NARCOLEPSY

Narcolepsy is a disorder characterized by sleep attacks and symptoms of rapid eye movements occurring at inappropriate times during the day. This is considered an abnormality of the brainstem property of Rapid Eye Movement (REM) sleep and overrides the right-brain function of vigilance or wakefulness. An inherited disorder in children, this condition is different from sleepy state often observed in ADHD children as shown by the lack of clinical manifestations of abnormal REM activity such as hypnotic hallucinations, sleep paralysis, and cataplexy (i.e., loss of muscle tone without loss of consciousness). However, it is interesting that the primary treatment for narcolepsy has involved the use of stimulant medications.

ANEMIA

This condition is defined by a reduction in the number of circulating red blood cells or in hemoglobin, or in the volume of packed red cells per 100 ml. of blood, or in a combination of two or more of these factors *(Taber's Medical Dictionary)*. Symptoms of anemia may include dizziness, drowsiness, headache, as well as other autonomic nervous system symptoms that may appear as "arousal problems." As noted by Goldstein and Goldstein, studies have correlated anemia with "personality disturbance, conduct problems, feelings of inadequacy, and immaturity."

FRAGILE-X SYNDROME

This is a chromosomal disorder associated with a fragile site on the end of the X chromosome. It is the second most common cause of mental retardation with mostly males being affected; females are potential carriers. Associated learning and attentional problems have been noted clinically and reported by Haperman and associates in a 1985 study. However, since only four cases were studied, little can be generalized to children and adolescents with ADHD. Symptoms of Fragile-X include a prominent nose and jaw, long ears, and epileptic seizures along with impairments of interest, attention, and behavior.

MOVEMENT DISORDERS

A simple chorea, such as Sydenham's Chorea, is characterized by irregular involuntary movements of the face and extremities that may appear one to six months after a streptococcal infection. This condition may be accompanied by irritability as well as obsessive and compulsive symptoms, some of which could be confused with symptoms of ADHD.

THYROID DYSFUNCTION

Hyperthyroidism is caused by excessive secretion of the thyroid glands which increases the basal-metabolic rate. Symptoms of hyperthyroidism that may be mistaken for ADHD include tremor, increased nervousness (overactivity), and signs of autonomic nervous system activity (e.g., sweating and rapid heart beat).

SLEEP APNEA

According to Stoudemire, there are two types of sleep apnea (SA)—obstructive SA and central SA. In obstructive SA, the pharyngeal walls collapse repetitively during sleep, causing intermittent upper airway obstruction and cessation in ventilation or apnea. In central SA, cessation of ventilation is related to loss of inspiratory effort. The major symptoms of sleep apnea include loud snoring, pauses in respiration during sleep, daytime hypersomnolence, weight gain, disturbed sleep, and deficits in attention, motor efficiency, and pyschomotor ability. Findley reported problems in concentration, complex problem solving, and short-term recall; all related to the severity of hypoxemia (insufficient oxygenation of the blood).

SINUSITIS

Similar to sleep apnea, sinus infections may result in decreased airflow through the nasal passages and may produce some of the same symptoms as those of sleep apnea. Likewise, one may expect to see decreased alertness manifested by poor attention and perhaps overactivity, due to hypoxemia.

PINWORMS

Pinworms infect the lower small intestine and large bowel, and often produce anal itching and result in restlessness or overactivity. Obviously, this may also serve as a distraction, making it difficult to engage in activities involving sustained attention. However, this condition is not typically of major concern in accounting for ADHD symptoms, especially with adolescents.

HEAD INJURY

The National Head Injury Foundation defines traumatic brain injury as "an insult to the brain, not of degenerative or congenital nature, but caused by external force, that may produce a diminished or altered state of consciousness." Problems with attention have been noted in numerous studies on children and adolescents who have suffered head trauma. Likewise, both hyperactivity and attention problems have been noted by parents of head-injured children and adolescents. Problems with sustained attention and performance speed also have been noted. Of course, many other cognitive skills may be affected by a head injury, including intellectual performance, motor skills, visual–motor skills, language, memory, and academic skills.

EPILEPSY

Even when anticonvulsant medications are used appropriately to treat epilepsy, there is still the continuing possibility that seizures may recur. Seizure activity has been related to organic lesions, metabolic disorders, drugs, toxic substances, fever, infections, and vitamin deficiency—as well as head injury—for children, adolescents, and adults. Some seizures are also apparently genetically based, of unknown etiology (idiopathic). The common effects from seizure activity are some reported psychological changes, but more clearly there are associated changes in EEG activity generally observed over a period of time. There are various types of seizures. These have been listed in the International Classification of Epilepsies of Childhood.

International Classification of Epilepsies of Childhood*

1. Primary generalized epilepsies

   True petit mal

   Tonic–clonic major seizures (grand mal)

   Combined petit/grand mal

   Primary myoclonic epilepsy

2. Secondary generalized epilepsies

   Associated with diffuse brain disease, including epilepsies secondary to specific encephalopathies and nonspecific encephalopathies (infantile spasms and Lennox–Gastaut syndrome)

3. Primary partial epilepsies

   With motor, sensorimotor, affective, or visual symptoms

4. Secondary partial epilepsies ("lesional")

   With elementary symptomatology

      with motor symptoms

      with special sensory or somatosensory symptoms

      with autonomic symptoms

   With complex symptomatology

      with impairment of consciousness only

      with cognitive symptoms

      with affective symptoms

      with psychosensory symptoms

      with psychomotor symptoms (automatisms)

The material in this section is adapted (with permission) from Spreen. Most seizures involve motor activity. In the classic seizure there is a sequence of tonic and clonic movements. In *petit mal* seizures, there is a sudden interruption of activities that may be accompanied by nystagmus, slight muscle contractions with the head moving backwards along with brief loss of consciousness and dropping of the head. In *myoclonic* seizures, there is loss of muscle tone along with jerky movements of arms and facial muscles. With *absence* seizures, there is a sudden loss of consciousness.

---

*From *Developmental Neuropsychology* by Otfried Spreen, Anthony H. Risser, and Dorothy Edgell. Copyright © 1995 by Oxford University Press, Inc. Used by permission of Oxford University Press, Inc.

Focal seizures (or *partial* seizures) frequently occur on one side of the body but can spread. With focal motor seizures, the precentral or motor gyrus of the brain may be involved, and symptoms of rigidity and clonic movements are seen (Jacksonian Epilepsy). In *complex partial* seizures (or psychomotor seizures), auras may involve complex experiences, mood changes, or even hallucinations. In some cases, consciousness may be compromised; there may also be confusion that follows the seizure.

Temporal lobe seizures are the most common of all partial seizures. Because of the close proximity and relationship to visual, auditory, and limbic system structures, the disorder may involve complex auditory and visual experiences as well as automatic behaviors that would certainly affect sustained attention or concentration. Even during periods of no demonstrable seizure activity from behavioral observation, there may be some evidence of "kindling" where repeated subthreshold electrical stimulations in the brain may lead to subsequent development of seizures. Thus subclinical disorganized abnormal electrical activity may occur periodically and may result in some behavioral changes that appear as ADHD symptoms.

In 1978, Walt and Forsythe noted that almost one-quarter of children and adolescents with epilepsy may have ADHD as a co-morbid condition.

ADHD ASSOCIATED WITH PSYCHOLOGICAL CONDITIONS

From one-third to one-half of teens with ADHD will have additional behavioral/emotional problems that will require psychiatric outpatient services. Other disorders may have many symptoms that mimic ADHD behavior. These psychological conditions may thus appear independent of or co-morbid with ADHD. (See page 49.) There are nine diagnostic categories under this rubric that may be further described as either acute or chronic psychological conditions.

ADJUSTMENT DISORDERS

According to DSM–IV, this category of disorders involves "the development of clinically significant emotional or behavioral symptoms in response to an identifiable psychosocial stressor or stressors. The symptoms must develop within three months after the onset of the stressor(s)." Obviously, the symptoms or the consequences of ADHD behaviors are stressful; alternatively, a stressor (e.g., head trauma) might precipitate both the adjustment disorder and ADHD behaviors. Also, adjustment disorders may be considered when ADHD children experience significant stress in the classroom but do not manifest a pattern that would be consistent with a diagnosis of anxiety, depression, or other psychiatric disorder. Many clinicians may use this category to describe such secondary reactions to the neurophysiological condition of ADHD.

ANXIETY

The essential feature of Generalized Anxiety Disorder is excessive worry (apprehensive expectation) about a number of events or activities occurring a majority of the time over a period of at least six months. Because severe anxiety may result in excessive agitated movement, impair one's attention and concentration, and cause errors of misjudgment in one's responding, some of these anxiety disorders may mimic ADHD behaviors. It is estimated that about 25% of teens with ADHD experience anxiety.

In addition to Generalized Anxiety Disorder, another co-morbid condition sometimes associated with ADHD is Post-Traumatic Stress Disorder (PTSD). PTSD is a delayed distress response pattern to an atypical and severe traumatic event. Associated features include depression, anxiety, disturbance of conduct, withdrawal, and interference with one's personal life, work, or academic adjustment.

Worry may appear similar to daydreaming, as one's fantasies to deal with anxiety-provoking stimuli may cause fixation of thought patterns and a generally introspective façade. Focusing on the child's fears, worries, and possible source of anxiety may aid in the differential diagnosis. Because ADHD and anxiety appear to be at opposite ends of the arousal continuum, there is an infrequent chance that the two may truly co-exist. When they do co-exist, it is found more often in the primary inattentive type of ADHD.

There are many anecdotal reports of some people responding with panic while others remain calm and goal-oriented during emergencies. Perhaps this state of relative calm during emergencies represents a shift of arousal gears that occurs when the low-arousal ADHD child or adolescent encounters a highly stimulating situation that would overwhelm any normal person. For comparison of symptoms, again refer to Figure 2.1.

The two conditions of anxiety and ADHD may automatically manifest different somatic reactions to states of emergency with the same underlying process (i.e., an increase in arousal). While one state reflects overarousal and confusion, the other (ADHD) reflects an optimal arousal state and thus more effective reaction. Conners has cited evidence to suggest that ADHD and anxiety may interact with anxiety factors minimizing manifestations of impulsivity, hyperactivity, and aggression.

DEPRESSION/DYSTHYMIA

Some ADHD characteristics have been noted with depressive disorders; depressive symptoms may be associated with ADHD in teenage and adult years. With the presence of depressive symptoms, there may be interference with thinking, and certainly in some cases where one is preoccupied with depressive thought patterns, there may be an interference with sustained attention. Furthermore, in depressive states there may be sleep difficulties similar to that experienced in ADHD. With agitated depression, there is the possibility of motoric restlessness similar to hyperactivity. With reference to the DSM–IV, it would be unusual for ADHD children to meet the full criteria for depression/dysthymia. In DSM–III-R, ADHD was listed as a predisposing factor for dysthymia;

now it is simply noted that ADHD may be associated with dysthymia as well as other conditions such as learning disabilities or mental retardation.

Teens who act out aggressively, engage in substance abuse, or run away from home and skip school may be manifesting some prodromal signs of significant depression, which may result in more dangerous self-destructive behavior and possibly suicide. From 25% to 30% of adolescents with ADHD may experience serious depression. Some of the warning signs indicative of serious depression are: (a) an attitude of complete indifference, (b) acting out aggression towards others or self, (c) erratic behavior across many situations, (d) rapid changes in mood, (e) irritability and a strong sense of edginess, (f) thoughts of death reflected in verbal or nonverbal communications (i.e., statements or pictorial drawings), (g) difficulty sleeping characterized by either excessive sleep or extreme restless agitated sleep, (h) a significant change in eating habits, (i) fatigue or general lack of energy, (j) loss of enjoyment of activities where there was prior involvement, (k) a significant change in academic performance, (l) complaints of aches and pains or obvious signs of difficulty, (m) giving significant possessions away, (n) difficulty in making even simple decisions, and (o) withdrawal from others.

According to the American Association of Suicidology, there are three general categories of clues to teen suicide: (1) verbal statements (e.g., "I don't want to live"), (2) behavioral changes (e.g., a change in academic performance), and (3) situational losses (e.g., loss of a loved one, important relative, or significant possessions). Teachers may make observations in significant communications from the adolescent. For example, writings may center around "death themes" or art work may reflect morbid preoccupations.

In lieu of significant symptoms of depression, the clinician may discover that the adolescent's mood disorder may meet the criteria for the cluster of "Sadness Problem," which is a subclinical variation of a major depressive disorder. Detail criteria for this cluster appears in the *Diagnostic and Statistical Manual for Primary Care (DSM–PC)*, Child & Adolescent Version, from the American Academy of Pediatrics (1996).

The DSM–PC represents a collaborative effort between the American Academy of Pediatrics and the American Psychiatric Association. It has two sections: the first dealing with the child's or adolescent's environment; the second focusing on how the child or adolescent responds to that environment. This format is useful in depicting difficulties in attention/concentration and behavioral inhibition/self-control as falling on a continuum. This DSM–PC compilation also appears useful in the classification of the more subtle forms of ADHD symptoms.

BIPOLAR DISORDERS

In DSM–IV, there are four categories of Bipolar Disorder (or Manic Depression). These include Bipolar I (marked by one or more Manic Episodes or Mixed Episodes); Bipolar II (marked by one or more major Depressive Episodes, accompanied by at least one Hypomanic Episode); Cyclothymic Disorder (marked by a chronic fluctuating mood disturbance involving numerous periods of hypomanic symptoms and numerous periods of depressive symptoms); and Bipolar Disorder (Not Otherwise Specified, or NOS). In general, the presence of either manic or hypomanic symptoms defines Bipolar Disorders.

During the manic phase there is irritable, expansive, or elevated mood with associated symptoms including hyperactivity (gross motor), racing thoughts, distractibility, and high risk-taking behavior. In hypomania, manic behaviors may be present within the context of a less severe mood disorder. The hypomania episode is marked by hyperactivity, silliness, giddiness, cheerfulness, distractibility, inattention, moments of rudeness and crudeness, and fluctuating cheerful to irritable moods.

It should be noted that in DSM IV, "ADHD and Hypomanic Episode are both characterized by excessive activity, impulsive behavior, poor judgment, and denial of problems." ADHD is distinguished from hypomanic episode by the characteristic early onset of ADHD (i.e., before age 7 years), its chronic rather than episodic course, its lack of relatively clear onsets and offsets, and the absence of abnormally expansive or elevated mood.

According to Dr. A.L. Robin, a diagnosis of Bipolar Disorder might best be made after working with the adolescent for some period of time (e.g., several weeks or months). Until recently, it was not considered possible for young adolescents to have Bipolar Disorder or to have it conjointly with ADHD. When it is found to co-exist, there appears to be an exacerbation of behavior problems with violent temper outbursts that may result in hurtful and/or destructive aggressive acting-out behaviors.

MENTAL RETARDATION

Mental Retardation (MR) is defined as below-average intellectual functioning (IQ 70 or less) on an individually administered intelligence test, together with deficits in adaptive behavior and having an onset prior to 18 years of age. According to DSM–IV, "the most common associated mental disorders are ADHD, Mood Disorders, Pervasive Developmental Disorders, Stereotypic Movement Disorder, and Mental Disorders due to a general medical condition (e.g., Head Trauma)." According to Barkley, when an individual who is mentally retarded meets all of the diagnostic criteria for ADHD relative to his or her mental age, then the additional diagnosis is warranted.

LEARNING DISABILITIES

The degree of overlap with learning disabilities (LD) is significant for ADHD. It has been estimated that about 10% up to 50% (average of 25%) of ADHD children may have a learning disability. However, Safer and Allen (1976) estimated 80% of ADHD in the LD population. Goldstein and Goldstein point out that while attentional factors are necessary, they are not sufficient for learning as the child or adolescent with a learning disability has difficulty processing information. Thus, they contend that although medication stimulates the attention center deep within the brain, it may "have little effect on the cortical ability of the brain to process information." Consequently, both ADHD and LD children have academic problems but for different reasons.

The general definition of learning disabilities is one of exclusion. To wit, LD excludes learning problems that are associated with sensory or motor difficulties, mental retardation, emotional disturbances, and cultural or environmental factors. Typically, a learning disability is operationally defined as a significant discrepancy between the child's or teen's general level of mental ability and his or her academic achievement in such areas as reading, math, spelling, handwriting, and language development.

Dr. Russell Barkley has noted that this discrepancy approach (i.e., IQ–Achievement Standard Score difference of 15 or more points) may result in an overestimation of LD in those children and adolescents who are in the superior range (i.e., IQ of 130 or above) with regard to ability (i.e., IQ), even though they have average reading skills and are functioning normally in school. However, his achievement cut-off approach (i.e., achievement test scores 1.5 standard deviation below the mean) may identify borderline mildly retarded individuals as LD. A combination of these two approaches appears to be most efficacious.

Most of these LD types involve a verbal factor. Whatever their disability, when placed in the classroom, these LD children and adolescents experience considerable frustration and may thus exhibit excess motor activity and poor attentional skills. Behaviors may be similar to those of the child or teen with ADHD but are reactive (i.e., secondary) to the child's or teen's primary disorder—learning disabilities.

Likewise, children and teens with ADHD may have learning disabilities because of their difficulty in focusing and sustaining their attention; they may process only bits and pieces of information that is not sufficiently repetitive. Conners has also suggested that many children and adolescents with LD exhibit ADD (without hyperactivity)—many of these are females who show some impairment of right hemisphere functions (e.g., poor organizational ability). In contrast, others have noted that those with ADHD (mostly males) have more frequent peer difficulties, fewer LD problems, but more conduct disturbance (CD) traits. Therefore, a comprehensive method of differential diagnosis is needed, especially when the co-morbid LD condition is suspected in addition to ADHD.

CONDUCT DISORDER (CD) AND OPPOSITIONAL DEFICIT DISORDER (ODD)

It has also been noted that in clinical settings, at least two-thirds of patients with ADHD also have oppositional defiant disorder (ODD) or conduct disorder (CD). Roughly 30% of the children and adolescents who meet diagnostic criteria for both ADHD and CD/ODD and are referred for treatment, reportedly tend to have an earlier age of onset, exhibit a greater total number of antisocial behaviors, and display more physical aggression toward both people and animals, along with destruction of property, theft, and other serious violation of rules. It has also been found that the greater the number of ODD/CD symptoms, added to characteristic symptoms of ADHD, the greater the risk for problems driving for such teens. Furthermore, it is noted that of all children and teens with ADHD, those with co-morbid conduct disorders are virtually the only ones at risk for antisocial behavior and drug use as adults.

However, there are two groups of conduct-disordered teens: (1) an "early onset" condition where symptoms appear prior to age 10 years (this group is likely to manifest antisocial behaviors throughout the lifespan); and (2) a "late onset" condition, where symptoms appear after age 10. This group's problems are not so longstanding or pervasive as the first group and, in all likelihood, will not continue past adolescence. However, in both cases, early intervention is essential to behavior, substance abuse, and criminal behavior, especially for those in the "early onset" group.

The ODD category generally describes milder forms of chronic behavior problems than those seen in conduct disorder. ODD appears to be more prevalent in males prior to puberty; thereafter, an equal number of females may be diagnosed. However, children and adolescents with ODD are seen as at risk for the development of a conduct disorder. Children with ODD display a pattern of stubborn negativistic, hostile, and defiant behaviors, but in contrast to CD, without serious violation of the rights of others. Roughly 40% to 65% of those with ADHD have ODD (the most frequently occurring co-morbid disorder). Many of the attentional problems of those with CD/ODD are associated with their persistent behavior.

It has become increasingly clear that while those with CD/ODD often exhibit some of the same behaviors as those with ADHD, these groups represent different types of disorders. According to Shaywitz and Shaywitz, the CD/ODD group seems to be found in older children and adolescents who have experienced some psychosocial disadvantage. This group is similar to one described by Weinberg and Emslie of children who exhibited both ADHD and CD/ODD characteristics. These children have evidence of repeated early abuse or neglect by multiple caretakers or inadequate or little parenting. The authors also describe two other groups, including one involving frontal lobe functioning and the other a family history of characterologic disorders. A third group is noted to be secondary conduct disorder, who manifests only behavioral disturbance during episodes of affective illness. They point out that some children and teens with episodic conduct disorder, ADHD, and affective irritability may develop a bipolar disorder.

OBSESSIVE COMPULSIVE DISORDER (OCD)

This disorder is characterized by recurrent and intrusive thoughts or images together with ritualistic behavior (e.g., hand washing), mental activity (counting, repeating words), and irresistible motor behaviors (touching, repeating other's behavior). These thoughts and actions are recognized as excessive, yet the person maintains contact with reality. Clearly such intrusive thoughts and behaviors may certainly disrupt one's ability to focus attention on task, and result in slower performance, missed information, and inappropriate responses due to lack of information. However, a common area of the brain, the orbitofrontal cortex, has been implicated in both ADHD and OCD. It has been further noted that some compulsive behaviors have been produced by amphetamines and other psychostimulants. Just as in the case with general anxiety disorders, OCD may be more frequently associated with the primarily inattentive form of ADHD.

DIAGNOSIS vs. ASSESSMENT

The evaluation of teens with ADHD is perhaps even more complex than with younger children. In many cases an adolescent may be referred for evaluation with a long history of several evaluations. In other cases, an adolescent may be referred for the first time. When prior evaluations are available, this can be quite helpful. Perhaps a diagnosis has been made in the past and the current evaluation was requested to document what changes have occurred. Or, perhaps prior evaluations simply focused on diagnosis and not a complete assessment.

While it may be important to arrive at a diagnosis, especially for legal or insurance purposes, the diagnosis by itself does not say much about how to treat the adolescent. It provides little information that can be used in treatment planning. Consequently, the term *assessment,* while sometimes used synonymously with *evaluation* and *diagnosis,* will be used here to denote a comprehensive evaluation of not only ADHD, but also co-morbid conditions. This type of evaluation may provide a diagnostic impression, but more important it can provide an assessment of strengths and weaknesses, as well as provide information that can be used to plan and implement a treatment program.

Use of the DSM–IV criteria places the emphasis on impairments or weaknesses, and may obscure the teen's strengths. For example, Dr. Arthur Robin has pointed out that impulsive individuals may actually excel in situations that require quick thinking. He explains further that when primitive man was a hunter, this characteristic may have been an asset. Also, the hypersensitivity that often develops from being criticized may heighten the person with ADHD's empathy towards others and may make them excellent helpers in times of distress.

The emphasis will be on a comprehensive evaluation of all components of the problems. In most cases involving ADHD, there is not a simple diagnostic pattern but typically several. One might then consider what is the *primary* diagnosis; what is the *secondary* diagnosis; and what is the *tertiary* diagnosis. Like levels on a three-tier layer cake, all must be assessed to get the total clinical picture. By adolescence, it is not unusual to discover that the pattern of ADHD with co-morbid conditions is even more complex than reported on prior evaluations.

Consistent with the basic treatment orientation to be discussed in Chapter 3, it is necessary to mention the use of the symptomatic approach. If our assessment is to be of value in treatment, there must be a direct linkage. Specifically, it is essential that the assessment provide a picture of each component of the problem, the pattern of deficits targeted for remediation, and the pattern of strengths to be used conjointly during the treatment process.

An in-depth discussion of the use of each teen's pattern of strengths will be elaborated on in later chapters. Detailed information will be needed on the teen's abilities, achievements, specific academic skills, motor, visual, visual–motor, visual–spatial, memory, attentional skills, executive control skills, and his or her behavioral/emotional characteristics. This type of comprehensive evaluation is essential for the survival of the teen with ADHD.

An analogous situation might be the teen who has just had a serious auto accident. There are suspected head, back, and internal injuries. It would be ludicrous for the treating physician to ask, "Now I believe we can evaluate and treat only one of these problems for him to survive." The parent would, of course, state that all problematic conditions should be evaluated and treated to give the teen the best chance of survival and to return to as normal a life as is possible.

The same scenario might be involved with the teen undergoing evaluation of ADHD. It is critical to assess all problems that may affect the teen's academic and personal life to provide the optimal chances for survival and productivity. The conditions that we are discussing here should be considered as life threatening and as serious as an auto accident. It is certainly no time to "cut corners," save money, and just do the minimum required. The teen's future is at stake.

In many cases, medication may be prescribed without behavioral interventions. This minimal treatment program may be supported by a "managed care orientation" to treatment, but may fail seriously in the long run when the accumulated effect of skill deficits are realized. Medication is critical in many cases, and this will be discussed in Chapter 3, but skill training and other interventions should also be considered crucial and their assessment should be included from the very beginning.

SCREENING EVALUATION FOR ADHD

In some cases, clinicians may face a situation where, due to financial, time, or managed-case constraints, it would be advantageous to conduct a screening evaluation than to have no evaluation at all. The minimum requirements for such a screening include: (1) a good history, including the teen's developmental background; (2) parent, teacher, and teen ratings; (3) brief testing to include: (a) a short ability test (e.g., KBIT), or an abbreviated form of the WISC–III, along with (b) the WRAT-3 achievement test, and (c) the Jessness Inventory; and (4) other brief clinical procedures, such as the human figure drawings (including the family), a sample of handwriting (on a sentence completion test), and a brief interview with the teen. Comprehensive treatment planning will be compromised, but some of the major problems may still be addressed.

Chapter 3

Medical and Clinical Interventions for Adolescent ADHD

Following the theme of assessment of ADHD symptoms and skill deficits for adolescents, treatment components should be linked to assessment findings. There are, however, levels of decisions that need to be made with respect to our evaluation.

The first question is, "Does this adolescent need to be hospitalized?" Significant depression with suicide potential would certainly warrant such placement. Assuming that there is no need for such a crisis intervention, the next question is, "Does this teen need to be referred for some additional work-up?" The teen who exhibits some indicators of a possible seizure disorder may certainly need to have a neurology consult. Likewise, if some other medical problem is suggested (e.g., anemia), this would also warrant a medical referral to rule out relevant physical factors.

Additionally, the clinician may ask the question, "Does this teen need to be referred for a medication consult?" Whether the teen is referred to his family physician, neurologist, or psychiatrist may depend on what conditions are suspected or associated with ADHD. While the family physician may deal with a wide variety of behavior disorders, those conditions that have a possible neurological implication (e.g., explosive personality) may best be referred to the neurologist. Those that have a strong behavioral–emotional implication (e.g., Bipolar Disorder) may best be referred to the psychiatrist for evaluation and medication consultation.

The Symptomatic Approach—Following the above sequence of decisions, the clinician must prepare a treatment plan that includes specific targets or goals for therapeutic intervention. Whichever techniques are selected, there must be a list of problematic behaviors or symptoms to address. This will include some of the traditional symptomatic characteristics of ADHD during the adolescent years, together with a unique set of skill-deficit areas to habilitate. The term *habilitate* is used to distinguish this training from rehabilitation. While the training may be similar in nature, in the latter case the skill has been acquired (learned), then lost perhaps through brain injury; the term *habilitation* thus refers to the development of a skill that theoretically should be acquired by the adolescent years (to some degree), but has failed to develop due to a lack of neurological development of an area of the brain that subserves that skill, a lack of opportunity to develop the skill, or some factors that interfere with the development of that skill. Regardless of the reason for the lack of development of these skills, deficit areas must be changed so that the teen may better achieve success in each area.

The overall goal is to maximize the teen's ability to adapt and cope rather than to "cure ADHD." Treatment will focus on medication, behavioral intervention, and educational accommodation and procedures. In addition to the use of multiple interventions, it will be essential that the teen's progress/status be periodically monitored. This means that every 3–6 months during the first year or two, the teen should be reevaluated to determine whether there has been progress. Thereafter, and assuming that the teen shows progress, less frequent check-ups may be scheduled (e.g., one to two times a year). If needed, revisions of the teen's program may be made or the teen may be maintained on the same program.

Use of Multiple Impact Therapies—This refers to the utilization of different approaches to the same target problem behavior or skill-deficit areas. The concept is much like that of multisensory learning for the remediation of various learning disabilities. Since each teen may process information differently, it is best to (a) repeat the information to provide more learning experiences, and (b) to provide the information in different formats. For example, the teen might read about skill development, have a verbal and visual presentation about it, and may experience it directly by actually doing it.

Since it is not known which may be the most efficient way to acquire impulse control skills, there may be many different approaches to develop that skill. The teen might develop some cognitive awareness of control through structured exercises in a game-like format. Alternately, the teen might learn these skills through some medium such as training in karate. The teen may also learn to improve self-control by developing some cognitive mediation strategy. Finally, the teen may improve self-control by direct reinforcement of better and better demonstrated self-control. Alternative therapeutic interventions will be discussed throughout this book as needed.

Periodically, there may also be other issues to address. If the teen is discovered using marijuana or alcohol, there must be a commitment to stop. The parents might then need to have a plan to monitor any substance use. Inspections of the teen's room, backpack, etc., may be conducted periodically. Likewise, random drug screens may be conducted or breathalyzer tests used when alcohol use is suspected. When the teen is unable to control the use of these substances, referral to a substance-abuse program would be warranted. It would thus be imperative to get control over the more serious substance-abuse problems before returning to address the ADHD characteristics. When the use of various substances is controlled and possible self-medication factors addressed, the use of appropriate medication may be planned.

Therapeutic Orientation—In this approach to managing teens with ADHD, treatment may be directed toward general characteristics of ADHD (symptoms), problematic behaviors, and skill deficits in the adolescent. Concurrently, training (treatment) may be provided parents in the form of parent-training programs, or for teachers in the format of workshops, inservice training, or personal consultation on ADHD. Therapeutic interventions may therefore address various aspects of symptomatic behavior in the adolescent, or may address how others react to the teen with ADHD.

Therapeutic Modalities—There are several modalities that may be used in treatment. These will include medications for ADHD and related conditions; behavioral interventions at home and at school; and other clinical interventions that are offered in clinics or other settings outside of the home and school environment.

This chapter focuses on medications and other clinical interventions that are typically conducted outside of the home/school situations, in a clinic or counseling setting. The various behavioral interventions that are both unique to the home and school setting, as well as those that are different in these settings, are discussed in Chapter 6.

There may be considerable overlap in approaches to problematic behavior that may be similar yet different in two different settings (e.g., home and school). In general, this is, in part, another conceptualization of a multi-modal program that addresses problematic behavior from different perspectives using different modalities.

MEDICATION INFORMATION

The information in this section does not replace personal medical consultation. No change in medication schedule or dose should be made, nor should any medications be added to the teen's medication regime without prior consultation with the child's physician. The author is also indebted to Kevin Passer, M.D., Board Certified Child Psychiatrist, and David Dugger, M.D., pediatrician, for their critical reading of the manuscript on "Medication Information."

The use of medication for ADHD began over 50 years ago. Stimulant medication was shown to be effective in 1937, but was not used to any large degree until around 1957 when methylphenidate (Ritalin®) was introduced. Many carefully controlled studies indicated that this medication was *safe* and *effective*. Despite occasional attacks by the media and a strong campaign against Ritalin® in the late 1980s by the Church of Scientology, this medication has survived both early and current attacks.

Much fear was generated for parents of children with ADHD when Ritalin® was implicated with brain damage, high blood pressure, confusion, murder, emotional disorders, Tourette's Syndrome, neurologic seizures, agitation, depression, and suicide. Many doubts were created in the professional community with demands for medication by teachers described as unable to cope with their students' behavior and psychiatrists who were considered "money hungry." Problems still periodically surface, but it is now generally accepted that stimulant medications are often quite appropriate for some, absolutely needed by others, and basically safe.

Drs. DuPaul and Stoner have noted that 750,000 children have been placed on stimulant medications. Production quotas of stimulants have exceeded written prescriptions. There is now good information that indicates the six-fold increases in stimulants from 1990–1995 were actually production quotas and not written prescriptions. A more accurate two- to three-fold increase has been prescribed. Also, the rise in use has been reportedly limited to those in the middle school and high school population, which is the focus of this section.

In 1996, Dr. Safer noted some reasons for the increase in stimulant prescriptions: (1) More children continue medication through the adolescent years; (2) The more subtle types of ADHD (Inattentive) are being identified and treated; (3) More girls with ADHD (again mostly Inattentive type) are being identified; (4) The general image of using stimulant medication has changed with more positive media exposure; and (5) Adults are being treated more now than in the past.

THE STIMULANTS

There are three primary medications that fall into this category: (1) methylphenidate (Ritalin®); (2) Destrostat® or dexamphetamine (Dexadrine®); and (3) pemoline (Cylert®). A fourth medication containing Dextroamphetamine saccharate and sulfate with amphetamine aspartate and sulfate (Adderal®) was previously used in adults for weight control (Obitral) and recently FDA-approved about three years ago as a treatment option for ADHD. Finally, methamphetamine (Desoxyn®) is also available, and is sometimes used for refractory patients.

Miller (1996) has noted that a review of over 155 controlled studies with over 5,000 children and adolescents treated indicates that stimulant medications are effective about 70% of the time, with a range from 60% to 90% effectiveness. However, only seven of these 155 studies involved adolescents. Results of these studies on teens indicate a positive response about 50% of the time, 20% lower than the reported 70% for children in general. Clearly more studies are needed with adolescents before concluding that stimulants are less effective for this age group.

Compared to ADHD, the percentage of all children with ADHD without hyperactivity showing a positive response is substantially lower at about 30%. In general, these stimulants reduce restlessness (and overall arousal), help children and teens to maintain their work effort so they may complete tasks, enhance the accuracy of their work and their ability to plan tasks, and improve their overall productivity in the classroom. As Barkley (1996) has noted, stimulants can increase a child's ability to show what he or she has learned. A decrease in impulsivity and disruptiveness, along with improved control of emotions (including aggressiveness), better interpersonal relations, better handwriting, and a general sense of calm have been observed. Some additional good side effects include more positive relationships with peers, siblings, and family, along with enhanced self-esteem. Stimulants have also been shown to be helpful with retarded children who have ADHD symptoms, if the retardation is not severe.

It is important, however, to note here that no stimulant medication will "cure" ADHD. Currently, there is no cure for ADHD. These medications help children and teenagers with ADHD to more closely approximate their potential abilities and their capacity for social relationships. While these medications improve a teen's present level of functioning, they do not have any apparent long-term effects other than to allow the teen to better acquire the skills he or she will need in the future. There is evidence that many teens who are treated with stimulants are better able to complete their education and probably have a lower risk of substance abuse in the future, but much depends upon the additional behavioral programs employed.

Essentially, the teen must perceive that he or she has the ability and skills to cope with problem situations. If a teenager has gotten the message that "what you need to do to improve your (school) work is to take this pill," an unfortunate association is established. It is clear that a "pill teaches no skill." It is essential that the teen also be given structured learning experiences that focus on his or her abilities to cope and adapt to many situations both academic and social, and that these skills must generalize and be utilized in future vocational, work, and social areas. Medication should, therefore, be combined with behavioral procedures to provide the adolescent with useful, adaptive skills that will be used throughout life.

In the past, there have been many concerns regarding the use of amphetamines for fear of "addiction dependency," or an increased risk for later substance abuse. First, the medications are used to enhance awareness and to improve attention and concentration; in contrast, much addictive drug use focuses on escape from reality or distortion of one's awareness of it. Second, teenagers with ADHD have been shown to exhibit a lower than normal level of arousal in the nervous system. Much of their hyperactive–restless behavior therefore makes sense—the teen is simply attempting to increase activation in the brain to a normal level, making the self-stimulation unnecessary. In short, when teenagers with ADHD take an appropriate dose of stimulant medication, they do not get high—they get to feel "normal"—since the arousal level is increased to a more normal range.

Some concern has also been experienced over possible appetite suppression, along with weight loss and stunting of growth. This can be a problem which is minimized when medication is taken with meals or shortly after a meal. It is especially not a problem during the teen years. Recent studies over a period of several years revealed that these medications do not result in stunting of growth, especially when excessively high doses are avoided. Untreated children with ADHD have been found to be generally somewhat shorter pre-pubertal than normal. Growth does occur later, post-pubertal, and the discrepancy disappears whether they are on or off medications. Actually, having ADHD affects their eating habits more than the medications. It has been reported that some youngsters eat better on medication as they can sit down at the meal and pay better attention to eating. While the medication does slow down the growth rate, it is highly variable. Also, larger children seem to be more affected than smaller ones. There is, however, no effect on puberty or rate of pubertal growth. Monitoring of height and weight is suggested on a monthly basis but not more frequently, unless weight loss has been identified as an issue.

There are, however, some side effects that should be considered causes for concern. Some of these include becoming socially withdrawn, overfocused, lethargic, agitated, teary, and emotionally upset. Often these side effects may appear when the medication is first introduced or when it is increased to a higher dose. They signal that the dose may be too high, but may resolve within a few hours after stopping the medication. When a stimulant causes these effects, the dose may be lowered or the teen may be switched to another medication. The rebound effect may be observed when the stimulant begins to wear off. At some point, the teen may become more irritable, crabby, teary, or hyperactive; this is basically related to a drop in level of arousal below that of the premedication level. This problem may be avoided by administration of a light dose of medication just prior to the time of rebound, changing to a longer acting, smoother stimulant, or selecting an additional agent, which can provide a "soft landing."

The possibility of tics and the appearance of Tourette's Syndrome have been cause for concern in the past. ADHD and Tourette's are fairly closely associated. While this may have been a contraindication for the use of stimulant medication in the past, it does not evoke so much concern today, and many physicians will proceed with stimulant medication, but perhaps with closer monitoring. At worst, the medication may exacerbate the manifestation of the behavior that would have been exhibited sooner or later. It is estimated that about 50% of these children with tics also have ADHD; some researchers and clinicians believe these two disorders may be on the same gene. In many cases, the ADHD symptoms may be manifested first. Tics may appear later in the sequence. Many children who show these tics will improve, some showing tics at low doses only to disappear on a higher dose. Tics are fairly common between the ages of 6 and 12 years and when the child is under a high stress level. The stimulant Ritalin® has, however, been known to lower the threshold for tics, thus increasing the probability of their occurrence.

Some teenagers may report headaches; this is generally rare and could be temporary or may necessitate a change of medication. Similar problems may occur with stomachaches, although this complaint is usually resolved if the teen takes food with the medication. It also appears that the complaints are more like "butterflies" and may last only about 45 minutes.

A statement on the use of medication from the Academy of Pediatrics as of August, 1996, is as follows: "Medication may be indicated when difficulties clearly affect school performance, social adjustment, or are associated with a significant behavior disorder. These difficulties may result in academic failure, inability to fulfill potential and give poor self-esteem, or social maladaptive behavior. Medication is not a panacea or a cure-all and should not be continued unless there is clear cut benefit." While the stimulants are basically safe, with Cylert®, baseline liver function tests are essential prior to starting this medication, as well as in regular intervals later. Currently, Cylert® is not indicated as a first-line treatment because of potential liver toxicity.

HOW DO STIMULANTS WORK?

The exact mechanism of action is still not known. However, available research indicates that increases in the availability of neurotransmitters in the synaptic cleft results in the desired changes in ADHD. Some experts speculate that such increases may occur when these neurotransmitters are blocked from re-uptake in the pre-synoptic region. It is known that specific regions of the brain, especially in the frontal and prefrontal areas, are rich in dopamine and norepinephrine receptors. These are the areas that are involved in behavioral inhibition that is a characteristic problem for those with ADHD.

THE DECISION TO MEDICATE

So many parents have voiced concerns over the use of stimulant medications that it is important to know who makes the decision on medications and on what basis the decision is made. Concerns have been raised even when parents understand the neurophysiological nature of ADHD and know the function of the medication. Knowing this, as well as the safety and effectiveness of these medications, may still raise concerns and many parents express the wish that their teen might not *need* the medication. Some teenagers with mild ADHD (Inattentive type) may be able to cope without medications, primarily using education resources, behavioral/cognitive techniques, and perhaps counseling/coaching when needed. Some parents have even turned to remedies described as "natural" and found in health stores. One substance called Pycnogenol has many anecdotal claims, but absolutely no research to back its effectiveness or its safety for use with children or teenagers. Some British studies have found that the "Oil of Evening Primrose" improved hyperactivity, but had no apparent effect on grades with teens. Future studies are needed to document its effect on other symptoms. Consequently, none of these so-called natural remedies are recommended. However, the use of such substances does reflect the parents' needs for alternative treatments that are safe and effective. It should be noted that just because a substance is natural does not make it safe.

When a decision is made to use a stimulant medication, it is done so with the parent's acceptance. In essence, *the parent makes the decision.* This decision will basically depend upon the seriousness of the ADHD condition and how it affects the teen's academic *and* social life. Frustration experienced by the teen and by teachers who must deal with his or her behavior is critical in making a decision. It is most important that there be cooperation from all parties—parents, teachers, and professionals, as well as the patient. Consideration must also be given to potential and actual side effects that may sometimes dictate whether a stimulant or some alternative medication should be used. While the presence of tics and even a seizure disorder are not absolute contraindications to the use of stimulant medication, the presence of glaucoma or cardiovascular problems may be clear contraindications.

Many experts indicate that stimulant medications exert greater behavior-changing effects when combined with other effective treatments such as behavior modification. It has also been noted that such combined treatment may minimize medication dosage.

Some factors noted by DuPaul that appear to enter into the decision to medicate include:

➠ the apparent severity of the ADHD symptoms and the presence of disruptive behavior

➠ prior treatments (e.g., behavioral) that may have failed

➠ the presence of anxiety (which lessens the probability of stimulants being successful)

➠ the parents' attitude toward medications

➠ the adequacy and competency of adult supervision

➠ the teen's attitude towards medication

Compliance may obviously be compromised by some of these factors.

Once a decision is made to use a stimulant medication, the only way to determine whether it will be successful is to conduct a careful *clinical trial*. Many physicians will not start medication at the beginning or end of the school year or during holidays. An *open* trial is typical where everybody knows that the teen is on medication. A *double-blind* trial, where no one knows whether the teen is getting a placebo or the actual medication, may be conducted if the results of the open trial are equivocal. It should be noted that about 10% of children who have ADHD don't respond positively at first. It is also known that stimulant medications may help anyone to focus better. Therefore, response to medication should not be used as a diagnostic indicator of ADHD.

Some physicians will also have access to the use of a continuous performance test (CPT)—for example, the Gordon Diagnostic System or the Test of Variables of Attention (TOVA)—to aid in predicting response to a medication. However, the ultimate test is to have baseline ratings from teachers, start the medication, and, at some point, obtain repeat teacher ratings. Parent observation and ratings of behavior change, as well as side effects, is also documented. Typical rating scales of effects and side effects are found in Figures 3.1a and 3.1b.

Often the physician begins medication on a weekend and observations are noted. If there are no significant side effects, the medication may be given for a few days, stopped, and then readministered. When behaviors vary with the changes and behavior improvements are noted with medication, the physician may then adjust the dose.

Figure 3.1a

MEDICATION EFFECTS RATING SCALE

Child/Teen Name _____ Age _____ Grade _____ Sex _____ Date _____

Instructions: Please rate each category of effects over the last week(s) from MUCH WORSE (1) to MUCH IMPROVED (5) by placing an X in the appropriate column for each item. If there has been no change in behavior for any specific category of effects, please rate SAME (3). If you have not been able to observe an effect, make no rating.

Category	Medication Effects	MUCH WORSE 1	WORSE 2	SAME (NO CHANGE) 3	IMPROVED 4	MUCH IMPROVED 5
ADHD	Attention/Listening					
	Impulsivity/Self-control					
	Hyperactivity/Restlessness					
SOCIAL	Cooperation					
	Social Interaction					
EMOTIONAL	Mood					
	Affect					
	Aggression					
ACADEMIC PERFORMANCE	Reading					
	Math					
	Handwriting					
CLASSROOM	Work/Behavior					
	Completed Work					
	Organizational Skills					
	Rule Compliance					
	Gets Along with Others					
	Subtotals					
	Total					

Rater's Name_____ Rater: Parent _____ Teacher _____ Other _____

How long have you known this child/teen? _____

How long has this child/teen been on medication? _____

List known medications: _____

Over what period are these ratings made? _____

Figure 3.1b
MEDICATION SIDE EFFECTS RATING SCALE

Child/Teen Name_____ Age_____ Grade_____ Sex_____ Date_____

Instructions: Please rate each category of side effects from NOT PRESENT (0) to PROFOUND (5) by placing an X in the appropriate column for each item. Base your ratings on observations of the child/teen over the past week(s). If you have not been able to observe an effect, make no rating.

Category	Medication Side Effects	NOT PRESENT 0	VERY MILD 1	MILD 2	MODERATE 3	SEVERE 4	PROFOUND 5
SLEEP/AROUSAL	Nightmares						
	Insomnia/Sleepiness						
	Excess Daydreaming/Staring						
EATING	Decreased Appetite						
	Increased Appetite						
	Weight Gain						
	Weight Loss						
GI SYMPTOMS	Stomachache						
	Dry Mouth						
	Constipation						
	Nausea						
MOOD	Irritability						
	Sad						
	Prone to Cry						
	Euphoric/Unusually Happy						
ENERGY	Fatigue						
	Sedation/Zombie-like						
CARDIO-VASCULAR	Rapid Heart Beat						
	Low Blood Pressure						
INTERPERSONAL	Talks Less with Others						
	Uninterested in Others						
NERVOUS & SYSTEM REACTIONS	Agitation						
	Dizziness						
	Tics/Twitches						
	Anxious						
	Bites Fingernails						
	Tremor/Shaking						
	Headaches						
	Skin Irritation (Patch)						
	Subtotals						
						Total	

Rater's Name_____ Parent_____ Teacher_____ Other_____

Over what period are these ratings made? _____

REBOUND EFFECT

The key here is to obtain maximum control while minimizing side effects, as well as any possible cognitive interference associated with some of the higher dose levels of medications. When the teen appears irritable, weepy, and more difficult to manage than prior to starting medication, this may be the *rebound* effect, especially if it occurs after four to five hours from the last dose in the case of methylphenidate, but later in the longer-acting stimulants. Normally this may be a problem when the teen comes home from school and this effect may make it very difficult to get homework completed. If the teen is weepy, exhibits a dazed look, and is restless, this may indicate overmedication and typically appears after about two hours from the last dose. At these times, the teen may also complain about "feeling weird."

One of the problems with Ritalin® and Dexedrine® is that when the medication wears off, there is a significant drop in the arousal level in the nervous system (sometimes even lower than pre-medication baseline). This can result in a marked increase in behavioral problems. This phase of medication effect has also been related to sleep problems. A simple solution to this problem may be to provide a mild dose of the stimulant in the afternoon. Adderal®, being a combination medication of several forms of dextroamphetamine, tends to have far fewer rebound effects.

Some experts have discussed a kind of "sleep window" that extends from 30 minutes prior to the end of the stimulant medication dose to about 60 minutes beyond the end of the dose. It may also be possible to time the drop in blood level of the last dose to correspond more closely to the time when the adolescent would go to sleep. Another possible intervention is a small dose of stimulant medication at bedtime. Other behavioral control techniques may also be helpful, such as a relaxation exercise at bedtime, or to provide music that may gradually change to slower rhythmic patterns over time.

DECIDING ON WHICH STIMULANT TO USE

As previously noted, there are options with regard to brand names and there are options regarding the length of time the medication is effective. For example, with the short-acting form of Ritalin® or Dexadrine®, a change may be noted after 15 to 30 minutes following ingestion of the medication. The improvement, if obtained, may last for about three to five hours—and on the average, four hours. This means that if the morning dose is taken with breakfast, by lunch time a second dose may be needed to allow the behavioral improvement to be maintained until the end of all classes. A third dose may, however, also be needed to obtain adequate cooperation and productivity during homework.

There is a tremendous individual response to the medications and how they are metabolized. Thus, while many teenagers are placed on three doses per day, others may require two and some need four. A fourth dose may sometimes be given at bedtime in lieu of an alternative medication. It may seem paradoxical that a teen may go to sleep easier and more quickly with a light dose of stimulant medication, but clinically, this may be an effective alternative. (This is not surprising when one considers that many adults—perhaps with adult ADHD—are capable of rapid sound sleep just after having a cup of coffee.)

Some factors that may influence the decision to use one stimulant over another include:

1. *Age.* Some pre-teens and teens resent taking the dose at lunch and request a long-acting medication. While Ritalin-SR® (sustained release) is stated to be 20 mgs, only 12–15 mgs are released over a period of 5–7 hours. However, it takes 45–60 minutes before Ritalin-SR® starts acting. It should also be noted that Ritalin-SR® tabs should not be broken as its slow-release properties may be destroyed. While Ritalin-SR® should last up to 8 hours, its effects often cover much less (average 6 hours). This form also appears to have fluctuating effects and when first taken may result in a spiking effect. Probably more patients fail to respond to Ritalin-SR® than to any other stimulant. However, this failure does not necessarily mean that regular Ritalin® will not work.

   Adderal® is reported to last 8–12 hours and is a smoother medication. Dexedrine Spansules® has often been noted as the medication of choice for adolescents. Such long-acting preparations are effective and show fewer side effects than Ritalin®. Since its duration of action is long, elimination of a noon-time dose is preferred by the teen.

2. *Rebound.* Fewer problems are noted with Adderal® vs. Ritalin®.

3. *Depression.* Ritalin® has a higher rate of dysphoria (an unacceptable side effect).

4. *Tics.* Ritalin® appears to lower the threshold for tics.

There have been only a few studies on Adderal®, and none have focused on adolescents. Like Dexadrine Spansules®, this medication may not have to be taken at school since it may last 5 to 6 hours. However, from clinical experience, it appears that most teens with ADHD will need two doses per day. This medication is as effective as others, but without the undesirable embarrassment of the noon-time dosing.

Unlike other stimulants, Cylert® has few cardiovascular side effects. It has therefore been desirable for teens with ADHD who are recovering from substance-abuse problems. The drawback is, however, liver function tests are needed at least every 3–6 months as there have been reported cases of liver toxicity with the majority of problem cases (11 out of 13) reportedly resulting in death. Recently, Cylert® has been indicated to be a second-line medication.

WHEN TO GIVE STIMULANT MEDICATIONS

Stimulant medications are just as effective when given with meals. Miller (1996) suggests not giving the medication with orange juice—it alters the effect. Since these medications do suppress appetite, it is best to avoid giving these medications in the two-hour period prior to a meal. Sometimes it's given just prior to breakfast. The medication can then enter the system more rapidly and not decrease appetite. If the teen resists taking the medication, it may be given with pudding or some other soft food.

Many physicians begin with either a half or a whole tablet (Ritalin® is available in 5-mg, 10-mg, and 20-mg tablets; Dexadrine® in 5-mg, 10-mg, and 15-mg tablets); Dexadrine® equals one-half to two-thirds the dose of Ritalin®. Some physicians use quarter tablet increases (but mostly for younger children). The teen may show little effect on a half-tablet, experience side effects on one tablet, but may find that a three-quarter tablet is optimal.

A study in 1996 by Dr. Rappley estimated the most common dose at 10 mg twice daily. The exact dose requirements will, of course, vary for each teen. Unique metabolic factors, severity of ADHD symptoms, number and type of co-morbid conditions, and factors in the home or school environments may all affect compliance and influence decisions on the dose and type of stimulant selected.

Most of the difficulty with stimulants may be encountered in the beginning when attempting to regulate the dose or when an increase is needed. Most practitioners believe that if the correct dose is given up front, there should be little change required for most children and teens. Although tolerance is not generally seen, some teens may cease to show a positive response for some unknown reason. In these cases, the medication may be suspended and the teen observed; other options may then be considered.

Some practitioners may start the teen on a low single dose in the morning. If there is a positive change in behavior that disappears about four hours later, the effectiveness is confirmed. A school-age child may begin at 5 mg and then go to a 10-mg or 15-mg dose. A teenager may start on 10 mg, then go to a 15-mg or 20-mg dose. The preschool child may start at 2.5 mg and go to 5.0 mg or 7.5 mg Ritalin®. A typical dose pattern is 10 mg (morning), 10 mg (lunch), and 5 mg (afternoon).

Miller has noted that Dexadrine® is not equivalent to Ritalin®. It's estimated that 10 mg Ritalin® is equal to 5–7.5 mgs of Dexadrine®, which equals 37.5 mg Cylert®. She notes that the *Physician's Desk Reference (PDR)* is incorrect in describing Cylert®. Specifically, it takes 48 hours to start working and it has to be taken every day starting at 37.5 mg, *not* 18.75 mg. Sometimes Cylert® may require a full week to build up in the body and get the full effect. It may also be noted that Cylert® may last 2–3 days after the last dose is given (i.e., stopped). Cylert® is therefore not recommended as a first-line medication for ADHD. Manifestations of hepatitis cannot be predicted by routine blood work for liver function tests. Thus, parents should be warned that signs of nausea, vomiting, chronic abdominal stress, lethargy, or jaundice should indicate a problem with this medication.

What About Monitoring?

When a teen is placed on stimulant medication, it is important to obtain a response rate every 3–4 months, according to Barren. He suggests that the patient be seen and given a physical exam each time. When on Cylert®, some physicians may have previously required a test of liver functions every 3–6 months; there are new guidelines from the company. Barren also believes that it is important to use rating scales to provide information about behavior changes in the classroom.

After the teen is placed on medication, behavior should be monitored on a weekly basis. It is often best to have the teacher rate the behavior and academic performance in school, and the parents rate the side effects at home. A number of options exist for these ratings:

1. Combinations of the abbreviated forms of the Conners Parent Rating Scale–Revised, Conners Teacher Rating Scale–Revised, along with the Teen's Self Report and the Academic Performance Rating Scale.

2. The BASC Monitor for ADHD (Teacher and Parent Ratings and a Student Observation System) combined with the Academic Performance Rating Scale.

3. The recently published Spadafore–ADHD–Rating Scale Medications Monitoring Form that allows the teacher to rate ADHD symptoms, social symptoms, and academic and classroom behaviors. A Medication Side Effects Rating is combined on this form. The ADHD Observation Form may also be used for direct behavioral observations in the classroom. However, there is no companion parent form; a different parent rating scale would need to be selected.

4. The ACTeRS may be used for teacher ratings in combination with the Academic Performance Rating Scale and the abbreviated Conners Parent Rating Scale–Revised. It is best to select instruments for monitoring that have been co-normed and determined to be consistent with those used in the initial evaluation process so that the effects of test variability may be minimized. Consequently, the first two combinations (i.e., [1] and [2] above) now appear to offer greater benefits and ease of interpretation. It is, of course, best to remain consistent and use the same monitoring devices over time for more accurate comparisons and documentation of treatment effectiveness. While demonstrating adequate dose sensitivity, computerized CPT results may allow for interesting comparisons (and research), but these CPT measures are best considered secondary to the ratings.

5. One of the most recent monitoring systems was developed by Dr. David Rabiner. This system may indicate a need for or change in medication. In addition, other areas including academic performance, behavioral/emotional, and social functioning are tracked. All three areas are noted on a weekly monitoring form. This information can be quite helpful in making decisions about when to make changes in the treatment program.

6. The Brown Scales may also be especially useful for monitoring the teen's response to treatment medication and/or behavioral programs. Both the significance and the magnitude of the improvement may be monitored. If the total score is lower than the limits of a 90% confidence interval of the teen's pre-treatment score, then the change is significant.

7. Last, the clinician may wish to use Curriculum Based Assessment (CBA) to monitor changes in academic performance in specific areas of reading, spelling, arithmetic,

and handwriting, as these assessments may have greater ecological validity in short-term comparisons that will reflect medication effects. An example of such a measure would be the number of words read correctly over a one-minute period. For details about the CBA, see Roberts and Landau (1997).

SIDE EFFECTS OF STIMULANTS

There can be some physiological reactions to stimulant medication that may be a source of caution. Each one of these must be considered when prescribing a stimulant for the teen.

First, its effect on blood pressure and intraocular pressure. Second, cardiac arrhythmia, especially when other stimulants are used (e.g., caffeine or nicotine) and with alcohol. Each teen may be affected differently. Third, tics are possible but are more likely to develop in younger children. The existence of co-morbid Tourette's Syndrome may require additional neurological or psychiatric consultation. Fourth, while rare, some teens may exhibit a psychotic reaction or significant depression with stimulant medication.

Other side effects may include headache, stomach pain, dizziness, insomnia, irritability, appetite suppression, and weight loss. While cardiovascular and possible glaucoma side effects are clearly serious and may contraindicate the use of stimulants, other effects may be controlled or managed with stimulant use.

Most adolescents do not get unduly concerned about these side effects. They are much more concerned about how the medication makes them feel or how it may change their personality. This may be especially true when the teen is seen to use this medication. He or she may be teased and become embarrassed about appearing different to other teens. It should also be noted that the side effects of appetite loss, mood and affect problems, along with withdrawal are seen primarily when higher doses of stimulants are used. In general, most side effects encountered are mild and, with dose management, optimum results can be obtained with regard to the control of ADHD symptoms; positive effects can be quick, working within 30 to 60 minutes in some individuals.

The objective when placing a teen on medication is not simply behavioral control. If a once-restless teen becomes passive but shows no other improvements in social interactions, completed work, or enhanced academic performance, then the current medication regimen/dose may be questionable. Many years ago, it was noted that the optimal dose of Ritalin® needed to manage social behavioral problems is higher than that required for adequate cognitive functioning. In addition to changing the dose and/or schedule, it is also clear that "pills do not teach skills." It is, therefore, essential to combine the medication regimen with other behavioral interventions such as skills training and perhaps adjunctive behavioral remediation programs. A teen who continues to be unproductive academically, even when placed on medication, may be suffering from an undiagnosed and unrecognized learning disability, dysgraphia, or neurological or emotional problem that impairs his or her ability to function.

ABUSE OF STIMULANTS

A recent study of adolescent substance abuse revealed that teens are much more likely to abuse substances such as alcohol, cigarettes, or marijuana than any type of amphetamine. The teens who do abuse Ritalin® may crush the tablets and inhale the powdered fragments. In general, stimulants raise the teen's arousal level to a normal range (since pre-medication levels reflect a state of low arousal). Thus, the stimulant produces a calm, focused state and not euphoria. Further, it has often been noted that ADHD by itself is not closely associated with later drug use. However, the additional co-morbid conduct disorder may contribute to inappropriate drug use, as well as behavioral and social problems.

HOW LONG SHOULD STIMULANTS BE GIVEN?

The answer to this question is both simple and complex. The simple answer is that medications should be administered as long as the teen needs them. This may be six months or several years. As these medications become more accepted for adults, they may also continue to be used for a part of adult life, again as they are needed. The complex answer, however, is that a decision on the continuation of medication may depend on the severity of the ADHD condition, the presence of side effects, and the availability of viable alternatives to medications.

Occasionally, a parent forgets to give the medication or runs out of it. If there is little effect upon behavior and/or academic performance, it is perhaps time to consider stopping the medication. To confirm the effectiveness, baseline teacher ratings are obtained while the teen is on medications; the medications may then be suspended for two weeks, given in the second week, and then stopped again. This procedure should give sufficient evidence to continue the medication or to stop it, using feedback from teachers and their ratings of the teen on and off medication.

Some experts suggest stopping treatment annually for one or two weeks about one month after the beginning of a new school year to allow time for adjustment to going back to school (October is suggested for a trial stop). With stimulant medications, it is possible to stop and start the medication; with alternative medications used for ADHD, a gradual weaning off the medication is required, which, of course, needs to be done under medical supervision. Stopping some of the alternative medications abruptly or even missing a scheduled dose may be risky and clearly should be avoided.

WHAT ABOUT DRUG HOLIDAYS?

Some physicians recommend that stimulant medications be given only for school days or perhaps for significant social events. Others do not stop the medications as long as behavior is a significant problem. Some will argue that the medications are just as important for social interpersonal relationships and should be continued even during summer vacations. In general, the medication helps the teen with life, not just school. There is even one study that demonstrates a benefit when playing baseball.

There is no evidence that continued use of medications is harmful, especially if they are monitored. Any decision regarding such "drug holidays" should be weighed against the potential harm that may result and the delay in development of critical skills that would occur without medications. This balance of possible benefits versus possible problems should be kept in mind with regard to the use of any medication. Any medication may have side effects, and any medication may precipitate unique medical problems for a specific individual. It's important to remember, however, that this is true of any medication that one may be given, including the over-the-counter medications.

FACTORS INFLUENCING MEDICATION EFFECTIVENESS

1. *Generic Ritalin® (Methylphenidate).* This has been reported to be less effective than the brand name. While some respond adequately to it, others will not. Miller has noted that only about 30 percent of ADHD teens do well on the generic form; it is estimated to be about two-thirds as potent. If the medication appears to have stopped working, check to see if your pharmacy switched to the generic form.

2. *Use of Sedating Medications.* Whether prescribed or over the counter, these medications may counteract the effect of the stimulant. Allergy and cold medications and some antidepressant medications may cause drowsiness. There will be a lack of stimulant medication effectiveness until the sedating medication is changed or stopped.

3. *Ritalin® with Orange Juice.* When stimulant medication is taken with orange juice, its effectiveness may be modified. In fact, any citrus, cranberry fruit, and juices, as well as vitamin C, can result in stimulant medication being removed from the system more rapidly and reduced in the blood level. This may be resolved by taking the vitamin C in the evening or at bedtime. There may even be increased stomach problems using citrus.

4. *Dramatic Events.* These events may change the need for stimulant medications. It is not unusual when highly stressful events or changes occur within a family (e.g., introduction of a foster child) that a teen who was on a well-adjusted dose level now appears to show an increase in ADHD behaviors.

5. *Minor Changes or Transitions.* These can also disrupt the level of adjustment to stimulant medications. Such changes (e.g., a family move, getting a new car, or changes in time during spring or fall) can all trigger a reaction that makes the child appear unmedicated.

6. *Dose Level.* Some say that very few children respond to doses of 5 mg. A typical dose ranges from 10 mg to 15 mg.

FACTORS INFLUENCING MEDICATION EFFECTIVENESS   *(Cont'd)*

7. *Medications.* Some medications used for treatment of asthma (e.g., Theophylline) may cause severe behavior problems and worsen attention problems and hyper-activity. For stimulants to be more effective, it may be necessary to switch to another medication for asthma. Likewise, some medications for seizure disorders, such as phenobarbital and anticonvulsants like clonazapem, phenytoin (Dilantin®) may generate more severe ADHD behaviors, making it more difficult to manage with the same level of stimulant that produced adequate control prior to introduction of one of these additional medications.

8. *Compliance.* Some children and even teens may have difficulty swallowing certain pills, or may actively resist taking the medications either because they have been teased about it or because of the reaction they have to it. These problems must be sorted out and discussed with the child's physician.

THE ANTIDEPRESSANTS

The following antidepressant medications will be discussed:

⇒ Tofranil® (imipramine)

⇒ Norpramin® (desipramine)

⇒ Pamelor® (nortriptyline)

⇒ Wellbutrin® (bupropion)

Alternative medications for ADHD may be used when there is a problematic reaction to a stimulant, significant side effects, a lack of positive response, or multiple problems to address. In many cases, the teen may be unable to tolerate stimulants. Other possible indications for the use of an antidepressant are the presence of significant anxiety or depression. According to Barren (1996), 30% to 40% of the children show a response to these antidepressant medications. However, others report a response of up to 70%.

The antidepressants have several noticeable benefits. Decreases in impulsivity and hyperactivity have been observed, along with diminished emotional instability. While these medications have only limited effect on attentional processes, there is often observed improvement in mood and anxiety, as well as improved sleep. Other advantages as noted by Wilens (1996) include: (a) a long half-life; (b) they don't exacerbate tics; and (c) they are especially good when there is anxiety and/or mood problems present as well as ADHD.

The typical side effects are dry mouth or constipation, sedation, dizziness or confusion, and changes in cardiac conduction. It should also be emphasized here that overdosing can be very dangerous.

Prior to the use of an antidepressant, it is critical to monitor and pretest for the following as suggested by Miller: (1) Syncope must be ruled out and it should be determined whether there is a family history of sudden death; (2) A baseline EKG should be obtained and repeated with each increase in dose (but not necessary with Wellbutrin®); (3) Blood levels should monitor the metabolism of the medication and not the response (except for Wellbutrin®); and (4) A long QT syndrome (i.e., the QRST complex reflecting changes in heart rhythm) can be difficult to diagnose without an EKG baseline and a repeat EKG. Significant problems can result with changing of the heart rate by medication. It should be noted, however, that the American Academy of Pediatrics has not found that EKGs are absolutely necessary.

In the past, the most frequently used antidepressant medication for ADHD was Tofranil® (imipramine); this one will be discussed in more detail. First, in general, the antidepressants are, as a group, less effective than stimulants, but there are contradictory studies. This group of medications is most often used when there is a mood problem (i.e., depression or aggression) associated with ADHD.

Tofranil® is longer acting compared with stimulants. Its half-life ranges from 10–20 hours and it also can be given once per day, typically at night so that sleep may also be improved. Some teenagers develop a tolerance for Tofranil® and the medication may be increased, but should additional increases be warranted, most physicians will turn to another medication.

For older children and teens, the dose may start at 10–25 mg and increase by 10–25 mg in increments up to 100 mg per day. While distribution of doses during the day may provide more even levels of the medication, this must be weighed against sedation effects. This may be particularly evident in the beginning of treatment and may gradually improve; however, this effect can recur with each increase in dose. Sometimes behavior changes occur within a few days; in other cases, it may take several weeks.

Sudden cessation of the medication may cause a flu-like withdrawal reaction with possible nausea, vomiting, headache, lethargy, and irritability or even emotional reactions like crying, sadness, or nervousness. Such problems can be avoided by a gradual weaning of the medication over several weeks. On rare occasions, heart rate and blood pressure can be affected. Plasma levels of the medications may be monitored, especially at higher doses. Some physicians will perform a routine electrocardiograph (ECG) as a precaution.

According to Wilens, Pamelor® (nortriptyline) is given by the dose schedule of 2 mg/kg/day, with an average dose at 75 mg/day. His suggestion is that if this medication does not work, don't increase the dose, just terminate it. However, others have suggested that the level should be monitored to reach an effective dose in a "therapeutic window."

According to Barren, Wellbutrin® (bupropion) may be helpful for those older adolescents and young adults in the 18- to 25-year age range. It has been reported to be mildly effective on aggressive and hyperactive behaviors. However, there have been only a few basically insignificant comments about "the way it makes the person feel." In general, it appears to be an excellent medication. Wilens points out that it is somewhat like a stimulant and the dose must be started very low. Hunt notes that this medication is good for "Anergic Depression" where there is not much energy and there is a need to be activated. According to Spencer (1996), Dr. Keith Conners found this medication to be effective for children. There is some reported risk of seizures with the older form (about 4 per 1,000 cases), but this is not significantly greater than that seen with other antidepressants (about 1 per 1,000 cases); it is also not found with the SR form.

THE ANTIHYPERTENSIVES

The following medications make up this category:

⇒ Catepres® (clonidine)

⇒ Tenex® (guanfacine)

Antihypertensive medications benefit the teen through decreases in over-arousal, hyperactivity, and impulsivity. In addition, there is often a significant lessening of aggressive and oppositional tendencies, as well as some general improvement in socialization functions and sleep. There is, however, limited effect on attentional processes. A skin patch is available for a more even distribution of the medication as absorbed by the body.

Some of the pitfalls and drawbacks of these medications include sedation effects and occasionally contact dermatitis when the patch is used on a daily basis. In addition, a t.i.d. dose (i.e., given three times per day) is often needed with pills. Sometimes a fourth dose is given at bedtime. These medications, like the antidepressants, must be increased or decreased slowly and gradually.

Clonidine is perhaps the most frequently used medication in this category, but Tenex® is fast becoming popular. Clonidine is useful with teens who are ADHD and aggressive. This medication has little effect on attention and distractibility; thus, a stimulant may often be combined with clonidine. However, many physicians avoid using this combination because of concerns about possible cardiac side effects.

If forthcoming, improvements may be seen within 4–6 hours with effects lasting up to 12 hours. Some sedative effects may be noticed during the first hour and a half after administration of this medication. A positive response may not occur until two weeks for some; it is unusual when the full peak effect is not realized within two months.

Again, sedation with resulting sleepiness may be the primary side effect for this medication. This may improve over a period of several weeks for a small percentage of ADHD children and teens. Use of the patch may still produce sleepiness, and it is sometimes difficult to keep the patch on. Some children and teens may also have headaches, appear confused, or exhibit an increase in aggressive outbursts. Hypotension and hypoglycemia are potential problems, the latter of which can be controlled by taking the medication with food. Clonidine may also affect heart rate; thus, exceeding the recommended dose can be *dangerous*. Stopping this medication should be done gradually over several weeks. Rebound hypertension may occur when stopping this medication suddenly and is potentially dangerous.

Many professionals report as many as 70% of the hyperactive, impulsive, aggressive children and teens respond well on this medication. Since this medication is more likely to result in improved compliance, it is perhaps best used when such problems are greater at home than at school. Dr. Hunt believes this medicine may be most appropriate for those children and teens with ADHD who are also very oppositional, defiant, or who present evidence of conduct disorder.

Tenex® is less potent than clonidine and thus considered to be a smoother medication. Given one to two times a day, it is less sedating. Reported dose levels range from 0.5–3.0 mg per day, and when given one to two times a day can last up to 10 hours in children and teens. Wilens also reports that it is more effective on attentional processes and less effective on impulsive and hyperactive behaviors. Barren calls this a "more arousal modulating medication." The overall effect is to decrease arousal and increase inhibition. Hunt believes that Tenex®, in combination with Adderal®, may be safer than clonidine. He explains that while the stimulant medication "increases the strength of the signal, Tenex® decreases the noise." The overall result is seen in the improvement of the signal-to-noise ratio, making noisy classrooms less distracting and allowing the child or teen to focus more clearly on the teacher's communications. As with clonidine, blood pressure assessment is recommended on all patients being considered for this medication. Clonidine and Tenex® are also useful when Tourette's Syndrome is seen with ADHD. These medications can help in treatment of the tics.

MEDICATIONS UNDER INVESTIGATION

Many medications are currently being researched for their possible application to problems of the child with ADHD. These include:

SEROTONIN RE-UPTAKE INHIBITORS (SSRI)

Prozac® (fluoxetine): Barren believes that this medication does not help ADHD symptoms. He does, however, believe that it helps with symptoms of depression and anxiety, and notes that some hyperactive behavior may be obsessive–compulsive behavior. One study, according to Spencer, showed it was helpful for depression associated with ADHD. This medication should not be used within six weeks of taking any MAO inhibitor such as Nardil®, Parnate®, or Marplan®.

Zoloft® (sertraline): Leventhal (1996) notes that this medication has been helpful for depression in adolescents. Combined with a stimulant, it has been used in regulating mood and irritability.

Paxil® (paroxetine): When combined with a stimulant, it has been helpful in regulating mood and irritability, like Zoloft®.

Effexor® (venlafaxine): Barren states that this medication should not be given to any child under 18 years of age. Leventhal indicates that this medication may be effective for teens with ADHD, especially in those cases with depression. The most common side effect of Effexor® is hypertension.

In general, the SSRIs have received recognition for the treatment of depression, anxiety, and Obsessive–Compulsive Disorder.

MOOD STABILIZERS

Tegretol® (carbamazepine): Barren notes that this anticonvulsant medication is used by more psychiatrists as a mood stabilizer. However, Leventhal believes that it is not especially effective for patients with ADHD.

NEUROLEPTICS

Mellaril® (thioridazine): According to Barren, this antipsychotic is milder so that the symptoms of tardive dyskinesia (involuntary rhythmic movements of the tongue, jaw, or extremities) are lessened or nil. He notes that it may be used in younger children after stimulants have been found to be ineffective. He further explains that this medication has been used with some aggressive children where other drugs haven't worked. In contrast, Leventhal does not recommend any antipsychotic medication for ADHD. However, some have noted that these medications are superior to stimulants in those with ADHD and low IQ.

BETA BLOCKERS

Inderal® (propranolol): Barren indicates that this can be an anti-aggressive medication, and that it has been useful with "post traumatic" aggressive children and teens. However, continued regular monitoring of heart rate and blood pressure is required. This medication can cause mood changes and depression.

ATYPICAL ANXIOLYTICS

BuSpar® (buspirone): Barren notes that this medication is appropriate for adults and anxious teens. It addresses impulsive and restless behavior, plus anxiety. It is a fair anti-anxiety medication and reportedly has helped some anxious or even aggressive ADHD children and teenagers.

Lithium carbonate: Barren notes that this medication has worked with some aggressive children. In combination with a stimulant, it can be an anti-manic mood stabilizer, and is indicated for Bipolar Disorders. Side effects are many, but may be controlled using a potassium supplement; this medication is best monitored by a psychiatrist.

OTHER MEDICATIONS

Auroix Maclobemide: Barren states that this MAO inhibitor has been studied in Germany and appears to be a good second-line medication. It reportedly helps most

ADHD symptoms and shows some improvement with attentional problems. It is not approved in this country at this time.

Depakote: This is a mood stabilizer according to Barren. Studies have shown that it sometimes helps aggressive behavior.

Haldol: Barren suggests that this medication may be used with Ritalin® or Dexedrine® when tics/Tourette's Syndrome (TS) are present. Leventhal suggests that the stimulant medication be used to determine if the tics get worse. In most cases, he reports that they do not worsen. This may be combined with a stimulant when both ADHD and TS are present. This medication has also been noted to be superior to stimulants in those with ADHD and low IQ.

Klonopin: Barren notes that this medication is different from Valium®, but still similar. He notes that there are no problems with addiction and it can be used for panic attacks, tics, and aggressive attacks.

Risperdol: According to Barren, this medication has unique anti-seritonin effects. It has been helpful for tics, but with longer duration of use, "kids seem to need more of it." He reports that it is not good for aggressive behavior and that there are no good studies of the medication in children. Some studies do show a positive effect on behavior; however, a significant side effect is weight gain.

DISCONTINUATION OF MEDICATIONS

It is clear that most children with ADHD will require medication throughout their teenage years. If medications are stopped during the summer vacation, most feel it is best to start the new school year on medications. This procedure may thus avoid potential harmful effects of an unmedicated state. Difficulties may occur rapidly and it may be quite stressful trying to play "catch up" when putting the teen back on medications. This is especially true of the nonstimulant medications that may not have their peak effect for up to two months.

Parents should inform the teacher that their teen is on medications or that there will be a medication change. Preparations may therefore be made to cope with the teen's adjustment to the change. Baseline teacher ratings are essential. Additional ratings should be obtained on a periodic basis (every three to six months) and when there are changes in the teen's medication schedule or therapeutic program. Follow-up medical visits should occur every three months.

WHAT TEENS SHOULD KNOW ABOUT MEDICATIONS

Information about the purpose of the medications the teen is taking is important. It is essential that explanations be given that are consistent with the teen's developmental level and his or her capacity to understand. It is critical to stress that the medication is used as an aid to help the teen in areas that are important to him or her. School work, social activities, and homework are all areas in which the teen must be made aware of problem behaviors to be dealt with. It is equally important to stress that it is not the medication that does the work; it is the teen who should be given credit. In other words, it is important to stress "internal attributes," giving credit to the teen's efforts rather than to "external attributes" (i.e., the medication alone).

Bowen, Fenton and Rappaport (1990) noted two factors that affected the teen's perception and willingness to take medication. These involved: (1) the perception that taking medication means that something is "wrong with them," and (2) the embarrassment when seen taking medication (e.g., being teased when seen taking meds at the school office). Sometimes it may be helpful for the teen to problem-solve with these two perceptions and to develop a list of pros and cons for/against medication.

Be sure to emphasize this point to the teen by comparing the use of medications to other problems that need treatments. For example, one wears glasses to correct a problem with vision, or a hearing aid to hear better. Other medications may be shown to help with allergies or asthma and thus allow the teenager to function like everyone else. Conners has noted that the teen may be encouraged by the statement "the real you" that shows itself when the medication is working.

Another important point must be stressed. Medications are used as long as they are needed. While the teen is taking medications, he or she may also be working on appropriate skills. Just as a teen who must use crutches while he has a broken leg or a wheelchair while she learns to walk again, the same is true of the teen with ADHD. The adolescent should realize that there may be some point in time when he or she will no longer need the medications or may need less medication. The teen must also be made to understand that medications should not allow the teen to avoid consequences for inappropriate behavior. At times, some children or adolescents may say, "I did it because I haven't had my medicine." There needs to be more recognition for positive behaviors and less emphasis on the negative ones.

Two good books for teenagers that describe the purpose of medications, their effects, and their use include: *I Would If I Could: A Teenager's Guide to ADHD/Hyperactivity* by Michael Gordon (New York: GSI, 1991) and *ADHD: A Teenager's Guide* by James Crist (King of Prussia: Center for Applied Psychology, 1996).

WHAT PARENTS MUST KNOW ABOUT MEDICATIONS

Parents must know the purpose and general use of the medications that are prescribed for their teenager. Knowledge of the effects of the drug, side effects, and possible complications is important. The parent must know what to expect from the medication and when to expect it (i.e., time course for effectiveness of the medication). Parents must be good observers of their teen. All changes, overt or more subtle, must be noted, and in many cases, formally recorded. These observations may be very useful for the prescribing physician.

Parents need to know about adjustment on medications, possible changes, rebound effects, and other issues that may be addressed with medications. Parents should also be instructed in the primary purpose of the medications, and that medication is not going to solve all problems. They should know that "pills do not teach skills." Many teens with ADHD are deficient with regard to specific skill areas that may affect their academic and social life. These deficiencies must be remediated through educational and therapeutic programs. Parents must remember that the best long-range outcome will be for those teenagers who have not only had medications, but also have had behavioral programs and skill training.

Parents *must* refrain from making comments about a teen's need for medication (e.g., "Boy, you sure need another pill now!" or "If you don't behave, I will have to take you back to the doctor for more pills"). It is also critical that parents think about these prescriptions as medication and not "drugs" in order to distinguish the prescribed substances from associations with effects of "street drugs."

It is equally important for the parent to remember that the medication is given for the teen's needs, *not* the parent's needs. One child stated, "When I take my medicine, everybody else gets better." Those around the child do change, and may react differently to the teen, but this is a secondary benefit. The teen must also know that the changes are for his or her benefit, not the parents'.

WHAT TEACHERS NEED TO KNOW ABOUT MEDICATIONS

Many teachers seem to think that if a student is on medication for ADHD, then nothing else needs to be done. It is important they know that even though medications may make it more likely that a teen will stay "on task," there are many occasions when the teen will not be on medication. Also, many behaviors are not influenced by the medications.

Teachers should also be aware that some medications may help the teen, but are useful only to a point; additional medication may actually interfere with learning. Thus, academic performance may be compromised at a dose level that is most effective in controlling unacceptable behavior. Lighter doses have therefore been generally more effective when combined with behavioral programs (Carlson et al., 1992). Sometimes less than a full dose of medication may be used. Research has also shown that more medication is not always better (Pelham et al., 1985), and that the dual approach of medications and behavior modifications works as a very powerful combined program. Furthermore, research has consistently shown better outcomes when the child has had both a medication regime and a behavior modification approach (Pelham and Murphy, 1986).

It is also important to note that the teen may rarely rely on medications indefinitely; having a learning component to improve "on task" behavior will thus be beneficial when the medication regime is terminated. It is possible, in some cases, to reduce or "wean" the adolescent from medications with the assistance of the behavioral program. It is generally agreed that the less medications used, the better. While most medications for ADHD are safe, there is always some risk with any medication, and side effects should be considered. Risk factors and side effects should, in fact, always be considered when designing the "dual-approach" treatment program. In some cases where the teen cannot take a certain medication because of a conflicting medication or simply because of a prior adverse reaction to the ADHD medication, comprehensive behavior programs are essential.

Typically, the pediatrician evaluating for ADHD will send out rating forms to both teachers and parents and should include a list of possible side effects when the teen is placed on medication. In this way, the pediatrician may get feedback on what is happening with the teen who is on a specific medication. See the medication chart in Appendix 13 for a list of possible side effects, and effects for various medications. This handout would be appropriate for either parents, teachers, or clinicians.

EXERCISE AS A THERAPEUTIC MODALITY

Exercise has many benefits for different individuals. Improvement in cardiovascular functions and weight management are two primary benefits. Exercise can also be beneficial for stress management, improved attention and concentration, and reduction of hyperactive–restless behavior. It has been noted that endorphin levels are lower in the brain for those with ADHD. Stimulation increases the level of endorphins, as does exercise. The result is that the teen with ADHD may appear more calm, logical, communicative, and "reasonable" following exercise. The only drawback, as Dr. Harvey Parker notes, is that it lasts for only about 60–90 minutes. However, a more relaxed exercise program must be used while attempting to adjust the dose of stimulant medication or false feedback may be given.

COACHING FOR TEENS WITH ADHD

Most teens with ADHD may have little difficulty maintaining attention to situations that are novel and intrinsically interesting, and which bring about some significant consequence. Many teens with ADHD can spend hours playing Nintendo™ with its stimulating graphics and rewards; many teens with ADHD may have little trouble with some courses where there is strong interest (e.g., music) or where the instructor presents the material in an interesting and perhaps humorous manner. However, according to Dr. Russell Barkley, the problem arises when there is a conflict between immediate and long-term delayed consequences. In short, these adolescents respond impulsively.

Students may have difficulty maintaining an image of a goal, devising a plan to follow, coping with frustration, motivating themselves, and varying their strategies in order to achieve a goal. All of this requires "executive skills" to select a goal, develop a plan to reach it, and maintain goal-directed activity (i.e., motivation).

Using a proactive approach, some teachers have been able to manipulate novelty, interest, and reinforcement to increase sustained attention. However, some of these successes are often short lived because some students with ADHD may satiate rather quickly and become bored. However, interventions that are designed to facilitate achievement of long-term goals may be more effective.

In 1998, a program was published by Drs. Peg Dawson and Richard Guare entitled *Coaching the ADHD Student.* Its application to adolescents is reviewed here. In coaching, students are asked to identify long-term goals and to develop action plans to achieve these goals. Daily coaching sessions follow this long-range goal-setting session and draw on "correspondence training" research. An application of this training was applied to ADHD by Dr. Paniagua. Simply, it was noted that when the individual makes a verbal commitment to engage in a behavior at some later time, the likelihood that they will carry out this behavior is increased. Teens with ADHD may thus be asked to report what tasks they intend to accomplish before the next coaching session, and to specify when they intend to accomplish them. The two-stage coaching process prepared by Drs. Dawson and Guare appears consistent with Dr. Barkley's model of behavioral self-regulation.

In *Phase 1,* the primary issue is "long-term goal setting." Demands and expectations change for teens with ADHD, especially for older teens in high school. While they may have greater range of course selection, they must have specific credits in various subject areas to graduate and perhaps attend college. It's essential that the teen look at what he or she wishes to accomplish in high school and beyond. Thus, plans are discussed regarding graduation and college. With younger adolescents (e.g., middle school), long-range goals may not go beyond high school for the present. However, some shorter-term goals such as passing courses to play sports may be of primary concern.

The following six steps are outlined by Dawson and Guare: (1) Describe Long-Term Goals; (2) Determine the Steps to Achieve Long-Term Goals; (3) Discuss Obstacles to Addressing Long-Term Goals; (4) Develop Ways to Overcome the Obstacles; (5) Identify Ways to Enhance the Likelihood of Success; and (6) Ensure That the Plan Is Realistic.

In *Phase 2,* there are daily coaching sessions. In addition to a review of the long-range goals initially selected, other longer-term obligations may be discussed. This latter group may include upcoming tests, quizzes, long-term assignments and projects, as well as other obligations to clubs, job, etc.

The successful use of this multifaceted model for coaching teens with ADHD appears to depend on the following components: (1) The long-range goal-setting may be the most useful component. (2) The relationship between the coach and the student underscores the need for an ongoing connection with a positive supportive adult, which may be even more important than the goals or plans made. The coach is a mentor, a cheerleader, and a conflict mediator, a person the teen can turn to during crises and earlier to avert crises. (3) The system of daily "check ins" may be essential for the teen who tends to procrastinate or has difficulty with time management. (4) The link between coach and teacher, checking with teachers on a regular basis, ensures that problems can be identified early (e.g., to prevent students from being overwhelmed by too many outstanding assignments). (5) The use of a creative problem-solving model not only addresses a current problem, but also provides a model for future problem-solving applications. (6) The developmental appropriateness of this model—the need for independence may be nurtured during this process when a coach allows the teen to operate independently and competently away from parents.

The development of mutual respect in the student–coach relationship may be a unique experience for many teens with ADHD. This is especially the case where parents have perceived the teen with ADHD (and perhaps rightly so) as being inadequate and unable to cope with problem situations without their directive control. However, many students who have been exposed to this type of coaching program have achieved success in high school characterized by improved grades, reduction of truancy, and a decrease in behavior problems.

This program attempts to help the teen with ADHD to internalize the kinds of executive skills needed to learn independently, develop plans, and to set and achieve goals in high school and beyond. Dawson and Guare point out that coaching is not a "cure all," and it is apparent that many additional interventions and strategies may be needed in some cases. The outline of this program is not meant to be exhaustive, and those interested may wish to review the manual and forms directly. (See Dawson and Guare, 1998.)

SMALL-GROUP EDUCATIONAL FORMAT

Teens with ADHD will generally not do well in large groups or in groups that do not have some structure and format. Their need for stimulation will make it more likely that each member will be synergized by the others, resulting in a group process that may best be described as chaotic.

While there is a need to limit the number in the group, as well as to put a limit on group sessions, the theme of the group may vary. For example, Dr. Arthur Robin has facilitated the establishment of "teen forums" through CH.A.D.D. Groups have been conducted not only at national CH.A.D.D. conferences, but in various parts of the country. Such groups were not geared to provide a specific education program, but were set up to facilitate group interaction among adolescents regarding coping with ADHD. These groups were held once for 1 1/2 to 3 hours with a maximum enrollment of 30 teenagers. Separate groups for middle, high school, and college-age teens appear to work best. Discussion leaders are teens with ADHD who have successfully coped with ADHD and who have good leadership skills, as well as being able to speak well and self-disclose about themselves.

Dr. Robin reports that a CH.A.D.D. group of Eastern Oakland, California conducted a 90-minute meeting. During the first part a 20-minute video by Dr. Schubiner (1995) entitled *ADHD in Adolescence: Our Point of View* (available from the ADD/ADHD Resource Catalog) was shown. During the second half of the meeting, there was an open-ended discussion. The first meeting of the CH.A.D.D. National Teen Forum (organized by Dr. Robin) provided basic information about ADHD, medication, study strategies, family issues, and high-risk behavior. These groups may be facilitated by a high-profile sports or entertainment figure who is able to disclose his or her ADHD.

Other creative uses of this small-group format may focus on additional issues such as (a) vocational selection and preparing to enter the work force or (b) application for a college education. Many of the issues addressed in the one-on-one coaching program may be adapted to this type of group format.

THE SUMMER CAMP

During the school year, it is sometimes difficult to arrange a sufficient number of situations in which social skills can be trained. However, the summer camp experience can provide numerous situations to work on social skills as well as other skills. Teens can participate in daily activities involving interpersonal skill groups, sports with skill training, discussions regarding adolescent issues along with problem solving regarding these issues, and job skill training.

Adolescents may also participate in a middle/high school type classroom to develop note-taking and test-taking strategies, and to work on other classroom issues related to ADHD. A well-established model has been provided by Dr. William Pelham dating back to 1980; programs are reportedly modified slightly for adolescents. This basic model has been adapted in many locations; a similar program is also offered by the ADD Clinic in Biloxi, Mississippi under the direction of Dr. Grad Flick.

Many of these summer programs are quite intense for as long as eight weeks. Such a full-time program will offer the equivalent of six years of therapy on a once-weekly basis. Some of the specific skills covered during this time period include: (a) Problem Solving, (b) Communication, (c) Organizational Skills, (d) Coping Skills, (e) Social Skills, and (f) Study Skills.

Results of summer camps have revealed that over 90% of the students of various ages were rated at least somewhat improved, compared with the 50% to 70% overall improvement that is typically noted in outpatient treatment studies. Such improvements were not only in "rule-following" and "classroom productivity," but also in self-esteem and sports skills. Self-perception ratings reflected improvements in all domains (indicating greater competence). Global self-esteem ratings were twice as great with the summer camp experience, compared with behavior changes from medication along.

Furthermore, parent ratings on the Disruptive Behavior Disorders Scale showed a 24% decrease on the ADHD scale, a 28% decrease on the ODD scores, and a 35%

decrease on Conduct Disorder (CD) scores. More parents who initially reported significant aggressive behavior stated that they were helped more than parents who reported less aggression as a problem.

Dr. Pelham has explained that the intensive nature of the program with good behavior-management techniques is the kind of program needed to modify the problematic behavior of ODD and CD which involve significant aggression components. It may be that the summer program is the treatment of choice for teens with ADHD and ODD/CD. Follow-up treatment year-round would, of course, be essential to reinforce and maintain learned skills and to ensure that generalization to other situations at home and school is maximized. While most summer camps focus on pre-teen behavior, there are an increasingly greater number for teens including the program at the ADD Clinic in Biloxi.

In addition to the summer program, other intensive "in-home" programs, such as Henggeler's Multisystemic Therapy (1990), are available to address the more difficult-to-manage behavior disorders. There is some evidence from research studies to support the use of these approaches when restoration of parental controls is indicated.

While school and home-based programs comprise the primary components of the teen's treatment program, there are many skill-training programs that may involve a home, school, and clinic integrative approach. While some programs may be primarily coordinated by a clinician, there is certainly a need for home and school involvement with training. The greater the number of learning experiences in diverse and different situations, the faster the skills will be acquired and the better they will be generalized to other situations. Other programs may be coordinated by the home or school with reinforcement of learned skills occurring in the other situational contexts.

SKILL DEVELOPMENT AT HOME, AT SCHOOL, AND IN THE CLINIC

Skill development may involve activities that are not carried out primarily for entertainment, but to shape and establish some specific skills. In formal skill development, the selection of the activity depends upon the particular skill to be developed, and the primary purpose of the activity will be to shape, enhance, or establish that skill. Each activity listed below addresses some lack of skill development and has some relevance to the teen's overall problems and difficulties in adjustment. These activities are divided into specific areas that are critical for the teen with ADHD to function well in the classroom, at home, and in society in general. Specific skills, often deficient in children and adolescents with ADHD, are the focus of formal training, which is most likely to be carried out by a teacher or mental health professionals; however, it is anticipated that such training will also be available for parents to use in the home situation. Attention training and the training of social skills are already available for home use. By training across many different situations, the teen learns more rapidly because of more learning trials, and the teen will also tend to generalize or apply his or her learned skills in more situations.

Although there is not a great deal of research on skill training of ADHD children in specific deficit areas, some training tools are available for clinical application to these problem areas of skill development in adolescents:

1. Attention

2. Social Skills

3. Organizational/Study Skills

4. Anger Control

ATTENTION TRAINING

Attentional processes are more complex than we sometimes think. Teachers tell parents, "Jimmy just needs to 'pay attention' in class; he doesn't keep his mind on his work." This all-too-common statement complains simplistically about a complex process. One may ask, "What does 'paying attention' mean?" The teacher may believe that he has communicated a specific problem to the parent, but a host of questions arise from this general statement about not paying attention.

Specifically, a parent may wish to know: When does the problem occur? In a specific class or in all? With one teacher or all? Only in one subject area (e.g., reading)? How long can the child attend? Does it matter where the child is seated? Does it matter how well the teacher is organized? How well he communicates? Are attentional problems only evident when changing from one type of task in a subject area to another? Did this problem just develop or has it been evident for some time? (While the focus is on attentional problems in this section, one might ask many of these same questions for other problem areas to be addressed.) At times, these difficulties with attention may be evident both at school and at home; for some teens, however, they may appear primarily at school.

The complexity of attentional problems has been documented in neuropsychological research, and the breakdown of attentional processes into subtypes is based on the work of Sohlberg and Mateer (1987). The attention training games called Attend-O™ Attention Training Games, developed by Dr. Flick at the ADD Clinic in Biloxi, represents a hierarchically arranged set of increasingly more complex tasks that involve attentional processes as complex as those encountered in real-life situations.

The Attend-O™ Attention Training Games evolved from a review of the neuropsychological rehabilitation literature in treating individuals who have sustained some type of brain injury, lesion, or dysfunction that has affected their basic abilities including: attention, memory, language, visual–motor, and other higher cognitive functions. The current emphasis is on the treatment of attentional deficits. (See Figure 3.2, Description of the Attentional Games.)

Figure 3.2
DESCRIPTION OF THE ATTENTIONAL GAMES

	THE ATTENTION TRAINING GAME	
Game Type	*Sensory Modality*	
	Visual	Auditory
FOCUSED ATTENTION	Every time you *see* a <u>RED</u> card, click the mouse.	Every time you *hear* the word <u>RED</u>, click the mouse.
SUSTAINED ATTENTION	Every time you *see* a <u>RED</u> card follow or come after a <u>BLACK</u> card, click the mouse.	Every time you *hear* the word <u>RED</u> follow or come after the word <u>BLACK</u>, click the mouse.
SELECTIVE ATTENTION	[A 3″ × 5″ array of colored cards is on the screen.] Every time a <u>RED</u> card follows a <u>BLACK</u> card, click the mouse. [Cards appear randomly in the 3″ × 5″ array. Various colors act as visual distractors.]	[A series of colors will be heard coming randomly from the right and left speakers.] Each time the word <u>RED</u> follows or comes after the word <u>BLACK</u>, click the mouse. [Various colors heard act as auditory distractors.]
ALTERNATING ATTENTION	Click the mouse every time a <u>RED</u> card follows a <u>BLACK</u> card (20″). Then click to <u>BLACK</u>-follows-<u>RED</u> (20″), then again click to <u>RED</u>-follows-<u>BLACK</u> (20″).	Click the mouse every time the word <u>RED</u> is heard to follow the word <u>BLACK</u> (20″), then click to <u>BLACK</u>-follows-<u>RED</u> (20″), then again click to <u>RED</u>-follows-<u>BLACK</u> (20″).
DIVIDED ATTENTION (I)	[Visual and Auditory presented at the same time.] Click the mouse when you *see* a <u>RED</u> card or *hear* the word <u>RED</u> (focus only on <u>RED</u>).	
DIVIDED ATTENTION (II)	[Visual and Auditory presented at the same time.] Click the mouse when you *see* a <u>RED</u> card follow a <u>BLACK</u> card or *hear* the word <u>RED</u> follow the word <u>BLACK</u> (more complex task).	
DIVIDED ATTENTION (III)	[Visual and Auditory presented at the same time.] Click the left mouse button when you *see* a <u>RED</u> card follow a <u>BLACK</u> card; click the right mouse button when you *hear* the word <u>RED</u> follow the word <u>BLACK</u> (the most complex task).	

Theory-based Attention Training—The model for attention training used here is that provided by Sohlberg and Mateer (1987). Their clinical model suggests that there are five subtypes, or varieties, of attention: (1) focused, (2) sustained, (3) selective, (4) alternating, and (5) divided attention. Based on cognitive theories and clinical observations of individuals with traumatic brain injuries, Sohlberg and Mateer hypothesized that one may experience difficulties in attention at one or more levels within each of these hierarchically arranged categories of attention. The following provides a refined and modified description of each of these five attentional components as they are used in this Attention Training Games program for treatment of attentional deficits in ADHD children, adolescents, and adults.

1. *Focused attention* is the most basic form of attention that involves the teen's ability to respond to a specific stimulus (visual or auditory) or to stay on one topic without a shift in attention.

2. *Sustained attention* reflects a teen's ability to maintain attention and persist on task until completion. This would also include the notion of vigilance and resistance to lapses in attention for an adequate period of time. Further, it is involved in the teenager's readiness to respond to some stimulus event. At the highest level, this also would incorporate the notion of holding and manipulating information as one might do in mental arithmetic.

3. *Selective attention* involves the teen's ability to maintain a specific cognitive set in the face of competing distractions. For example, selective attention is involved when the teenager recognizes that the parent's voice during instructions is the main focus of attention, *not* others' comments or noises. It should also be noted that the distractors may be "external" (e.g., noise) or "internal" (e.g., one's thoughts or feelings).

4. *Alternating attention* includes the idea of "mental flexibility," as when there is a need to shift attention between tasks that access different modes of information processing or different response patterns; for example, the student who has to listen to the teacher and take notes alternately, while holding the information intact. This situation requires that the teen switch from looking at the teacher (processing the information both visually and auditorially), and then transferring it in an abbreviated form through verbal expressive functions in writing. Some continuity of the flow of ideas and words must be maintained (i.e., a mental holding process) so that appropriate concepts, ideas, and facts may be reconstructed in notes.

5. *Divided attention* requires the ability to respond almost simultaneously to two or more tasks having different demands. This process may involve rapid alternation of attention or a somewhat automatic or almost unconscious processing responsivity on one of the tasks. Attention may be divided into any combination of visual, auditory, or kinesthetic (movement) stimuli, but more commonly there is a visual and auditory combination. The task or response requirements may be as simple as a

single unitary response or a complex one (e.g., two different visual–spatial [right versus left] response patterns). Such complex response patterns are not infrequently associated with complex attentional processes when one interacts with sophisticated machines (e.g., task demands of a pilot in the cockpit that is filled with gauges, auditory sounds, and multiple-response switches).

Training Program Applications—Before describing the Attend-O™ Attention Training Games, we must consider other available software and/or training programs for application with children with ADHD.

First, the Attention Process Training (APT) program developed by Sohlberg and Mateer (1987, 1989) has been used with children as young as 7 years of age. One study by Williams (1989) with a small group of children 8 to 11 years old showed improvements in attentional process but with questionable generalization to their natural academic settings. Other successful training has been noted by Campbell (1990). Most of these training modules would, however, be appropriate for most adolescents with ADHD.

Computer-based programs have been described by Bracy *(Soft Tools,* 1983), Sandford *(Captain's Log™, 1985),* Williams *(Cool Spring Software,* 1992), and Podd *(NeurXercise™,* 1989). According to a recent survey, only a few of these programs had been used with children or adolescents who have ADHD. At present, only *Captain's Log™* has been reportedly used in some preliminary studies with ADD children (Fine and Goldman, 1994; Sandford, 1995; Kotwal, et al., 1994). To date, none have reportedly been used with teens.

Over the last ten years, neuropsychologists have been developing these cognitive-stimulation techniques primarily to rehabilitate adults who have experienced some type of brain insult that produced impairments in specific skill areas involving attention, memory, visual–motor skills, and other functions that have affected their adaptation to daily-life routines. The emphasis in these techniques has been on rehabilitation as the attempt is made to repair or recover skills that have been lost or altered in some way.

Some of these same techniques are beginning to be used with children and adolescents who have ADHD or LD (learning disabilities). While these persons have not lost skills, they have failed to develop them. While no gross abnormalities of brain tissue or neurochemical processes have been fully documented, there is such a similarity of behavioral characteristics with those individuals who have sustained actual brain injury that the application of cognitive neuropsychological remediation techniques to the child or teen with ADHD or ADHD/LD seems clearly worthwhile.

In a recent study, Kotwal and others (1994) have shown that training with the *Captain's Log™* program with 20–35 training sessions resulted in some improvement on the Conners Parent Rating Scale (for ADHD) and a structured questionnaire, along with some general improvement in grades. An article in *CH.A.D.D. Magazine* (Fall, 1994) pointed out the value of using computers to help children and teens with ADHD.

Computerized training programs look quite promising and may become a useful tool in planning comprehensive treatment programs for older children and teens with ADHD. Extension of some training exercises from the clinic into home and school settings would certainly help to increase generalization of learned attentional skills to those critical environments in which the child or teen must function. Additionally, the increase in the number of practice trials would enhance the rapidity with which these skills are required.

Criteria for an Attentional Training Program—According to Sohlberg and others (1993), there are six basic tenets of the approach in addressing cognitive impairments.

1. *Use of a theoretical model.* The current attention training programs utilize the clinical model adopted by Sohlberg and Mateer (1989).

2. *Programs are hierarchically organized.* This guarantees a broad range of tasks and ensures a gradient of difficulty level that may be linked to real-life events.

3. *The necessity for repetition.* This series of programs is promoted to be used in a number of situations involving clinic, school, and eventually home use.

4. *The program series is data-driven.* Simply stated, progress through these programs extends from the simple to the most complex of attentional tasks, with movement determined by the person's performance (i.e., percent correct–percent errors).

5. *The program should plan for generalization.* The ultimate goal of this behaviorally based attention training system is to affect real-life attentional problems of the teen with ADHD. Utilization of ratings that monitor changes in corresponding areas of attentional deficits will facilitate documentation of the effectiveness of the specific training components. Overall improvement in ancillary rating scales (e.g., Conners, ACTeRS, etc.), along with improvements in grades and performance on specific neuropsychologically based attentional tasks, will be monitored. Also, there is now available an Inventory of Attentional Deficits (IAD) for teachers to rate the teen on areas of focused, sustained, selective, alternating, and divided attention (Flick, 1999), and an objective computerized assessment of these attentional deficit areas in a diagnostic program entitled *Test of Attentional Deficits (TOAD)* by Flick (1999). Both of these measures may help to not only document the pattern of each individual's attentional deficits, but also monitor change (and especially improvement), as a function of treatment (i.e., training, medication, or both). The generalization factors will certainly be addressed by the use of extended training in different situations, and effectiveness of this procedure monitored for change.

6. *Ultimate success will be determined by changes in school functioning.* This factor will simply represent the end process of training as reflected by improved functioning in real-life situations that are meaningful for the child with ADHD. The

Inventory of Attentional Deficits (IAD), available through *The ADD/ADHD Resources Catalog,* will be most helpful in documenting these changes.

Plotting Improvements—First, a clinician must obtain baseline measures of performance (i.e., pretraining phase). This may be primarily rating scale information, but could also involve performance on a computerized test of attention (e.g., TOAD). During the training phase, the clinician keeps a record of percentage of correct responses and the percentage of errors. This may be plotted (see Figure 3.3) to show an improvement on each task and to show that the teen is learning the skills. This graph also shows that each time the task is made more difficult (e.g., shifting from 1 card/2 sec to 1 card/sec and from there to 2 cards/sec) performance drops as expected. It is, in short, a good example of the learning process as applied to the acquisition of attentional skills. Post-training assessments, after a period of approximately three months, may reflect overall positive changes in ratings, psychological and neuropsychological test performance, and indirectly in classroom academic work.

If a general behavioral program is established at home, the adolescent's scores may be translated into points (using a positive system only); this will provide additional motivation on these tasks. Improvement in attentional skills may be influenced by (1) the number of practice sessions and (2) the number of situations in which practice occurs.

Like any habit development, and especially for children and teens with ADHD, tasks must be repeated frequently. For this reason, it is desirable for the teen to practice these tasks at home, at school, and at the clinician's office. In this way, the skills will be acquired faster and they will be better generalized across home and school situations. This means that the teen will be better able to apply the learned skills in situations other than the one where they were learned.

BEHAVIORAL INHIBITION TRAINING

As part of the Attend-O™ series, Behavioral Inhibition Training (BIT) exercises have been developed by Dr. Grad Flick in 1999 as an extension of the Attention Training Games. The assessment of BIT has been available with the Conners CPT program and more recently has been included in the overall assessment of attentional deficits in Flick's Test of Attentional Deficits (TOAD)—Attend-O™ Volume 1.

The BIT exercises are based on the assessment model by Sohlberg and Mateer previously described. In BIT exercises, the adolescent must click the mouse on each non-target (e.g., black cards) and refrain or inhibit responding (i.e., clicking) to targets (e.g., red cards). When errors of comission are made, the teen is signaled by a "ding"; errors of omission where the teen fails to click the mouse on some nontarget receives no direct and immediate feedback—it is counted as an error in the results summary of the session. Just as with the attention training exercises, the failure to inhibit on the target must be considered a more serious error reflecting failure of behavioral inhibition.

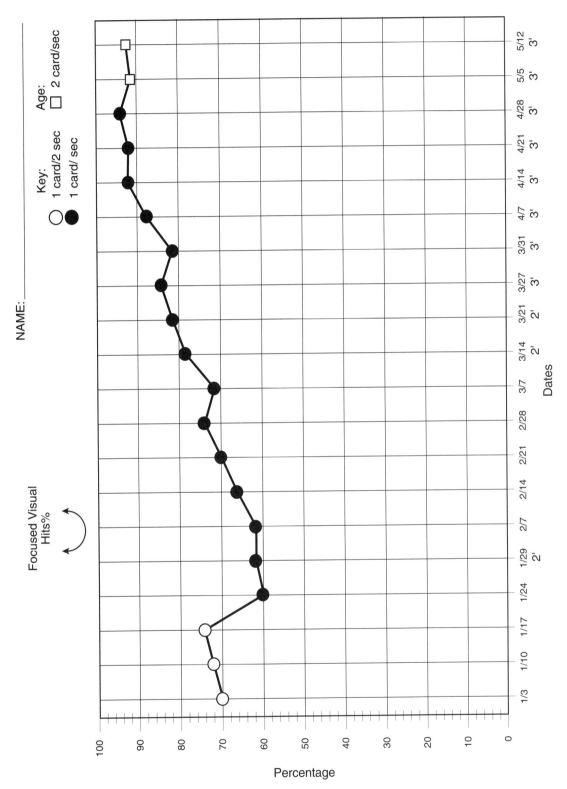

Figure 3.3   PLOTTING IMPROVEMENT

Although there is no research on this procedure at present, it appears to provide an objective means of investigating various parameters that will affect the acquisition of learned behavioral inhibition. Since behavioral approaches have been used with a wide range of behaviors—both molar (overt) and molecular (covert physiological responses)—there is no reason to believe that its use in developing behavioral inhibition skills would not be a viable application.

Some of the work on other computerized programs (e.g., *Captain's Log*™ and *NeurXercise*™) may best be described as habilitation. However, note that there have been few studies with teens in this area up to this point in time. This area is thus fertile grounds for research.

Neuropsychologists have, over the last ten years, been developing techniques to rehabilitate individuals (primarily adults, but some children) who have experienced some type of brain insult that produced impairments in specific skill areas involving attention, memory, visual–motor skills, and other functions that have affected their adaptation to daily life routines. The emphasis in these techniques has been on rehabilitation as the attempt is made to regain or recover skills that have been lost or altered in some way. Some of these same techniques are beginning to be used with children and adolescents who have ADHD or LD.

While these teenagers have not lost skills, they have failed to develop them. Consequently, their psychological test pattern looks similar to the adult or teen with certain types of brain injury. While subtle differences in brain structure and function have been noted for teens with the so-called "invisible handicaps," notably ADHD and LD, no gross abnormalities of brain tissue or neurochemical processes have been fully "documented." "Documented" is emphasized as there are many sources pointing to a biological structural or neurochemical basis for the behavioral characteristics of ADHD. There is a lack of definite evidence.

Nevertheless, there is such a similarity of behavioral characteristics with those individuals who have sustained actual brain injury that the application of cognitive neuropsychological remediation techniques to the child with ADHD or ADHD/LD seems clearly worthwhile. The bulk of outcome statistics are with individuals who have had actual brain damage, but these techniques have begun to be applied recently by several clinical researchers (including the author), and some results have been published.

One such program of training materials has been computerized and is entitled *Captain's Log*™. The program was developed by Sandford and Browne (1988). This system was nicknamed a "mental gym." The explanation for this nickname is simple: The system provides a series of cognitive training exercises in several critical areas, including modules for attention, visual–motor skills, conceptual skills, numeric concepts/memory skills, and a newly added attentional program involving components that address visual scanning, concentration and inhibition, both visual and auditory attention (discrimination), as well as visual organization, memory, and attention to detail. The complete program is far too complex to explain in detail in this book and should be used only under the guidance of a clinical neuropsychologist familiar with such rehabilitation procedures.

Other computerized cognitive neuropsychological programs are also available (e.g., *NeurXercise*™) that primarily have been used, to date, with adult head-injured patients, but have more recently been applied to ADHD behavioral symptomatology. No research studies have been found with the *NeurXercise*™ program, which was developed by Dr. Marvin Podd, et al. (1989). Perhaps some training exercises may also be extended for use with home and school computers. This would certainly help to increase generalization of learning skills to those critical environments in which the teen must function. However, these home and school programs should perhaps best be used as adjuncts to primary training programs that are conducted under the supervision of a clinical neuropsychologist experienced in the use of neuropsychological rehabilitation programs.

SOCIAL-SKILL TRAINING

There are a number of relevant social skills on which to concentrate. Of course, just learning to play any of the games by the rules is helpful for the teen who has relationship difficulty with peers and siblings. Several games and programs designed to teach social skills are available (and some overlap with other areas of skill training). A board game that may be used with younger adolescents (13–14 years) is entitled the *School Behavior Game,* available through *The ADD/ADHD Resources Catalog.* Employing a cognitive–behavior orientation, young teens may learn appropriate self-talk to deal with various situations they encounter going to school (e.g., bus ride, classroom, playground, and lunch room), all of which may have rules of behavior. Students may be trained to effectively deal with transitions from one situation to another—a problem for many students in junior high or middle school who are faced with these new demands. The establishment of a cognitive map for a behavioral routine and knowledge of the rules in different situations will be essential. A program for the enhancement of generalization to the student's natural environment is also available.

With the current increase in school-related violence, programs have been developed for teachers to work with youths to improve self-control and social behavior. A number of programs are available, including Dr. Hill Walker's *ACCESS (Adolescent Curriculum for Communication and Effective Social Skills).* This program teaches 31 skills in 3 areas: (a) relating to peers, (b) relating to adults, and (c) relating to self. Some of the specific skills taught, using a small-group format, include: listening, greeting others, offering assistance, eliciting attention from an adult, how to disagree with an adult, and obeying class rules. This program may be used in private clinics as well as in schools.

A second type of group focuses on specific content with structured training exercises. Since social skills are best developed within a group format, several programs may be used.

An excellent program was developed by Dr. Janet Giler, which is designed to teach children and young adolescents with ADD and/or LD ten basic social skills and self-evaluation techniques. Her *ADDept* curriculum uses structured learning over a 10-week period to train and evaluate ten essential social skills. This "pull-out" program teaches the LD/ADD student to master: (1) listening and responding, (2) showing interest by smiling and asking questions, (3) greeting others, (4) giving compliments, (5) understanding body language and vocal tones, (6) understanding personal space and appropriate touching, (7) learning to join an ongoing activity, (8) sharing and cooperating, (9) ignoring teasing, and (10) managing anger appropriately. Groups are limited to 4 to 6 students, all of whom are preferably in the same grade or within one grade of each other. As Dr. Giler points out, these students learn better in small groups outside of their classroom for several reasons: (1) Some LD/ADD student may have sequencing problems that may interfere with learning in a large group; (2) LD/ADD children need a multi-modal approach that includes role-playing (more difficult to do in the class); (3) An LD/ADD student may make errors interpreting body language requiring immediate feedback to make self-corrections (this would also be more difficult in regular class); and (4) LD/ADD students already fear ridicule. These students need the safe environment that the "pull-out" program uses to facilitate learning without fear of recrimination.

The Prepare Curriculum by Dr. Arnold Goldstein (1988) is a ten-week comprehensive program for use with elementary-level students and adolescents. It focuses on problem solving, interpersonal skills, anger control, moral reasoning, and stress management as major areas of problems for students who are aggressive, withdrawn, or generally weak in social competency. Games, role-playing exercises, group discussion, and other activities are used in the training process.

The *Job Related Social Skills (JRSS)* program covers a number of job skills: prioritization of job responsibilities, understanding directions, giving instructions, asking questions, asking permission for things, asking for help, accepting help, offering help, requesting information, taking messages, joining in a conversation, giving compliments, being convincing to others in apologizing, accepting criticism, and responding to complaints. These skills cover a wide range of both basic and specific social skills as they relate to job situations.

An interactive multimedia CD-ROM is being developed by Dr. Richard Goldsworthy at Indiana University (personal communication), which focuses on the development of social skills in young adolescents. The program will allow teens to make problem-solving decisions about various social situations, and then to explore the consequences of their decisions. Such software may be used by both schools and parents to train at-risk teens in social problem-solving strategies. A full course in social skill instruction is planned. Computerized programs such as this one may provide valuable training with minimum staff involvement.

ORGANIZATIONAL AND STUDY SKILLS

The *Skills for School Success* program developed by Anita Archer and Mary Gleason (and available from Curriculum Associates) provides an excellent resource to teach several appropriate classroom behaviors as well as organizational and study skills. Rather than focusing on remediating their deficiencies, these procedures focus on developing skills that teens with ADHD need to succeed in the classroom. Behavior appropriate before and after class, and time/materials management are covered. Learning strategies that focus on completing assignments, memorizing, proofreading, and taking notes are just a few of the areas discussed. In addition, study strategies and discussions about how to take tests are covered. Using reference material, and reading and interpreting graphs and tables are also highlighted. This program covers grades 3–6 with guidelines for a downward extension to grades 1 and 2. Advanced programs for grades 7–12 are now offered.

Also available is a workbook program entitled *Study Strategies Made Easy: A Practical Plan for School Success* by Leslie Davis and Sandi Sirotowitz with Harvey C. Parker. The focus of this series of exercises is on grades 6–12. It covers organization, learning styles, reading comprehension, communication, note taking, homework, stress management, memorization, and test taking. It is designed to be used as a program, but the clinician may wish to focus on specific sections that are critical for an individual child. A video with the same title is also available for training purposes.

ANGER-CONTROL TRAINING

Goldstein (1988) cites a refinement of Novaco's (1975) three-stage sequence into a chain where the teen learns (1) *cues*—both physiological and kinesthetic that signal anger arousal, (2) *triggers*—both internal and external factors that provoke anger, (3) *reminders*—self-instruction statements to reduce anger arousal (e.g., "I can work out a plan to handle this"), (4) *reducers*—techniques in combination with reminders to reduce anger (e.g., deep breathing, backward counting), and (5) *self-evaluation*—the opportunity to self-reinforce and/or self-correct (depending on the success of the preceding steps).

In 1998, Arnold Goldstein, Barry Gleck, and John Gibbs published a program entitled *Aggression Replacement Training (ART): A Comprehensive Intervention for Aggressive Youth* (Champaign, IL: Research Press). ART was initiated in 1987 with Skillstreaming as its behavioral component, Anger Control Training as its emotion-targeted component, and Moral Reasoning Training as its cognitive component. Skillstreaming consists of 50 skills in 6 categories that are taught by lecture, modeling, role-playing, and feedback. In Anger Control Training, there is an analysis of triggers, cues, and anger reducers with evaluation of the "Hassle Log." This latter device basically describes a sequence of events starting with what happened (e.g., somebody teased me), what was the reaction (what did you do? e.g., cried, ignored it, ran away, etc.), and what were the consequences. Modeling, role-play, and coaching are used in this program. In the last component, the student moves from Immature Moralities with Stages Power and Deals to Mature Moralities with Stages Mutuality and Systems. Efficacy evaluation suggests that ART is an effective intervention for aggressive youth.

An anger-control program is available for adolescent males 14 years and older. This program, entitled *Controlling Anger and Learning to Manage It (CALM),* was designed for adolescents who are incarcerated or who are on probation. However, it may actually have broader applications. CALM is a cognitive behavioral group-training program that is intended to reduce anger, violence, and emotional loss of control for certain groups of adolescents. Over 24 two-hour sessions, the CALM program teaches delinquent teens to monitor and understand underlying emotional reactions to prevent and control problematic behavior. Based on cognitive behavioral theory, CALM not only teaches skills necessary to reduce the frequency, intensity, and duration of anger, but also addresses the management of other strong negative emotions including jealousy, anxiety, and depression. Sessions are highly structured, sequential, and designed to be delivered to groups of delinquent males who are at risk for inappropriate, violent behavior.

Techniques such as modeling, role-play, teamwork, personal assignments, self- and peer-evaluation, as well as constant participant involvement, are used to promote change in inappropriate and unproductive thought and behavior patterns. The program may be led by a paraprofessional who completes a short training program. The workbook for participants has a sixth-grade reading level. Various scripts are offered with the flexibility of modification to adapt to various situations. This program appears to be easily adapted to many different situations. In addition to the participant's workbook, there is an audio tape of relaxation exercises and education game scripts to be used in the sessions.

A computer-based CD-ROM program entitled *SMART/Cool*™ is also available to help students in middle and junior high school define violence, understand the consequences, and discover strategies for avoiding confrontations in their daily lives. The interactive software focuses on two segments each with focus activities.

In the first segment, entitled "Managing Anger," teens learn about how angry feelings develop and how to express anger appropriately. Situations and locations that are most likely to trigger anger are presented. Specific strategies for confronting an angry person include staying calm, engaging in some alternative behavior, walking away, or talking out problems instead of pulling weapons. Acting on impulse versus "thinking it through" are compared in a game-like format.

In the second segment, entitled "Resolving Conflicts," conflict situations are presented so that the teen may compare his or her decisions about what the people in the scenes were thinking. In another section on celebrity interviews, the teen can compare his or her thoughts with those of well-known people. In teen interviews, several teenage role models discuss conflict-resolution and mediation strategies.

Finally, there is some focus on problem solving. Typically conducted in a school setting, the discussion group leader—typically a teacher or school counselor—may provide a context where teens can brainstorm. For example, some models may be given to provide the basis for change. Students focus on how they may have learned old habits (e.g., unlearning old swimming habits when he or she joins the swim team, or learning new basketball techniques when a new coach comes in). This latter part can be quite beneficial in reinforcing or developing and maintaining appropriate cognitive strategies around anger and conflict resolution. It could best be carried out in an ongoing group for continued role-play and discussion about using the techniques discussed and getting reinforced for doing so.

STRESS-MANAGEMENT TRAINING

Stress-management and relaxation training has many benefits for students with ADHD, as well as parents and teachers. There are many possible formats to conduct such training. One such format may involve some general introduction to concepts and principles of stress management, followed by specific relaxation exercises and/or training.

A good introduction to stress management may be obtained using the *HELP–Stress*™ program developed by Dr. Mark Johnson and associates. There is an adult (over 18 years) version and a youth version (for adolescents 13–17 years). It can be administered in 30-minute weekly sessions over an 11-week period. Topics covered include an introduction about stress, how it may be assessed, the affect of thoughts and how to change distorted thinking, environmental factors, and a kind of "stress inoculation" procedure. Following this series, the adolescent may be provided some specific relaxation exercises (available through *The ADD/ADHD Resources Catalog)* developed by Dr. Flick. Similarly, following the adult version, parents or teachers may use specific relaxation tapes developed for them by Dr. Flick.

In general, stress-management and relaxation training exercises have been proven to be quite beneficial for anger control, anxiety, sleep difficulties, depression, and one's general health and well being.

SELF-ESTEEM TRAINING

Although related to social skills, training in self-esteem has widespread applications to many other skill-development areas. It has been the focus or central issue involved in the concept of resiliency as noted by Dr. Robert Brooks. A computerized training program entitled *HELP–Self-Regard*™ has been made available by Nancy Chaconas, M.A., and the Multi-Health Systems staff. This is an interactive program that assists adolescents 13–17 years of age with their self-image. The program teaches teens to identify and challenge self-defeating thoughts, to take action and accept responsibility, to develop effective use of words, to create personal affirmations, to develop mental visualization skills, to set goals, and to use relaxation techniques. Computer-generated reports on sessions allow the school or clinic to check on the student's progress.

UNDERSTANDING AND ACCEPTING ADHD

Understanding the nature of ADHD behavior is critical for the parent or teacher to deal effectively with it. First, it is important to understand that the basic behavior is driven by the teen's neurophysiology. This can alleviate much guilt and fault finding, self- and other-blame that many parents and some teachers look to in their early attempts to deal with ADHD behavior. Second, it is essential to understand that the most consistent finding about ADHD behavior is inconsistency. Thus, the teen's good days and bad days, which may be so puzzling to both teachers and parents, may become more readily accepted. It is not at all unusual for parents to comment that, "His teacher said he did all of his work yesterday, but none today. If he did it one day, she knows he can do it." This inconsistency frequently sets up students for unreasonable expectations because of parents' and teachers' lack of understanding of the teen's inconsistent work or behavioral pattern. The adolescent's neurophysiology changes from one day to the next and may be affected by his or her stress events, food and drink intake, sleep patterns, environmental changes, and by both prescribed and over-the-counter medications. Whatever affects the teen's neurophysiology also affects his or her behavior.

It is of paramount importance for the parent to learn to distinguish which behaviors are a function of the ADHD and related conditions, and which behaviors are not. If a request is given to a teen (e.g., "Please pick up your clothes and put them in the closet"), and the adolescent fails to do it, you may simply ask the teen to repeat to you what you asked him or her to do. If he or she is able to repeat the request, this is an example of outright *noncompliance,* **not** *inattention.* Many parents have been told their child is "just a normal child" or "don't worry; the child will grow out of that stage." Now during adolescence, the behavior remains unchanged. Others comment that, "Well, the father said he was just like that when *he* was a child, and he'd get a beating every day." Parents are often confused by what others tell them and as a result sometimes deny that their teenager has a problem. This is indeed unfortunate, as the longer the problem goes untreated, the more difficult it is to deal with it. Older children and adolescents with ADHD frequently have many additional problems to deal with including poor self-concept, a long history of failure in school, depression, and, at times, "acting out" of aggressive behavior. Ultimately, this may result in the adolescent dropping out of school or necessitating some type of residential placement to impose limits and control behavior. Early understanding and acceptance of ADHD will clearly have a greater effect on the success of treatment. It is critical to know that, at this time, there is no "cure" for ADHD. It is a condition that can, however, be managed once it is recognized, understood, and accepted.

Behavioral training programs for parents and teachers may be offered in different formats. First, there are many clinics, both private and university affiliated, that offer behavioral programs for parents. Often such programs are combined with treatment of the identified child or teen with ADHD. Second, both parents and teachers may receive either separate or combined behavioral training instruction in workshops. Dr. Grad Flick of the ADD Clinic in Biloxi, Mississippi offers several one- or two-day workshops for parents and teachers. Such workshops may be offered in-house or out-of-state at some prearranged facility. Many such workshops are now available, and some are offered through CH.A.D.D. during its international conference each year. Most such workshops (even those over a two-day period) serve as a good introduction to begin work on behavioral changes. A good comprehensive reference book to use in addition to such a workshop, or even in lieu of one, is Flick's *ADD/ADHD Behavior-Change Resource Kit* (1998). Now, let's turn to a discussion of parent and teacher training programs.

BEHAVIORAL TRAINING PROGRAMS FOR PARENTS

Parent training programs developed over a ten-year period beginning in the early 1980s. These behavioral programs targeted the difficult-to-manage behaviors involving aggression, defiance, and the *most difficult* conduct disorders. The addition of oppositional behaviors and/or conduct disorder behaviors make the typical teen with ADHD even harder to manage. Since very few of these complex aggressive behavior patterns respond to medication, behavioral counseling or parent training programs in behavioral techniques have become increasingly more important. In addition to workshops offered by Grad Flick, there have been many other experts in this clinical area who have also offered workshops and parent training programs in their clinic work with children who present complex patterns of ADHD. Conners's program as well as Barkley's program are modeled after a program originally developed by Connie Hanf (1969). For example, in Conners's program parents receive 14 sessions over a 12-week period with "booster sessions" provided on a once-a-month basis. Group sessions utilize lectures, modeling, and role playing. Information about ADHD is provided along with specific information on behavioral techniques, including those needed to set up a home token economy. Homework is assigned and telephone calls are made during the week to literally prompt parents to use the techniques.

In many hospitals, clinics, and some schools, parent training programs are now offered to assist parents in understanding some of the special needs of the child with ADHD and to teach those techniques and general behavioral principals that have been shown to be helpful. While there has been an abundance of research and considerable clinical evidence that such parent training in behavioral techniques can be beneficial, it appears that the only measures of change have focused on the teen. While this is certainly a critical point, there has been, to date, no instrument available to document changes in "knowledge of behavioral techniques" or general information about the use of such procedures with ADHD children.

An instrument has been developed by Dr. Grad Flick at the ADD Clinic in Biloxi which provides a type of content-based assessment of such knowledge. This instrument, entitled *Flick's Survey of Behavioral Practices & ADD/ADHD*, assesses a wide range of information that is common to most all behavioral programs. It also assesses general factual information about ADHD. Although much of the information surveyed is based on the content as discussed in this author's book, *Power Parenting for Children with ADD/ADHD*, the majority of this information would be commonly found in most all current books with material on either behavioral modification and/or the ADHD behavioral syndromes.

Some sample items are as follows:

T F	1.	Good and appropriate behavior should be rewarded.
T F	2.	Bad and inappropriate behavior should be punished.
T F	3.	It is important to reward a good behavior or punish a bad behavior as soon as possible after it appears.
T F	4.	Physical punishment is generally not effective in the long-run with children who have ADD/ADHD.
T F	5.	Use of time-out for bad behavior will always work with the ADD/ADHD child.

This instrument is intended to be administered prior to parent training and then following the training. It might also be used prior to reading this book or *Power Parenting for Children with ADD/ADHD,* and then taken again following completion of the book. Repeated assessments may also indicate where parents may wish to refresh their memories regarding certain techniques. Although it may be used, at present, as a measure of general knowledge of behavioral principles, it is anticipated that future research may allow for a description of a profile of practices so that parent training and/or behavioral counseling programs may target specific areas of weakness, thus saving much time and expense. Knowledge of remaining weakness or confusion regarding certain issues would certainly be best cleared up prior to the parent implementing behavioral programs as opposed to initially operating on the basis of misinformation. In summary, this instrument may improve the efficiency and the effectiveness of behavioral programs following various types of parent training or behavioral counseling programs.

BEHAVIORAL TRAINING PROGRAMS FOR TEACHERS

It is not uncommon for teachers to receive brief inservice training on managing ADHD behavior and related problematic behavior. Yet today many teachers remain woefully inadequate when it comes to the issue of classroom discipline. Managing difficult and sometimes dangerous behavior is one of the most stressful tasks teachers face in our schools. In fact, some authorities agree that it is often this very issue that precipitates "teacher dropout." It is not often that teachers feel inadequate in curriculum content; it is frequently noted, however, that they feel ill-equipped to cope with difficult behaviors often associated with ADHD, Oppositional Defiant Disorder, and Conduct Disorder.

Many workshops are usually available for teachers. However, the old adage "a little knowledge is a dangerous thing" would seem to apply. Too often, these "workshops" range from a half-hour lecture to a one-day program. While some of these may be helpful to some, they may provide little basis for teachers changing the way they respond to students with ADHD and other problems. Sometimes a brief change may occur, but because this new way of dealing with the difficult behaviors may be weak, the teacher may quickly revert back to a prior ineffective strategy. Let's face it. Change is difficult. Changing habitual ways of behaving takes some effort, support from others, and reinforcement in order to maintain the change. Persistent and well-established problematic behavior of teens with ADHD can often easily weather any attempted change by teachers, and may actually reinforce the teacher for a return to old ways of coping. In short, old habits "die hard" as there is some comfort in them—even if they continue to prove ineffective.

Workshops offered through the ADD Clinic in Biloxi by Dr. Grad L. Flick provide teachers with one to two days intensive training on (a) basic behavioral techniques and (b) specific applications. Most important, teachers must receive information on the underlying nature of ADHD problematic behavior, for it provides the foundation on which many behavioral interventions are based. Practical applications of these techniques may require rehearsal and role-play procedures, as often the techniques may be misinterpreted and thus poorly implemented in actual classrooms. In the ideal world, training should not stop at this point. Instead, there should be feedback and refinement of the direct application of techniques until such techniques can be used accurately and consistently in the classroom. At present, the ADD Clinic offers follow-up consultation to these workshops to deal with some of the problems encountered.

To provide some measure of knowledge of behavioral principles and ADHD, an instrument entitled *Flick's Survey of Behavioral Practices and ADD/ADHD* is available. This assessment may be given prior to and again following the training workshop. Such an assessment may provide information about cognitive changes regarding coping with problematic behavior, but not a measure of actual changes in the teacher's response to the problematic behavior.

COMPULSIVE BEHAVIOR TRAINING

It has been noted by Faigel and colleagues (1995) that "In most settings, adolescents who learn to be compulsive in completing tasks as part of their cognitive therapy are the ones who succeed. Those who do not will be more likely to fail." This compensatory pattern of a rigid routine may establish sufficient structure in tasks so as to enhance the probability of their being completed accurately. This pattern has also been noted by Flick (1996, 1998) in earlier publications.

The major issue facing cognitive therapists is one of moderation. It may be neurophysiologically impossible to go too far—creating additional problems instead of adaptive behavior. Truly, obsessive–compulsive disorders appear to have some neurophysiological basis that may be modified through medication. For teens with ADHD, it may be possible to train compulsive behavior by reinforcing a routine procedure of checking work performance to ensure completeness and correctness. Essentially, a habit of checking one's work may be established as a habit. To conduct such training, one must have a well-defined task that may submit to a checklist analysis. Once the checklist is established, it is only necessary that there be a reinforcement when each step of the checklist has been checked. While such a procedure could be conducted with a paper-and-pencil checklist, it would be best conducted with a computerized routine where each step could be reinforced through feedback and a grand feedback provided at task's end when it is clear that all items were checked. This type of procedure would lend itself quite nicely to checking the accuracy of a series of math problems. However, it is also obvious that numerous other applications may be made.

FAMILY THERAPY

Being a parent of an adolescent with ADHD is difficult. Feelings of guilt, withdrawal, or anger in response to the teen's behavior may erode the adolescent's self-confidence and self-esteem. Some parents who understand the biological basis for the behavior may accept the teen's behavior or at least overcome their feelings of hostility toward it and are able to provide love and unconditional positive strokes to nurture their teen's good feelings about him- or herself.

Even though the adolescents with ADHD are able to learn that they are not at fault for their problems, there is still much difficulty accepting how they are different from their peers. Parents likewise need to understand that their teen's difficulties are not attributable to deficient parenting, but that relationships can be improved with the use of effective behavioral techniques.

By the time their child reaches adolescence, parents are often overwhelmed and sometimes feel a sense of helplessness and hopelessness. They often state, "I tried everything and nothing seems to work"; they are often seen at the stage of "learned helplessness" and have just about given up. Some have viewed themselves as failures. Some have become overly stressed in attempts at dealing with their teen's behavior and some have become casualties of intramarital stress. After so many arguments where each spouse is blamed for the teen's trouble, there is little time for their marital relationship.

Family therapy approaches attempt to first better understand the nature of their teen's ADHD behaviors and how they have reacted to it. With counseling in behavior-management techniques, training to enhance communication, and instruction in problem-solving procedures, parents may become better equipped to develop strategies to cope with disruptive behaviors and to use more positive approaches in helping with sibling concerns and conflicts. By reframing perceptions of family members, improving the basic family structure within which to operate, and by using the most effective and appropriate behavioral procedures, family life can improve and the chance for a successful outcome for the teen with ADHD may be increased.

THERAPEUTIC PROSTHETICS

While not a therapeutic modality in itself, the use of various devices may aid the teen with ADHD in dealing with several problem areas. For example, many teens with ADHD have difficulty inputting information into memory storage due to distractions or inability to shift attention from one thing to another. Various electronic devices may "bypass" such difficulty by tracking assignments, keeping a record of appointments or projects due later, as well as commitments (e.g., meetings, engagements, etc.).

Electronic notebooks can solve the teen's problem of keeping track of complex schedules, assignments, data, etc. A less expensive format may be found in the daily planner, yet more is required of the student in using such a planner.

"White noise" generator can create a background that may mask distractions and enhance concentration. Of course, wearing headphones will also reduce room noise.

ELECTRONIC REMINDERS

DEVICES

An electronic device called the MotivAider™, invented in the early 1980s by Dr. Steve Levinson, can provide a signal or cue for the teen to engage in some specific appropriate behavior. Looking very much like a beeper, it is worn on the belt or carried in the pocket. It can be set to deliver a two-second vibration (perceptible only by the teen) that may occur from once a minute to once every several hours. The cue (the vibration) is directly associated with a special "private message" that only the adolescent will know. For example, the teen may be told that when she feels the cue, that is a signal to "pay attention" or "get back to work if you are off task," or perhaps something more general as to just "check to see if you are doing what you are supposed to be doing!" With improvement, the device may be set to vibrate less frequently and may eventually be phased out. The MotivAider™ appears to be a unique self-monitoring device that is appealing and "relieves teachers and parents of the need to nag."

Another more sophisticated and computerized system is called the Tickle Box®, manufactured by ADDAPTIVE Learning Company. This type of paging system provides an external cue (vibration and a visual signal from the pager) for things on the teen's "to do" list. It has some built-in goal rewards involving colorful graphic animations and audio feedback (e.g., "good job") when the adolescent successfully completes a task. Weekly award certificates are built into the program for use as back-up reinforcers for the teen. Although no formal studies are available at this time, the device would seem to appeal to adolescents; the authors state that "because paging systems are commonplace, the teen does not feel ostracized by using this adaptive device." Wearing a pager would be quite unique and might create a feeling of importance. While the at-home software is fairly inexpensive, the addition of the pager (with activation fee and pager airtime) obviously poses a financial hardship for many potential users of the system.

The Watch Minder® is a training and reminder system that looks much like a digital watch. It has different modes or functions. In the training/self-monitoring mode, a message is selected (e.g., PAY ATTN); this is displayed periodically (e.g., every 10 minutes), accompanied by a 2-second vibration. Other messages include: RELAX, GOOD JOB, and STOP. In the reminder mode, multiple messages can be selected from a list of 60 preprogrammed, to be displayed at specific times throughout the day. For teens, these may include: GO SCHOOL, BACKPACK, DO HW, TAKE MEDS; and for older teens: GO WORK, CK E-MAIL, CALL HOME. There are other specific messages that can be programmed. All of these functions are provided in a sports watch that has a large easy-to-read display for time, date, stopwatch, training, and reminder functions. The silent alarm provides private reminders of the personal messages.

The teen with ADHD is quite sensitive to various sounds in the classroom. With hearing generally more sensitive than other children, they may be distracted by even subtle and soft sounds that are typically not noticed by normal teens. An electronic device called the Easy Listener, manufactured by Phonic Ear™, reportedly can help to create a better listening and learning environment by reducing the noisy distractions of air conditioners, squeaking chairs, and chatting neighbors, and clarifying the teacher's voice with mild amplification. The overall result is an improvement of the signal-to-noise ratio. This device sounds appealing, but there are no available studies as yet to determine the effectiveness in actual classroom situations. The primary drawbacks, however, are that it is quite expensive and not only does the teen wear a unit (receiver), the teacher must wear the transmitter. Another similar device is called HEARIT®, and is promoted as a "new effective auditory tool for learning disabilities." It also reportedly reduces distractions to allow the adolescent to stay on-task more often and to sustain attention for longer periods of time.

HEARIT® is described as a user-friendly "personal communicator" device that provides critical enhancement of higher consonant-range frequencies of spoken language. The adolescent can reportedly "pluck out" speech in the presence of noise while sustaining auditory processing abilities. The device may be tested on an individual basis to determine whether it may be beneficial to try in other situations (e.g., the classroom). The benefits of using this device include:

➠ increased phonological awareness for improved focus and comprehension during reading

⠶ reduction of distractions for improved on-task time

⠶ improved auditory discrimination in remediating articulation errors

It is also noted that this device meets the demands of the Americans with Disabilities Act of 1990 to provide reliable accessible communication. There is, however, no known research on the use of this device with teens with ADHD, and the high price would likewise limit its general use.

Another similar device is available at a much lower and reasonable cost. The Noisebuster Extreme® from Educational Solutions reduces background noises. An electronic chip analyzes incoming offensive noise and a precise anti-noise sound wave is generated through the stereo headphones. This device provides 15 decibels of noise reduction, canceling noise between the 20–1,500 Hz frequency range. There is also a slide bar adjustment to vary the amount of noise cancellation. It may be used in the classroom or at home during homework. The Noisebuster Extreme® has been tested clinically and research evidence is reportedly forthcoming. However, the cost, design features, and technological basis for the instrument make it an interesting alternative to consider for some adolescents.

Another unique device that is now commercially available is called TV Allowance®. Each child in the family is given a code number so that TV times and programs may be tracked. With this device, the parent can easily provide extra time for cooperative behavior around TV time, while subtracting time for teen hassles over TV programs. One device can manage up to four children; each child uses his or her own code to view his or her programs. TV Allowance® was designed to limit the amount of time children watch television or play video games.

TAPE RECORDERS

Small tape recorders can be useful in school and at home. At home, the teen may use one to record spelling words. It provides an additional sense modality (auditory) through which learning can occur. Thus, the teen can write the words (kinesthetic mode of learning), visualize them (visual mode of learning), and hear them spelled out in his or her own voice (auditory mode of learning). This procedure may develop internal auditory cues that will be very useful when the adolescent has a spelling test. As most spelling tests are dictated, associating the sound of the words with their visual and kinesthetic cues would certainly benefit the teen. It is also a procedure that allows the teen to practice writing and learning words in the same manner he or she will be tested.

Since many adolescents with ADHD have handwriting problems, they may find the tape recorder useful in recording stories and paragraphs that they are assigned to make up and write. This procedure of saying and reading words thus reduces the pressure of writing (which may slow down cognitive thought processes), frees the more relaxed creative right-brain thinking, and enables story construction to be more interesting. This technique, however, depends entirely on acceptance and approval of the use of the tape recorder by the teen's teacher.

Computers

Most all teens appear more motivated when using computer programs to learn skills and tend to stay on-task for longer periods of time, according to research findings by Mary J. Ford et al. (1993). The fascination of a computer that talks, using organizational software, will certainly hold the teen's interest. The teen could, for example, type in reminders for rules or projects and have the computer tell him or her to carry out the instructions. It's like having a coach available at the touch of a button.

Mnemonic Devices

Memory aids have been very helpful for adolescents with learning disabilities and can be used for teens with ADHD. For example, teens may be taught to use visual images, rhymes, and rap songs to associate specific lists on chains of information. Another specific mnemonic procedure is termed the "write–say" method. This simply involves having the teen *write* and therefore *see* misspelled words several times while spelling them *aloud*. In this procedure, visual, auditory, and kinesthetic modes of learning are involved. Such multi-modal approaches have been quite effective not only for spelling, but also in learning multiplication tables in math.

Small electronic devices may also be used by the teen to record important information in class for later replay at home. The only constraint is that such devices have limited capacity except for some of the more expensive ones.

Special Techniques and Procedures

A self-monitoring system designed by Dr. Harvey C. Parker to improve on-task behavior is entitled *Listen, Look and Think: A Self-Regulation Program for Children.* It is available through the ADD Clinic. This system features an endless loop cassette tape that plays an audible tone at variable intervals (every 30 to 60 seconds). As soon as the beep is heard on the headphones, the teen marks a sheet to indicate whether he or she was on- or off-task. Depending on the length of the task, the teen may mark the sheet 1–20 times. This procedure is based on research and, although it may sound as if it would be distracting, it has worked well with many students to reduce off-task behavior as well as to control distractions. Perhaps wearing the headphones also reduces auditory distractions in the teen's classroom, homework, or study environment. A copy of the recording sheet is found in Figure 3.4.

Another device that has helped improve on-task behavior is the Attention (Response Cost) Trainer, developed by Dr. Grad Flick, and also available through *The ADD/ADHD Resources Catalog.* The teen begins with a specific number of points (e.g., 30) for a 20-minute assignment. Each time he or she gets off-task, a point is subtracted by flipping over a card. Points are on cards on a flip-top stand. This alternate procedure employs 3x5 cards numbered from 1 to 30 and placed on a flip-type photo stand. This stand is preferably placed on the teacher's desk, but within the student's view. Only one teen can be monitored at a time to avoid confusion.

Figure 3.4

SELF-RECORDING FORM

NAME: _____

DATE: _____ SUBJECT: _____

Listen to the program tape as you do your work. Whenever you hear a beep, stop working and ask yourself, *Was I Paying Attention?* Mark your answer (✓) below and go back to work.

Was I Paying Attention?		*Was I Paying Attention?*	
Yes	No	Yes	No

Self-Evaluation Form

1. Did I follow the directions?	Yes	No
2. Did I pay attention?	Yes	No
3. Did I ask for help if I needed any?	Yes	No
4. Did I finish my work correctly?	Yes	No
5. Did I check my answers?	Yes	No

From *Listen, Look and Think: A Self-Regulation Program for Children* by Harvey C. Parker, Ph.D. Used by permission of Specialty Press and distributed by A.D.D. Warehouse (1-800-233-9273).

At the beginning of the assignment, the teen is told that she has 30 points. Each time the teacher observes that the teen is off-task, a card is flipped over, thus deducting one point from her total. A clicker can also be used to signal the loss of a point. This system is reviewed with the teen in advance so that she is clear about what to expect. It is not known whether any research-based comparison has been made between this inexpensive system and a similar electronic device, Dr. Gordon's Attention Trainer™.

While the procedure is similar and falls within the "response cost" procedural category, it does lack the total nonverbal message delivered by the electronic Attention Trainer™ (available from Gordon Systems, 301 Ambergate Road, De Witt, New York 13214). The only ways to give the child feedback on whether he or she was off-task are to: (1) call out the child's name and when he or she looks up point to the cards as one is flipped or (2) use a clicker and discuss what this signal means prior to using the system. These appear to be the only ways to inform the teen he or she was off-task and have a "loss of a point"; feedback may prompt the teen to return to work. Naturally, this system, as well as the electronic Attention Trainer™, needs to have some back-up consequences (i.e., rewards) other than just knowing how many of the total points were retained. The Attention (Response Cost) Trainer is available from *The ADD/ADHD Resources Catalog.*

A procedure that is often helpful in academic work is called *self-instruction.* For example, a parent can teach this procedure to a young teen for use during homework. The parent simply models the way the teen might "think out loud" using self-instruction (self-talk), verbalizing each logical step needed to solve a problem or to complete a task. Adolescents not only learn that it is okay to talk to themselves while working, but they also acquire a process of asking questions about what the next step is and telling themselves, "What I need to do next is . . ." Having such self-talk appears to help the teen who otherwise tends to rush through homework. This technique is especially useful for math problems and writing. Verbal descriptions of the task must be quite detailed—almost to the point where one can visualize the result simply by listening to the verbal description. This slow-down procedure helps to modulate the teen's impulsive tendencies, while at the same time improving his or her attention to detail and accuracy, especially during written work.

DECISION ON ALTERNATIVE TREATMENTS

Some of the novel procedures described here were, of course, never intended to be used as a sole treatment of ADHD, and some would certainly be combined with other procedures in a typical multi-modal treatment program. With the incidence of other problems—such as learning disabilities, depression, anxiety, and conduct disorders—so high, it is necessary to address each problem. Thus, a multi-modal treatment program is a generally accepted standard. It will behoove the parent or teacher to pick and choose techniques and procedures for specific applications. It is also important that parents or teachers feel comfortable with these procedures and techniques selected.

Chapter 4

FAMILY ISSUES FOR TEENS WITH ADHD

A large-scale study of 20,000 teens indicated that 80% interacted well with parents; 20% had difficulty with depression, suicidal thoughts, and/or risk-taking behavior. Families with teens who have ADHD experience more conflict and must deal with more problems than typical families with adolescents. While parents don't actually cause ADHD behavior, the way they handle it can make life harmonious or discordant. Communication problems, emotional problems (especially anger and depression), stress problems, and conflicts requiring almost constant problem solving may all appear at some time during adolescence.

All of these difficulties vary in degree and number for any specific family with an ADHD teen. It is also clear that problems especially with one family member (e.g., the ADHD teen) may result in some problematic behavior in another family member (e.g., parent or sibling). Given that the attention deficit disorder is predominately genetically based, there is a greater likelihood of volatile interactive problems between siblings, or between parent and siblings. In short the whole family is affected even when there is just one member with ADHD.

In addition, if one or more parent has had a history of ADHD along with Conduct Disorder, all of which has evolved into characteristic antisocial behavior, such parents are not only likely to use hostile–aggressive actions toward the teen member, they are also more likely to pull away from the teen and spend less time attempting to teach any of the mainstream values in a positive and productive manner. Co-morbid disorders such as ODD and CD have often been attributed primarily to poor parenting, parental personal problems (psychiatric disorders), and marital disharmony. However, one must always look at the interactive nature of the parent–child relations to sort out whether marital disharmony may have resulted in some of the behavioral problems in the teen or whether the teen's ADHD behavior with either ODD or CD caused the marital distress.

The interactive nature of ADHD problematic behavior does not begin during adolescence. Unless the ADHD characteristic has resulted from some brain disorder (i.e., an acquired form of ADHD characteristic), there has probably been a long history of interactive problem behavior. As described in detail in the *ADD/ADHD Behavior-Change Resource Kit* (Flick, 1998), there is a pattern of escalation of restrictive commands that, in the long run, fails to bring about adequate compliance.

Instead of describing the interaction between parent and child (with ADHD) as parent dominated, this interaction is more adequately described as bi-directional. Their "two-way" interaction now means that the child may have just as much influence on the parent as the parent has on the child. As the child grows there may be a long history of many interactions in which the child has "won." This may have resulted in parents giving up and relinquishing authority and allowing the child to "control" the parent–child interaction.

There are children who perceive that they are dominant and can do as they please. Of course, when the child makes the decision to "eat candy for breakfast," to defer to that decision may cause only personal harm (i.e., poor nutrition, dental problems, etc.). However, as a teenager, when a decision is made to "build a bomb," to defer may cause harm to many. Thus, when teens with ADHD decide that they can do as they please, parents may decide to step in and attempt to change their pattern. To change any pattern of behavior that has existed for some time would be difficult, but to change the pattern referred to would be extremely difficult. Now, this scenario may be an extreme and infrequent one, but there are others less extreme and less frequent that are still quite difficult to change.

ASSESSMENT OF PROBLEMATIC BEHAVIORS

The first step in making any change is to recognize that problem(s) do exist, and to have a better understanding of these problems, especially with regard to how they develop and how they are maintained. In *Power Parenting for ADD/ADHD Children* (Flick, 1996), it was anticipated that with a good understanding of the nature of Attention Deficit Disorder and knowledge of effective behavioral techniques, parents could be empowered and could deal more effectively with their children. The same can be true with adolescents who have ADHD. However, the problem behaviors may be somewhat different; many of the problematic behaviors have a longer history and are thus going to be more difficult to change; and the effective techniques may be modified somewhat, and some techniques may even be discarded as ineffective with teens. However, it is still believed that behavior changes are possible—just somewhat more difficult to achieve. Finally, it may also take longer to modify some of these "difficult-to-manage" behaviors.

The problematic behaviors are not discussed in any particular order—their severity and frequency may vary from one family to another. In general, where there is an adolescent with ADHD in the family, conflicts are characterized by negative communications (e.g., mutual accusations, defensiveness, interruptions, poor eye contact, poor attention to others, and considerable reactive lecturing), along with many problem-solving difficulties (e.g., power struggles and general lack of negotiation).

Parents who use an authoritarian directive-control approach to problem solving may initiate a cycle of escalating "coercive" interactions. This increases the likelihood of oppositional behavior (i.e., aggression). One or more of the following problems may exist.

COMPLIANCE

Teens with ADHD may be noncompliant to a much greater extent than in childhood. Basic problems of inattention, memory difficulty, distractibility, or passive resistance to some rule or directive may each account for some incidents of defiance. Likewise, striving for independence may play a role. These issues may need to be discussed with the teenager to arrive at some consensus about compliance. In short, if the teen has more input into decisions regarding these issues, compliance can be enhanced. There will be a more in-depth discussion of rules; suffice it to say now that it is better to have only a small number and to differentiate between negotiable and nonnegotiable rules.

IMPULSE-CONTROL

The basic characteristic of ADHD seems exaggerated in teens with ADHD. The sequence of "I think—I react" is a frequent one describing how quickly thoughts can lead to actions, and even more often actions before thoughts. Such teens may then say things that are embarrassing, spend their money as soon as they get it, and generally have much trouble with "delay of gratification." Parents may control this problem only indirectly by managing those situations that are associated with impulsivity (e.g., don't tell him or her things that you would not want broadcasted to others).

ATTENTION

Another basic problem is that of inattention. Continued difficulty with one or more of the subtypes of attentional deficits may result in difficulty staying focused, maintaining attention to task completion, attending to a changing pattern, and dividing their attention to two or more things. Thus, such teens with ADHD may have trouble listening to a teacher, following changes in math, or attending to their driving so that they don't speed or have an accident. Of course, as parents and teachers we sometimes give the adolescent with ADHD too many things to remember, or we may possibly provide information in such a manner as to create "boredom." Knowing that a teen with ADHD continues to have trouble processing information means that we must present the information in a preferred mode of information processing (i.e., visual, auditory, or kinesthetic), and we must limit the amount of information presented, and check out whether the teen got that information before proceeding to present new information.

MEMORY

Sometimes noncompliance may result from difficulty with attention and/or memory. Teens with ADHD appear so forgetful (and even more so than teens in general) that it creates considerable frustration for most parents and teachers. At times being forgetful can mask some intentional defiance. One of the most common complaints is that the teen with ADHD forgets to do his chores (and especially to clean his room). In all probability these are longstanding problems with habits that are either poorly developed or nonexistent. To develop better habits regarding chores, it will be necessary to post various types of cues or reminders, to perhaps make some things contingent on completing the chore(s), and to always positively reinforce behavior that is either in the appropriate direction (i.e., partial completion) or for completion of the whole chore.

ORGANIZATION

Chaos and disorder are hallmark characteristics of teens with ADHD. Their rooms, desks, backpacks, etc., are "messy." Numerous possessions may be lost or placed in some type of "black hole" never to be seen again. Footballs, jackets, jewelry can all disappear regardless of the importance of that item to the teen. There are some practical solutions to these problems, such as putting a name on clothing and other items, or just buying "cheaper stuff" and expecting it to be lost.

Of course, parents and teachers may review routines to help with developing better organization, but remember that some parents are really "adults" with ADHD and they too have trouble with this problem area as well as other problems on this list. It may be necessary to review and model what is meant by "clean your room." To some teens with ADHD, that means only that you must clear a path to be able to walk through the room. Show first, and then have the teen complete the task under some supervision. If you refuse to leave until it's completed, you will reinforce task completion by leaving at the end (removing a thorn or splinter feels good). Your leaving terminates a mildly aversive situation, and reinforces the task completion. However, it may also be important to decide whether this chore is of sufficient priority to follow through in this manner. A more in-depth discussion of priorities will be forthcoming. One option is to simply close the door to the teen's room so that you can't see it.

TIME MANAGEMENT

Those with ADHD have difficulty with time; the teen with ADHD seems to have more serious problems in this area, perhaps because of general resistance to authority during this period of his or her life. Several important areas of the teen's life may be affected. First, there is frequent, and at times apparent blatant, disregard for curfews and other time constraints. Late for appointments, his job, his projects, this teen with ADHD seems to live with procrastination. There is also difficulty judging time needed for task completion or to finish a test; there is difficulty getting up in the morning and difficulty with bedtime. Partly due to organizational problems, but also related to time problems in the teen, is trouble planning ahead to finish special projects for school, or that special gift for "Mother's Day" finished instead for a Christmas gift. Solutions vary for these problems—some parents invest in a cheap wristwatch or beeper (not so cheap), and others try to develop the habit of using planners and establishing a routine way of dealing with time-related issues.

EMOTIONAL REACTIVITY

Just as in younger children, teens with ADHD may have a lower level of frustration tolerance and may be quick to respond emotionally. Quick to express anger, quick to cry, these adolescents are described as "wearing their emotions on their sleeve." It is, however, difficult to know and predict what the reaction might be as the response is capricious, spontaneous, and labile. Such teens are quite sensitive emotionally as they are neurologically.

Following impulsive emotional acting-out, such teens are generally embarrassed and experience a sense of guilt. This is not always the case, however, especially with teens who have ADHD and Conduct Disorder or Oppositional Defiant Disorder. To some degree these reactions are related to ongoing physiological changes (i.e., hormones). Many of the acting-out episodes may also bring about a period of introspection and wonder—whether they might be "crazy" or "different" in some way. Perhaps the worst is for the teen to imagine that he or she is "different" and can't handle these "problems" or situations, leading to feelings of inadequacy and depression.

AGGRESSION

Parents and teachers alike have many complaints centering around this issue. "He argues, curses, talks back and is generally disrespectful" are frequent statements made by many parents and some teachers. Keep in mind that the person with ADHD maintains a need for stimulation to compensate for the lower level of arousal in the nervous system (documented by many different measures in many different studies). It is not unlikely that teens with ADHD will engage in some behaviors that will likely "stir things up."

Cursing, sexual gestures, dress, grooming, and teasing all carry some emotional impact and may generate a reaction—especially if the parent or other sibling also has ADHD. This is a set-up for volatile exchanges. These are also most likely to occur in the family; school reactions may occur in relation to other students who have ADHD or with teachers who have ADHD. It is noteworthy that those teachers (with ADHD) who developed a rigid obsessive–compulsive approach and adherence to rules may create the most friction in relationships with the teen who has ADHD. Thus, while such compulsive strategies may have helped the teacher cope with underlying problems, those same strategies may generate conflict with the teen who has ADHD.

Many parents and teachers might overlook or ignore some of these inappropriate behaviors. If they do not get a reaction, they will literally "die on the vine" and become extinct. To respond to the teen's attempt to "hook" you into a full-blown conflict will only result in further deterioration of your relationship and does not solve the problem. It only gets worse. Disengagement is the general recommendation for this situation. When the teen is angry, he or she needs space. Walk away and come back when the teen has calmed down. Communicate to the teen, "I'll be back when you've calmed down and are in better control of yourself," saying this in a cool nonemotional tone. It's important to recognize the emotional upset and to state that whatever disrespectful behavior was shown (e.g., cursing) is not acceptable. Also, it is impossible to problem-solve when emotionally upset. When both parent and teen have calmed down, it will be feasible to sit and discuss the issues to problem-solve.

ACTIVITY STIMULATION

While the teen with ADHD is not typically "hyperactive," there is often a residual level of over-activity that is characterized by restlessness and for some being over-talkative. Facial expressions, slouching and re-slouching postures, purposeless movement (e.g., tapping a pencil), eye rolling and similar behaviors, all reflect boredom—a need for some type of stimulation. There may be a need to be doing something all the time, yet it is often not any goal-directed purposeful activity.

Just like their younger counterparts, the ADHD teen may seek out novelty and excitement. Many adult activities are, however, perceived as totally "boring" and are usually avoided. It is important for parents and teachers to recognize and understand that many of these behaviors are not meant to be disrespectful although they may certainly have that appearance. For the parent or teacher it provides a cue to shift gears and perhaps interact with the teen to discover what interest may be pursued. It may be especially useful to sequence activities so that the "boring" ones may be followed by the more interesting ones.

SOCIAL SKILLS

Because of the many difficulties associated with ADHD, teens may continue to have problems in various social relationships both in and out of the family. In some extracurricular activities such as sports, the teen with ADHD may have trouble attending to instructions, controlling impulses, adhering to rules (or even remembering them), modulating emotional responses; some may continue to experience frustration associated with poor coordination. Thus, their basic problems may make it difficult to engage in sports or some specific social activities. Likewise, their general immaturity may affect their judgment and influence their acceptance or rejection by the social group. There is also much difficulty in family social interaction as the pace is typically slower and perceived as "boring." Sitting still for a long period may be as difficult in family gatherings as it is in school.

Some more serious social problems may develop as a result of continuing rejection (lack of peer acceptance) by others. In such cases, the teen with ADHD may develop the self-perceptions as an "outcast or loner." The mechanism is not clear, but teens with ADHD who show this pattern tend to find other teens with similar problems. Association with similar individuals may result in a synergistic effect on inappropriate behavior. Thus, any pre-existing inappropriate behavior may be exaggerated. This can lead to the engagement of various "dangerous" risk-taking behaviors.

RISK-TAKING

Usually parents of teens with ADHD will have considerable experience with emergency rooms at hospitals, sometimes knowing these doctors by their first names. Such accident proneness, and careless and reckless behavior seem to be exacerbated during adolescence. These teens with ADHD not only break their bones—they break others' possessions. Having difficulty with planning and foresight, there is only a loose association between behavior and consequences. (Personally, I recall trips to the hospital to remove a fishhook imbedded deep in our son's hand and another occasion for multiple cuts that resulted from walking through a plate glass door.) Much of this behavior again relates to basic problems in ADHD together with a lack of awareness of personal space and surroundings.

NARCISSISM

Most all adolescents are "wrapped-up" in themselves, being concerned about their appearances, their clothes, what material possessions they have, and their own personal gratification. I recall that our son did not wish to leave the house until his hair was perfectly combed. It is therefore not unlike the teen with ADHD to show an exaggeration of such problems as they fail to remember birthdays and special events. While sometimes oblivious to others' needs, they can focus on their own needs and wants to excess. Callous comments may go unnoticed as they seem to show little concern for others' feelings. However, in some cases, perhaps where the teen with ADHD is struggling to be accepted by others, he or she may appear overly generous—especially with others' possessions. It was not surprising to find several important things missing when we returned to our house one day. (Our son had given credit cards and jewelry to his "friends.")

Fitting into the perception of an exaggerated sense of importance, it is not unusual for the teen with ADHD to quickly satiate with some new possessions only to request replacements. Outside of Nintendo™, many gifts are quickly put aside with requests for something new. Perhaps such tendencies relate to the lack of personal accomplishments, and the need to enhance their personal perceptions and perceptions by others. There appears to be an exaggeration of the notion that "the person with the most toys at the end wins."

BOUNDARY

Much sibling conflict arises when teens with ADHD violate boundaries of space and the personal time of others. Siblings complain when their room is entered and their possessions are taken without permission. To the dismay of parents and siblings, not only are their things taken but they also are often returned broken. The teen's sense of importance and lack of concern for others also appear to surface in their problems.

Violations of personal time by interruptions often reflect selfish motives. There is a lack of perceptiveness regarding the appropriate time and the appropriate manner to communicate with others, especially parents. There may even be a general lack of awareness about the inappropriateness of their intrusive behavior as they have difficulty reading social cues of frustration and disgust.

SLEEP–WAKE DIFFICULTIES

These are directly related to the underlying physiological differences of the teen with ADHD. In fact there is often chronic sleep problems. First, there may be difficulty going to sleep as many teens with ADHD are more alert at night compared with daytime. Also, many have developed techniques of cognitive stimulation to keep themselves more alert during the daytime, but may have trouble turning off this technique at bedtime. For some teens, relaxation exercises at bedtime may help; for others, a mild stimulant may help.

Teens with ADHD may also have trouble waking up. This is perhaps a more common problem for parents. Should the teen only have this difficulty during the school week, but not on weekends, this is probably not a sleep problem, but rather a lack of enthusiasm about getting ready for school because of the degree of frustration and failure generally experienced in school. These problems must be addressed with medication and behavior interventions. One very useful procedure regarded by many parents is to give half the morning dose of stimulant medication before the teen gets out of bed (usually about 30 minutes before he or she is to get up). When the teen does get up, there are fewer hassles before going to school or work. This stimulation may be sufficient to address this problem.

Another behavioral intervention might involve a behavior generally for lateness. Thus, if the teen drives, he or she could lose driving privileges or some other preferred privilege might be reduced. Sometimes a second medication may be added at nighttime to aid in facilitating sleep induction and to address other problems as well. For example, Tofranil® or clonidine has not only helped to improve sleep but also helped to address moody, irritable, and aggressive daytime behaviors. Of course, it is reasonable to expect better mood as a result of improved sleep alone.

Excessive sleeping may not just be a symptom of ADHD and this condition's generally low arousal; teens with ADHD typically become depressed. Their general lack of energy and excessive sleeping may thus reflect depression. This should be checked out, especially if there are other symptoms of depression. (See pages 55–57 for more details on dealing with depression.)

Minor depressive episodes may be helped with additional targeted medication, but it is possible that some added physical exercise might benefit, especially if the teen has a fairly sedentary activity level. Running has been shown to be especially effective. Prior to any intervention, it is best that the teen get a physical exam. Some medical problems such as allergies, anemia, or other illness/infections may lower the energy level.

IDENTITY

During the process of evolving identity, some difficulties may arise in addition to the common issues that address the question of "Who am I?" The development of independence and autonomy coincide with the increase in responsibility that the teen will gradually assume. However, teens with ADHD are notoriously "late bloomers" with regard to overall maturity.

It has been estimated that teens with ADHD are generally 2 to 3 years behind their normal teens. This translates into difficulty accepting responsibility. One author, Paul Olsen, M.S. (1996), talked about a "responsibility deficit disorder." This might range from problems admitting guilt over some transgression (e.g., getting into a fight) to denial of having homework when he does. Lying is therefore common, as is the act of apologizing. Perhaps these difficulties relate to the problems many teens with ADHD have when it comes to admitting they were wrong or they made a mistake. Such issues are problems for teens in general as they do not wish to appear different. Teens with ADHD have similar investments in protecting themselves, but they are even more sensitive to such issues and rather than admit to another failure or shortcoming, protectively and perhaps automatically at this point in their life, quickly deny everything that would implicate them.

Lying is a difficult problem to cope with since the teen who effectively avoids unpleasant tasks (i.e., homework) may be directly rewarded each time the lying behavior "works." Consequently, there may be a long history of "rewards" for this inappropriate behavior. If the teen eventually tells the truth and is then "punished," it is "truth telling" that is discouraged by punishment and not "lying behavior." It is the last behavior in the sequence (i.e., truth telling) that is punished. This would certainly encourage the teen to get better at lying and not to tell the truth.

SELF-CONCEPT AND SELF-ESTEEM

This is a major area of concern for most parents and teachers. A teen's perception of self is critical to survival. If the teen with ADHD perceives himself as "dumb or stupid" because he has difficulty completing his work, learning the teacher's lecture, or remembering information to respond to test questions, the failures he experiences will contribute to negative self-esteem. It is essential that such a teen be helped to experience more positive strokes, building on strengths, and coping with weakness. It is through such positive experience that teens with ADHD develop *resiliency*, a construct that has become increasingly more important in working with persons who have ADHD.

Over a period of time it is apparent that those with ADHD who survive almost devastating life experiences and achieve success may do so because of some "islands of competency" as noted by Dr. Robert Brooks. It is the recognition of the teen's strengths that is most important. One can therefore unequivocally state that the primary cumulative effect of a long history of negative comments such as "he could do better if he would only try," or "need to improve math skills," or "if he would only pay attention in class his grades could be better" is quite detrimental to self-concept and self-esteem. There is nothing positive about these comments, nothing encouraging in these comments, and certainly nothing that suggests a strategy to change anything. The primary effect these comments have is to further erode the already weak and fragile self-esteem and reinforce the teen's own perception of himself as "stupid." It's the only reasonable conclusion since many students have tried to meet the expectations of parents and teachers, only to "fall short" each time.

Once parents and teachers recognize some of these problem areas, these difficulties may be addressed by order of severity. Parents and teachers are encouraged to use the Problem Summary Sheet (see Figure 4.1) to get an overview of the teen's problems as the first step in addressing them. Each problem is rated by parents and/or teachers. The top three problems may be listed with specific interventions to address these problems. Separate ratings for home and school may reveal different sets of problematic behavior. There may be many different ways to view or conceptualize problems. By examining these different views of behavior problems, some creative interventions may be designed.

In addition to recognizing problem areas, it may be helpful to parents to have some structure on which they may understand parenting styles. According to Alexander-Roberts (1995), there are four types of parenting styles for children and adolescents. These include: (1) domineering or overly controlling parents—teens with this style of parenting are likely to have trouble with anger, be rebellious, and be disrespectful of authority; (2) neglectful parents—teens turn out insecure, rebellious, and show little self-esteem; (3) lenient parents—these teens have general difficulty with all of society's rules; and (4) firm and loving parents—a most beneficial form of parenting, which results in the teen being able to function independently in society with a positive self-concept and high self-esteem.

Clearly, some style in parenting will shift with the age of the child so that what is appropriate and best for young children (i.e., firmness, direction, and love) may not at all be best for the teenager who needs not only love but also a more democratic approach to parenting for the development of responsible and more independent behavior. In this whole process, there are some clearly dysfunctional parental styles (i.e., Patho-Parenting), which will be outlined by Dr. Alma Lott Flick in the following section. She has conducted basic behavioral training with parents of children and teens with ADHD, and has developed the following conceptualizations based on this work. A general descriptive framework based on both transactional analysis and behavioral concepts is utilized.

Figure 4.1

PROBLEM SUMMARY SHEET

Name_____ Age_____ Grade_____

Parent(s) Completing Ratings_____

Instructions: Please rate the identified teen for each problem area using the key below for your rating. Rank order the top 10 problems and then pick the first three for initial intervention.

Key: 0 = DOES NOT APPLY   3 = SEVERE
1 = MILD   4 = PROFOUND
2 = MODERATE

Rating

Problem Area	0	1	2	3	4	Rank ▪ 10
Compliance						
Impulse Control						
Attention						
Memory						
Organization						
Time Management						
Emotional Reaction						
Aggression						
Activity Stimulation						
Social Skills						
Risk-Taking						
Narcissism						
Boundary						
Sleep-Wake Difficulties						
Identity						
Self-Concept/Self-Esteem						
Overall Severity (Sum)						
Problem	Intervention(s)					
(#1)						
(#2)						
(#3)						

PATHO-PARENTING STYLES

The term "Patho-Parenting" is used in the context of this chapter to describe parental relationships with the teenager that produce unhealthy (patho) or negative behavior and fail to correct the problems it attempts to address with the teen. It doesn't address the main issue and stops the development of positive relationships between parent and teen. So why does the parent continue to use what doesn't work effectively? Habit, ADHD physiology on the part of the parent, and lack of information on how to address the problem and solve the issue. Perhaps all three and no more excuses.

Patho-parenting styles actually reinforce the bad behaviors the teen displays because they reward the behavior with attention and stimulation. This section attempts to isolate some typically common patho-parenting tactics that often signal trouble between the parent and their teen. First, however, there are some important things that must be addressed to offer a foundation to begin changing.

PARENT–TEEN COMMUNICATION

The key to understanding behavior and resolving problems between parent and teen lies within the parent's understanding of communication and its complexities. Communication is determined by many levels of functioning within the personality of the parent and within the personality of the teen, both on an unconscious and a conscious level. To help demonstrate the complexities of communication and to decode what is really being said to your teen, study carefully the following information.

How many times have you felt there is another person inside you who takes over when you think, parent your teen, or feel anger at a ball game instead of just having fun? Energy systems make up our personality, and each seems to have a specialized function. The "grown-up person" inside of us does the thinking, logical reasoning, and decision making. The "little boy or little girl" inside of us is the feeling, creative, pleasurable or fun side of us. There is also the "parent" side of us that stores the guidelines organized into beliefs that are the result of our early training from significant others in our life; in fact, we may actually look and gesture like our parents of origin when disciplining our own teenager. It is in the "computer" of our programmed personality from which we parent our child and the patho-parenting tactics are unfortunately carried down through the generations. This explains one reason why parents continue to use the same patho-parenting tactics that repeatedly do not work.

The first step to change for the parent and teen is for the parent to become aware of behaviors that they use over and over again with their teen that result in the same predictable negative results, and to literally *stop* and to apply the change of pattern that will work. There is often great resistance to change on the part of both the parent and the teen for they will be forced to find other more appropriate ways of getting positive attention from each other. It is, however, worth the risk and it changes future generations of parenting styles when you do. If you choose to take charge of your teen with effectiveness and love, you must first take charge of the little boy or girl within you. There is no such thing as successful parenting when you have the little person (child) part of you disciplining the little boy or girl inside of your teenager. There has to be an adult around to deal with solving the problem rationally and effectively.

The words used within the context of language cue you to the personality state you are into (parent, adult, or child within). Listen to yourself and words like "you always, never, have to, should do, have to do" are indicative of the parent or authority state that is demonstrated. The first reaction of any teenager to a parent or a critical parent is to turn them off and run. Instead, consider using more adult words like "would you be willing, will you, etc." This small shift of wording changes the context of the request and may more likely be heard, especially by the older teen. Remember, the primary object of communication is to send a message that will be received by the teenager.

Let's take a look at the developmental issues that must be learned in adolescence: (1) communicate with others directly and effectively, (2) establish personality boundaries so that the adult part of the teen has the information to deal with adult life issues, and (3) the protection from parents to recycle all emotions and to deal with them rather than acting them out. Actually, the real issues of adolescence have to do with testing out parental rules, often with rebellion, to check and see if the parents really do care, and to test whether the parents' values and beliefs really do suit the teen. To help the teen accomplish this developmental phase, it would be helpful for the parents to have worked out their own feeling and rebellion and control issues; however, this is not always the case, for parents often have problems that prohibit them from effectively parenting their teenager.

The following patho-parenting behaviors have been isolated that signal problems within the little boy or girl of the parent, which impede effectively parenting the teenager and seeing them through this predictable emotionally volatile stage of development with the adolescent: (1) the persistent loud yeller, (2) the impulse responder, (3) the critical emotional abuser, (4) the rigid obsessive, (5) the over-protector, and (6) the buddy syndrome.

1. **Old Yeller.** Yelling for the purposes of communication serves no purpose, but it is something that has probably persisted for years. By now the parent has modeled the behavior of yelling that it is performed perfectly with no results, yet it continues and the noise level increases with booming changing voices of the teen. Yelling is an ineffective passive behavior (because nothing but noise level is achieved), and it is a child-to-child transaction (the child of the parent to the child of the teen). To change this pattern is simple; stop the yelling and find another way to make the request. The request may still not be responded to by the teen but it will get the attention redirected. Interestingly, teens with ADHD seek stimulation, and yelling is stimulating to the noise levels and vocal chords. As in the case of all ineffective passive behaviors, once the behavior is terminated, there must be found a new way to get positive stimulation. Try a touch or a hug, by accident, of course.

2. **The Impulse Responder (the ADHD Parent).** The teens of the ADHD parent have more privileges removed for such a long time that no one can possibly remember. This adultless or no-think tactic actually serves to reward the bad behavior of the teen for it gets both attention and stimulation, and the threats and punishments are not carried out. The teens are almost on constant restriction and yet the problems are never addressed, except for punishment administered only when the parent is angered. The permission is for the parent to think instead of react; exactly what you are attempting to teach your teen.

3. **The Critical Emotionally Abusing Parent.** Parents who have received critical, angry parenting in their own life will use the same patho-parenting tactics with their children if they don't change the pattern. Angry words poorly executed by the parent are abusive and self-confidence blowing to their teen. Words like "stupid," "ignorant," etc., are often the basis for the teen to fail to develop a positive self-image of him- or herself. Hateful words and criticism often hook the rebellious and acting-out part of the teen; although compliance may be granted by the teen, it is often done with fear and dislike of the parent. Stop the behavior and pick up the pieces of your relationship with your teen.

4. **Rigid Obsessive Parenting.** These styles become control issues between parent and teen that have no positive resolution other than the teen acting out negatively in some way to defy authority. There is no way to have a perfect teenager and his or her room will often be a disaster—and that is a fact. Control issues are difficult to stop on the part of the parent for it goes so far back in their own belief systems from their families of origin. In adolescence, rules may be broken to check them out. Parents must offer safety and the freedom to experiment within the bounds of security and love. Parents must also clearly specify which rules can be negotiated and which ones cannot be negotiated.

5. **The Over-protector.** The parent who fails to allow the teen to think for him- or herself is creating a dependent, angry adult who will have difficulty making decisions and finding motivation and direction in his or her life. Their motto is "You do the thinking for me." Learning to take responsibility for consequences is a valuable part of life training. Teens who are protected from learning about the natural and logical consequences of their behavior and how that behavior affects others may be unable to discriminate those limits that are imposed by others, and those that are self-imposed. Overly controlling parents give teens two choices: (a) oppose the parent and act out or (b) give in and fail to develop adequate identity. Neither of these options is healthy. In general, it is recommended that parents give advice only with permission, and give compliments and positive recognition when appropriate but as often as possible.

6. **The Buddy.** Adolescents need a parent, not a friend, at this stage of development. They need the parent to be a parent and provide caring and protection through

structure and discipline. Teens need reasonable rules to break and parents to love them even when they goof up, while providing appropriate consequences for their misbehavior. Normally in adolescence there is a lot of emotional scatter; one moment the teen is almost adult in his or her behavior, in the next moment the teen is a child again. It is because of this mood swing that teens need a strong predictably loving parent who is a parent and not just a friend.

Successfully parenting the ADHD teenager requires willingness to shift gears, that is, to be flexible, practice consistency, and have a good support team from your spouse or significant other adult in the household. Ideally, whether single or jointly, the parents will work together as a team for assuredly you will be tested and played against each other by your teenager. Marital problems will be reflected in the patho-parenting by setting up alliances, secrets, and often underhanded tactics by parents.

It is also a fact of life that mental illness does abound and there are addictions of all kinds, including workaholism, that take the positive stroking out of the life of the teen so that he or she acts out negatively to get attention and often to call attention to the problems that parents have. If indeed you identify any patterns suggestive of patho-parenting, know that professional assistance does help: It is a sign of strength to reach out and change your life.

GENERAL PARENTAL STRATEGIES FOR ADHD TEENS

Considering the number of problem areas that may need to be addressed, the adolescent with ADHD must be nurtured and guided through a veritable maze of problems. Adolescence is certainly a critical period in life. There must be resolution of some of the basic problems that may have existed for years, together with new life challenges at just about every turn. In essence, there are only a few years to develop and acquire the skills that will allow this teen with ADHD to progress and meet the upcoming challenge of an independent and responsible adult.

It is still not a matter of "outgrowing" the ADHD characteristics for these will most likely be around to challenge the teen when he or she is an adult. Thus, it is important for parents and teachers to use some general and specific strategies to assist the teen with one or more of the aforementioned problems. Parents especially may use some of these techniques, procedures, and general strategies discussed in the sections on communication, problem solving, and conflict resolution. Some basic and essential orientational components that are most general and cut across all techniques will also be described.

FAMILY STRUCTURE AND ORIENTATION

The following points are essential for parents of teens with ADHD. These provide a basic orientation and structure in the family with an ADHD teenager. *First and foremost,* there is a need for a generally *positive orientation to problems.* In all probability, the teen with ADHD has experienced a long history of negative comments, critical attitudes, and failure in school and perhaps other areas of life (e.g., social, sports, etc.). If there has been much parental conflict and hassles, constant nagging, and critical verbal statements, change will not be easy.

Recognition of these problems is, however, an essential first step in the process of turning things around. Accumulated negative approaches to the teen's behavior may have already fostered poor self-concept and low self-esteem, along with feelings of depression and anger. Some distance may have developed in the relationship with the adolescent such that communication and closeness may be rarely experienced. However, it is never too late to begin to focus on the teen's good behaviors and strengths. It is not too late to begin to structure situations to encourage more of the appropriate behavior.

For each inappropriate behavior, there are alternative behaviors (i.e., opposite behaviors) that can be developed and maintained. For example, when siblings get into hassles, it is possible to punish both by imposing a restriction (i.e., take a privilege away). It is more important, however, to make positive comments (i.e., praise) when siblings cooperate on some task, and in fact, to arrange some pleasant consequence for each when this happens (i.e., some small reward in addition to praise).

Second, it is important that teens with ADHD recognize that *it is their behavior that is disliked, not them.* Thus, when parents focus on behavior they can communicate to the teen, "I love you; I don't like your behavior." Separating behavior from the "person" is essential. Unconditional love can be given to the person with the underlying goal of changing the behavior.

Third, it is critical that parents of teens with ADHD *learn as much as possible about ADHD.* As with younger children, it is felt that when parents understand the behavior and have the knowledge about which techniques or strategies are most effective in dealing with problematic behaviors, they can be empowered. It is never too late to acquire more knowledge about ADHD and the techniques and strategies that are effective in coping with ADHD problem behaviors.

Additional information may be needed to deal with teens with ADHD but, to reiterate, it is never too late to acquire this information. Many books, tapes, videos, and workshops are offered on ADHD. See *The ADD/ADHD Resource Catalog* in the section on resources for additional information on resources for parents, teachers, and clinicians. It is also important for parents to know about the teen's legal rights to special accommodations and interventions in school.

Fourth, it is essential that parents provide *structure for appropriate behavior* to develop. It is not sufficient to just have a positive orientation, it is also necessary that the parents have rules about behavior with clearly communicated consequences. Teens with ADHD may impulsively make wrong decisions even when they know the rule. However, it is necessary that parents start with the structure of rules and deal with violations that follow.

Employing a democratic process to discuss and establish house rules works best. By involving the teen in this process, parents are less likely to make rules that are unrealistic and too difficult for the adolescent to manage. Such family meetings encourage a collaborative problem-solving process that allows teens to see themselves as a contributor to the solution of problems instead of being perceived as the cause of the problems. Agreements that are established in this manner will make it difficult for the teen to manipulate one parent against the other, as all parties will be clear on what is allowed. Should disagreements arise, no decision is rendered by either parent until there is a meeting to discuss and renegotiate the issue.

The appropriate parenting style would therefore emphasize negotiation instead of trying to dictate the rules. Working together, it is possible to establish mutually agreed-upon rules and limits, rewards for appropriate behavior and compliance, as well as to delineate the consequences for inappropriate behavior and noncompliance. It would, however, be important for parents of teens with ADHD to be explicit and definitively state which issues will be negotiable and which ones will not be negotiable. Firm parental standards here are essential.

Rules can be classified as either negotiable or nonnegotiable rules.

EXAMPLES OF NONNEGOTIABLE RULES:

1. No alcohol or drugs
2. No cursing
3. No violence
4. No smoking
5. No taking others' possessions
6. No curfew violations
7. No unprotected sex
8. No skipping classes or school

EXAMPLES OF NEGOTIABLE RULES:

1. Homework time
2. Driving privileges
3. Curfew time
4. Dress and appearance
5. Extracurricular activities
6. Work schedules
7. Chores
8. Cleaning one's room
9. Dating behavior
10. Telephone privileges
11. Allowance

Conflict resolution and problem solving address issues relating to these rules. In those cases where the teen is involved in establishing the rules, there will most probably be greater compliance. If there is agreement on use of the car for 6 hours on Saturday and 4 hours on Sunday, any violation of driving behavior may result in loss of driving time of this agreement. For example, if the teen comes home 2 hours past curfew one night, 2 hours may be subtracted from the teen's use of the car next Saturday and Sunday. This would mean that the teen would have the car for 4 hours on Saturday and only 2 hours on Sunday. This "response cost" type of procedure works quite well with teens, and especially teens with ADHD. It's very important to use fair consequences. It is not necessary, nor is it effective, to take driving privileges away for weeks. It is, however, essential that the parent follow through with consequences for such inappropriate behavior.

Fifth, it is critical that parents *be consistent in their relationships* with teens. Of course, this would be true for a child at any age, but it is so important that teens not develop manipulative strategies that can change parental decisions. When such strategies become well established, they can be quite detrimental to the adolescent's future relationships in his or her vocational/occupational, social, marital, and personal life.

Sixth, problem behaviors *need to be handled when they occur.* It is therefore critical that parents react quickly with consequences to rule violations and other inappropriate behavior. Established consequences should be made known to the teen for rule-violation and perhaps for other problematic behaviors that have occurred in the past. Immediate consequences are most effective, and of course this also applies to appropriate behavior. Most important, parents and teachers as well need to act on misbehavior but they *must avoid lectures and nagging.* To lecture the teen following an inappropriate behavior will only provide excess attention that serves to reinforce or strengthen the inappropriate behavior and not discourage it. Old habits are hard to break, but this is an important one to change.

Seventh, practice *understanding of ADHD behavior* by recognizing that the teen with ADHD may repeatedly engage in some inappropriate behavior as part of one of the basic underlying physiologically-determined ADHD characteristics. It may therefore require more time to effectively cope with this behavior. Understanding can be communicated by stating that "I know that it is hard to control your temper. By fighting with your sister you have lost your driving privileges for one day." It is sometimes surprising how different your teen's behavior may appear when it is viewed from this "disability perspective." Reframing is a general technique that may be helpful in several ways, but it has a most important use here for parents.

Eighth, model especially the appropriate behavior you wish your teen to show more often. Thus, when parents show respect for others and their property, are honest by saying what they mean and meaning what they say, and by demonstrating responsibility and good moral values, such behaviors are more likely to be adopted than by lecturing about them. Teens and children in the family will therefore *do what you do* rather than *do what you say.* If you show caring behavior, teens will be more likely to show it.

Ninth, it is also important for parents to *check on their teen's behavior and provide consequences* when needed. It is essential that parents check out to see if a teen really doesn't have any homework as he or she stated. Thus, parents must enforce rules. Establishing rules is useless if there is no follow-up on compliance. In contrast to normal teens, parents of teens with ADHD cannot adopt the position that "If he doesn't do his work he'll just fail" and that will be his consequence. Teens with ADHD don't *plan to fail*—they simply *fail to plan.*

It is sometimes surprising when teens with ADHD discover they may be unable to use sufficient foresight to enable them to predict what will happen when they continually fail to turn in homework. There may be denial that the homework counts or unrealistic expectations that they can "make it up with good grades on the final exam." Mandatory homework and classwork is essential from the beginning to the end of the school year.

Too often, parents are notified that their teen with ADHD is failing late in the school year when it may be impossible to remediate the problem. While these teens may complain of close monitoring regarding such activities as homework, and might engage in significant hassles with the parent, it is important for the parent to enforce the rules. It is not sufficient to adopt an attitude of "If he fails, he fails!" When the teen has demonstrated responsible behavior by completing homework, the parent may back off. Parents must also be able to rule out basic academic problems that might account for failure experiences or resistance to complete work. Basic visual, hearing, handwriting problems, or significant academic deficits should be ruled out.

Teens must also be monitored in other areas of their life—where they go, who they are with, what they are doing, and when they will be home. Such close monitoring allows the parent to reinforce the teen's good decisions quickly and to possibly avert unpleasant or troublesome outcomes by cuing a review of predictable outcomes and use of good judgment.

Tenth, be your teen's *best advocate.* There is no one else who has a greater investment in your teen's success and survival in life. The teen with ADHD experiences so much negative feeling from criticism, frustration, and failure that the family and home should become a refuge from outside forces. Family unity should therefore act as a buffer against the outside influences. However, it is not sufficient to just provide safety and comfort in the home situation. The teen needs to deal with these outside influences and problems and must learn strategies to function more independently. Help will be needed and the parent must act as the child's primary advocate. Certainly teachers, relatives, friends, coaches, and others may also act in this capacity. Yet, much assistance and persistence will be required to obtain needed accommodations and other services to which the teen with ADHD has a legal right. Parents must remain positive and supportive, encouraging the teen during periods of frustration to overcome obstacles; the parent(s) need to be the best coach they can be for their teen.

SHIFTING CONTROL

When children are young, parents "get in the habit" of telling them what to do, when to do it, and how to do it. As the child matures, parents must learn to "shift control" gears. It becomes increasingly more important to gradually relinquish control. Parents must now start to *guide* their teen's behavior, not *direct* it.

There are some important differences as well as similarities in how the parent must act in interactions with the teenager. Discussion about issues with the adolescent should begin with a request to talk instead of giving orders or directives. In general, parents should also respect the teen's privacy and enter his or her room only if they seriously suspect that drugs are being used. As there is a serious issue to discuss, parents should avoid direct confrontations that may easily escalate into violent arguments. If it is an issue that has already precipitated an emotional upset, the parent should avoid any attempts to talk about the issue at that time. Remember that it takes two to argue. If the teen attempts to continue with arguments, it would be important for the parent to flatly state, "I will not argue with you about _____. When we can sit down to discuss the problem let me know." Say, "I'll talk to you at some other time" and then leave the area.

SPECIFIC PARENTAL STRATEGIES FOR ADHD TEENS

There are two categories of specific skills needed by parents of teens with ADHD. These skills include: (1) Communication and (2) Problem Solving/Conflict Resolution (Negotiation). These are the essential skills needed beyond some of the general strategies previously listed.

Communication—Good communication among family members is essential to how adequate the family functions. It is essential for making decisions providing structure—solving problems and promoting emotional health in the family. Communications may be positive or negative; verbal or nonverbal.

Communication is the input to the system. If the input is faulty, the process or operation of the system is dysfunctional. The idea of reciprocity in interpersonal communications was noted by Dr. Gerald Patterson in 1982. The principle of reciprocity is simple—it states that "you get what you give." In short, this means that if parents engage in negative communications with their teen, so will the teen with them.

Families that have difficulty communicating can profit from training in communication skills. First, there are some general guidelines for good communication. According to Dr. Arthur Robin there are four important points to summarize here:

1. Listen to others without pressure. Be receptive to when the teen wants to talk and don't try to force him or her to talk. Many teens turn to peers when they perceive that their parents won't listen—believing that they might just get a lecture.

2. Use active listening where the parent paraphrases what the teen says back without any judgment. This communicates understanding without critical comment.

3. The parent should express how he or she feels about what is discussed using "I" statements (e.g., "I get concerned when you're not home on time").

4. Deal only with truly negative communications. This refers to intentional critical demeaning comments aimed at others' weaknesses and intended to manipulate others in doing what the teen wants. Use of sarcasm, name calling, ignoring, ridicule, snickering, mocking, interrupting, threatening, laughing at, "weird" expression, reflecting annoyance or boredom are just a few of the negative actions that may impair communications.

Typically, the teen's use of these actions tend to bring about negative reactions from others such as parents or teachers. Such negative reactions might include lecturing, hogging the conversation, making light of the adolescent's feelings or statements, and getting off the topic to bring up old issues that were the cause of earlier conflicts. Such a process may only result in an escalation of negative (bad) feelings, and very likely no resolution of the initial problem or conflict. Family members can communicate in many ways. The key is to get each member to show respect, patience, understanding, and compassion in this process.

According to Dr. Robin, systemic communication training involves the following: (a) Make family members more aware of their negative communication and how they affect the family; (b) Focus on some of the most obvious negative communication; (c) Teach family members to use positive communications that can be developed from instruction, modeling, behavior rehearsal, and feedback on practice; and (d) Encourage family members to practice these new communication skills at home.

The first assignment is to identify some of these negative communications. A list of negative communications is provided in the form of a handout (see Figure 4.2). The items may be divided up—each family member reads some and, when finished, there is a discussion about which ones apply to the family in question. Second, once the critical items on the list are identified, each family member takes a turn acting out one negative and one positive communication. Third, all family members need to agree to practice positive communication at home during the next week. It is best that these practice sessions be tape-recorded. During the next session, discussion should center on how well the practice session progressed.

With continued practice and feedback on the adequacy of the communications, improvement may occur. Positive comments about better communication will result in continued improvement. Recognition for improved communication given in a framework of respect will provide dramatic results. Parents can now use these improved communication skills to aid in negotiations, problem solving, and conflict resolution.

Problem Solving—Using a clearly outlined series of steps, this approach has been demonstrated to be helpful in resolving conflicts with ADHD teens. According to work by Drs. Arthur Robin and Sharon Foster, who have researched conflict resolution with adolescents, this model has been recommended. There are five steps in this problem-solving sequence:

1. Identify the problem.
2. List all potential solutions.
3. Evaluate each solution and pick the best.
4. Plan to implement the best solution.
5. Monitor and evaluate the plan.

Figure 4.2
FAMILY NEGATIVE COMMUNICATION HANDOUT

Check if your family does this:	Try to do this instead:
1. ____ Call each other names.	Express anger without hurt.
2. ____ Put each other down.	"I am angry that you did _____."
3. ____ Interrupt each other.	Take turns; keep it short.
4. ____ Criticize too much.	Point out the good and bad.
5. ____ Get defensive.	Listen, then calmly disagree.
6. ____ Lecture.	Tell it straight and short.
7. ____ Look away from speaker.	Make eye contact.
8. ____ Slouch.	Sit up, look attentive.
9. ____ Talk in sarcastic tone.	Talk in normal tone.
10. ____ Get off the topic.	Finish one topic, then go on.
11. ____ Think the worst.	Don't jump to conclusions.
12. ____ Dredge up the past.	Stick to the present.
13. ____ Read others' minds.	Ask others' opinions.
14. ____ Command, order.	Request nicely.
15. ____ Give the silent treatment.	Say what's bothering you.
16. ____ Make light of something.	Take it seriously.
17. ____ Deny you did it.	Admit you did it, or nicely explain you didn't.
18. ____ Nag about small mistakes.	Admit no one is perfect; overlook small things.

NOTE. From *ADHD in Adolescents: Diagnosis and Treatment* by Arthur L. Robin. Copyright 1998 by The Guilford Press. Used with permission.

These steps may be used by the parents and teen to resolve problems, but limit the focus of each problem-solving session to one problem. Using the outline of this problem-solving approach (see Figure 4.3), parents and teen may proceed and try the *Problem-Solving Exercise* in Figure 4.4. Some general guidelines and rules of order may be discussed prior to each session. These are:

➠ Talk without yelling.

➠ Talk without accusations (i.e., no put downs, name calling, blaming).

➠ Talk using "I" statements.

➠ Talk using brief statements.

➠ Should any session become too emotionally charged, terminate and reschedule.

The purpose of setting these ground rules is to maintain order and focus during the problem-solving session. Now let's return to the outline and Step 1.

1. **Identify the problem.** Each person should define the problem. For example, Mother might say, "I get very angry when you don't call us to let us know where you are and why you'll be late." Then ask Teen to paraphrase what was said to be sure that there was understanding of the problem. Father can then state his definition of the problem, followed by Teen's statement of the problem.

2. **List all potential solutions.** In this segment, all potential solutions are listed without regard to evaluation or comment. Creative brainstorming is useful here; all ideas are written down.

3. **Evaluate each solution and pick the best.** Mother, Father, and Teen take turns evaluating each idea. Each will explain how that solution would affect them and others in the family. If it is a workable solution for that person, a rating may be given. (It will work = 2; It will not work = 0; It may work = 1.) For each solution, sum the ratings and select the best solution. If there is no best solution, go back to revise some items where a "compromise" is possible. Use items rated as 1 or 2 by Teen to begin looking for possible compromises.

4. **Plan to implement the best solution.** At this time it will be necessary to put down on paper the specifics regarding how this solution will be carried out. Write what each person will do. Also determine what the consequence will be for noncompliance, but more important, what will be the consequence for compliance. When these specifics are worked out, decide on a period of time to test the solution. Depending on opportunity, set a time to meet to evaluate the solution. For some ideas this may be a week; others may require a longer evaluation period. One parent should keep a record of success or failure experiences. These events should be chronicled for future discussions and revision of the solution as needed.

Figure 4.3

OUTLINE OF PROBLEM-SOLVING PROCEDURE

1. Identify the problem.

A. Each family member states problem as he or she sees it.

B. Teen paraphrases what parents say.

C. Parents paraphrase teen's perception of the problem.

D. A general statement of the problem ensues.

2. List all potential solutions.

A. Each family member provides a solution.

B. Brainstorm with creative, even wild ideas.

C. Don't judge or evaluate any solution.

3. Evaluate each solution and pick the best.

A. Each family member states how each solution would affect other family members.

B. Each solution is rated by each family member: 2 = WILL WORK; 1 = MAY WORK; 0 = WILL NOT WORK.

C. If no best solution, pick items rated 1 or 2 and discuss compromises.

4. Plan to implement the best solution.

A. Put down on paper specifics about how the solution will be carried out.

B. Decide on a test period to evaluate the solution.

C. Set a time to meet again to evaluate success or failure of the solution.

5. Monitor and evaluate the plan.

A. Each family member comments on how the solution . . .

B. Details for consequences for compliance/noncompliance need to be clearly stated and perhaps put in writing.

C. If the plan was not successful and agreeable to all family members, the solution may (1) be modified by suggestions from each family member, or (2) a new problem-solving process started to select a new solution.

D. If the plan was successful, a celebration may be planned.

Figure 4.4

PROBLEM-SOLVING EXERCISE

Date _____

Note: Use this form to guide the family in going through the problem-solving process.

1. *Identify the problem (one problem per session).*

Mother: _____

Father: _____

Teen: _____

General Consensus: _____

2. *Potential solutions.*

Mother: _____

Father: _____

Teen: _____

Additional: _____

3. *Evaluate each solution.*

Mother states how each will affect others   *Rating*

Solution 1: _____   _____

Solution 2: _____   _____

Solution 3: _____   _____

Solution 4: _____   _____

Father states how each will affect others   *Rating*

Solution 1: _____   _____

Solution 2: _____   _____

Solution 3: _____   _____

Solution 4: _____   _____

Figure 4.4

PROBLEM-SOLVING EXERCISE *(Cont'd)*

Teen states how each will affect others   *Rating*

Solution 1: _____   _____

Solution 2: _____   _____

Solution 3: _____   _____

Solution 4: _____   _____

Sum of Ratings (*by the highest sum)

Solution 1: _____   _____

Solution 2: _____   _____

Solution 3: _____   _____

Solution 4: _____   _____

4. Plan to implement the solution.

Mother will: _____

Father will: _____

Teen will: _____

5. Monitor and evaluate plan.

Mother says: _____

Father says: _____

Teen says: _____

5. **Monitor and evaluate the plan.** Records of the success or failure of the plan may be discussed, adhering to the same ground rules as previously set. Each person may take turns responding to the reading of the success or failure as noted. A decision must then be made to either (a) modify this solution, or (b) go back through the problem-solving process to select a new solution. If the plan is successful, then a little celebration is in order. If there is need of a modification, a new date is set for a reevaluation of the modified solution. If a new process is indicated, that might begin with this session.

Once this process is established, it may be used to solve many types of problems that vary in severity and importance. In other words, a problem may be infrequent but of serious concern (e.g., violation of curfew) that would take precedence over a more frequent problem (e.g., excessive use of the telephone) but with less serious implication. It is therefore helpful to have some way of ranking these problems so that they can be addressed in order of priority.

Additionally, as Dr. Robin has pointed out, some problems are traditionally "ADHD problems" and if parents attempted to address every one they would have time for little else. Parents need to pick and choose their battles. A list of some of the types of relevant problems that need to be addressed are provided in Figure 4.5, along with some of the minor "ADHD type problems" that may not typically be addressed using the problem-solving format. No attempt is made to suggest which problems may be most significant; this issue must be determined by each family. In a relative sense, some problems rated as mild in one family may be rated as severe in another family. If a problem does not apply, it is not rated. Rated items are compared and ranked in order from HIGHEST (10) to LOWEST (0) for ten problems.

Breakdowns in the Problem-Solving Process—Difficulties may arise in the course of using the problem-solving process. These difficulties may occur at any level but need to be resolved for one process to be effective. Some potential difficulties are:

1. **Breaking the ground rules.** When a meeting escalates to yelling and cursing or using any other negative communication, it is important to immediately terminate the meeting. By refusing to continue to engage in such inappropriate and destructive behavior, the parents send the message that this problem will not be resolved until it is worked out within the guidelines of ground rules of acceptable behavior. This will result in the teen having no opportunity to engage in such problematic behavior until the problem is resolved. Thus, if the problem is one of curfew, the teen is essentially grounded until this is resolved. Engaging in acceptable behavior will therefore facilitate the achievement of a solution and the return to dealing with the curfew solution. Of course, if it is the parent who violates the ground rules, it is only fair to allow the teen freedom to go out without the grounding restriction.

Figure 4.5
PROBLEM-SOLVING ISSUES

Problem Area	Problem Activity	Mild	Moderate	Severe	Profound	Rank—10
School	Homework					
	Study Time					
	Class Preparation					
	Procrastination					
	Tardy					
	Skips Class					
Chores	Completion					
	Unfair Assignment					
	Unprompted					
Driving	Speeding					
	Accidents					
	Rule Compliance					
	Use of Car					
Time	Home Late					
	Late/Misses Appts.					
Relations	Clothes					
	Fights with Siblings					
	Uncommunicative					
	Disrespectful Talk					
	Disrespectful Behavior					
Other Problems	Drugs					
	Smoking					
	Sex					
	Money					
	Hurtful of Others					
Write-in						

2. **Difficulty with problem definition.** Sometimes the way a problem is defined is inaccurate. On occasions a problem may mask underlying difficulties. Until the surface problem is addressed, the underlying difficulty remains. Perhaps the teen has been failing to turn in his math homework. Attempts to implement a plan for him to complete math homework may fail if the real problem is that the teen is deficient in math and really needs a tutor. Many real problems may go unnoticed or may be masked because the teen may be too embarrassed to admit that he doesn't know how to do the work.

3. **Solution planned is too complex.** It may be discovered that it is too difficult to even monitor the solution selected because of the parent's schedule. For example, the solution may be that the teen may use the telephone for 30 minutes of talk time to friends or 10 minutes long distance only after homework is completed. However, if neither parent comes home until 5 P.M., it may be discovered that long-distance calls have been made prior to 5 P.M. on several occasions; it is obvious that this plan will not work. Parents must be able to monitor the planned solution and be able to provide consequences for either compliance or noncompliance. The above situation may have persisted for some time; if the teen's long-distance calls are not caught, it is obvious that such a monitoring system is inconsistent and will not work. Another solution must be worked out.

4. **Parental problems interfere.** When a point system is designed, there may be some difficulty keeping up with the system because those parents who have ADHD may experience some difficulty paying attention to points. They may not always be consistent in giving points or being able to let the teen know if he has sufficient points to use them. In general, parents with ADHD have more difficulty in all aspects of behavior management. This includes following routines, setting limits, and following through on consequences. Their expectations for the teen may also be unrealistic. There may be failed promises, and even some difficulty maintaining attention during conversations about issues and problem solving. Fortunately, not all parents with ADHD present problems such as this, but when this occurs, alternate strategies for running the behavioral programs will need to be developed. In essence, the parents must be trained as well as the teen.

5. **Severity of the teen's problem.** Sometimes the teen with ADHD will have severe behavioral/emotional problems that may preclude working in the aforementioned framework. In such cases, it may behoove the clinician to work directly with the whole family with more intensive family-oriented therapy. If needed, a referral may be made for this approach. When some gains are realized, the family and teen may again be supervised in the problem-solving approach.

Chapter 5

EDUCATIONAL ISSUES FOR ADHD TEENS

SURVEY OF PROBLEMS AND CONCEPTS

Just like their younger counterparts, teens with ADHD often have difficulty paying attention and completing class work, sometimes rushing through their work, sometimes daydreaming because they perceive school work as boring. While in school, they think of other things like dates, meeting and hanging out with friends, playing Nintendo™—anything to escape the boredom of the class. As the teen moves up the grade ladder from middle to high school, more is expected. Students have increasingly more work, more things to organize, and more teachers with whom to deal. Instead of planning and problem solving for responsible action, they often respond to capricious thoughts.

Teens with ADHD typically experience difficulty in the areas of homework, long-term projects, getting accurate assignments, bringing home materials needed for homework, taking notes, taking tests, organizing everything, managing time, and planning for future vocational and personal goals. Given just the number of these problems, there is increased risk of failure, which is sometimes as high as three times that of students without ADHD. About one-third will drop out of school.

About 25% of teens with ADHD have problems with aggressive acting-out behavior, including fighting, substance abuse, and other delinquent behaviors. Overall achievement is generally lower than that of classmates, and the majority lag behind in some academic areas by at least one year.

What are some of the warning signs that the teen is in trouble? The following are but a few of the possible problem areas:

1. poor grades
2. threatens to drop out
3. messy work samples
4. restless overactivity
5. doesn't complete work
6. skips classes
7. often late for class
8. complains of boredom
9. seems lost in class
10. doesn't bring books to or from school
11. talks resentful of teachers
12. shows no interest in school
13. hangs out with similar students
14. shows poor self-concept with negative critical comments about self
15. fails to do homework
16. disorganized for time and work

As indicated in the *CH.A.D.D. Educator Manual* by Rowler (1995), "ADHD adversely affects educational performance to the extent that a significant discrepancy exists between a child's intellectual ability and that child's productivity with respect to listening, following directions, planning, and organizing to complete academic assignments which require reading, writing, spelling, or mathematical calculations." However, there is often some difficulty in documenting impairment; for example, how much work should a teen of average ability be able to complete. This would be a measure of productivity. There are no pre-existing standards. A curriculum-based assessment approach would be informative. Local norms for percentage of work completed may be used for each class to determine the productivity of the teen with ADHD. This measure may be affected by basic ADHD symptoms, but may also reflect interference from co-morbid disorders and their characteristics.

In order that the teen with ADHD be productive, he or she must be able to: (a) Process information from reading assignment and lectures; (b) Be able to recall and reconstruct such information in expressive writing or through verbal reports; (c) Function independently in academic work while demonstrating appropriate social interactive behavior with others; and (d) Be able to demonstrate sufficient motivation to maximize performance and to maintain that level of motivation with feedback on the adequacy of his or her performance. In short, the teen with ADHD may be impaired at any level from (a) to (d). Academic failure may certainly affect motivation and contribute to feelings of inadequacy, a poor self-concept, and low self-esteem. Such difficulty may lead to behavior problems and associations with others who have similar difficulties. Ultimately, this progressive deterioration of the teen's attempt to adapt to his or her educational environment may result in expulsion or dropping out of school with further escalation of delinquent and perhaps antisocial behavior.

Parents and teachers will need to be aware of these problems, and others not listed, that reflect on poor adjustment to the demands and expectations of their academic level. Parents and teachers will need to work together to deal with these problems. Students left unattended with such problems may escalate to more serious resentment, aggression, and acting-out impulsively of this aggression.

A multi-faceted program may be needed to turn these problems around. Several options are available to provide the student with the best possible education. Every student, whether that teen is currently experiencing difficulty or not, has a legal right to an appropriate education. What follows is the current state of affairs with regards to the students' legal rights.

SUMMARY OF IDEA, 504, ADA, AND IEP

There is often much confusion over the legal rights of students with ADHD. Federal laws ensure that all disabled persons, without regard to the nature and severity of disability, must be provided a free and public education (FAPE). These laws also dictate that such students be educated along with those students who are not disabled. Furthermore, these disabled students need to be identified, evaluated, and provided appropriate services. There are three basic approaches: IDEA, 504, and ADA.

1. **IDEA** represents *Individuals with Disabilities Education Act.* Evolving from the *Education for All Handicapped Children Act of 1975,* its purpose is to provide financial support to states to provide adequate and appropriate services for disabled students up to age 21. Recently amended in 1999, provisions were specified to include ADHD as a disability under the other health-impaired category.

2. **Section 504 of the Rehabilitation Act of 1973** states that no individual can be discriminated against based on his or her disability. Section 504 applies to all public and private agencies that receive federal financial aid.

3. **ADA** refers to the *Americans with Disabilities Act of 1990.* This Act ensures equal access to employment, transportation, public accommodation, and services for all. Federal civil rights protection is provided for those with disabilities in either public or private sectors.

These three sets all have the general purpose of protecting disabled students from discrimination and to allow for the aforementioned FAPE. The three are compared in a reprint (see Figure 5.1) from *ERIC Digest* (E537, dated June 1995); it was written by Kelly Henderson, M.Ed., former staff member of the Council for Exceptional Children, Department of Public Policy.

GENERAL SUMMARY

According to a recent 1999 review by Matthew Cohen, attorney and legal consultant with CH.A.D.D., "Section 504 provides a faster, more flexible, and less stigmatizing procedure for obtaining accommodations and services for children with disabilities." He explains that with broad eligibility criteria, less information may be needed to meet eligibility requirements and this can be done "without the stigma and bureaucratic procedures" associated with IDEA.

Figure 5.1

OVERVIEW OF ADA, IDEA, AND SECTION 504

Americans with Disabilities Act of 1990 (ADA)	Individuals with Disabilities Education Act (IDEA)	Section 504 of the Rehabilitation Act of 1973
TYPE/PURPOSE		
A civil rights law to prohibit discrimination solely on the basis of disability in employment, public services, and accommodations.	An education act to provide federal financial assistance to State and local education agencies to guarantee special education and related services to eligible children with disabilities.	A civil rights law to prohibit discrimination on the basis of disability in programs and activities, public and private, that receive federal financial assistance.
WHO IS PROTECTED?		
Any individual with a disability who: (1) has a physical or mental impairment that substantially limits one or more life activities; or (2) has a record of such an impairment; or (3) is regarded as having such an impairment. Further, the person must be qualified for the program, service, or job.	Children ages 3-21 who are determined by a multidisciplinary team to be eligible within one or more of 13 specific disability categories and who need special education and related services. Categories include autism, deafness, deaf-blindness, hearing impairments, mental retardation, multiple disabilities, orthopedic impairments, other health impairments, serious emotional disturbance, specific learning disabilities, speech or language impairments, traumatic brain injury, and visual impairments.	Any person who (1) has a physical or mental impairment that substantially limits one or more major life activities, (2) has a record of such an impairment, or (3) is regarded as having such an impairment. Major life activities include walking, seeing, hearing, speaking, breathing, learning, working, caring for oneself, and performing manual tasks.
RESPONSIBILITY TO PROVIDE A FREE, APPROPRIATE PUBLIC EDUCATION (FAPE)?		
Not directly. However, (1) ADA protections apply to nonsectarian private schools, but not to organizations or entities controlled by religious organizations; (2) ADA provides additional protection in combination with actions brought under Section 504 and IDEA. Reasonable accommodations are required for eligible students with a disability to perform essential functions of a job. This applies to any part of the special education program that may be community-based and involve job training/placement.	Yes. A FAPE is defined to mean special education and related services. Special education means "specifically designed instruction, at no cost to the parents, to meet the unique needs of the child with a disability..." Related services are provided if students require them in order to benefit from specially designed instruction. States are required to ensure the provision of "full educational opportunity" to all children with disabilities. IDEA requires the development of an Individualized Education Program (IEP) document with specific content and a required number of specific participants at an IEP meeting.	Yes. An "appropriate" education means an education comparable to that provided to students without disabilities. This may be defined as regular or special education services. Students can receive related services under Section 504 even if they are not provided any special education. Section 504 does not require development of a plan, although this written document is not mandated. The Individualized Education Program (IEP) of IDEA may be used for the Section 504 written plan. Many experts recommend that a group of persons knowledgeable about the students convene and specify the agreed-upon services.

Figure 5.1

OVERVIEW OF ADA, IDEA, AND SECTION 504 *(Cont'd)*

FUNDING TO IMPLEMENT REQUIREMENTS?

No, but limited tax credits may be available for removing architectural or transportation barriers. Also, many federal agencies provide grant funds to support training and to provide technical assistance to public and private institutions.	Yes. IDEA provides federal funds under Parts B and H to assist States and local education agencies to meeting IDEA requirements to serve infants, toddlers, children, and youth with disabilities.	No. State and local jurisdictions have responsibility. IDEA funds may not be used to serve children found eligible only under Section 504.

PROCEDURAL SAFEGUARDS

The ADA does not specify procedural safeguards related to special education; it does detail the administrative requirements, complaint procedures, and the consequences for noncompliance, related to both services and employment.	IDEA requires written notice to parents regarding identification, evaluation, and/or placement. Further, written notice must be made prior to any change in placement. The Act delineates the required components of the written notices.	Section 504 requires notice to parents regarding identification, evaluation, and/or placement. Written notice is recommended. Notice must be made only before a "significant change" in placement. Following IDEA procedural safeguards is one way to meet Section 504 mandates.

EVALUATION/PLACEMENT PROCEDURES

The ADA does not specify evaluation and placement procedures; it does specify provision of reasonable accommodations for eligible students across educational activities and settings. Reasonable accommodations may include, but are not limited to, redesigning equipment, assigning aides, providing written communication in alternative formats, modifying tests, redesigning services to accessible locations, altering existing facilities, and building new facilities.	A comprehensive evaluation is required. A multidisciplinary team evaluates the child, and parental consent is required before an initial evaluation. IDEA requires that reevaluations be conducted at least every 3 years. Reevaluation is not required before a significant change in placement. For evaluation and placement decisions, IDEA requires that more than one single procedure or information source be used; that information from all sources be documented and carefully considered; that the eligibility decision be made by a group of persons who know about the student, the evaluation data, and placement options; and that the placement decision serves the student in the least restrictive environment. An IEP review meeting is required before any change in placement.	Unlike IDEA, Section 504 requires only notice, not consent, for evaluation. It is recommended that districts obtain parental consent. Like IDEA, evaluation and placement procedures under Section 504 require that information be obtained from a variety of sources in the area of concern; that all data are documented and considered; and that decisions are made by a group of persons knowledgeable about the student, evaluation data, and placement options. Section 504 requires that students be educated with their non-disabled peers to the maximum extent appropriate. Section 504 does not require a meeting for any change in placement.

DUE PROCESS

The ADA does not delineate specific due process procedures. People with disabilities have the same remedies that are available under Title VII of the Civil Rights Act of 1964, as amended in 1991. Thus, individuals who are discriminated against may file a complaint with the relevant federal agency or sue in federal court. Enforcement agencies encourage informal mediation and voluntary compliance.	IDEA delineates specific requirements for local education agencies to provide impartial hearings for parents who disagree with the identification, evaluation, or placement of a child.	Section 504 requires local education agencies to provide impartial hearings for parents who disagree with the identification, evaluation, or placement of a student. It requires that parents have an opportunity to participate in the hearing process and to be represented by counsel. Beyond this, due process details are left to the discretion of the local education agency. It is recommended that districts develop policy guidance and procedures.

From *ERIC Digest*, 1995, E537

In comparison, IDEA does offer a wider range of services, along with better protection and safeguards than Section 504. Also, parents may participate in each step of evaluation, placement, or change that is recommended.

Students who exhibit less serious problems and where the "child's needs are limited to easy classroom modifications" may be best served by Section 504, instead of IDEA. Many school districts prefer Section 504 as they have "greater administrative latitude and less accountability than under IDEA." Schools also "have less discretion to use regular discipline" under IDEA than with Section 504. Consequently, "many school districts are unwilling to consider eligibility for children with ADHD under the Other Health Impaired category of IDEA" even when entitled to services.

Parents must be aware of their legal provisions, determine their student's specific needs as well as assess how well the school district has provided services in the past under the 504 plan. Only then can the best option be selected. If needed, parents would also be encouraged to seek consultation from knowledgeable professionals, and perhaps legal advice.

IDENTIFICATION, EVALUATION, AND PLACEMENT PROCEDURES

The following is an outline of the steps involved from identification to placement of the student with ADHD:

➡ Referral

➡ Evaluation

➡ Assessing Eligibility

➡ Developing an IEP or 504 Plan

➡ Due Process for Grievances

➡ Resolution

Now, let's consider each one briefly.

Referral—Any of the student's teachers may make the referral in writing; subsequently, the school principal will call a committee meeting with the teacher making the referral and others who might be involved with the child (i.e., therapist). At this meeting the student's progress is reviewed to see if a formal evaluation is needed. Before conducting the evaluation, some interventions or suggestions may be discussed especially when the problems are not considered serious. If an evaluation is recommended, it may be conducted by a school psychologist. Parents are informed, in writing, of any decision made.

Evaluation—This considers the severity and complexity of presenting problems. Ability, achievement, speech and language, visual–motor skills, and behavioral/emotional functions may all be addressed. With IDEA, the evaluation must be conducted by a multidisciplinary team. With Section 504, evaluation guidelines are broader. Information may be obtained from parents, teachers, and medical sources to determine if there is evidence of ADHD; a complete psycho–educational evaluation may be done under IDEA. Comprehensive evaluations may address not only primary problems of ADHD, but also secondary co-morbid problems.

Assessing Eligibility—With IDEA, a complete, written report is generated and sent to a review committee to assess eligibility for special education services. The student may meet criteria for one or more conditions (i.e., ADHD and LD). Judgments are made regarding the primary handicap; if this is not possible, the student may be classified as multi-handicapped and referred for Special Education.

The Individualized Education Plan (IEP)—If the student is declared eligible for Special Education, an IEP must be designed. This plan will specify the services that the teen will receive. These services must address the student's individual educational needs. The IEP specifies placement, goals and objectives, relevant services and the duration of services, as well as the means to monitor progress. This IEP must be reviewed periodically. Those contributing to the IEP are: a regular education teacher, a special education teacher, a school district representative, the school psychologist (or outside consultant), parents, and, when appropriate, the adolescent.

Section 504 Plan—To receive services under Section 504, there must be a 504 Plan. A 504 Plan might be satisfied by an IEP, but may best provide a list of accommodations. See the section on accommodations in Appendix 12. A guiding principle is that the student should be educated in the least restrictive environment and, for most, this means inclusion in a regular class. A case manager oversees the student's progress.

Due Process—With either IDEA or Section 504, a due-process procedure is available. If there has been disagreement between parents and the school regarding evaluation, placement, or services, such grievances can be impartially examined by the hearing officer. Parents may also appeal any due-process decisions.

Due process cannot be employed to either change the student's teacher or to modify the teacher's behavior. Some of these issues are best resolved in an informal meeting with school officials.

Resolution—Prior to requesting a due-process hearing, conflicts may be addressed more informally through meetings and negotiation. In many cases, it is best to bring in some potential solutions to these conflicts. Mediators have been helpful in bringing about resolution of many conflicts, but should the issues not be resolved, a due-process hearing can be scheduled.

Readers interested in a comprehensive guide through the legal maze regarding educational rights may refer to a special chapter by Zigler-Dendy (1995) in *Teenagers with ADHD: A Parent's Guide,* or the chapter on legal rights by Dr. Harvey Parker (1999) in *Put Yourself in Their Shoes.*

SUGGESTIONS FOR PARENTS

The following suggestions have been adapted from recommendations made by CH.A.D.D. regarding the writing of IEP and Section 504 Plans.

1. *Do your homework.* Before attending an IEP or Section 504 Plan meeting, learn as much as you can about how your child is functioning and what he or she needs. Whether your child has been evaluated privately or by the school system, get feedback on the results and be clear about the findings and recommendations relevant to school (i.e., accommodations).

2. *Study the options.* Be sure you understand the difference between IDEA (special education) eligibility and eligibility under Section 504.

3. *Know what your child needs.* Be clear about what accommodations and services may be available from the school before you attend the meeting. IEP goals and objectives need to be specified as relevant, realistic, and measurable.

4. *Be prepared for the meeting.* Know the purpose and who will attend. You are entitled to a written advance notice with the above information clearly stated.

5. *Bring all requests.* Feel free to offer your own ideas and to comment on the school's proposal, based on what you know about your child.

6. *Have all accommodations/services documented.* Get everything in writing to make it easier to obtain follow-up and enforcement.

7. *Bring a support person.* A spouse, relative, or friend may provide support and may help to record information.

8. *Bring your independent expert.* The person who evaluated and/or treats the child may provide valuable information and support.

9. *Ask questions.* You have a right to a clear explanation of any decisions regarding placement services, accommodations, etc., that are unclear. You may also request additional time in a second meeting, should time run out.

10. *Know details of the plan.* Know who will be responsible for implementing each aspect of the plan, and how it will be monitored and evaluated. You must have consistent involvement with periodic feedback on the effectiveness of the plan.

11. *Behavior problems must be covered.* If a behavior-management plan is needed, be sure that the focus in on positive (reinforcement) approaches. You are entitled to request a "functional behavioral analysis" to better understand the problematic behavior.

12. *Know OHI as an option.* Many schools only consider students with ADHD for a 504 plan. Under the Other Health Impaired (OHI) category, special education is also an option, depending upon needs.

13. *Get/keep records.* You should keep a file with the report of the meeting and the resultant IEP/504 plan. Also keep all report cards, meeting reports, correspondence, and behavioral disciplinary records. You may need these later.

14. *Work collaboratively with the school.* You should avoid adversarial positions if at all possible. Recognize positive efforts by staff and work out disputes using a win–win approach whenever possible.

When problems arise that cannot be resolved in a reasonable fashion, parents may first wish to contact either the local or national chapter of CH.A.D.D. The national organization has legal counsel and may have precedents for resolving the very same problem. If not, suggestions may be rendered as to the nature of legal advice that needs to be sought out. Hopefully, many of the problems encountered may be worked out before reaching this stage of development. Persistent parent advocacy and a good knowledge of legal rights regarding the issue of a free and appropriate education will be most helpful.

School Discipline

In consideration of the increase in violence and general behavioral disturbances in schools, many educators are adapting "zero tolerance" discipline policies. In a report on school discipline, CH.A.D.D. asserts that (a) there is little evidence that "children with disabilities are disproportionately responsible for school discipline problems" and (b) "there is no validity to the claim that special education procedural safeguards excessively interfere with the ability of school administrators to exercise appropriate discipline and contact in the schools."

Based on information provided by 35,000 CH.A.D.D. members on students with ADHD, many students with ADHD who require special education have not been recognized with a disability, and have been subjected to regular education discipline. Reports indicate that such students are often suspended or expelled without due process. Also, many students with ADHD, some of whom have not been identified, are transferred to alternative educational settings, which may offer little meaningful education.

In general, the needs of students with ADHD can be met through application of discipline that is instructional, consistently administered and applied only in the context of a consistent educational program that targets the development of socially appropriate behavioral alternatives.

Some of the basic principles for school discipline could apply to all students.

Proactive Discipline

CH.A.D.D. believes that many discipline situations can be anticipated and prevented. A proactive orientation must use ongoing training and enforce disciplinary standards, delineating which behavior is acceptable or unacceptable and focusing on the positive.

REASONABLE CONSEQUENCES

CH.A.D.D. further believes that all schools should have a variety of consequences and be able to document effective consequences that reduce inappropriate behavior.

POSITIVE REINFORCEMENT

CH.A.D.D. believes in the emphasis on positive reinforcement as more effective in developing appropriate behaviors; detention, suspension, and expulsion are unlikely to modify the student's inappropriate behavior.

LEARNING OPPORTUNITIES

Specific skill training is needed to facilitate the development and utilization of socially appropriate behavior. All students should be encouraged to take responsibility for their behavior and should get positive feedback, when successful.

CH.A.D.D. states that schools should be able to demonstrate that each "disabled student" has had appropriate accommodations and skill training to prevent unacceptable behaviors before considering disciplinary measures. Reasonable accommodations in disciplinary standards should be discussed with parents and the student. The application of disciplinary procedures can then be applied only after the student has been provided a consistent educational program that emphasizes the development of socially appropriate behaviors.

ACCOMMODATIONS FOR TEENS WITH ADHD

It is important to know the teen's legal rights to an appropriate education. It is also important to know how the teen with ADHD may be accommodated in the school. The following represent some of the accommodations possible at the middle and high school levels. Note that some accommodations may be appropriate only for young adolescents; others may cover the entire age range of adolescence.

ACCOMMODATIONS IN THE SCHOOL SETTING

As a teacher you will need a good understanding of the nature of ADHD-driven behaviors and a set of effective strategies to successfully manage these difficult behaviors and guide these students successfully. Some suggested strategies follow.

Adjust Student Seating—Standard classroom rows are least distracting; groups at tables may present problems for some teens. Seat ADHD students near the teacher or a student who models appropriate classroom behavior. Avoid seating the ADHD teen near distractions (e.g., noisy air conditioner and high-traffic areas).

Use Carrels—Study-type carrels and privacy boards reduce visual and auditory distractions and may be offered at times to all students. Teachers need to make it acceptable for students of all ages to be responsible for managing their own problems. Recognizing when they need a quiet distraction-free setting is essential. Effective teachers also use different environmental prompts to make accommodations within the physical environment of the classroom.

Hand Gestures—Use hand signals to communicate privately with an ADHD teen. For example, ask the teen to raise his or her hand every time you ask a question. A closed fist can signal that he or she knows the answer; an open palm can signal that he or she does not know the answer. You would call on the teen to answer only when he or she makes a fist.

Mechanical Timers—Note for the teen the time at which the lesson is starting and the time at which it will conclude. Set a timer to indicate to teenagers how much time remains in the lesson and place it at the front of the classroom; all students can check the timer to see how much time remains. Interim prompts can be used as well. For instance, students can monitor their own progress during a 30-minute lesson if the timer is set for 10 minutes three times.

Classroom Lights—Tuning the classroom lights "on and off" prompts students that the noise level in the room is too high and they should be quiet. This practice can also be used to signal that it is time to begin preparing for the next lesson. If noise is consistently high, the teacher may wish to explore the use of the Classroom Noise Monitor (available from *The ADD/ADHD Resources Catalog*). Effective teachers make accommodations in the learning environment by guiding students with ADHD with follow-up directions.

Follow-up Oral Directions—After giving written directions to the class as a whole, provide additional, oral directions for the class with teens who have ADHD.

Follow-up Written Directions—Provide follow-up directions in writing. For example, write the page number for an assignment on the chalkboard. You can remind the teen to look at the chalkboard if he or she needs additional review of the assignment. Effective teachers also use special instructional tools to modify the classroom learning environment and accommodate the special needs of their students with ADHD.

Highlight Key Words—Highlight key words in the instructions on worksheets to help the teen with ADHD focus on the directions. You can prepare the worksheet before the lesson begins or underline key words as you and the students read the directions together.

Use Pointers—Teach the teen to use a pointer to help visually track written words on a page. For example, provide the teen with a bookmark to help him or her follow along when students are taking turns reading aloud.

Adapt Worksheets—Teach a teen how to adapt instructional worksheets. For example, help a student fold his or her reading worksheet to reveal only one question at a time. The teen can also use a blank piece of paper to cover the other questions on the page.

Try Alternative Lighting—The "hum" of fluorescent lights may distract or annoy. Where possible, use an alternative lighting like incandescent. Note that a "strobe light" may be used with some students to create additional stimulation and thereby enhance alertness.

Provide Background Music or "White Noise"—Use headphones with selected background rhythmic music or "white noise" sounds for specified ADHD students to block distractions.

Use Tape Recorders—Use headphones to cue students using self-monitoring and to provide an incentive for "on cue" behavior.

Use a TV-type Monitor or an Overhead Projector—This type of lesson presentation can help students locate and follow important points.

TEEN-CENTERED ACCOMMODATIONS

You can teach and help the student practice desired skills frequently and within different contexts, often involving counselors and even parents.

Teach Self-monitoring—A periodic signal or cue (e.g., a beep on a tape recorder or other device) can help the student be aware of being "on" or "off" task. With practice this awareness can become automatic. Such a device may be used most effectively when the student is engaged in a private work session, and generally not in the context of the entire classroom.

Model Instructions—Have the student repeat and review complete directions (silently) to himself or herself to counteract impulsively starting assignments without a clear understanding of what is to be done. To teach this technique, simply give the directions and then ask a classmate to repeat them. It is not necessary that ADHD teens be called upon—asking other good students will appropriately model the procedure.

Model Problem Solving—Expand this self-talk technique to include questions such as: *What is the problem? Is there more than one way to solve it? Which solution is best? How can I best solve the problem using this solution?* This self-monitoring via self-talk teaches a step-by-step approach using periodic self-checks for accuracy.

Teach Organizational Structure—Demonstrate how large, complex assignments may be divided into a series of smaller assignments. The student may then use a step-by-step, logical progression from one to another until the whole assignment is completed.

TEACHER-CENTERED ACCOMMODATIONS

Classroom demands tend to exacerbate ADHD-type behavior, and teachers often encounter the same frustrations as parents—perhaps even more—when trying to discipline. When usual disciplinary techniques do not work to correct problematic behavior, take care that you do not, because of your own frustrations, use more restrictive or even punitive measures. Learn and utilize techniques of behavior management that *do* work, and adapt and modify some of your own behavior to work successfully with ADHD students:

1. **Become knowledgeable** about ADHD and understand the characteristic behaviors. A knowledgeable teacher is able to understand and deal effectively with ADHD behavior. For example, knowing that *inconsistency* is a hallmark behavior, the understanding teacher avoids comments like: "I know you can do this work because you did it all yesterday," or "You can do better—you just aren't trying." ADHD students can be very sensitive, and an aware teacher avoids public confrontations and finds alternative ways to address such things as test grades, medication issues, and misbehavior. Use of learned, alternative approaches results in less emotional pressure and stress for the student and the teacher.

2. **Be flexible** rather than rigid. Be willing to adjust "assignment loads" and "work span" to give the ADHD pupil a better chance at success.

3. **Take time when teaching.** ADHD students, particularly, can have trouble with rigid, fast-paced settings. Do not speed through lessons, but take time to show clearly the organization of materials. Provide a positive, flexible environment for student to learn in. Pay attention to more appropriate behavior.

4. **Provide structure and routine.** Have a fairly consistent daily routine (e.g., roll call, math, recess, reading, lunch, social studies, and music); this is not generally a problem at these grade levels. Help students develop daily expectations by keeping this same sequence of activities but provide variation within each activity (i.e., sometimes have an audio–visual approach, others a hands-on project, sometimes use a computer, etc.) to provide increased interest and stimulation.

5. **Prepare students** for a change in routines. For example, if a school assembly is planned or a special guest speaker is visiting your class, inform students in advance of the event.

6. **Integrate exercise** as part of your daily routine. For example, have students do stretching exercises as part of the daily schedule to help reduce stress, enhance alertness, and provide an opportunity for students to be active and to be free to move around, "with permission," after work is completed. Note that this becomes part of the daily routine.

7. **Avoid information overload.** Teach to the teen's capacity to attend and process information. As the teen better handles small segments of work, gradually increase the "work time" span, reinforcing the student for staying "on task" and then for "work completion."

8. **Establish behavior priorities.** Impulsivity and distractibility interfere with work output; some minor over-activity, however, does not and thus may be overlooked. For example, unusual postures, slouching, humming, or tapping might best be ignored if they do not interfere with the ADHD student's work or distract others.

9. **Use movement as reward.** Use permission to move around as a motivator (e.g., "When you finish this assignment, you are free to move around in the back of the class").

10. **Reinforce three types of behavior.** Teachers, aides, the principal, coaches, and counselors should focus as often as possible on three types of appropriate behaviors, especially when exhibited by students with behavior problems: (a) good or desirable behavior; (b) an improvement over past behavior; and (c) any neutral behavior (not doing anything inappropriate). As the appropriate behavior is observed, specific positive attention should be delivered in a warm, enthusiastic manner such that it cannot be perceived as simply mechanical. Avoid just "good" and say instead, "Josh, I'm glad you remembered to wait for your turn." Be specific.

11. **Provide consequences for inappropriate behavior, too.** Physical punishment does not work with ADHD behavior, and, of course, would never be used with teenagers. Other mild punishments such as a "behavior penalty" can be effective. However, it's important to confirm that the student did understand what he was supposed to do (or not do) and that he simply chose not to comply; do not punish if he missed some of the message or was truly confused about expectations. However, stay aware that such punishments do not inform the teen what *to do*—they only focus on what *not* to do.

12. **Redirect inappropriate behavior** (often more helpful with younger student). Remove the teen from a situation where acting out has started or is about to occur, and place him or her in a different situation. For example, move a pupil from one area to another to reduce aggressiveness shown toward the group in the first area.

13. **Use "success oriented" programs.** Realize that these build slowly on small successes and behavior improvements; there aren't rapid, major changes in behavior that are for the long term. Take comfort in knowing that slow and gradual behavior changes help develop life-long skills.

14. **Review rules frequently.** Rules for all situations—classroom, playground, lunch room, bus trip, etc.—should be kept simple and few in number; and they should be reviewed regularly and be posted. Additionally, to help a student move to a new situation, prepare him or her for transitions by briefly reviewing the rules and expectations for that new situation. (Refer to School Behavior Game from the ADD/ADHD Resources Catalog.)

15. **Use priming** to help the ADHD student keep focused. Before initiating a task, remind the students of some prearranged reinforcement from you to help them stay focused and "on task" until completion.

GENERAL INSTRUCTIONAL PRINCIPLES

Effective teachers help prepare their students to learn when they *introduce, conduct,* and *conclude* each academic lesson. These principles of effective instruction, which reflect what we know about how to educate all students in the class, will especially help a teen with ADHD to stay focused on his assigned tasks as he transitions from one lesson to another throughout the school day.

Students with ADHD benefit from clear statements about their ***teacher's expectations*** at the beginning of the lesson. Consider these strategies.

1. **Review previous lessons.** Review information about previous lessons on this topic. For example, remind teens that yesterday's lesson focused on learning how to work on solving an algebraic equation. Review several problems before describing the current lesson.

2. **Set learning expectations.** State what students are expected to learn during the lesson. For example, explain to students that a language arts lesson will involve reading a story about the Titanic and to answer questions.

3. **Set behavioral expectations.** Describe how students are expected to behave during the lesson. For example, tell students that they may talk quietly to their neighbors as they work on a seatwork assignment or raise their hands to get your attention.

4. **State needed materials.** Identify all materials that the teen will need during the lesson. For example, specify that students need their journals and pencils for journal writing.

5. **Explain additional resources.** Tell students how to obtain help in mastering the lesson. For example, remind the teen to refer to a particular page in the textbook to get help in completing a worksheet.

When conducting an academic lesson, effective teachers use some of the following strategies.

1. **Use audio–visual materials.** Use a variety of audio–visual materials to present academic lessons. For example, use an overhead projector to demonstrate how to solve an addition problem requiring regrouping. The students can work on the problem at their desks, while you manipulate pointers on the projector screen.

2. **Check student performance.** Question individual students about their mastery of the lesson. For example, you can ask a student doing seatwork to demonstrate

how he arrived at the answer to a problem or ask individual students to state, in their own words, how the main character felt at the end of the story.

3. **Ask probing questions.** Probe for the correct answer before calling on another student and allow teens sufficient time to work out the answer to a question. Count at least 15 seconds before giving the answer and ask follow-up questions that give the teen an opportunity to demonstrate what he or she knows.

4. **Perform ongoing student evaluation.** Identify students who need additional assistance. Watch for signs of lack of comprehension, such as daydreaming or visual or verbal indications of frustration. Provide these teens with extra explanation or ask students to work together on the lesson.

5. **Help students self-correct their own mistakes.** Describe how students can identify and correct their own mistakes. For example, remind students that they should check their calculations in mathematics problems and reiterate how they can do that, remind students of particularly difficult spelling rules, and how students can watch out for "easy-to-make" errors.

6. **Focus dawdling students.** Remind students who dawdle to keep working and redirect these students to focus on their assigned task. For example, you can provide follow-up directions or assign learning partners. These practices can be directed at individual students or at the entire class.

7. **Lower noise level.** Monitor the noise level in the classroom and provide corrective feedback, as needed. The classroom noise level may also be shaped using a behavioral format and the Classroom Noise Monitor (available from *The ADD/ADHD Resources Catalog*).

8. **Provide advance warnings.** Provide advance warning that a lesson is about to end. Announce five or ten minutes prior to the end of the lesson (particularly for seatwork and group projects) how much time remains. You may also want to tell students at the beginning of the lesson how much time they will have to complete it. Effective teachers may also help students prepare for transitions *when concluding a lesson.*

9. **Check assignments.** Check completed assignments for at least some students. Review with some students what they have learned during the lessons, to get a sense of how ready the class was for the lesson and how to plan the next lesson.

10. **Preview the next lesson.** Instruct students how to begin preparing for the next lesson. For example, inform students that they need to put away their textbooks to prepare for the next class.

The listed accommodations can be of significant importance to the teen with ADHD—sometimes meaning the difference between success and just survival. These adjustments do not require any significant increase in demands on the teacher's time.

Using a formal 504 Plan with accommodations specified in writing, and based on documented difficulties that were reported in the psychological and behavioral assessment, the student will be more likely to realize his or her maximum capabilities. The formal report will ensure that the critical recommendation will be carried out. It will also provide greater uniformity or consistency in providing recommended accommodations. The formal plan will also mean that someone in the school system will be called upon to serve as a case manager who will monitor the student's progress and document whether the implementation of these accommodations are effective. In addition, there will be required periodic meetings among teachers, parents, and student to document progress. With a formal plan and classification with disability, there should be no difficulty in obtaining special services as needed. In fact, the school must, by law, provide appropriate services for this teenager with ADHD. Should the student wish to continue education at a higher level, special accommodations may continue at that level as prior school records may clearly indicate a need.

PARENT-CENTERED ACCOMMODATIONS

Cooperation from parents who will learn and work with you to modify and manage the student's behavior will have synergistic, positive effects. Consider the following techniques or strategies.

DEVELOP A HOME–SCHOOL BEHAVIOR PROGRAM

Regularly monitor the student's classroom behavior and report to the parents in a cooperative behavior-management program. You may monitor behaviors such as completion of assignments, following instructions, obeying class rules, and getting along with others. Parents then record your feedback on a Home–School Behavior Chart (available from *The ADD/ADHD Resources Catalog),* and use the information as an integral part of this joint behavior-management effort. Share recommended reading and resources with parents.

TEACH PARENTS TO PRACTICE SIMULATED SCHOOL BEHAVIORS

Many home situations closely parallel school settings: obeying rules, following instructions, completing homework (or in school, class assignments), and getting along with siblings and friends (at school, with peers). Tell parents of the importance of *generalizing* behavior practice to help their teen learn desired behaviors and at home to:

⟹ Have a *routine.*

⟹ Establish and regularly post and review *rules.*

⟹ *Practice* at home to work on problems exhibited in school:

- If the problem is getting off task in school, practice staying on task for homework or chores.

- If the problem is talking loud in the hallway at school, review talking in a normal voice at home "just like in school."

➠ *Reinforce* appropriate behavior as the teen works on it.

➠ *Especially notice and reinforce* appropriate behavior that is spontaneous.

➠ *Use the same cues* the teacher uses in school to cue appropriate behavior, and to reinforce desired behavior at home:

- For example, if the teacher uses two fingers to remind student not to interrupt others, parents use same "cue" at home. Parents may also use written reminders in specific situations to cue chores or homework completion.

➠ If necessary, *use context or background similar to classroom* to practice at home:

- For example, a tape of classroom noises used at home during homework will help the teen generalize his or her newly learned appropriate behaviors, like staying on task to completion of work.

Many teens with ADHD may benefit from accommodations that reduce distractions in the classroom environment. These accommodations, which include modifications within both the physical environment and the learning environment of the classroom, help some teens with ADHD stay on task and learn.

SKILL TRAINING FOR SCHOOL SUCCESS

It is critical that students at this level of academic development experience success. If the teen with ADHD has had a long history of forgetting, failure, and frustration (the three F's), there needs to be an immediate turnaround with interventions geared toward success. If the teen with ADHD has already experienced success with accommodations at earlier grades, it is essential that continued success be ensured by implementing the accommodations and other programs that are critically needed. As a child matures, although his or her needs may change, sometimes the same accommodations may work; in other cases, some new or additional accommodations will need to be tried. Perhaps, the changes needed will require some additional programs or training that the school does not provide. In some special cases, parents may either work directly with their teen to provide such remedial training at home or may seek it out at some treatment center. This special training may be quite unique or it may be adopted for use in the school setting.

There are several types of skill training that may be established within the teen's academic setting. One factor that cuts across all suggested training is that *a positive approach is essential.* It is best that this approach be adopted schoolwide starting from the top down. Thus, the whole atmosphere of the school should be permeated with a positive "air of success" orientation. This may begin with implementation of accommodations, but is most characterized by daily positive interactions. Sarcastic, critical comments are totally avoided. This may also provide a positive model for appropriate social interactive behavior. It may further be characterized by a more relaxed, varied, and multisensory approach to learning situations. Time is structured for purposes of organizational interventions: developing a routine of writing assignments, reviewing assignments, pointing out what is important, and reviewing them again. This orientation is carried out in all subject areas all day. Students are not singled out; instead, questions may be posed in a general way. Students may be called on randomly, or students may be called on who are without ADHD. Their response models important information for the teen with ADHD, perhaps reorienting that student and providing feedback on a question he or she could not answer (if called on). Unison responses to questions may also not single out the teen with ADHD. Students may also respond with greater motoric involvement (e.g., raising hand to answer yes). This may actually provide some self-stimulation that may improve attention and response involvement. Use of movement may further create additional stimulation that helps to maintain alertness (e.g., students may stand to answer history [short] questions).

The following areas are of general concern for teens with ADHD. Some suggestions are given to aid the student in each area, and thus, enhance his or her chances of academic success.

ORGANIZATIONAL STRATEGIES

Disorganization is a monumental problem for teens with ADHD. It encompasses many areas of school functioning, including keeping track of school supplies and materials (notebooks, assignment book, etc.), as well as planning projects and keeping a schedule (i.e., time management). Some of the essentials include:

1. All students should have adequate and essential supplies for their schoolwork. This might include notebooks for each subject (preferably different colors), a three-ring binder with colored pocket dividers and a plastic pouch (zippered) for pens, pencils, etc. It is critical that the teen have a student planner book or Homework Assignment Book (available in *The ADD/ADHD Resources Catalog*) to record assignments, upcoming projects, etc. A dictionary is basic; an encyclopedia or Internet access would be an excellent addition. Miscellaneous supplies include pens, pencils, highlighters, hole punch, small stapler, paper clips, rubber bands, and hole reinforcers (papers will surely be torn and in need of frequent repair).

2. Model an organizational behavior pattern for the student to develop and adapt. For example, keep a neatly organized desk; planned lessons and activities; an "everything in its own place" classroom set-up for materials, adequate supplies and books. Also, the teacher may post assignments and review them orally to aid the student in copying them accurately.

3. Managing time also comes under organizational strategies. Many teens with ADHD lack awareness of time in general. Thus, they may have difficulty with appointments at scheduled times, knowing how long it will take to finish a task, or meeting deadlines and curfews.

4. Following directions may also be an essential skill that will aid the teen in general organization behavior. An interactive software program entitled "Following Directions" is available through *The ADD/ADHD Resources Catalog*.

To deal with this problem in the academic setting, there is a need to use schedules (to plan a week), a daily reminder ("to do" list), and a long-range planner. Perhaps the most important of these is the daily "to do" list. Many students find it helpful to not only list homework assignments in their book, but also put down some notes regarding homework, as well as other reminders of things to do before and after school. An example of a *"To Do"* List is found in Figure 5.2. When these items are completed, they can be scratched off the list. When the student says "Good, I finished that assignment," there is a (self-reinforced) sense of accomplishment. Each day, a new list is made and those items that are not completed carry over to the following day. Items that are most important are starred. A weekly schedule is critical in avoiding conflicts as most of today's teens have busy schedules with after-school activities and hobbies. Activities that are locked in to a specific time need to be entered first at the beginning of a new week. On Sunday, the student may put in class times, special events, practice sessions, and homework times for each day. By making these dedicated times clearly visible, the student is aided in planning other activities. A monthly list of planned activities is also helpful for long-range projects, ensuring that future conflicts of having to do two projects with the same deadline can be avoided. Use the *Long-Range Projects* planner in Figure 5.3.

Some general time-management suggestions include: (a) Setting priorities—do some of the most important, and sometimes most difficult things first, instead of putting them off. (b) Break down those tasks that are complex and do them in small, manageable steps. (c) At the risk of creating some parental resentment and havoc, learn to say "no," at least for the immediate time when you are perhaps already over-committed to various activities. You may wish to commit to do this task (at some future time after consulting with your long-range planned schedule). (d) Add extra time to those tasks for which you have estimated time for completion. (e) When needing to make appointments, begin with the appointment time and work backward to determine how much time you need to dress, eat, and travel to the appointment. Subtract time for each component and a little more to determine what time to get ready for the appointment. (f) If a teen is old enough to drive or uses public transportation, a small cassette player may be used to review notes, definitions, or whatever else the student recorded to prepare for school. (g) While in a doctor's office, the student can review notes or even use that time to plan new activities. (h) To avoid procrastination and complete tasks for deadlines, the student may need to develop the habit of "do it now."

Figure 5.2
"TO DO" LIST

Date _____

Items from Yesterday (Star Critical Items)	Comment
1.	
2.	
3.	
4.	
5	
6.	
7.	

Items from Today (Star Important Items)	Comment
1.	
2.	
3.	
4.	
5.	
6.	
7.	
8.	
9.	
10.	

Figure 5.3
LONG-RANGE PROJECTS

Date _____

#	Project	Date Due	Initial Draft	Revision	Final Draft	Date Completed
1						
2						
3						
4						
5						

Signs may be posted in various places, but the critical place may be the one in which homework and projects are done. Keeping long-range project components on the daily or weekly reminder list will also help. (i) Use an electronic reminder. In addition to a conventional watch with alarm, there are several devices that can serve as a reminder to do things. One special watch, the Watch Minder™ (available from *The ADD/ADHD Resources Catalog),* can be programmed to remind a student when to take medications, when to go to an appointment, when to come home, etc. Details of this device can be found in Chapter 3 under "electronic devices."

NOTE-TAKING STRATEGIES

Due to poor handwriting and disorganization frequently noted in those with ADHD, there is a need for extra effort to (a) write notes that can be read and (b) to get information down on paper that accurately reflects what the teacher said. Thus, the need for note-taking strategies. The student's job will be to write notes in the appropriate book for that subject and to use abbreviations for words to save time and space and to ensure continuity in writing. Some of these abbreviations include: pgs. (pages), e.g. (for example), w/o (without), # (number). Information on abbreviations, as well as other important techniques for students, can be found in a book entitled *Study Strategies Made Easy* by Leslie Davis, Sandi Sirotowitz, and Harvey Parker (available from *The ADD/ADHD Resources Catalog).* A student must also review notes after class, fill-in recalled information that was omitted, and highlight (yellow marker) important points or words to look up or define. Should the student have extremely poor handwriting (a form of LD called *dysgraphia),* he or she may request to use a tape recorder or obtain a copy of notes from the teacher or another student.

Use of the Directed Note Taking Activity (DNA) was investigated by Drs. Evans, Pelham, and Grudberg in 1995 with teens participating in a summer treatment program. Models provided students as to how notes should look in their notebooks. Students divided their notes into main ideas and details. In a very structured program, the teacher would make a point and then direct the teen to record it in his or her notes. Behavioral shaping of improved notes with a gradual fading of prompts resulted in general improvement of on-task behavior (taking notes) and better performance on class assignments by having notes. This procedure appears worthwhile to consider further application in high schools.

TEST-TAKING STRATEGIES

There appears to be an increase in test taking from elementary to high school. There are three basic areas to look at: (1) preparation for the test, (2) the student's approach to the test, and (3) taking the test. Let's consider each component.

Preparation for Tests—As part of the time-management problem, many students with or without ADHD plan poorly for most tests. The idea of "cramming" for tests is certainly not new. Despite reports of impaired performance and increased stress associated with cramming, this approach persists. All students should be encouraged and reminded periodically to prepare for a test by breaking down their study into a few or several component sessions as time permits. Reminding students to "put this in your planner/schedule" would be essential. Additional preparation for tests may include not only one's notes and highlighted book, but also old tests.

Approaching the Test—Some students fear tests, rushing through due to either a natural tendency or to escape from a task that is perceived as unpleasant. Some special treatment programs may be needed for test anxiety. Since teens with ADHD may miss some important points or misunderstand test questions, it is a good idea to train students in the habit of reading test questions more than once. It is also good to train students in other aspects of test taking. This includes developing priorities on test items that are worth more points (i.e., greater contribution to the total score) and to read over briefly all items and to answer those items first that are known best. Some of the most helpful training might consist of teaching students how to "take tests" by giving "practice tests." Our goal is to maximize a student's performance so that the student may demonstrate what he or she has learned.

Taking the Test—With adequate studying and knowledge of the best approach to test taking, the student is prepared. For teens with ADHD, the actual test conditions may also need to be considered. Specifically, there may be excessive noise or other distractions that may cause the teen with ADHD to get "off task."

A software program entitled *Test Taking Made Easy* is available through *The ADD/ADHD Resources Catalog*. This program focuses on how young teens can prepare for tests and follow test directions, as well as how to answer true–false, multiple-choice, and fill-in-the-blank test items. A unique printout describes the student's areas of strength and weakness, providing suggestions for further growth. Should the student have general difficulty with written exams, an appropriate accommodation for oral examination may be made within the student's 504 Plan.

MEMORY STRATEGIES

For many school subjects, the ability to memorize facts and dates may be essential to a good test result. For teens with ADHD, it is extremely frustrating to have difficulty remembering what they reportedly studied so hard. There are several important points that the student should know about memorization: (a) There is no substitute for repetition and especially to distribute the learning (practice) sessions over time. (b) The student needs practice in discriminating important from less-important information and facts. There must be effective selectivity regarding what is important and likely to be on a test. Sometimes the teacher will emphasize what is important by stating, "This is something you need to know." Also, using the SQ4R Method may be helpful in targeting essential information. This method is discussed in some detail on page 182. (c) The student might learn how he or she learns best (i.e., through visual, auditory, or kinesthetic sense modality). Visual is the most typical way of processing information, but sometimes it is best to use a multisensory approach combining modes of processing. This latter approach may be most useful for most teens with ADHD and especially when there is co-morbid LD.

There are different memory techniques for different learning styles (as noted in the book *Study Strategies Made Easy* by Davis, Sirotowitz, and Parker. See Table 5-1.) In this table, several different memory techniques are listed: (1) *Acrostics*—a series of words making a funny sentence is used to note a list, with each word representing an item on the list. For example, in remembering the 12 cranial nerves, we used "Over Old Olympus Towering Tops A Finn And German Vendored Some Hops." To this date, I still remember the sentence. (2) *Acronyms*—for example, HOMES to recall the Great Lakes of **H**eron, **O**ntario, **M**ichigan, **E**rie, and **S**uperior. (3) *Charting* provides a descriptive visual image. (4) *Visual emphasis*—may use lighting to emphasize something visually. (5) *Visualization* uses a visual image of an object(s) (often in a humorous situation) to describe an event. Sometimes motion can be added to make a kind of videotape. However, visualization might simply involve visualizing the printed words or graphs in a book. Adding pictures to words uses both sides of the brain to store information, increasing the chance of recall. (6) *Association*—visual or verbal connections may help remember words or a series of things. (7) *Recall questions.* (8) *Rehearsal* clearly helps to remember. *How* one rehearses may also be important. For example, if one can rehearse lines in a play by singing them initially, the use of the right brain again will aid recall. Other rehearsals might take place under similar conditions to actual test situations. For example, if one learns to spell words orally, but is tested by writing the words, recall may be impaired. The solution is to record the words so that the student may actually practice writing the words as would happen on the test in class. Similarly, learning words or facts under ideal conditions (i.e., quiet) may then be practiced under conditions of classroom noise. (A series of tapes of classroom noise is available through *The ADD/ADHD Resources Catalog.*)

Table 5-1. MEMORIZATION TECHNIQUES FOR DIFFERENT LEARNING STYLES

Technique	Learning styles		
	Auditory	Visual	Kinesthetic
1. Acrostics	xx	xx	xx
2. Acronyms	xx	xx	xx
3. Charting		xx	xx
4. Visual emphasis		xx	xx
5. Visualization		xx	
6. Associations	xx	xx	
7. Recall questions	xx	xx	xx
8. Rehearsal	xx	xx	xx

NOTE. From Davis, Sirotowitz, & Parker (1996). Copyright 1996 by Specialty Press. Reprinted by permission.

HOMEWORK STRATEGIES

Homework has long been a source of irritation and hassles between parent and teen. It is a problem that is magnified many times for teens with ADHD. In fact, the greatest academic difficulty for most teens with ADHD is completing all homework assigned and turning it in on time. In clinical practice, parents of teens with ADHD frequently complain about homework and many parents would rejoice as much as their children if homework were not given. Problems with homework often begin in school and continue until the work is returned to school the next day.

A Frame of Reference for Homework Problems—To begin, parents may need to explore their own attitudes and beliefs toward homework. Parents' beliefs and attitudes—whether they consider homework beneficial or not—are communicated to the teen in both conscious and subtle ways.

For example, as the parent of a teen with ADHD, you, too, may have had difficulty with homework issues when you were a teenager. How did this influence you? How is this reflected in your behavior *now* or by the way you handle your teen's problem(s) with homework? Have your childhood experiences made you more understanding or less understanding? It is likely that your teachers and parents were not very understanding about your failure to do homework or your forgetting it. Take a few moments to reflect and verbalize your own childhood experiences with homework.

You may have considered your childhood experiences and problems with homework to be unique; however, you may see some correlation between what you experienced as a teen and what your teen now experiences. Do you want your teenager to have the same experiences you had or do you wish for a better situation for your teen? Hundreds of parents have said that they want their teenagers to have an easier time and not experience some of the pain that they endured. Often, however, history repeats itself simply because we (a) are not aware that this is what's happening, or (b) don't know how to go about changing it. When we buy a new car, a manual outlines how to operate and care for the car; no such manual exists for teens. A step-by-step procedural manual for dealing with teens and their special problems (like homework) surely would help!

Assessment with the Homework Problems Checklist—To address homework issues, you should first become familiar with the various problems associated with homework. Fill out the *Homework Problems Checklist* in Figure 5.4. If needed, collaborate with some of your adolescent's teachers to get a complete picture about homework across general subjects.

By checking how frequently each problem is manifested, you can get an overview of your teen's problems with homework. These homework problems fall into one or more of the following twelve categories:

1. Fails to write down assignment. *(See item 2.)*
2. Writes the wrong assignment. *(See item 2.)*
3. Forgets the assignment book. *(See item 1.)*

Figure 5.4
HOMEWORK PROBLEMS CHECKLIST

Child/Teen Name_____Age_____

Parent's Name_____ Relation to Child_____

School_____Grade_____

Date _____Class Placement: Regular _____Special_____

PLEASE RATE EACH STATEMENT	Never (0)	At times (1)	Often (2)	Very Often (3)
1. Fails to bring home class assignment and essential materials (textbook, dittos, etc.).				
2. Unclear about what homework has been assigned.				
3. Denies having homework.				
4. Refuses to do homework.				
5. Whines or complains about doing homework.				
6. Must be reminded to sit down and to get started on homework.				
7. Procrastinates or tries to put off doing homework.				
8. Doesn't do homework satisfactorily unless someone is there to monitor him/her.				
9. Doesn't do homework satisfactorily unless someone sits beside him/her to help with the work.				
10. Daydreams or attempts to play with things (erasers, pencils, etc.) during homework.				
11. Easily distracted by noises or others' activities nearby.				
12. Easily frustrated by homework.				
13. Fails to finish homework assignments.				
14. Takes a very long time to complete homework.				
15. Responds poorly when asked to correct errors or sloppily done homework.				
16. Produces homework that is messy or sloppily done.				
17. Hurries through homework such that he/she makes careless errors.				
18. Critical of his/her production, even when he/she does a good job on homework.				
19. Forgets to bring homework assignments to class.				
20. Deliberately fails to bring homework assignment back to class.				
TOTAL SCORE				

From *Winning the Homework War* by K.M. Anecho and F.M. Levine, 1987, NY: Simon & Schuster. Reprinted by permission of the publisher.

4. Forgets materials needed. *(See item 1.)*

5. Takes hours to do minutes of homework. *(See items 10, 11, 12, 13, 14, 16, 17, 18.)*

6. Hassles about when and where to do homework. *(See items 4, 5, 6, 7, 8, 9.)*

7. Lies about having done homework. *(See item 3.)*

8. Fails to bring notes home concerning homework. *(See item 1.)*

9. Needs constant supervision with homework. *(See items 8, 10, 11, 12, 16.)*

10. Needs constant help with homework. *(See items 8, 15.)*

11. Forgets to get homework papers signed. *(See item 1.)*

12. Forgets homework at home. *(See items 19, 20.)*

Many other problems could be added to this list, but these are the major ones that often make parents feel like they are back in school. Parents of teenagers with ADHD often work with their teens each day on homework—struggling and experiencing frustration, anger, and perhaps guilt that drives them to assume responsibility for their teen's work. Some parents say, "I literally have to do it or it would never get done"; others state, "I eventually wind up doing it just to keep my sanity."

Dealing with Homework Problems—The following plan focuses on the homework problem areas. It is a behavioral approach that involves the development of habits or skills. Behavior becomes a habit only with repetition and practice over many learning trials, and you must be prepared to assume a supervisory role—like a very dedicated coach or teacher—working daily to bring about needed changes in one or more of these areas.

1. **Assignments.** First and foremost, each teen should have an assignment book. These may be purchased at many school supply centers, you may make your own, or use the *Homework Assignment Sheet* (HAS) (see Figure 5.5). Homework assignment sheets may be put in a brightly colored binder clearly marked Homework Assignment Book; it should contain enough sheets for each day of the week, and will be brought to and from school each and every day.

Many teens with ADHD have problems writing down assignments. However, if the teen is able to write, she can record each assignment in her Homework Assignment Book. Then the teacher need only initial the HAS in the appropriate box each day so that you will know the assignment, as written, is correct.* Your teen must learn to regularly and correctly record assignments. This habit will help him (1) begin to take more responsibility for his work and (2) develop greater independence in work at home and at school.

---

*Special provisions must be made if your child (a) writes so sloppily that the assignment cannot be read or (b) makes many errors in writing the assignment. These provisions might include use of a computer, prepared assignments, tape recordings, etc.

Figure 5.5

HOMEWORK ASSIGNMENT SHEET

Name _____

Date _____

Subject	Assignment	Teacher's Initials	Books/Materials Needed	In Bag	Finished/ Filed	Parent's Initials	In Bag	Specials projects to be completed
								Tests to study for tomorrow or future date (specify)
								Materials/clothes needed for special events
								Teacher notes or requests

Helping the Teen with ADHD Write Assignments. Consultation between parent and teacher is critical in helping the teen write assignments. Most teachers give homework assignments on a day-to-day basis. The goal for the ADHD teen is to foster development of the habit of consistently, accurately, and clearly writing his daily assignment in his Homework Assignment Book, and this goal is set to be reached in a specified period of time. Most teachers are happy to help the teen develop necessary skills—and check this task daily with the teen—as long as they know they're being asked to do this daily checking only for a specified length of time. They're especially willing to help when they realize the benefits to the student. Teachers should be encouraged to give assignments orally and in writing (on the board or projected on a transparency) so that the teen will use both *visual* and *auditory* senses to process the information.

A parent can assist the teenager in developing this habit of writing assignments by reviewing and practicing this process at home on an as-needed basis.

An additional underlying problem may make it difficult for the child to complete this task. Some teens write poorly and sloppily, perhaps because of:

1. poor training in handwriting

2. dysgraphia, when there is a neurological basis for poor writing that will affect how long remediation will be required

3. rushing through the task—they may see it as unpleasant, simply wishing to "get it over with as quickly as possible"

ADHD children and adolescents are also less attentive to detail in their writing, and even when asked to redo their work, they often do not improve. To deal with this problem, the teen may be (1) placed on a mild afternoon or evening dose of stimulant medication, or (2) taught a self-instruction "slow-down" procedure or bypass strategies, such as "use of the computer."

Teens with true dysgraphia experience significant frustration in writing. *Dysgraphia* is a disorder involving fine-motor coordination. For these students, written assignments may be perceived as "punishment," with associated anger directed toward the teacher, the school, and the parent. These students can have their assignments recorded (via tape recorder or mnemonic device), or obtained by other means while the teen is habilitated in this area of dysfunction. Expecting otherwise from a teen with dysgraphia is certain to spawn numerous other behavioral and emotional difficulties.

2. *Forgetting the Assignment Book.* The Homework Assignment Book is expected to be brought back and forth between home and school daily. Failure to at least bring the assignment book home and to school each day results in loss of all privileges for that day (or grounding) until the teen has caught up all the work assigned. Incorporate the teen's specific problem behavior (i.e., bringing the Homework Assignment Book to school and back home daily) into the

home–school program. Improvements and positive changes in this habit can thus be monitored and reinforced when positive changes first occur; these behaviors initially will be weak and must be strengthened.

3. ***Bringing Needed Material Home.*** In this behavioral program, whether formal or informal, all privileges are suspended until the teen is caught up on his or her work. Monitor this behavior daily. Should the teen fail to bring home materials needed for homework over the weekend, be aware of this on Friday so that privileges may be suspended over the weekend. To avoid this unpleasant situation, the teen must practice at home, asking himself what materials are needed for each homework assignment and then checking to be sure that he has loaded these items in his bookbag. Doing mock exercises on this routine will help make this procedure a habit for the young teen. The checklist procedure may be likened to an airplane pilot's checklist before take-off: Flying with insufficient fuel means not completing the trip successfully—just as trying to work math problems without the text means the assignment cannot be completed.

4. ***Taking Hours to Do Minutes of Homework.*** Just about every parent of children and adolescents with ADHD has complained of problems about homework taking too long. To help your teen with this problem, first check the amount of homework given. Many of these students are simply unable to complete large assignments. Consultation with the teacher may result in a shorter homework assignment; the teacher may realize that the teen with ADHD is bright and could demonstrate what she has learned with a shorter assignment. Also, you can teach your teen how to cope with large assignments that, at first, look impossible to complete; show your teen how to break up large assignments into smaller units that are more manageable. For example, 20 math problems can be divided into four groups of five problems each, and a short break can be offered as a reward after completion of each group. By developing such subgoals, your teen will learn to view large assignments and projects as "doable." Be aware that, to some extent, the teen's perception of difficulty is likely to be colored by the hassles he or she may have experienced in school just hours before. (How would you like to repeat your day's work at night?) This problem might be solved with a light dose of stimulant medicine in the late afternoon or evening.

An exercise that works fairly well in the classroom as well as at home is an auditory self-monitoring system. The child wears headphones and listens to a recorded tape (available in *The ADD/ADHD Resources Catalog)* for a periodic beep that occurs approximately every 30 to 60 seconds. Each time the beep is heard, the child marks the form to indicate whether he or she was on or off task at the time the beep was heard. The self-recording sheet is shown in Figure 3.4 on page 115.

While this procedure may sound distracting to the child, it has proved beneficial for many older children and some teens with ADHD, increasing awareness of being off-task and reducing auditory distractions while the headphones are worn.

5. ***Where and When to Do Homework.*** To foster the development of the homework habit, develop a routine that can be practiced each day. Several factors are involved; the two most important are "where" and "when" homework is to be done.

Where to Do Homework. Initially, homework should be done in an environment with very few distractions. Gradually, more distractions may be tolerated. This increased tolerance for distractions is important for such skills and habits to be successful in the classroom.

As with any play or sport, it is important to practice in a place that is similar to the one where the performance or game is to take place. First, a desk is suggested. Sitting at the kitchen table where others are passing by, talking, and so on, is just not conducive (initially) to good work. Second, there is some evidence that the place of study does not have to be totally quiet—and in fact, some background noise may actually be helpful; however, this factor may vary considerably from one individual to another. Basically, the teen needs to do homework in the same place each day.

When to Do Homework. The teen must have a homework schedule. This does not mean fitting homework into a busy schedule of piano, dance, volleyball practice, and so forth. While such social activities may be important, you and your teen must prioritize, organize, and develop a schedule centering around homework. With today's often-hectic lifestyles, parents may model activities that result in the teen's feeling overwhelmed. Homework must take priority and be scheduled at the same time each day. This regularly scheduled time should allow the teen some flexibility to engage in important outside social activities, but one should never sacrifice the time set aside for homework. A general recommendation is that the teen should devote at least two hours per night for upper-level grades through high school. In the absence of teacher-assigned homework, the scheduled time is spent doing some type of educational game, reading, or preparing for an upcoming test or project. Homework time should be viewed as sacred.

Teenagers should be allowed to choose the time for homework. A daily, weekly, and monthly schedule—visible at a glance—must be made. The teen may, for example, wish to do homework right after school so as to not miss favorite TV programs; or the teen may elect to go out, eat dinner, and then do homework. Schedules are best developed through collaboration of parent and teen.

Even with a designated place and a schedule for homework, there are often hassles over homework time. The teen shows resistance or avoidance when it is time for homework; this is sometimes related to some difficult work to be done. Teens who have a learning disability or problems writing may clearly wish to avoid tasks that elicit the disability and associated frustration and anger. The following suggestions may be used to make the task easier:

➠ Cut length of assignment.

➠ Use more interesting materials.

⟹ Break up the assignment.

⟹ Use of computer instead of writing.

⟹ Use the Premack Principle.*

The Premack Principle may be used to make difficult tasks more palatable. Suggest (1) doing the more difficult tasks first and (2) doing homework before an enjoyable activity. Essentially, when difficult work is followed by something that is less difficult and more fun, the first activity becomes more pleasurable; the teen is rewarded for completing the undesirable activity. Completion of homework may also be listed as one item in the home–school (point) behavioral program, and thus the homework habit is reinforced and strengthened.

6. ***Lying About Homework.*** Lying about homework is not unusual with teens who have ADHD. First, lying may allow the teen to escape an activity that is perceived as unpleasant. Second, the act of lying is a kind of "risk-taking" that creates some stimulation and excitement for this teen of low-arousal state in the nervous system.

Dealing with lying can be quite difficult for the parent. Some teenagers have practiced so much that they become quite adept at lying; it may even have become a habit, albeit a less desirable one.

The following sequence is a common one:

1. Teen lies about homework.

2. Parent suspects teen is lying.

3. Parent questions teen further.

4. Teen admits to lying and tells the truth about a homework assignment.

5. Parent says, "You lied—you are grounded—you won't be able to play in your baseball game tomorrow."

A parent may really believe she is punishing the teen for (1) lying and (2) not doing the homework. In reality, however, in such a scenario, the consequence for the behavior is punishment right after telling the truth. Thus, because in reality the truth-telling is punished, in future similar situations, the teen wants to avoid what he perceived as resulting in punishment and is likely to lie again—and even to develop a more convincing lie to avoid the punishment. An alternative response from you might be, "I really appreciate your telling me the truth about your homework. I know how difficult that must have been because I know how difficult it is for you to do that homework project. I'm really proud that you decided to be honest with me. I'll be around to help should you need it." In this case, the child is rewarded (praise) for telling the truth as well as learning that you understand his or her plight.

---

*The Premack Principle states that an action with a high probability of occurrence can be used to reinforce an action with a low probability of occurrence.

Proper use of the Homework Assignment Sheet is beneficial in keeping communications clear about homework. Also, this sheet can be used to give feedback to the teacher regarding how the teen worked on his or her assignment. At times, a teen may work the entire homework period and still not complete the assignment. With a short note from you (written on the HAS in ink), the teacher (who already has been consulted about this behavior program) will often accept the assignment as complete. The teen's effort and demonstration of knowledge should be rewarded; the teen should not, in such cases, be penalized for being unable to finish the task. This HAS system will foster improved communication between home and school.

7. ***Notes from the Teacher.*** The HAS includes a space for the teacher to indicate that a note accompanies the form. When a pocket folder is included in the binder for the HAS, personal notes, progress reports, discipline slips, and other communications can easily be sent home. There is also room on the HAS to write comments in place of a separate note. This box is at the bottom of the form. This ensures that such notes will reach home; if not, the teen may be grounded until the note is received. Providing this type of organizational structure will help the teen with ADHD develop strategies and habits for saving important documents. As with all of these procedures for homework, the ultimate goal is for the teen to develop skills he or she can use immediately and in the future.

8. ***Needing Constant Supervision and Help.*** According to Kathleen Anecho and Fredric Levine, parents should act as homework consultants. This means that you should not do a teen's homework nor should you be in the teen's presence every moment of the time spent doing homework. Once a teenager is familiar with the task, you need not stay directly by the teen. Answer questions if and when needed. It is very important for teachers to assign work that the teen can perform by him- or herself. (Many parents, unfamiliar with today's schoolwork, may actually provide misinformation to the teen and create even more difficult problems for the student in the classroom and in the parent–child relationship.) Assigned homework is clearly the teen's responsibility. If you provide excess help or actually do the work, the child is being set up to become overly dependent upon others, and when similar help is not forthcoming in the classroom, the teen may feel lost and confused. A teen who experiences significant coordination problems (e.g., dysgraphia) may find excessive written assignments difficult to complete, yet he or she may be quite capable of understanding and learning that same work. Use of computers and word-processing programs may greatly assist that teen in completing homework as well as prepare him or her for the future where writing per se may be replaced by laptop computers connected to worldwide information resources. (Voice-command computers are in their infancy, but they may virtually eliminate writing, as we know it. For some teenagers with ADHD, this changing future can seem like a miracle!) The goal of establishing and developing good work habits in the homework environment should carry over (generalize) to use these habits and skills in the classroom setting, too. You therefore must prepare the teen to work under typical classroom conditions and to meet expectations similar to those of the teacher.

With regard to supervising needs, teenagers with ADHD may require monitoring of their homework activity (but *not* of the homework itself). This may be accomplished in two ways. *First,* the teen may self-monitor. Using the stop, think, and listen program, the teen may record when he or she is on or off task as he or she hears a beep on the headphones. This procedure has been shown to be effective in recent research. Clinically, the procedure (developed by Dr. Harvey Parker and noted previously) has worked well with many teens.

Second, you may monitor the child's homework activity. By observing the young teen in an unobtrusive manner, you can record whether he or she was on or off task on the *Homework Check Card* (see Figure 5.6). Inform the child that you will randomly check to see if he or she is or is not working on the homework assignment. The teen does not know when you will observe him or her; such random checks should serve to keep the teen on task for a longer period of time. Perhaps 10 checks are possible each night; 50 checks would be conducted throughout the week. When the teen is off task, this number will be subtracted from the number of times he or she is on task. If the young adolescent survives with a minimum number of 30 points, she may earn a previously specified privilege for that weekend. (Questions and requests for assistance are *not* counted as being off task.)

Figure 5.6
HOMEWORK CHECK CARD

WORKING	Mon	Tues	Wed	Thurs	Fri	Sat	Sun
"On Task"							
"Off Task"							
Net Totals							
Grand Totals							

As an alternative to this self-contained weekly reward system, the teen's point total may enter an overall behavioral (point) system used both in school and in home situations. The issue of staying on task is reinforced both at home and at school, and the teen receives points for being on task for classwork *and* on task for homework. Reinforcing desired behavior in both situations results in:

➟ Faster learning

➟ More generalizing learning

➟ Strengthening of independent work habits

9. *Getting Homework Papers Signed.* Use of the HAS promotes better communication between home and school; teachers are able to indicate when parents are to sign homework papers. Your teen's failure to bring home papers to be signed results in grounding. Alternatively, your teen may be rewarded (e.g., praise) for bringing home test papers, even when they reflect poor grades. Remember, the focus here is on *habits* about homework and schoolwork. It is especially important to praise the teen for bringing home those test papers that reflect poor grades (imagine how difficult it is for your teen to knowingly share such information with you!), because such information is necessary to improve the home efforts and to develop remedial work activities.

10. *Forgetting Homework at Home.* "Forgetting" homework at home is really not a memory problem, but is rather a lack of organization. The HAS has a place to check when homework is completed and then filed in the subject binder, which is different from the Homework Assignment Book, and placed in the school bag. Homework for each subject is placed in its own section in a three-ring binder. This subject binder has pockets and sufficient room for many plastic dividers. A separate divider in front contains pencils, sharpener, marking pens, paper clips, small staples, or whatever else the teen's teacher requires. Once the homework for a subject (e.g., math) is completed, the HAS is checked as the work is filed in the binder and the binder is placed in the school bag. The Homework Assignment Book (i.e., five Homework Assignment Sheets for that week) is placed in the school bag when all assignments for the day are completed. Thus, the teacher will know that the work was completed, inspected, and filed by parent and teen.

Where should the teen place the school bag? The answer is simple—in the same place each night. This place should be very obvious (e.g., by the front door) for the teen to see in the morning and should ensure that the teen takes the school bag to school.

It is only through repetitive practice of a routine that the routine becomes established as a habit. Whether this newly developed habit is maintained will in turn depend on whether it is reinforced. How generalized the habit becomes will likewise be a function of how often it is reinforced and in how many different situations it is reinforced.

"How can I tell if my teen is developing these habits?" many parents ask. The answer can come in three basic ways. First, others—and particularly teachers—may comment that the teen is getting better at one or more of these homework-related behaviors. Second, you can monitor and record progress using the more structured behavioral program. Then, week by week there is a record of progress. (Refer to the section on point or token systems.) Third, periodically review the Homework Problems Checklist and compare current ratings with those from the first time the checklist was completed. The number and degree to which these areas are monitored may depend on the age of the teen.

OTHER FACTORS FOR SCHOOL SUCCESS

There are other factors that influence success in school. Three basic ones are discussed here:

Learning Style—As noted under the section of memory strategies, students learn through different modalities. Some learn best by what they view, some learn best by what they hear, and others learn best by doing. These three modes are generally called visual, auditory, and kinesthetic ways of processing information. For example, while some students learn to spell by reading and visualizing words (visual), others learn by hearing the word and spelling it out loud (auditory); still others may learn by writing (kinesthetic). Of course, the multisensory (MS) approach generally ensures quicker learning when the learning style (LS) is not known and especially when the student is learning disabled. The MS approach guarantees that one's LS will be tapped. Although there is not an exact method of discovering the preferred mode of learning, the Learning Style Inventory (LSI) (appropriate for students from high school through college) by Dr. Albert Canfield may be helpful. It is also useful for the student to note in which situation learning is more efficient—quiet or with background music. It is likewise good to know the teen's period of peak performance and learning. Many teens with ADHD actually learn best at night, yet they are asked to perform in daytime classes. The cycle of the biological rhythm of the body may, in short, be reversed in many students with ADHD.

Reading Comprehension—Beginning in middle school, there is an apparent significant increase in reading assignments. This steadily continues to be of greater importance to the student in high school and beyond. Information must be processed through reading and the student must understand or comprehend what was read. Certainly, this problem may relate to attentional factors, but there are strategies that may help the student read for greater understanding. It is understandable the frustration a student must experience when he loses his place in reading, skips words or lines, gets distracted at other times, and has trouble with short-term memory affecting the continuity of information processed such that he must read the same material over and over. Such problems can certainly be the cause for the student to wish to avoid such tasks.

Many techniques to help the student are listed in the book *Study Strategies Made Easy* by Davis, Sirotowitz, and Parker. However, it is worth reviewing one procedure called the SQ4R Method, which can be quite helpful in improving reading comprehension. SQ4R stands for *S*urvey, *Q*uestion, *R*ead, *R*ite (Write), *R*ecite, *R*eview. An outline of the SQ4R method is found in Figure 5.7.

Figure 5.7

STUDENT CHECKLIST FOR APPLYING SQ4R TO READING TEXTBOOKS

SURVEY each section to be read.

_____ Determine the organization of the chapter.

_____ Survey the first pages for basic information, such as the title, author, and table of contents.

_____ Identify any study aids, such as chapter objectives, introductions, illustrations, summaries, bibliographies, glossaries.

QUESTION the material.

_____ Say the chapter title aloud, converting the title of the chapter into a main idea question.

_____ Convert the heading or subheadings into questions.

_____ Add questions from the back of the chapter.

_____ Be sure to include questions requiring interpretation, integration, and application of ideas.

_____ Begin to answer the questions, using prior knowledge.

READ to find the answers to your questions.

_____ Circle key words or phrases that answer your questions.

_____ Read figures and tables, then relate them to the questions.

_____ Think about what you are reading and reread passages that are unclear.

_____ Try to visualize or create pictures in your mind as you read.

RECITE the answers to your questions in your own words.

_____ Restate, paraphrase, summarize the information in your own words.

_____ Elaborate about the main ideas and relationships between ideas, using examples.

[W]RITE the answers to your questions.

_____ Write brief answers in your own words.

_____ Use charts, diagrams, and symbols to help answer the questions.

REVIEW.

_____ Read questions; recite/write answers; refer to text; and add, correct, or delete information.

_____ Ask the teacher to explain ideas that you did not fully understand.

_____ Repeat the review after a week.

The following steps are involved: (1) the student skims (**S**) over the assignment to identify the general topic and its main points; (2) questions (**Q**) are generated and answered as the story unfolds; (3) the story is read (**R**) with the goal of answering the questions posed; (4) answers to questions are written (**R**); (5) the student recites (**R**) these answers paraphrasing them in his or her own words; and (6) the student reviews (**R**) what was done. This last phase helps to reinforce what was learned and aids in retention.

During the process of reading, the student is also encouraged to keep a list (written) of words that are not familiar.

Homework—While this area has been reviewed in detail elsewhere, it is such an important factor in school success that it would be helpful to review some strategies that may be useful for the teen with ADHD.

1. Teachers should write assignments on the board and review each one orally. Then the student may be directed to copy the assignment in his or her homework notebook or on the Homework Assignment Sheet.

2. Teachers may collaborate with parents to complete the homework checklist, a diagnostic indicator of where primary homework problems lie.

3. The teacher may regularly use training exercises to teach and reinforce techniques to correctly write assignments, to have necessary books and materials, and to return completed assignments to class.

The teacher may also wish to consider implementing a program entitled "Skills for School Success" by Anita Archer and Mary Gleason, developed and published in 1989. This program is published by Curriculum Associates.

HOME-SCHOOLING

There is a greater number of parents who are now teaching their children, including teens with ADHD, at home. Whether from concern over an increasing number of incidents of school violence or the inability of some schools to meet all of the needs of the teen with ADHD, to home-school is a viable option. There is greater use of computers in instruction, using software that allows for self-pacing of learning. Parents are finding that they can provide not only packaged materials to meet educational standards, but may also supplement many areas with in-depth instruction and, in particular, ensure that high-interest materials are used. Parents who wish to explore this option may begin by contacting the local school district. While perhaps initially stressful and certainly a new learning experience for parent and teen, there are clearly many opportunities to be exposed to material that the teen would not normally encounter in school.

FAILURE AND RETENTION

Many teens with ADHD have had considerable prior experience with failure and retention. To date, there is little evidence to argue the benefits of retention after failure. Those who have been held back exhibit poor self-concept, negative attitudes toward school, and generally lower levels of achievement. In other foreign cultures, it has been reported that less than 1% of the school-age population is retained; in the United States the rate is 50%. When a teen lags behind his or her peers, there is an increased probability of becoming a dropout. From all available evidence, parents should consider that there is no research showing the benefits of retention. Children and teens who are retained in the same grade have a generally lower self-concept, poorer attitudes toward school, and low achievement. When these children have learning problems as well, their drop-out rate is estimated as high as 54%. Parents may wish to explore other options such as tutoring, summer school, or perhaps, even home-schooling.

PROMOTE AND MAINTAIN SELF-ESTEEM

It is important to not only consider the perception of the self, but also the label and feeling states associated with it. Thus, one's perception of self with ADHD may be that of a "klutz," an "absent-minded professor," a "flake," "an unreliable person," and so forth. Many of these self-perceptions erode the self-concept and generate low self-esteem since these are all negative feeling states associated with the labels. Therefore, one must overcome the perceptions by modifying them and reframing the perceptions so that they might be processed differently. Many of these perceptions will generate feelings of anger, depression, inadequacy, hopelessness, and despair. As long as these self-perceptions with their associated feeling states exist, the person with ADHD may be weighted down with "excess baggage" that serves no useful function. It is crucial that with approaching adulthood, these perceptions and feelings be modified not only to improve the teen's personal life, but also to enhance his or her chances of success in later life. Should these early patterns persist, the teen is put in a disadvantaged position. All attempts at adaptation to life situations will be affected by this "aura of failure and negative feeling states."

The ways a teen perceives him- or herself constitute self-concept, and a teen may have several differing views of that "self." A teen with ADHD may realize he or she has poor social skills and poor math skills, but may also realize that she performs as an excellent soccer player. Such varying awareness is, indeed, fortunate; otherwise, the teen with ADHD could be devastated by his or her many difficulties, making such comments as, "I am really stupid in school" or "I really am a weirdo; I can't get along with anyone." Such a teen exhibits a lack of understanding of the important fact that he or she is a "person" and thus distinct from "what he or she does." The essential message to convey to this teen is "You are *not* your behavior." Don't criticize or put down the teen;

be aware of the teen's internal dialogue regarding such a negative message. Over time, adolescents with ADHD can accumulate quite a number of negative messages; the effect is a progressive erosion of self-perception to the point of a generally negative self-concept.

Self-esteem represents how the teen feels about himself or herself. It's a generalized feeling that develops over time and reflects the impact of his life experiences. Often, this feeling state is based not only on what the teen perceives but also on the expectations others may have of the teen. A teen with ADHD who is having a problem completing a task may be told "I know you can do this work; you completed it yesterday." Such performance inconsistency (characteristic of the ADHD pattern) sets up the teen to fail to meet the expectations of others, and thereby creates another negative weight on the self-esteem scale. The greater the number of failure experiences, the more negative, or lower, will be the teen's self-esteem. Despite the teen's effort in school, little is achieved. Even though there is a tremendous desire to be popular, many are treated like annoying outcasts. Although some do well in sports, others are banished to the sidelines and often criticized when they do play. Since the teen may encounter failures and disappointments in many areas of his or her life besides in the academic area, there is a general tendency for the teen to develop a poor self-image, or self-concept, and to have many negative feelings (low self-esteem). Along with these past failures and excess criticism is the feeling of always being treated unfairly. These teens must be taught how to change negative thoughts to positive ones. Separating behavior from self is quite important when the teen is taught to say "It is my behavior—not me that is being criticized." These teens may also be taught the "stop–think" procedure as they say to themselves "Stop! Thinking like this will get me nowhere—I need to think positive thoughts." Remember, too, that most teens with ADHD are exceptionally sensitive emotionally as well as neurologically. When teenagers with ADHD begin to believe they are retarded, lazy, or losers, these beliefs may become associated with feelings of hopelessness and a perception that putting forth effort in school, or in other situations, isn't worth the effort. When this leads to a pervasive sense of being "defective," there may be significant loss of motivation. Positive strokes are clearly needed!

GIVE POSITIVE STROKES

It is most important that parents and teachers of adolescents with ADHD provide numerous and frequent positive strokes to counteract the numerous negative ones they receive. Exercise 5.1 will help you develop an awareness of those things the teen does well so you can use this information to provide positive strokes.

If you have not named ten things, go back and add those "parts of" things the teen does well (even if the overall activity would not be described as done well). In other words, if only a single component of an activity is performed well, list that component; for example, teen works very hard on tasks (once these have been organized and put into proper sequence). This list will serve you later as a resource to provide positive strokes for the adolescent.

Exercise 5-1. POSITIVE STROKES

List all of the things the adolescent with ADHD does well.

1. _____

2. _____

3. _____

4. _____

5. _____

6. _____

7. _____

8. _____

9. _____

10. _____

The following is a list of sample positive strokes regarding what the teen does well:

Exercise 5-1. SAMPLE POSITIVE STROKES

1. I really liked the birthday present you got for me—that was a very caring thing to do.

2. I appreciate the way you helped to clean the house.

3. You are really helpful to me in taking care of your little brother.

4. You know, you are very good at drawing those pictures of race cars.

5. I was really impressed by your play in the baseball game—two home runs—wow!

6. Thanks for folding the clothes so neatly.

7. I can really count on you to take out the trash on Monday night.

8. You are doing well with your drum lessons—even our neighbors have commented.

9. I really like the way you have organized your baseball card collection—it is very impressive and shows that you have put a lot of work into it.

10. I know that math is not easy but I am really impressed by the way you have accepted extra assignments to work on. It is going to pay off.

IMPROVE SELF-ESTEEM

Parents of a teen with ADHD need to be almost superhuman to remain positive and supportive in the presence of the teen's difficulties and failures. The teen's perception of self-worth is influenced by the reactions of others. Parents, teachers, and others significant in the teen's life provide a mirror that shows the teen how he or she is appreciated; based on this, self-image is shaped. To maintain adequate self-esteem, the significant people in the teen's life must be aware and constantly emphasize the positive in what is said to the teen if he or she is to enjoy success.

You can affect self-esteem by the words you use and by how those words are used. Intonations of the voice, lack of interest in activities, failure to listen to what the teenager says, backhanded compliments, and statements that question competence may all erode the teen's self-esteem. Eventually, your perceived lack of interest may result in reduced or even closed communications with the teen. Remember that the teen with ADHD is quite sensitive to remarks of others. Accusations such as "You really annoy me" or "You always make such a mess" focus directly on the teen, *not* on the behavior. It is *not okay* to focus your criticisms on the teen; it *is okay* to state how you feel about his or her *behavior;* for example, "I really get upset when you interrupt my conversation." Sometimes a parent or teacher, who is aware that the teen has previously exhibited dangerous behavior and may simply want to "protect" the teen, may, in the very act of being (over) protective, inadvertently say things that recall to the teen his or her incompetency. For example: "Don't try to do that by yourself. You know you will hurt yourself." Sometimes it is very difficult to balance the need to protect the teen with allowing him or her to feel trusted in becoming more independent.

You must be careful to avoid comparisons with other relatives and classmates. When the teen with ADHD shows improvement and does his or her best work ever, it is important to *note that improvement* and avoid finding fault. Don't give backhanded compliments.

➠ *Example of backhanded compliment:* "This is a very neat and organized math homework page. You are really improving. Maybe next time you will get all the answers right."

➠ *Example of sincere, reinforcing compliment:* "This is a very neat and organized math homework page. You are really improving. Look, you have even gotten more answers right this time than last."

The language used is most important. Critical comments and destructive words (like "dumb," "stupid," "pest," and "worse") can all depress the teen's self-esteem. Everyone has negative qualities, but adults are allowed to promote their assets and hide their weaknesses; teenagers with ADHD are often forced to expose their difficulties in front of a class or on the ballfield. If these teens are to feel good about themselves, they must receive more attention for what they *do well now,* for their *effort,* and for their *improvements* in all that they do. Listen to this teen, acknowledge what he or she says, and be genuinely interested in his or her conversation.

Focus on any positive characteristics and emphasize improvements when they appear. For example, writing may be messy and words may be misspelled, but the teen's story may have good content. It is important to point this out, saying, "I really like the story you wrote." These teenagers must experience a sense of competency and be allowed to think and act in a more independent manner. Too often, in a need to get things done quickly, adults may simply tell the teen with ADHD what to do instead of allowing the teen to *think* of what he or she needs to do. While this seems to save time, it is at the expense of communicating to the teen that he or she is competent; it says instead that the teen must depend on others to tell him or her what to do. By not allowing the teen to come up with the answer or do a task simply because it will take a little more time, you may cause the teen to feel inadequate, to perceive that he or she cannot cope, and in general to develop a helpless, overly dependent attitude.

In the classroom, most teachers are aware that the teen with ADHD needs more attention and is especially sensitive in situations where his or her "differences" are made known. You must use methods and materials that will hold the teen's interest. Despite their sometimes rude and inappropriate behaviors, teens with ADHD are quite sensitive to comments made in the classroom. Be very careful of what you say. If a teen is misbehaving, it can be devastating to say, "Johnny, did you take your medicine this morning?" or "Beth seems to act so smart at times, let's see if she knows the answer to this question." Get and keep the teen's attention; offer many opportunities for small successes, and praise, praise, praise! Emphasize and bring out the "good stuff" for everyone to see.

AN EXERCISE PLAN TO COUNTERACT NEGATIVE THEMES

To help you learn to pay attention to this "good stuff," use a reminder system for cues to give more positive strokes. You may be cued by a watch that beeps on the hour or, preferably, on the half hour. Each time the beep is heard, look for something the teen has done that could be considered an occasion for a positive comment. A reward card system may be used to give positive strokes or checks (or punch out holes in the card). The number of strokes may be increased as you see an increase in the overall number of times the good behaviors appear. When any good, appropriate, or improved behavior is shown, it is rewarded more often, thus bringing about an increase in the number of these behaviors per day. This exercise is designed to counteract the generally negative themes that pervade most of the attention given to teens with ADHD. At the end of the week the number of strokes on the reward card may be traded for some prearranged consequence (i.e., no homework in one subject or a certain number will get a free ticket to a dance or sports game).

Finally, there is the issue of the effect of "grade retention" on the self-concept/self-esteem of the teen with ADHD. Dr. Mel Levine (1994) notes that retaining a teen in a grade can cause significant setbacks to the teen's pride. Retention in preschool and kindergarten may be acceptable, but may not be helpful after the first grade. Moreover, he points out that grade retention has not been shown to help any age child succeed in the future. Teenagers with a history of grade retention have a higher probability of leaving school without graduating and with a propensity to engage in activities that are detrimental to them. Dr. Levine believes that there are alternatives to grade retention. These may include extra help at home or at school, summer school, or after-school remedial programs. In short, there are many ways to counteract the negative impact of failure in school.

GIFTED TEENS WITH ADHD

A discussion of education issues would not be complete without including those teens with ADHD who fall within the gifted or very superior range of abilities. With an IQ of 130 or higher, these students are a real challenge to educators. Such students typically may have little trouble learning assigned material, yet, they too may show an inconsistent performance that may be reflected in their grades. The usual comments about their daydreaming or being lazy or simply not "trying hard" or "not using their abilities" does not seem to apply. Without treatment, such teens may either go completely unnoticed or "suffer in silence." Since many of these gifted teens with ADHD are able to "get by" and typically do not have associated behavior problems in class, such students may not be referred for evaluation. However, these students may develop serious behavior problems, depression, and/or a poor self-concept and low self-esteem. In the eyes of their teachers, parents, and even some professional counselors, they simply perceive themselves as people who have failed to live up to expectations.

The development of positive self-esteem is not only essential to succeed in school, but in other areas of the teen's life as well. While some compensation may be made by shoring-up self-esteem at home, getting positive strokes and recognition is extremely important at school. However, in the absence of recognition at school, such teens may build on recognition received outside of the school, at home, in sports, or in some area where the teen has specialized skills (e.g., computer science). In short, the gifted teen needs to receive attention and praise for his or her special skills and knowledge.

Chapter 6

BEHAVIOR MANAGEMENT FOR ADHD TEENS AT HOME AND IN SCHOOL

Behavioral interventions may be conducted at home or in the school. In addition, parents and teachers may work cooperatively on behavioral programs for teens. Some of the same procedures may be used by both parents and teachers; some may be discussed primarily for use by parents, but also reviewed briefly in discussing their application by teachers.

BEHAVIORAL INTERVENTIONS AT HOME

One of the most powerful treatment components that—for many teens is almost equal to medication—is behavioral interventions. In some cases behavioral techniques have been shown to be just as effective as medication; in some other cases, behavioral techniques may be the treatment of choice.

There are two basic behavioral approaches that may be used: (1) a general behavioral orientation to work with spontaneous behaviors as they occur, and (2) use of certain behavioral techniques that are planned with specific behavioral objectives in mind. Of course, it is not uncommon for parents and teachers to use both approaches.

As was previously noted, interventions will focus on behavior. There is less concern about diagnoses; however, there may be some behaviors that may respond differently to behavioral interventions because of their different origin. For example, while some behaviors that stem from neurological conditions may be similar to that found in ADHD, these behaviors may be slower to respond to interventions, and some will perhaps necessitate medical interventions before planned behavioral strategies will work.

Whether a parent or teacher is addressing specific behavior problems, a general A–B–C format should be used. This means that the parent or teacher must consider (a) the antecedents, (b) the behavior, and (c) the consequences.

A—ANTECEDENTS: WHAT COMES FIRST

Antecedents are those stimulus events that precede the behavior. They are the verbal requests, questions, gestures, nonverbal visual signals, classroom noise, etc., that lead to the behavior and perhaps trigger it. Antecedent events are very important, for they are the input into the system. If this input is unclear or incomplete, then surely the outcome will be compromised. Antecedent events can be classified as:

1. rules
2. expectations
3. communications

Together, they provide the basic structure (the input) in the teen's family or in the school environment within which the ADHD behavior can be monitored.

Many teachers and parents believe they have *rules,* but few rules are actually written down; most rules are so unclear (e.g., "Weekday chores must be done when you get home from school" could mean immediately, or after a snack, or before any TV, etc.) that it is not at all unusual for the teen to be confused. Thus, engagement in thought about rules and which ones are to be used would be extremely helpful for both parents and teachers.

When *communicating* requests, parents and teachers must not only be clear and concise, it is also critical that they have the ADHD teen's undivided attention when communicating; eye contact is essential when you face the teen.

It is also important to focus on the *style* of communication the parent or teacher uses. Both passive and aggressive styles are fraught with problems; an assertive approach, however, is most effective. More information about communication styles, including information on metacommunication, and a specific communication style exercise, are discussed later in this chapter.

B—BEHAVIOR: THE CENTRAL ISSUE

Behavior is *what the teen does.* Parents and teachers often make observations such as "he's lazy" or "he's just got a bad attitude," and believe they're truly describing behavioral problems that can be the focus of change. Not so; in all good behavioral programs, "behavior" means something that is observable, countable, and, of course, changeable. Conversely, "behavior" is *not* what the teen *doesn't* do (i.e., "not doing work" is not a behavior). "Playing with a pencil" while not doing work may be "the behavior" that we wish to diminish or extinguish (i.e., remove). Having the parent or teacher list classes of behavior, such as desirable vs. undesirable, helps to provide a frame of reference for defining and working with these behaviors. The appropriate and inappropriate behaviors may be further subdivided into those that appear (a) at home, (b) at school, and (c) outside the home or school.

You will come to realize that, for the most part, problem behaviors fall into four basic categories:

1. relationship with adults (primarily parents and teachers)
2. relationship with siblings
3. relationship with peers
4. relationship with self in personal areas pertaining to:
   a. safety
   b. morals
   c. habits
   d. emotional control and expression

C—CONSEQUENCES: REACTIONS TO BEHAVIOR

Consequences that are provided for these behaviors are of critical importance. It does not matter whether a behavior has been *elicited* by a specific request or *emitted* as a spontaneous variant of some behavior in which the parent or teacher has some investment.

Consequences may be classified as either *rewards* or *punishments.* There are many types of rewards, and also many variations of punishments. It is important to list consequences (both rewards and punishments and their subtypes), but it may be confusing, so let's look at a few examples.

First, let's look at *rewards.* There are two basic subtypes:

➠ giving a positive consequence: a thing, an activity, a social reward
➠ taking away a negative consequence: removal of a fish hook from the teen's foot

Likewise, *punishments* can take the form of either:

➠ giving an aversive consequence: slapping
➠ removing something positive: taking away a computer game or privilege

The antithesis of consequences, yet often also effective, is *no consequence* following a behavior. The absence of a consequence means that the behavior will not be strengthened or maintained. This, of course, is desirable (i.e., the absence of consequence) when we wish to weaken or extinguish certain inappropriate behaviors.

The last condition to consider in the areas of consequences is a concept called *shaping.* In this procedure, the focus is on a behavior that does appear to be an improvement (i.e., it is more like the "final behavior" the parent or teacher wishes to establish), although it is not yet the exact behavior that is desired. Since there is always some variation in how a behavior is exhibited, the parent or teacher need only wait until an even closer approximation to the desired behavior occurs and then reward it. This procedure is quite useful, too, in helping the teen develop new behaviors or strengthen a desired behavior that exists in some immature form. The simplest example of this process involves the development of speech and language skills. As the child develops, he receives positive feedback on the accuracy of his speech, and over time, he thereby shows more accurate productions.

Parents and teachers will find it quite helpful to develop an awareness of what is *rewarding to* and what is *punishing for* the teen with ADHD. Even more specifically, it is a useful exercise to be able to subdivide these consequences as has been described earlier (the positive and negative rewards, and the two forms of punishment). Listing specific behaviors that are appropriate for *extinction* (i.e., removal) and those that are targeted for *shaping* (i.e., improvement) is also helpful. In some cases, these will be opposite or alternative behaviors; in other cases they may be totally unrelated. Since social rewards are part of structured behavioral programs as well as informal ones, a special exercise focuses on the use and development of social rewards. In some families and classrooms, few forms of social rewards are used. However, it is possible for both teachers and parents to learn, practice, and develop skills in using social praise.

USING THE A–B–C SEQUENCE IN BEHAVIOR PROGRAMS

If parents and teachers share a general background of basic principles of behavior, they will be in a better position to deal with behavior problems, even when faced with the so-called "difficult to manage behavior" of the teen with ADHD. The basic principles are as simple as A–B–C. Figure 6.1 outlines this sequence used in later discussions.

Figure 6.1
ANTECEDENTS–BEHAVIOR–CONSEQUENCES

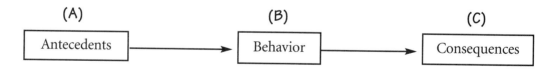

For appropriate and effective behavior management, it is essential to have a good understanding of these three components. Details of each of these three components will follow.

Here we note that some behavior may seem to occur capriciously without any apparent cue or trigger. Even in this instance, appropriate consequences are necessary. However, our focus now is to understand and develop skills that will bring specific behaviors under control of a specific stimulus (e.g., a verbal request). In this process you will have helped the teen develop a learned behavior. Ideally, the sequence might go like that shown in Figure 6.2.

Figure 6.2
STIMULUS–RESPONSE–STIMULUS

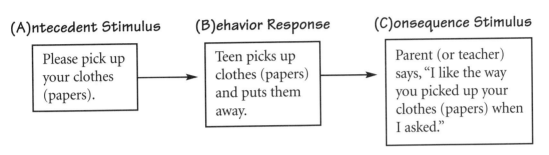

(A)ntecedent Stimulus	(B)ehavior Response	(C)onsequence Stimulus
Please pick up your clothes (papers).	Teen picks up clothes (papers) and puts them away.	Parent (or teacher) says, "I like the way you picked up your clothes (papers) when I asked."

The sequence may continue with the parent's or teacher's comment, which is a consequence, serving as a stimulus (A), triggering another behavioral response from the teen (teen feels good or happy, exhibits new behavior, a smile), which behavior has the consequence (C) of being a stimulus for the parent or teacher, who also responds (B) with a good feeling and a smile. Even without a technical analysis of this sequence, one can quickly see that more occurs than just a *learned response* to the request. The teen and parent experience good feelings from the interaction. This is in marked contrast to a sequence where the teen experiences pain, and the parent or teacher feels anger and frustration over the teen's failure to comply. Using the basic behavioral principles in the A–B–C format can lead to enhancement of the parent–teen or teacher–teen interactions, and, over time, to a more positive emotional bond between the parent and teen, or an enhanced relationship between teacher and teen.

ANTECEDENTS

THE FIRST THING THAT MAY NEED TO CHANGE

In the world of computers the acronym GIGO stands for "Garbage In—Garbage Out." It is quite relevant here to emphasize that if the wrong information is processed, the output may not make sense. Communications, rules, and expectations—and the manner in which these are presented to teenagers—may make the difference between compliance and noncompliance. This discussion of antecedents thus focuses on the basic structure of the family or within a classroom. It provides the foundation on which behaviors result. If requests, directions, rules, and expectations are not clearly specified, the teen's ability to respond appropriately is compromised. Granted that communicating with the adolescent is different from with younger children, but clarity of communication is essential at all ages.

WRITING RULES AND DEVELOPING EXPECTATIONS

Rules are everywhere. Driving a car, working, or even playing games would be difficult without rules. In families, rules are seldom explicitly stated or written down. Most often, rules are implied and seem to be discussed and stated primarily following the occurrence of some misbehavior. With ADHD teens who respond on impulse, it may sometimes make little difference even if the rule could be cited. Also, rules often imply what the teen *should not do* rather than what he or she *should do*.

The following is a list of situations where rule-governed behavior is typically found:

Awakening	Visiting
Talking	Dressing
Bedtime	Watching TV
Being home on time	Driving the car
Eating	Homework
Chores	Expressing anger
Greeting others	Dinner time

Try your hand at writing rules for some or all of the situations listed above for your teen.

Exercise 6-1. WRITING RULES

1. _____
2. _____
3. _____
4. _____
5. _____
6. _____
7. _____
8. _____
9. _____
10. _____
11. _____
12. _____
13. _____
14. _____

After you have written your rules, check them against the following examples.

Exercise 6-1. EXAMPLES FOR WRITING RULES

1. Remain at the table while *eating.*

2. Wait turn to *talk;* don't interrupt.

3. When driving the *car,* have seat belt on at all times.

4. Keep feet on floor and off furniture while *watching TV.*

5. Keep hands to self when *angry.*

6. *Greet* others by saying "Hello" or "Good morning."

7. First do *homework,* then go out.

8. *Bedtime* is 10:00 P.M.—no exceptions!

9. Be *awake* at 6:30 A.M.; *dressed* by 7:00 A.M.

10. When *visiting* always say "Please," "Yes, sir," and "No, thank you."

11. *Be home* by 5:00 P.M. for dinner.

12. Do all *chores* on list each week.

Notice that all rules are clearly written and are specific as to what the parent wishes. Several of these rules might apply equally well to the classroom (e.g., #5 and #12). Others may be specified for the classroom only (e.g., "Raise your hand to ask permission to go to the bathroom," or "Remain quiet and listen carefully when the teacher is talking").

Many rules could serve as the first statement in a *when–then* sequence. For example: "*When* you do all chores on your list for the week, *then* you may have weekend privileges" (that is, assuming there is no significant intervening punishment).

Note that not all of the preceding situations may be used. Some of these situations may be more appropriately discussed in terms of expectations for the teen.

In some situations, the parent or teacher may simply describe the desired behaviors. Somewhat different from rules, expectations may involve several components that describe a series of behaviors expected from the teen. Expectations may vary with the age of the teen as well as with the teen's ability to comprehend and retain what is said. A teacher might review expectations prior to entering a special event (e.g., a field trip). It is best to simplify these expectations and limit each to no more than three components.

Now write down some (at least three) sequences of events that involve some of your expectations for your teen in Exercise 6-2. Remember, keep these simple, concise, and straightforward. See the examples for developing expectations below for some ideas.

Exercise 6-2. DEVELOPING EXPECTATIONS

1. _____

2. _____

3. _____

Exercise 6-2. EXAMPLES FOR DEVELOPING EXPECTATIONS

1. In class I will expect you to listen to directions, follow them carefully, and complete your assignments.

2. When away from home I will expect you to treat other people and their property with respect.

3. When your cousin Bubba comes to visit I will expect you to keep your hands to yourself and control your temper.

These expectations may stand alone or be tied to consequences. In the preliminary stages of behavior management, these general expectations may be used to "test" the teen for degrees of compliance.

Rules and expectations provide important parts of the basic structure for behavior. Negotiable and nonnegotiable rules were discussed in Chapter 4. The next important step is to communicate this information about rules and expectations to the teen. If the teen doesn't get the right message, he or she can't make an appropriate response. Parents and teachers must not assume the teen knows better. This is especially the case with teenagers who have ADHD. It is often discovered that the "message sent" is not necessarily the "message received." Teachers, parents, and professionals must therefore focus on developing good communication skills.

DEVELOPING COMMUNICATION SKILLS

Getting the correct information to the teen may be the most critical part of the entire behavioral sequence. As many teens with ADHD are distractible and hear only parts of communications, it is most important to check out whether the teen has gotten the entire message.

Some of the basic steps in the communication process are:

1. **Get eye contact.** Give your message facing the teen or child at any age.

2. **Speak clearly and distinctly in a normal tone of voice.** You don't have to shout or give instructions like a drill sergeant. Most teens with ADHD are, in fact, quite sensitive in their hearing.

3. **Present your instruction or request in a simple, concise manner, emphasizing what you want the teen "to do."** For example, "Please pick up your clothes and put them in the dirty clothes hamper." Avoid giving negative commands (i.e., what you don't want).

4. **Verify that the teen has heard what you said by simply asking him or her to repeat what you said.** If the teen repeats it correctly, you have an opportunity to reinforce the correct perception of your words by saying, "That's exactly right. You got it. Now do it." If the teen has trouble repeating your words, give him or her the correct words and ask again for him or her to repeat them. If the teen still has trouble, it may be that this teen really has a hearing problem, the adolescent is engaging in passive–aggressive strategies, or the commands are too complex. Then you will need to simplify instructions or break them down into simpler components. Now we will focus on what a teacher or parent may actually say—the content of the message.

Exercise 6-3. DEVELOPING COMMUNICATION SKILLS

In this exercise, write down some of the commands, directions, requests, and instructions you use in communicating with ADHD teens. Please limit your responses to ten items.

1. _____
2. _____
3. _____
4. _____
5. _____
6. _____
7. _____
8. _____
9. _____
10. _____

Now review some of the following examples to compare with your communications. It sometimes takes a review of statements made orally—but now in written form—to determine how clear, concise, and positive the statements sound and how they might be perceived by the teen. Are these clear to others? Ask yourself: Would they know exactly what to do after hearing these communications?

Exercise 6-3. EXAMPLES FOR DEVELOPING COMMUNICATION SKILLS

1. Please put your dirty clothes in the clothes hamper.

2. Empty all of the trash cans and put the garbage out.

3. Take your math book out and turn to page 17.

4. This is important; be sure to write this in your notebook.

5. When you go to the store, would you fill the car with gas?

6. Okay students, clear off all books on your desk and put them in your bag.

LEARNING ABOUT COMMUNICATION STYLES

Dr. Harvey C. Parker, in *The ADD Hyperactivity Workbook,* has discussed three types of communication styles:

1. Passive

2. Aggressive

3. Assertive

Problems may be encountered in using the first two styles. The third alternative appears to work best for parents and teachers. Dr. Parker's discussion of these styles of communication is right on target and are summarized here in a modified form.

Passive Communication—Parents who use passive forms of communication typically have teens who are manipulative and controlling. Such parents have difficulty stating rules and enforcing them. Recognizing that the teen is in control, a typical communication might sound like, "Mary, it's your bedtime—do you want to go to bed now?" Of course, the parent hopes the teen will say yes. If not, the parent might say, "Well, it's late but you can play one more computer game—then it's time for bed." This process may continue either until the teen does get tired or until the parent becomes angry. If the latter should happen, the teen knows exactly what to say: "Dad, you're mean—you just aren't fair." This statement may certainly "push a critical button" and may result in some guilt (i.e., maybe I really am mean), or self-doubt (i.e., maybe I am too harsh—maybe she should be allowed to stay up later). Future communications may thus be less authoritative, more evasive, and less believable. Of course, during the later teenage years, parents will generally move towards a less autocratic or domineering position with the teen.

Some examples of passive communication include:

1. "Don't you think it's time to get ready for school?"

2. "How many times do I have to tell you to clean up your desk?"

3. "Don't you think you ought to be doing your work now?"

Very often these passive communications are given in the form of a question with the decision resting upon the teen. When one hears a communication like, "Young man, don't you think you should take your feet off that coffee table?", one expects to hear the teen say, "No! I'm not ready to do that."

Aggressive Communication—Parents who use this form of communication may be manipulative and controlling of others. They tend to be exceedingly strict and may use threats, severe punishment, derogatory names, or any other technique to exert their power and control. Any resistance to their rules and regulations would be quite threatening and would typically be met with even greater force. Such forms of communication have typically been associated with severe physical punishment in the past.

The association of physical punishment with these communications will result in "temporary control" or control only in the presence of that person or only until the teen is big enough to retaliate. Humiliating comments, name calling, or belittling may be made without regard for the teen's feelings. While compliance may result in the short-term, in the long-term accumulated suppressed anger in the teen may be expressed in a violent manner at some time in the future, often quite unexpectedly.

Some examples of aggressive communication include:

1. "You're lazy and no good—you're no son of mine!"

2. "You crack head—can't you think any better than that?"

3. "You never listen—do you know how to do that job I gave you?" (stupid is implied)

Very often these communications are like "verbal darts." One can just imagine how the teen might feel being on the receiving end of one of these communications. These communications are not limited to the home. Very often a teacher will create much embarrassment with questions such as, "John, did you forget to take your medicine again?" (stupid is implied) Another teacher called a teen "air head" since he couldn't possibly have any brains; if he did, he would know his place in reading. These comments or communications do little in terms of constructive feedback, and just simply devastate a teen's already weak self-concept. While the teen remains a victim, the aggressive communicator remains in control and "one up."

Assertive Communication—Parents who use this assertive form of communication are secure in their beliefs and can express their ideas, needs, and wishes in a clear and direct manner that is respectful of others' rights and feelings. These parents provide needed structure for their families by being explicit and fair in rules and expectations for their teenagers. They are also capable of enforcing these rules and standards in a way that allows the teen to think and act independently and to be responsible for his or her behavior. The parent is clearly in charge and assumes a leadership role in the family, modeling appropriate parental behavior for the teen.

Some examples of assertive communication include:

1. "When you finish your chores you can _____."

2. "Name calling is against the rules. Stop it or get your consequence!"

3. "Stop arguing immediately or (specify consequence) _____."

In these examples, the parent is quite clear about consequences. Also, the responsibility for change is placed upon the teen. In a similar manner, teachers may use the assertive form of communication. For example, providing a signal to a student who must then decide to (a) stop a behavior, or (b) accept the consequence (prearranged). Should the teen (self) control his behavior, he may be rewarded by the teacher who reinforces behavior change *and* maintains control in the classroom.

Now that you, the parent and teacher, have some familiarity with the assertive style, you may go back and rewrite some of your typical communications in this format.

Exercise 6-4. WRITING COMMANDS IN THE ASSERTIVE STYLE

1. _____
2. _____
3. _____
4. _____
5. _____
6. _____
7. _____
8. _____
9. _____
10. _____

Some of the typical characteristics that distinguish the assertive style, illustrated by Dr. Parker, are adapted as follows:

1. Say what you mean and mean what you say.

2. Give commands politely, yet firmly.

3. Make eye contact with the teen before a command is issued.

4. Follow through on your command with immediate supervision.

5. Don't ask the teen to follow a command. Remind the teen that the command *must* be followed. However, as the adolescent gets older, fewer directives are given. In

short, there are only a few directives that "must" be followed, as the teen develops greater independence.

6. If the young teen tries to talk you out of a command, stick to your guns.

These guidelines would apply to the nonnegotiable type of rules where the parent must retain authority. However, in some cases involving noncritical rules or expectations, it is more desirable for the teen to have input into decisions and to be able to resist following blindly authoritative commands.

Once you are able to communicate *clearly, concisely,* and *convincingly* (the three Cs) using the assertive style, move to the next step—determining which compliance problems may remain. In short, once you become more effective in communicating, some problem behaviors may literally "disappear." Essentially, these problems were probably related to ineffective communications.

METACOMMUNICATIONS

The term *metacommunication* refers to a communication about a communication—a higher level of communication that makes the original communication more complex. It may result in confusion on the part of the listener if conflicting messages are being sent. For example, when talking with a parent while his teen is present, the teacher or counselor may ask the parent to deliver a command to the teen. Even when the parent uses the appropriate content n the command, for example, "Please keep your feet on the floor," the manner or emotional tone in which the message is delivered will make a difference in how the message is perceived.

This same message may be delivered while the parent is smiling (nonverbal metacommunication) or it may be delivered in a very soft voice. Either metacommunication may imply that the parent is not serious or perhaps is weak and ineffectual. With these perceptions, the teen may ignore the message even though the content is appropriate.

On the other hand, extreme forms of metacommunication should be avoided (e.g., loud, booming voice and stern, threatening facial expressions). If the parent or teacher is to be effective with commands that have an assertive content, he or she must also present that content with an assertive style. The parent or teacher can practice some of the assertive commands by recording them and then replaying the tape for feedback on how he or she sounds.

BEHAVIOR

Behavior, at any age, falls into two basic categories: (1) desirable (appropriate), and (2) undesirable (inappropriate). The goal of any behavioral program would be to increase the former and decrease the latter.

It would still be appropriate to make a list of behaviors that fall into these two categories. First, make a list of all the desirable behaviors you would like your teen to show. Some of these may be behaviors that are occasionally exhibited; others may not yet exist.

List up to 12 of these in Exercise 6-5. Now, list up to 10 undesirable behaviors in the left-side column of Exercise 6-6. There is an alternative (appropriate) behavior for each undesirable behavior you may list either in the home or school setting. For those wishing to obtain greater detail on this form of behavior analysis, consult the *ADD/ADHD Behavior-Change Resource Kit* (Flick, 1998). These alternative behaviors will be quite important as parents and teachers need to focus far more positive attention on the teen's behavior. Any appropriate behavior will suffice. At the end of these exercises, the parent or teacher will have two basic lists: (1) all of the teen's undesirable behaviors and (2) all of the desirable behaviors that can be increased, some of the latter being opposite and incompatible with the undesirable behavior, and others simply being those appropriate behaviors that need to be established or improved. Now we'll first consider some of the possible consequences before turning to some direct behavior interventions.

Exercise 6-5. LIST DESIRABLE BEHAVIOR

Desirable Behaviors	
1.	7.
2.	8.
3.	9.
4.	10.
5.	11.
6.	12.

Exercise 6-6. ALTERNATE BEHAVIOR LIST

No.	Undesirable Behavior	Alternate (Desirable) Behavior
1.		
2.		
3.		
4.		
5.		
6.		
7.		
8.		
9.		
10.		

CONSEQUENCES

Consequences refer to whatever follows a particular behavior. These are the rewards and punishment for desirable and undesirable behaviors, respectively. Parents and teachers may have a fairly good idea about what their teens like to have either at home or in school. There may be some universal rewards—such as money or no assigned homework—but to obtain the best and most accurate information, the adolescent should be consulted. There is much evidence to suggest that when the adolescent participates in decisions about the behavioral program, its effectiveness is enhanced. Try your hand now to list some of the identified teen's likes and dislikes. Complete Exercise 6-7 on your teen's likes and dislikes.

Exercise 6-7. TEEN'S LIKES AND DISLIKES

Likes	Dislikes

Exercise 6-7. EXAMPLES OF TEEN'S LIKES AND DISLIKES

Likes	Dislikes
Playing Nintendo™	Cleaning room
Fishing on weekends	Taking out trash
Rock concerts	Written assignments
Use of car	9 P.M. curfew
Telephone	Visiting Aunt Martha
Money	Family picnics
Fashion clothes	Driving Mom to store

Behavioral interventions

Based on the list of desirable, undesirable, and alternative behaviors for the teen, a number of behavioral interventions may be employed to increase the strength and frequency of occurrences for desirable behaviors and to weaken or decrease the frequency of occurrence of undesirable behaviors. The simplest interventions will be discussed first, followed by more complex ones.

Positive Rewards

When we pay attention to a desirable (appropriate) behavior, it will become stronger and more frequent in occurrence. When a parent or teacher praises a behavior, the social praise (i.e., "I really like the nice work you did on your science project.") and the positive attention feel good. Although occasional tangible rewards are helpful, the bulk of rewards for adolescents will take the form of either social praise (i.e., good comments, pats on the back, your undivided attention, etc.) or privileges (i.e., giving permission for the teen to do something that you still control). Since social rewards can be given any time and any place, they are a good source to create good feelings and to enhance self-esteem. Parents and teachers should give these liberally whenever possible—look for any desirable behavior as often as you can.

Ignoring Some Behaviors

For some undesirable behaviors it may be best to ignore them. One cannot attempt to deal with all ADHD behaviors; parents and teachers must pick and choose the ones that are most important. Is it really important that the teen not slouch in his chair in class or that he forgets to put his shoes neatly away in the closet? Most would say probably not. Attending to a behavior reinforces it and makes it stronger; ignoring a behavior is mildly punishing and weakens that behavior (i.e., contributes to its extinction).

You may wish to now make a list of behaviors that could be ignored. Refer to Exercise 6-8. From this list select one or two that you could ignore. Once you decide to ignore these behaviors, you must do so completely. Some experts call this *Active Ignoring* because the parent or teacher must actively be involved with something (e.g., reading a newspaper or book) to ensure that he or she doesn't attend to the behavior. Expect that behavior to increase in frequency and intensity since the teen will experience frustration over the withdrawal of attention. It may be essential for the parent or teacher to use a kind of self-talk procedure to remind themselves that the annoying behavior that is being ignored will become more annoying.

Ignoring must be complete until the behavior in question is extinguished, or the annoying behavior will be reinforced at a more intense level. In addition, if the parent or teacher "gives in" and pays attention to the behavior at the more intense level, the teen will be reinforced for being persistent and holding out until attention is delivered.

Exercise 6-8. **LISTING THOSE BEHAVIORS TO BE IGNORED**

Behaviors to Be Ignored (Extinction Process)	
1.	11.
2.	12.
3.	13.
4.	14.
5.	15.
6.	16.
7.	17.
8.	18.
9.	19.
10.	20.

Exercise 6-8. **SAMPLE BEHAVIORS TO BE IGNORED**

Behaviors to Be Ignored (Extinction Process)	
This following sample list is provided for you to use as a guideline. Ignoring does not imply avoiding dealing with the behavior. It is, instead, a viable technique to weaken and remove these behaviors.	
1. Complaining	8. Swearing (for reaction)
2. Loud talking	9. Inappropriate noises
3. Repetitive demands	10. Repetitive questions
4. Repetitive requests	11. Clowning
5. Burping	12. Inappropriate eating (occasional noise)
6. Passing gas	13. Rolling eyes (when punished)
7. Screaming	14. Begging

This tendency may then be generalized to other annoying behaviors in different situations, thus establishing a pattern for the development and maintenance of additional annoying behaviors. At the adolescent-age level, there may be several of these behaviors that are well-established. Compare your list of behaviors to be ignored with some of the sample behaviors that the parent or teacher would best ignore. Be sure to prepare for general exacerbation of the intensity of some of these annoying behaviors—especially those that are well-established.

INSTRUMENTAL BEHAVIOR PLANS

When a behavior leads to some reward, it is termed an *instrumental behavior.* This is a variation on the old "grandma's rule" theme, "first you eat your supper, then you get your dessert." It is also a variant of the behavior contract to be discussed later. Another description is that the teacher or parent may present the teen with a "when–then plan." Examples are numerous: "When you finish your homework, then you can have phone privileges," or "When you complete your chores, then you are free to go out." It is important to never reverse this plan, i.e., never say, "Yes, you can go out, but you have to promise to do your chores." It is also important to have fair expectations about what is to be done in return for privileges. Behavior contracts are just a bit more formal specifications, put in writing, and will be discussed next.

WRITING A BEHAVIOR CONTRACT

A behavioral contract (see Figures 6.3 and 6.4) is a written agreement between the parent or teacher and the teen, wherein the parent or teacher agrees to give to the teen something that is desired after fulfilling some specified expectation of the parent or teacher. While writing such a contract sounds simple enough, be sure to determine carefully whether the teen is capable of meeting the expectation *and* whether the consequence (i.e., reward) is appropriate for that accomplishment.

Figure 6.3
BEHAVIORAL CONTRACT

I, _____ , agree to _____

_____

(perform some task expected by parent/teacher). This is to be completed by (date)

_____*. In return, I would like _____

(some wished-for reward). I therefore agree to the contract specified above.

_____   _____
      Parent/Teacher Signature   *Child's Signature*

*If no deadline is set for completion of the contract, put NA (Not Applicable).

Figure 6.4
SAMPLE COMPLEX BEHAVIOR CONTRACT

I, _____, agree to do the following:
(Student's Name)

1. Complete written assignments with 80% accuracy or better.
2. Remain quiet and keep my hands to myself when at lunch.
3. Write the assignment for homework for each period.
4. Have homework completed.

Each day that I do the above things, I may choose one of the following:

1. Use the class computer for 20 minutes.
2. Choose the next available class job (e.g., errand) the next day.
3. Twenty (20) minutes free time at the end of the day.

Completion of one week of the above daily list will earn one of the following:

a) one hour extra use of car on weekend
b) renting a selected movie
c) release from one weekend chore (i.e., folding clothes)

I agree to fulfill this contract.

Signed:

_____   _____
Student Signature   *Teacher Signature*

_____   _____
Parent Signature   *Date*

This contract is in effect as of _____. It will expire on _____.

At the end of this contract, a "new contract" may be written.

Generally, behavioral contracts are most appropriate for older children and adolescents (ages 10 to 15), yet such agreements may be used with some brighter younger children, even as young as 8 years of age. Since many teens with ADHD are immature, they may be used with even older adolescents. While these contracts may be somewhat tricky to develop, they can serve as a good motivation for the teen to accomplish short-term goals. The word "tricky" is emphasized because we may expect too much or perhaps have a payoff that is insufficient to maintain goal-oriented behavior. For example, it is not uncommon for parents to offer something significant (e.g., color TV) in return for all A's on the next report card. While this may seem very attractive to the teenager at first, over a period of time this reward may seem quite distant and perhaps even impossible to achieve. Because the expectation (all A's) may be too great or too distant in the future, motivation will eventually be diminished. This type of motivational approach is insufficient to maintain adequate work effort until the goal is achieved.

In the typical behavioral contract, our expectation may involve either academic behavior (e.g., completing homework) or some other behaviors (e.g., remaining quiet in class)—more realistic and attainable short-term behavioral goals, and readily realized goals. You are now encouraged to write some examples of behavioral contracts and to compare these with the examples provided. It should be noted here that there is no punishment or negative teacher or parent feedback to the teen if the teen does not uphold his or her part of the contract; the reward is simply not realized. It is imperative that the parent or teacher fulfills his or her part of the contract as agreed.

WRITING A BEHAVIOR PENALTY PLAN

Behavior penalty or response cost involves taking a privilege away from the teen for a short period of time. There are some advantages to the use of behavior penalty. Outside the home, time-out and other procedures may be more difficult to employ and some may be developmentally age-inappropriate. A behavior penalty does not require a special place; it can be administered anywhere, anytime. Misbehavior while riding in a car, in a shopping mall, or while visiting a friend can easily be dealt with using a behavior penalty.

The following are general guidelines for the use of a behavior penalty:

1. Make a list of those behaviors that may be difficult to deal with using other techniques (maximum of three). See Exercise 6.9 on page 212. List some of the teen's major misbehaviors.

2. Talk with your teen about which behavior will result in a behavior penalty. Select three of the major misbehaviors (A, B, and C).

3. Make a list of privileges that can be taken away for a behavior penalty. List all privileges in Exercise 6-9 (right-hand column). Pick three to be associated with the three major misbehaviors.

4. Remember to review with the teen the consequences for one of these misbehaviors, as well as to note the consequences for appropriate behavior. If misbehavior has occurred while riding in the car in the past, the teen is informed which privilege will be lost should the misbehavior occur and what the reward will be should the teen show alternative appropriate behavior instead. Refer to Exercise 6-10, an Alternate Behavior Plan. List alternate behaviors for each of the three major misbehaviors. Next to each alternate (i.e., opposite desirable behavior) list a positive consequence (i.e., reward). Be sure to discuss which consequence may be effective with the teen. Input from the adolescent will help to make the procedure effective. This technique, called "priming," will increase the effectiveness of the consequences and provide some cognitive link of past consequences to behavioral control at present. There will be some internalization of what consequences will follow either misbehavior or appropriate behavior. It is also assumed that, given a choice, the teen would prefer the positive consequence (reward) for appropriate behavior.

5. It is wise to give the teen some predetermined signal (preferably nonverbal) to serve as a warning and to allow him or her to develop self-control, which may subsequently be rewarded. One signal might be to hold up two fingers for the teenager to see. This will serve as a signal to decide either: (1) to change the current misbehavior or (2) to accept the consequences. All of this is reviewed prior to being in these situations, and you can even have a rehearsal of the procedure.

6. Once the signal is given, say, "__name__, look here" (while holding up two fingers) and give the teen a few seconds to respond. It will be far better for the teen to develop and gain control over his or her behavior.

7. If control is achieved, you may say, "John, I'm very proud of the decision you made to stop teasing (annoying, hitting, or anything else) your sister. I like the way you are now sitting quietly with her, keeping your hands to yourself." If you have set up a point system (as in the next section), then points may be given. The teen should, however, be reminded that you will be pleased to see good behavior continue.

8. Be consistent and follow through with the procedure. If you don't, the teen will see that you often say things you don't mean.

Exercise 6-9.   **BEHAVIOR PENALTY PLAN**

Major Misbehaviors*	Privileges to Remove
1.	1.
2.	2.
3.	3.
4.	4.
5.	5.
6.	6.
Three Major Misbehaviors	**Associated Loss Privilege**
A.	
B.	
C.	

*Significant misbehaviors that may be difficult to deal with using other procedures.

Exercise 6-10.   **ALTERNATE BEHAVIOR PLAN**

	Misbehavior	Alternate	Positive Consequence
A			
B			
C			

DEVELOPING AN EFFECTIVE GROUNDING PROCEDURE

Grounding has almost universal stature in discipline, especially among teens, even though its effectiveness is often questionable. There are so many complications surrounding this procedure that it often does not work. One common problem is that when the teen is grounded, so, too, is the parent who must supervise him or her. The parent may wish to terminate the grounding and let the teen go; this is often done capriciously and does not follow any appropriate behavior. If there is some reason to terminate, be sure the teen performs some task or chore prior to termination.

A second problem is that often the teen may be restricted to the home but have privileges intact (e.g., stereo, TV, Nintendo™). If so, the situation is not that unpleasant. Third, grounding is often far too severe. As with any punishment, the best way is to use limited time. If too lengthy, the teen may develop a hopeless feeling about regaining privileges, and this may simply lead to additional misbehavior, which in turn leads to additional grounding. The vicious cycle almost never ends and neither does the misbehavior.

If a teen is to be grounded, use a short-term plan. In addition, don't allow him or her to just hang around the house. Select three extra chores for the teen to perform; when they are completed, the grounding may end (assuming no other misbehavior has occurred). When appropriate behavior appears, the termination of grounding will serve to reinforce that appropriate behavior. The purpose of the grounding is not just to weaken the undesirable behavior but to facilitate the development and maintenance of alternative desirable behavior. During the period of grounding, there should be no privileges (TV, telephone, etc.) allowed.

PRACTICING APPROPRIATE BEHAVIOR HABITS

One assumption often made when misbehavior occurs is that the "teen simply doesn't know better." Thus, if the teen slams a door closed when entering a room, a parent or teacher may assume that the teen doesn't know how to close the door. Although this is a very simple concept, it is really quite complex. For example, you may first ask the teen, "Would you show me the appropriate way to close the door?" If the teen does it correctly, say, "Yes, that's exactly right, but apparently you need a bit more practice doing this so that it will be automatic." Then the teen is asked to go out and come in again, closing the door appropriately each time for a few practice trials. This is called "positive practice." If the teen does not initially demonstrate that he or she knows how to close the door (baiting you), you then model this for the teen saying, "Let me show you the proper way to close the door." No lecture, no emotional outburst. Following the demonstration, go through the practice steps, having the teen close the door appropriately three times. If during one of those trials the teen slams the door, then three more additional practice trials are added.

On some occasions, a teen's misbehavior may be disrespectful to you. In this case, he or she might go through the "positive practice" phase and then have to provide "restitution" to you for speaking in a disrespectful manner. Restitution may involve having the teen perform an added chore. This general procedure has been termed *overcorrection with positive practice and restitution*. If the teen requests something in a disrespectful manner, then following the overcorrection procedure, he or she is allowed to ask for the requested item or favor in an appropriate manner. At this time, say, "Yes, that is the appropriate way to ask. You may have . . ." This overall procedure may best be used with young adolescents. It would also be appropriate to use this procedure privately with the teen, *not* in front of a class. It is therefore best used with young adolescents in the home situation.

POINT SYSTEMS

A behavioral system involving points is a kind of *token economy,* which sets specific behavioral goals to be met using well-defined rewards (points), and punishments (fines or loss of points). It is fairly objective, does not require a great deal of decision making for parent or teacher (once set up appropriately), and presents well-defined guidelines for the teen who may previously have thought it impossible to get rewards and privileges on a consistent basis.

Many teenagers, both normal and those with ADHD, have worked unsuccessfully with these programs—particularly in school—and often become frustrated and angry or depressed when the teen never reaches the desired goal. This can happen when ADHD children and teens are placed in competition with non-ADHD children and teens in the classroom. Clearly, the teen with ADHD is unlikely to reach the criteria set for most non-ADHD teenagers.

Point systems are excellent balanced behavioral programs, as they focus on both reward and punishment. It is also possible to deal with several behaviors (appropriate and inappropriate) at the same time, but don't attempt to deal with too many behaviors at once. If you do, the system becomes too complex and, with frustration for both you and the teen, the program is often dropped.

A point system provides the teen with valuable experience that will be important later in life, for example, a checking account. This system also provides the teen with opportunities to plan ahead (i.e., to determine how many points are needed for an array of privileges) and to make decisions (i.e., with only so many available points, the teen may have to choose which privileges are to be selected). Of course, these experiences provide an excellent introduction to events in adult life where similar decisions must be made at different levels. The point behavioral system may therefore provide a wide range of experiences that have an affect on the teen's life as an adult.

LISTING BEHAVIORS FOR REWARDS AND FINES

Basic to all point systems with older children and teenagers are the following:

1. Listing the behaviors we wish to see more often—to earn rewards.

2. Listing behaviors we wish to see less often—to receive punishments (fines).

3. Listing the privileges and fines—the source of motivation for the program.

Exercise 6-11 helps you begin the process. This exercise provides you with a list of behaviors that you may use in setting up a program.

Exercise 6-11. LISTING BEHAVIORS FOR POINT SYSTEMS

Desirable and Appropriate (1A) Behavior	Undesirable and Inappropriate (1B) Behavior
1.	1.
2.	2.
3.	3.

Following selection of appropriate and inappropriate behaviors, the next step is to set the reward value (points) so the teen knows what the payoff will be for exhibiting those appropriate behaviors and what punishment, or fine, will be encountered should he or she exhibit the inappropriate behavior. See the sample listing of behaviors.

Exercise 6-11. SAMPLE LISTING OF BEHAVIORS

Desirable and Appropriate (1A) Behavior	Undesirable and Inappropriate (1B) Behavior
1. Complies with requests	1. Noncompliance
2. Greets others	2. Ignores others
3. Completes chores	3. Leaves before completing chores
4. Dresses for school at 7:45 A.M.	4. Remains in bed after alarm
5. Puts dirty clothes in hamper	5. Throws dirty clothes on floor
6. Home by 6:00 P.M. for supper	6. Late for supper
7. Makes bed	7. Leaves before making bed

Privileges are the tangible rewards, social interactions, and specific activities that the teen finds enjoyable and that serve to reinforce the behavior that allowed for them. Privileges are the known reinforcers that provide an incentive or motivation to perform behaviors that may seem difficult or even unpleasant. You probably have a pretty good idea of what is reinforcing for a teen, as he/she will typically engage in that activity whenever possible.

By completing these lists, you focus on all behaviors that need to change—either to develop and strengthen the appropriate ones or to weaken and remove the inappropriate ones. While this example is of behaviors at home, a similar list can be made of school behaviors. By making these lists, you can organize your thinking about these two categories of behavior and make it easier to select those behaviors to be included in the more formal behavioral programs.

SAMPLE SELECTING PRIVILEGES

Privilege	Unit of Time/Money	Points
1. Playing Nintendo™	Per ½ hour	4
2. Fishing trip	Day trip	15
3. Skating trip	Per trip	15
4. Eating at pizza restaurant	Per trip	20
5. New fishing lure	Max $5.00	15
6. Renting movie	About $3.00	10

In addition to listing the privileges, you must also describe the unit of time or how much money may be involved in that privilege. This unit of time or money will also be important in determining the points required for that thing. Teachers can compile a similar list appropriate to the school setting.

For extended events and for those things that cost money, we can roughly estimate the number of points required for that thing. Thus, "eating at pizza restaurant" is estimated to be 20 points. One must take into consideration how important is the privilege, and how often the teen would like to have that privilege.

Throughout all of these behavioral programs where points or tokens are used, it will be essential to keep the points assigned to behaviors, fines, and privileges as low as possible to make it easier for the parent to run the program. It is also important to remember that these points assigned to privileges are only our initial estimates. It will be important to determine how many points the teen is generally able to earn and then to make sure that some of the privileges are able to be obtained. The points assigned to behaviors, fines, and privileges can be revised once we know what the teen can earn. It should also be remembered that some privileges are daily while others are weekend (e.g., fishing trip). It is most critical that the teen be able to earn the daily ones. Keep in mind that the primary criterion for any behavioral program is that it be successful. Nothing is gained from making it too difficult for the teen.

As DuPaul and others have noted, it is important to use reinforcers that are viewed as "necessities" by the teen (e.g., TV, playing video games, renting a movie), rather than reliance on "luxury" items that he or she could live without (e.g., eating lobster at a fine restaurant). Carr (1981) has some suggestions regarding identification of significant reinforcers.

1. Observe the effects of the reinforcer on the teen. Something may be reinforcing if:
   - the teen asks for that reinforcer again;
   - the teen seems happy during the time he or she has the reinforcer;
   - the teen seems unhappy when the reinforcer ends; and
   - the teen is willing to work to earn that reinforcer.

2. One may note the teen's choice on various inquiries regarding reinforcers. Again, a reminder to discuss with your teen which privileges should be listed.

PLANNING POINT SYSTEMS FOR ADOLESCENTS

Programs may be modified according to the teen's chronological age or mental age. Variations in the point systems will be discussed here.

Points—A point system may be used with children ages 6 through 12 years, and can be modified for teenagers. Again, keep in mind that these are simply rough guidelines. Some very effective programs have been conducted with immature adolescents. Children 9 to 12 years of age and beyond may work with both appropriate and inappropriate behaviors.

If the child is older (9–12 years of age and up), let's take a look at a behavioral program for that age level. The form used for the home/school behavior program is found in Figure 6.5. The major difference between this chart and ones for younger children will be that of adding inappropriate behaviors to the lists; they will receive fines. Also, you may be able to work with a few additional behaviors; however, start with a fairly simple program, especially if you are a novice at setting up and managing such programs. Other behaviors can always be added, still within limits.

On the Home/School Behavior Chart, notice that there are several places to put appropriate behaviors for development, but only a few spaces for the inappropriate behaviors that will be fined. The reason is simple; you want to avoid emphasizing the negative, the inappropriate, the undesirable behavior. Unless you do, a teen may be burdened with so many fines that a negative balance of points is obtained; this would be very discouraging and should never be allowed to happen.

A negative point balance might occur due to carelessness or other unusual circumstances, but this condition may result in a runaway system, where a teen may begin to feel hopeless, depressed, angry, and a failure. This may clearly affect his or her self-concept and self-esteem. This type of system is undoubtedly faulty in design; terminate such a program immediately. Note that many parents may not be able to set up and manage this type of behavioral point system; they will need direct supervision and guidance from an experienced behavior therapist.

Figure 6.5

HOME/SCHOOL BEHAVIOR CHART

Name _____ Age _____ Grade _____ Sex _____

Date started _____

POINT SYSTEM

Date								
Behavior	**Points**	**Mon**	**Tues**	**Wed**	**Thurs**	**Fri**	**Sat**	**Sun**
Bonus								
Total Points Earned								
Fines	**Points Lost**	**Mon**	**Tues**	**Wed**	**Thurs**	**Fri**	**Sat**	**Sun**
Total Points Lost								
Points Available to Use								
Privileges	**Points Used**	**Mon**	**Tues**	**Wed**	**Thurs**	**Fri**	**Sat**	**Sun**
Total Points Used								
NET POINTS								

Figure 6.5

SAMPLE HOME/SCHOOL BEHAVIOR CHART

Name ___M.G._____ Age __14___ Grade ___8___ Sex ___F____

Date started ____4/20_____

POINT SYSTEM

Date		4/20	4/21	4/22	4/23	4/24	4/25	4/26
Behavior	Points	Mon	Tues	Wed	Thurs	Fri	Sat	Sun
Brings note home	2	2	2	2	2	2		
Follows instructions	† V(0-6)	6	4	6	6	6		
Completes classwork	† V(0-6)	6	4	6	6	5		
Obeys class rules	† V(0-6)	6	4	6	6	4		
Gets along with peers	† V(0-6)	6	4	6	6	6		
Completes homework	10	10	10	10	10	–		
Bonus	2	111(6)	11(4)	11(4)	1(2)	1(2)	111(6)	111(6)
Total Points Earned		44	32	40	38	25	6	6
Fines	Points Lost	Mon	Tues	Wed	Thurs	Fri	Sat	Sun
Name calling	10							
Failure to complete HW	20							
Late for supper	6							
Total Points Lost								
Points Available to Use		44	32	40	38	25	6	6
Privileges	Points Used	Mon	Tues	Wed	Thurs	Fri	Sat	Sun
Skating trip	20					20		
Computer time (1/2 hr.)	6	11(12)			11(12)		111(18)	111(18)
Movie selected (rent)	20						20	20
Pizza	20		20					
Watching TV (1/2 hr.)	10		10	30		10		
Special treat	4					4		4
Total Points Used		12	30	30	12	34	38	42
NET POINTS		64	66	76	102	93	61	[25]*

*Savings in brackets   † (V = Variable)

SCHOOL NOTES

The use of a home–school note is an essential part of the Home/School Behavior Chart system. It is best to use a form that can report the results of several classes with regard to work performance and academic behavior over a period of one week. At times, it may be necessary to use a daily report system, but this may become cumbersome especially when the teen has several teachers.

A sample of the weekly report is shown in Figure 6.6; a sample of a daily report that could be used with adolescents is shown in Figure 6.7.

There are several important factors that should be considered when using the home–school note system with teens: (1) It is important to monitor/rate the appropriate (positive) behaviors that we want to establish, develop, and maintain. (2) It is essential that teachers rate the teen's academic performance and related academic behavior, as well as those appropriate (alternative) behaviors. (3) It is best to keep the number of behaviors small and manageable. (4) It is essential to involve the teen in the planning stage of this program. (5) Behavioral ratings should be the primary report; narrative comments should be kept to a minimum, and teachers should be encouraged to maintain a positive framework when making comments (i.e., it's best to say nothing if you can't say something positive). This last point is extremely important as teens with ADHD may have serious problems with self-image by the time they reach high school due to their long history of receiving negative comments. (6) It is critical that the goals or behavioral objectives be clearly specified in the behavior program (i.e., the criteria for success and what consequences will result). (7) All details must be clearly specified with regards to the procedure for handling the home–school note. Who will have it, where it will be filled out, what will happen if there is a substitute teacher, etc.

Once you have finished setting up your point system, refer to the completed program in the example depicted in Figure 6.5. Use the suggestions provided to modify your program where needed. Remember that the only criterion is that the teen be successful at the program.

You can indicate with slash marks how many times a behavior was observed or how many events of privileges were used. At the end of the day, or any time the teen wishes to use privileges, the point totals may be calculated. Points used are subtracted from points earned to give net points for that day. The teen starts each new day with *zero points.* However, the remaining *net* points from each day will carry over to the weekend (Saturday and Sunday) where the teen may have fewer opportunities to earn points. This will be especially true when many of these points are earned in school. Note that on Saturday the total points come from (a) points earned that day and (b) net points left over from each weekday. The teen will also need to develop the idea of saving some points on Saturday so that she will have points to use on Sunday; otherwise, the teen may repeatedly ask for something that could be completed for points.

Figure 6.6
WEEKLY SCHOOL NOTE

Name _____   Date _____

Dear Teacher:

Please rate this student in the areas below in the following scale: Excellent = 4, Good = 3, Fair = 2, Poor = 0 or NA (Not Applicable) for each day of the week, mornings or afternoons, IS = In-School Suspension, OS = Out-of-School Suspension.

Morning	MON	TUES	WED	THUR	FRI
Followed instructions					
Completed work					
Obeyed class rules					
Got along with peers					
(write in)					
(write in)					
Afternoon					
Followed instructions					
Completed work					
Obeyed class rules					
Got along with peers					
(write in)					
(write in)					
Time-outs					
Detentions					
Suspensions (IS/OS)					
Lunchroom behavior					
Recess behavior					

Positive Comments:

_____

_____

_____

_____

_____ Teacher's Initials _____

Figure 6.7

DAILY SCHOOL NOTE (MULTIPLE CLASSES)

Name _____   Date _____

Dear Teacher:

Please rate this student in each class period in the areas listed on the following scale: Excellent = 4, Good = 3, Fair = 2, Poor = 0 or NA (Not Applicable). Also indicate whether the class is in the morning or afternoon and initial at the bottom.

Note: IS = In-School Suspension; OS = Out-of-School Suspension

CLASS PERIODS

AREA	1	2	3	4	5	6	7
Followed instructions							
Completed work							
Obeyed class rules							
Got along with others							
(write in)							
(write in)							
A.M./P.M. Class							
Time-outs							
Detentions							
Suspensions (IS/OS)							
Teacher's initials							
Lunchroom behavior							
Recess behavior							

Positive Comments:

_____

_____

_____

_____

_____

_____

_____ Teacher's Initials _____

© 2000 by The Center for Applied Research in Education

Another possible way for the older child and teenager to earn extra points is the use of *bonus points,* awarded for *special good behaviors.* There will be sufficient incentives to motivate the child to earn more points. This may also carry over into future weeks of the program, as the teen may wish to have an abundance of points, especially on weekends. Any points left over at the end of the week will go into "savings." (See the bracketed points in the example, Exercise 6-5.)

The concept of savings must be taught and developed. At some point, you state, "Okay, you've worked hard for several weeks and you have *X* points in savings. I think it's time to use these points for something special." For example, a parent can then arrange for a special trip (e.g., a movie), a special event (e.g., renting a Nintendo™ game), or anything that the teen enjoys, within some reasonable limit.

The question of how long the program should run is often asked. There are no exact rules, but in general continue the program until there is at least 80% improvement—when an appropriate behavior is shown eight times in ten possible situations. Remember that perfection is not the goal. A program continues if other behaviors not originally addressed now seem more important, or when a new behavior must be targeted and included. When it is time to stop a program, have a kind of "graduation party." This will emphasize again how well the teen has done. Although the formal program may be stopped, continuing feedback on the teen's behavior must be provided in the form of praise. Providing verbal praise and maybe pats on the back will be crucial in allowing for a continuation of improvement.

In this system, you are reinforcing several appropriate behaviors and punishing (i.e., fining) a few inappropriate behaviors. It is always important to list more appropriate behaviors than inappropriate ones. For several of the behaviors, there is an inappropriate behavior and its opposite, alternative appropriate behavior. This will provide a very powerful program to get some of the inappropriate behaviors under control fairly quickly.

Typically, during the beginning phase of the program, there is considerable variability; it may even seem as if some inappropriate behaviors get worse. The teen will often test the system to see if you mean what you say. This is especially evident when the teen, faced with a low number of points, plans how he or she will earn a sufficient number to have access to desired privileges. Again note that on Friday the net points carry over to Saturday, and Saturday's net points carry over to Sunday. This is the only time that the points will carry over. During weekdays, each day starts at zero points. Just as in the first example, all points remaining from Sunday go into savings (in brackets). After a period of time and accumulated points, these "savings" may be used in a special celebration.

If a teen gets a number of fines, it is best to set a maximum number (e.g., 5). If that number is exceeded, there is total loss of privileges for that day. It is essential, however, that you avoid negative point balances. If they occur, reassess the program and start over with new point values assigned. The sole criterion for this point system is that it be successful. If a parent does not have success in three attempts, he or she should request professional consultation and cease all such behavioral programs.

BEHAVIORAL MOMENTUM

A new behavioral approach to studying the allocation of behavior under changed environmental constraints is termed "behavioral momentum." The model of "behavioral momentum" was originally proposed by Nevin, Mandell, and Antak in 1983, but has surfaced more recently (Ploud and Garther, 1995), focusing on the use of high probability requests as a proactive procedure to reduce noncompliance. It has been used to improve medication-taking behavior, attempting hard tasks, self-injury, and aggressive behaviors.

The underlying principle of behavioral momentum is fairly simple. Many experienced salespeople have used it for years. Each time the salesperson asks a series of questions (posed so that anyone would answer in the positive), once you have answered "yes" several times, there is positive agreement momentum making it more likely that the person would answer yes to the last question, "Would you like for your family to have this _____?" Once there is momentum, there is an increased likelihood of getting a positive response. In recent studies, it was found that getting compliance with "give me five" and "give me a hug" (high probability requests) increased the probability of getting retarded subjects to "put your lunch box away" (a low probability request).

How to Implement Behavioral Momentum

1. A parent or teacher would first select a series of behaviors that a student/teen would like to do at least 75% of the time.

2. The parent or teacher then would ask the student/teen to do several of the high probability behaviors before asking him or her to complete the low probability behavior. Asking for two to three of the likely behaviors will increase the probability that the student/teen will complete the unlikely behaviors. This procedure is ideally suited for noncompliant teens, or for that matter, any-age noncompliant student or teen.

3. Behavior momentum can be used at home or in the school. Parents may start with two or three simple requests before making a request that may be normally rejected. Likewise, teachers may arrange the order of activities in their classroom so that two or three easy activities are completed before asking the student to complete a more difficult one. Such a classroom procedure would be essential in a class where there are several students who are typically noncompliant. What teen would refuse when a parent says, "Please go get my purse/wallet over there so I can give you some money"?

In Exercise 6-12, the parent or teacher may write down some easy (high probability) and hard (low probability) requests for practice.

Exercise 6-12. **Behavioral Momentum Exercise**

Parents	
High Probability Requests	Low Probability Request
1.	
2.	
3.	
Teachers	
1.	
2.	
3.	

Positive Response Program

One of the main problems with noncompliant teens is that they rarely give any response to requests. If a positive response can be trained, it may act very much like the behavioral momentum program. The basic idea here is to teach the student/teen to make any positive response to a request. The student/teen may even make a choice of which response he or she would like to use.

Some suggestions for a positive response are: (1) "Sure," (2) "Okay," (3) "Yes, I will," and (4) "No problem." Any other response can be accepted as long as it is not inappropriate in some way. Students are asked directly to give one of the agreed-on responses when a request is made of them. This procedure is adapted from one described by Rhode, Jenson, and Reavis (1996) in their book *The Tough Kid Book*. Initially, each time the student/teen responds with one of the selected responses, it is verbally reinforced. Later, after an initial period of one to two weeks, the response is reinforced randomly. The effect of saying the response appears to cue or help start the requested behavior and generally reduces noncompliance. Teams can compete with one another, with each team selecting a different response. One team may be the "OK Team," another may be the "No Problem Team," and so on. Teams compete for some payoff (e.g., team with highest number gets no homework). This program therefore utilizes peer support and encouragement to motivate students for increased compliance.

This positive program may also be combined with a response-cost procedure. For example, points are earned for each team when a student gives a positive response, but lost when the requested behavior is not completed. Under this combination program, the team with the most points may be eligible for some larger consequences, such as no homework one night or one weekend. Generally, the solely positive program should be sufficient to motivate students to comply. The response-cost component may only be introduced if needed.

The teacher's method of dealing with ADHD adolescent behavior in the classroom and other school settings is, in general, similar to those employed with younger children. However, there are some adjustments needed for (a) use of reinforcers that are appropriate to the teen's age (or mental age); (b) some developmental changes that occur in the manifestation of ADHD in adolescence; and (c) employment of specific techniques of discipline that are more commonly used with older students. This does not mean that those procedures that have been used for younger students do not work; it simply gives the teacher a wider range of procedures from which the most useful, acceptable, and effective ones may be selected.

POSITIVE BEHAVIORAL ORIENTATION

A generally positive orientation should actually be ubiquitous. School, work, play, and family settings are all occasions for use of a positive behavioral orientation, where the general focus is on what are appropriate expectations (i.e., "do" as opposed to "don't" rules). This communicates to the student what behavior is important and desired, and sets the stage for making any mild punishment more effective. As with younger students, it is important to view classroom management of adolescents with ADHD across two dimensions: (1) the A–B–C sequence of Antecedents, Behavior, and Consequences, and (2) the focus of modification on (a) the environment (e.g., the classroom), (b) the teen's skill deficits, or (c) the teacher's response to the teen. In a positive behavioral orientation, the focus on antecedents and modification of the environment both deal with the establishment of structure. Teens with ADHD need continuing emphasis on structure whether imposed by others or requested by the teen. In many cases the teen must depend on the teacher or other school personnel to provide these adjustments or accommodations. These accommodations, together with the structure of effective communication with the ADHD teen, comprise the antecedents in the behavioral sequence.

GENERAL CLASSROOM BEHAVIOR MANAGEMENT

MODIFYING ANTECEDENT—ACCOMMODATIONS

There are several areas to address that will serve as proactive measures in preventing problematic behavior in the classroom. Accommodations are essential if the performance of a teen with ADHD is to be maximized. Statistics indicate that without such adjustments, the risk of school failure may be 2–3 times greater than that for teens without ADHD. About 50% of those students with ADHD will fail; about one-third will eventually drop out of school.

Adjust Student Seating—Research has shown that using the standard rows or a semicircle of desks is least distracting; groups at tables may present problems for some children as well as adolescents. Adolescents identified as having ADHD often function better if they are seated near a student who models appropriate classroom behavior. The teacher should avoid seating the student with ADHD near distractions, such as a noisy air conditioner or high-traffic areas. Teens should not, however, be placed next to a teacher's desk as might have occurred at a younger age.

Use Carrels—Study-type carrels or privacy boards lessen visual and auditory distractions. These need not be used solely by the ADHD child or adolescent; at times, many other students may elect to use these areas of the room if they are made available.

Alternative Lighting—The "hum" of fluorescent lights may induce some distraction or annoyance. If it is possible, consider using an alternative lighting source. On another note, periodically using a "strobe light" has been effective in creating additional stimulation to enhance alertness and may not create a "distraction" as one might believe.

Provide Music Background—Some students have benefited from rhythmic background music or even "white noise." Headphones can be used for specified ADHD students so that other students are not disturbed and so that distractions are blocked out for the student wearing them. Headphones may also become an integral part of behavioral programs that emphasize self-monitoring. A tape of recorded "beeps" may be used to cue and provide greater awareness of "on-task" behavior. This procedure may be limited to younger adolescents; it might be embarrassing for older teens.

Use an Overhead Projector—The use of an overhead projector may aid any student, who typically gets distracted, visually. This allows the ADHD student to easily locate and follow important points that are emphasized with a pointer.

Accommodations are also found in Chapter 5. For a detailed list of accommodations in higher education, consult Gordon and Keiser (1998). Also, parents and teachers may refer to Appendix 12 for a handout on accommodations that would be appropriate for teens and may be supplied to the school along with the psychological report.

MODIFYING ANTECEDENT—RULES, EXPECTATIONS, AND COMMUNICATIONS

The First Thing that May Need to Change—Communications, rules, and expectations, and the manner in which these are presented to teens may make the difference between compliance and noncompliance in the classroom. This discussion of antecedents thus focuses on the basic structure within a classroom. It provides the foundation on which behaviors result. If commands, directions, rules, and expectations are not clearly specified, the teen's ability to respond appropriately is compromised.

RULES AND EXPECTATIONS FOR SCHOOL

Just as there are rules at home, there are rules in the classroom, school grounds, and in transportation to and from school on the bus. Rules often imply what the teen should not do rather than what the teen should do. It is best to state rules in a positive framework, and it is still important to review rules often, even with teens.

The following is a list of situations where rule-governed behavior is typically found in school:

Sitting in class	Changing classes
Eating lunch	Taking tests
On the school bus	At school assembly
During P.E.	During a field trip

The following are some examples of rules:

1. Remain quiet in class.
2. Raise hand to ask questions.
3. Keep hands to self.
4. Use appropriate language.
5. Remain seated on bus.
6. Keep food on plate or eat it.
7. Return lunch trays.
8. Be on time for bus.
9. Be on time for class.
10. Keep feet on floor during class.

Notice that all rules are clearly written and are specific as to what the teacher or parent wishes. Rules may be specified for the classroom only (e.g., "Raise your hand to ask permission to go to the bathroom" or "Remain quiet and listen carefully when the teacher is talking."). For young teens who may not fully understand the rules, role-playing may be used to model the appropriate behavior and/or cues may even be provided in the form of pictures that depict the correct behavior associated with each rule. Some of the preceding situations may be more appropriately discussed in terms of expectations for the teen.

In some situations the teacher may simply describe the desired behaviors. In general, students with ADHD have much difficulty meeting expectations. Over time the gap between what teachers expect and the student's performance widens. In addition to academic expectations, there are also behavioral expectations. Somewhat different from rules, behavioral expectations may involve several components that describe a series of behaviors expected from the teenager in school. Expectations may vary with the age of the teen as well as with the teen's ability to comprehend and retain what is said. For example, a teacher might review expectations prior to entering a special event (e.g., a field trip). It is best to simplify these expectations and limit each to no more than three components.

The following is a list of sequences of events that involve some of your expectations for the adolescent.

EXPECTATIONS

1. While we are visiting the Governor's House, I will expect you to:

   a. Greet the Governor appropriately (i.e., "Good morning, Governor _____.")

   b. Walk quietly and orderly from and back to the bus.

   c. Keep your hands to yourself (i.e., no fighting).

2. When you go to assembly on Friday, I will expect you to:

   a. Keep your hands to yourself.

   b. Sit quietly during the presentation.

   c. Ask appropriate questions.

These expectations, which will also vary for young versus older teens, may stand alone or be tied to consequences. In the preliminary stages of behavior management, these general expectations may be used to "test" the young teen to see if he or she is capable of compliance or to test the level/degree of compliance.

Rules and expectations provide important parts of the basic structure for behavior. However, the next important step is to communicate this information to the teen. If the teen doesn't get the right message, he or she can't make an appropriate response. Teachers must not assume the student "knows better." This is especially the case with a teenager who has ADHD. It is often discovered that the "message sent" is not necessarily the "message received." Teachers must therefore focus on developing good communication skills with their students.

COMMUNICATION SKILLS—TEACHER AND STUDENT

Similar to the home situation, getting the correct information to the student may be the most critical part of the entire behavioral sequence. As many students with ADHD are distractible and hear only parts of communications, it is most important to check out whether the teen has gotten the entire message. Much of this information was discussed in the section of this chapter dealing with parent communications, so it will only be briefly reviewed here.

The following is a review of some of the basic steps in the communication process:

1. **Get eye contact.**

2. **Speak clearly and distinctly in a normal tone of voice.**

3. **Present your request or directive in a simple concise manner emphasizing what you want the teen "to do."**

4. **You may wish to verify that the teen has heard what you said by simply asking the teen to repeat what you said, either exactly or in his or her own words.**

Now we will focus on what a teacher may actually say—the content of the message. Review some of the following examples on communications. It sometimes takes a review of statements made orally—but now in written form—to determine how clear, concise, and positive the statements sound and how they might be perceived by the student. Are these clear to others? Ask yourself: Would they know exactly what to do after hearing these communications?

DEVELOPING COMMUNICATION SKILLS

1. "Put your old test papers in the trash can."
2. "Please turn off the lights in the classroom."
3. "Would you help me put this ice chest in the back of the room?"
4. "Take your math book out of your bag."
5. "Take out a pencil and writing pad for this next assignment."
6. "Clear off all books on your desk and put them in your bag."
7. "Write down these pages for your reading assignment."

COMMUNICATION STYLES

Teachers need to remember the three types of communication styles discussed by Parker (1992):

1. Passive
2. Aggressive
3. Assertive

Problems may be encountered in using the first two styles. The third alternative appears to work best for the teacher.

Passive Communication—Teachers who use passive forms of communication typically have difficulty stating rules and enforcing them. Recognizing that the teen is in control, a typical communication might sound like one of the examples that follow.

Some examples of passive communication include:

➠ "Don't you think it's time to get ready for assembly?"

➠ "How many times do I have to tell you to clean up your desk?"

➠ "Don't you think you ought to be doing your class work now?"

Very often these passive communications are given in the form of a question with the decision resting upon the young teenage student. When one hears a communication like, "Young man, don't you think you should get started on that assignment?" one expects to hear the teen say, "No! I'm not ready to do that."

Aggressive Communication—Teachers who use this form of communication may be manipulative and controlling of others. They tend to be exceedingly strict and may use threats, severe punishment, derogatory names, or any other technique to exert their power and control. Any resistance to their rules and regulations would be quite threatening and would typically be met with even greater force. Such forms of communication are often associated with severe punishment. Humiliating comments, name calling, or belittling may be made without regard for the teen's feelings. While compliance may result in the short-term, in the long-term accumulated suppressed anger in the teenager may be expressed in a violent manner at some time, often quite unexpectedly. The teacher would be best to avoid such confrontations.

Some examples of aggressive communication include:

⮕ "You're lazy—it must be hard to keep your head up."

⮕ "With a brain like yours, I'm not surprised—can't you think any better than that?"

⮕ "You never listen—do you know how to do that assignment I gave you?" (stupid is implied)

Very often these communications are like "verbal darts." One can just imagine how the teenage student might feel being on the receiving end of one of these communications. Very often a teacher will create much embarrassment with questions such as, "Brian, did you forget to take your medicine again?" (stupid is implied) Another teacher called a teenager "air head" since he couldn't possibly have any brains; if he did, he would know his place in reading. These comments or communications offer little in terms of constructive feedback; they simply devastate a teen's already weak self-concept. While the young teenage student remains a victim, the aggressive communicator remains in control and "one up."

Assertive Communication—Teachers who use this assertive form of communication are secure in their beliefs and can express their ideas, needs, and wishes in a clear and direct manner that is respectful of others' rights and feelings. These teachers provide needed structure for their students by being explicit and fair in rules and expectations for their teenagers. They are also capable of enforcing these rules and standards in a way that allows the young teen to think and act independently and to be responsible for his or her behavior. The teacher is clearly in charge and assumes a leadership role in the classroom, modeling appropriate authoritative behavior for the teen.

Some examples of assertive communication include:

⮕ "When you finish your assignment, you can go."

⮕ "Name calling is against the rules. Stop it or get your (pre-arranged) consequence!"

⮕ "I need for all students to listen to these directions."

In these examples, the teacher is quite clear about what is requested and/or the consequences. Also, the responsibility for change is placed upon the teenage student. The teen can: (a) decide to stop name calling or (b) receive an extra (pre-arranged) assignment. Should the teen (self) control his behavior, he may be rewarded by the teacher who reinforces behavior change *and* maintains control in the classroom.

Once teachers are able to communicate *clearly, concisely,* and *convincingly* (the three Cs) using the assertive style, they can move to the next step—determining which compliance problems may remain. In short, once teachers become more effective in communicating, some problem behaviors may literally "disappear." Essentially, these difficulties were probably related to ineffective or inappropriate communications.

Metacommunications—The term *metacommunication* refers to a communication about a communication—a higher level of communication that makes the original communication more complex. It may result in confusion on the part of the listener if conflicting messages are being sent. For example, a message may be delivered while the teacher is smiling (nonverbal metacommunication) or it may be delivered in a very soft voice. Metacommunication may imply that the teacher is either not serious or perhaps is weak and ineffectual. With these perceptions the young teen may ignore the message even though the content is appropriate. On the other hand, extreme forms of metacommunication should be avoided (e.g., loud, booming voice and stern, threatening facial expressions). If the teacher is to be effective with commands that have an assertive content, he or she must also present that content with an assertive style. The teacher may wish to practice some of the assertive commands by recording them and then replaying the tape for feedback on how he or she sounds.

MODIFY THE TEEN'S BEHAVIOR/SKILLS

This second area focuses on "teen-centered accommodations" where the adolescent with ADHD is taught to better deal with some of his or her difficulties. While these skills may be developed in the classroom, they are acquired more rapidly if they are also practiced in different multiple contexts (e.g., in the counselor's office, home, and at school).

1. **Model instructions.** Teach the young teen to repeat and review directions silently to him- or herself. This habit of repeating instructions or directions can counteract the tendency to impulsively start assignments without a clear understanding of what is to be done. To teach this technique, simply give the directions or instructions and then ask a student to repeat them. It is not necessary that teens identified as having ADHD be called upon—asking other good students will appropriately model the procedure.

2. **Model problem solving.** An extension of the first technique, this includes additional self-directed questions such as: (1) What is the problem? (2) Is there more than one way to solve the problem? (3) Which solution is best? (4) How can I best

solve the problem using this best solution? Basically, this process is a step-by-step approach with periodic checks on accuracy. Self-talk and self-monitoring are encouraged throughout.

3. **Teach organizational structure.** Demonstrate how large, complex assignments may be divided into a series of smaller assignments. The teen may then use a logical progression from one step to another until the entire assignment is completed. Students with ADHD should also be encouraged to organize other critical areas of his or her life. The two most critical ones are the backpack and the locker. By periodic inspection, the student can receive feedback and coaching on more effective ways to organize things. It will, however, be difficult to function in this role if you, as a teacher, have trouble with organization. In addition, teachers may review with students what is needed with regard to school supplies. While this may seem age-inappropriate, teachers must remember that students with ADHD are immature and often appear to function more like students about two years younger. It is also good to review things that need to be done now or to schedule activities to be done later in some type of daily, weekly, or monthly planner.

4. **Teach self-monitoring.** The teenage student with ADHD can be taught to monitor his or her own "on-task" behavior. Giving a periodic signal or cue (sometimes provided by a beep on a tape recorder or beeper-type device) can make the young teen more aware of whether he or she is "on" or "off" task. There is much research to demonstrate the effectiveness of this procedure once it has been reinforced, practiced, and become automatic.

5. **Learning from mistakes.** The teen with ADHD can profit from a review of prior tests and work. Quick feedback on tests, class work, or homework will be most helpful. Teaching students how to use such information from the analysis of mistakes on tests and assignments can help the student to improve performance on future tests and assignments.

MODIFY THE TEACHER'S RESPONSE TO THE TEEN WITH ADHD

At times, teachers may experience the same sense of frustration and stress that some parents have experienced in their relationship with the teen with ADHD. Whether at home or in the classroom, difficult-to-manage behavior may result in similar escalation of disciplinary techniques that typically become more restrictive, more emotional, and perhaps even punitive. The latter punitive reaction is, however, less likely to occur with ADHD teens, often out of the teacher's fear of retaliation by the teen. In addition, it would be developmentally inappropriate. Clearly, the demands of the classroom continue to elicit ADHD behavior even in the teen years, especially if the teen has failed to learn how to cope with these demands. There are a number of factors that influence the student–teacher relationship, and may affect the frequency and severity of problematic ADHD behavior. Modifications by the teacher and how the teacher relates to the teen with ADHD can make a significant difference. Some of these points follow:

1. **Make sure to have a good knowledge and understanding of ADHD.** A teacher's understanding of the behaviors of a student with ADHD is probably the most significant factor in how he or she will deal with that student. For example, inconsistency is a hallmark characteristic of ADHD behavior, exhibited when the student does well one day and poorly the next. If the teacher does not understand this characteristic inconsistency, he or she may set up the student for undue pressure by saying, "I know you can do this work because you did it all yesterday." However, by understanding and even expecting this characteristic inconsistency in performance, the teacher can use alternative approaches that cause less emotional pressure and stress, and she or he can make fewer comments that erroneously suggest to the student, "You can do better—you just aren't trying." Inconsistency is but one of many behaviors characteristic of ADHD. A knowledgeable teacher is much better able to deal with these issues than a teacher who does not understand the dynamics of ADHD behavior.

2. **Be flexible.** When a teacher is more flexible than rigid and is open to adjustment of "assignment loads" and "work span," the ADHD student has a better chance at success. Likewise, an aware teacher knows that a student with ADHD may be very sensitive, so he or she avoids public confrontations and finds alternative ways to address such things as test grades, medication, or misbehavior.

3. **Take time in teaching.** There are many ways in which a teacher can send students a message to "Hurry!"—speeding through lessons, not taking time to clearly show the organization of material, not showing attention to "good behavior," and using an authoritarian approach. All of these can result in conflicts with ADHD students, who generally have trouble with fast-paced, rigid, rule-governed expectations and settings.

4. **Provide structure and routine.** The teacher should have a fairly consistent routine of daily activities (e.g., roll call, math, recess, reading, lunch, and music). How each activity is conducted might vary, but the sequence of activities should remain the same. Having such a routine develops daily expectations, while the variation within each activity (e.g., audio–visual, hands-on project, computer use, etc.) provides increased stimulation.

5. **Integrate exercise.** Having students stretch or simply stand periodically as part of the daily schedule may help to reduce stress, enhance alertness, and provide an opportunity for students to be active with permission. While more direct applications may be used with younger teens, older teens may still benefit when there is greater active involvement in learning. In lieu of exercise, perhaps greater movement or a more "hands-on" approach to learning may be integrated with conventional procedures.

6. **Avoid information overload.** Teach to the student's capacity to attend and process information. As the student better handles small segments of work, the teacher may gradually increase the "work time span," all the while reinforcing the student for staying "on task" and also at the end for "work completion."

7. **Establish behavioral priorities.** Overactivity or restlessness, per se, does not necessarily interfere with work output; it is impulsivity and distractibility that impair performance. Thus, some restless overactivity may be overlooked. For example, assuming unusual postures or some humming and tapping might be best ignored, as long as it does not interfere with the ADHD student's work or become distracting to other students. In fact, permission to move around may actually be used as a motivator (e.g., "When you finish this assignment, you are free to move around in the back of the class").

8. **Reinforce three types of behavior.** All those involved in the classroom, including teachers, aides, the principal, and counselors, should focus as often as possible on appropriate behaviors exhibited by students. For the teen with ADHD, this includes any one of three types of behavior: (a) a good or desirable behavior, (b) an improvement over past behavior, and (c) any neutral behavior (i.e., the student is not doing anything inappropriate). When a student is exhibiting appropriate behavior, it is best to compliment him or her specifically, saying exactly what you liked about the behavior (not just saying "that's good" or "you did good"). This specific positive attention should be delivered in a warm, enthusiastic manner and should never be perceived as mechanical.

9. **Provide consequences for inappropriate behavior.** Many teens with ADHD receive much negative attention in the form of disapproval and indirect verbal comments. It is now fairly well accepted that mild punishments—such as time-out for young teens or behavior penalty for most all teens—can be effective. However, the teacher must first check to see if the teen understood what he was supposed to do and simply did not do it (noncompliance) or whether he missed part of the message and was confused. If the student was, in fact, disobedient, then a mild punishment such as time-out (young teen) or a behavior penalty (any teen) can be an effective consequence.

   However, with so many variations, the behavioral procedure of time-out may be poorly understood. Sometimes overused and ineffective in the school setting, time-out, like other punishments, never tells the teenager what to do—only what *not* to do. Unless it is used in a general positive, rewarding environment, it becomes totally ineffective. Behavior penalties may be quite effective, especially when the student may lose a favorite activity for a short period of time.

10. **Redirect inappropriate behavior.** Redirection is often helpful with younger students but may sometimes be used effectively with teens. This strategy simply involves removal of the student from one situation, where acting out has started or is about to occur, and placing that student in a different situation. Moving a student with ADHD from one table to another may reduce the teen's opportunity to exhibit annoying behavior toward one group of students or toward one student. Placing the student with those who are more likely to ignore the annoying behavior may prove beneficial.

11. **Use "success-oriented" programs.** Nothing is learned from repeated failures. The goal is to work for small successes in behavioral programs, rather than to expect major, rapid changes. Build on these small improvements and take comfort in the knowledge that slow and gradual behavioral changes are more likely to result in the development of lifelong skills that will aid the teenager as he or she matures.

12. **Review rules frequently.** To prevent problems that arise when the student moves from one situation to another, prepare him or her by briefly reviewing the rules that are appropriate for the new situation. Rules in all situations—classroom, P.E., playground, lunch room, bus trip, etc.—should be kept simple, few in number, and reviewed on a regular basis. Posting of the rules for each situation is also important, especially for younger teens. It is also important to state what the consequences will be for rule violations.

13. **Use priming.** The use of "priming" may help keep the teen with ADHD focused. Reminding students of some arranged reinforcement for a task prior to the performance of the task will help them stay on task and complete it.

14. **Maintain interest.** Perhaps one of the most important characteristics that maintain interest of ADHD students is the teacher's style of teaching. Most students with ADHD have expressed greater interest when teachers are visibly dynamic, use humor, change voice inflections, interact by kidding the class, and move around the room. Teachers who talk in a monotone from an overhead projector with the room lights off are likely to "put the student with ADHD to sleep." It is recommended that when hand-scheduling classes, the student with ADHD should be paired more often with dynamic teachers and less often with the latter type described. The student's work performance might also be improved by the type of assignments given. Dr. Sydney Zentall and colleagues at Purdue University have shown that teachers can make work assignments more interesting to ADHD students by adding novelty to the assignment.

DEALING WITH DISRUPTIVE/INAPPROPRIATE TEEN BEHAVIOR IN THE CLASSROOM

Disruptive behaviors vary on a continuum from those that are mildly annoying to those that pose serious threat to persons and property.

First, it is important to discuss the issue of "What are disruptive behaviors?" and then to explore some of the procedures that the teacher may use to deal with them. Some mildly annoying behaviors may be ignored; others must be dealt with using procedures that are generally effective, especially when used within a positive behavior orientation. For example, when the teacher has a positive relationship with the student and provides many positive strokes for appropriate behavior, attention from the teacher comes to be associated with good feelings. When it is withdrawn, the student will probably feel a loss and wish to reestablish the teacher's attention and the good feelings it brings. In contrast, when a teacher's attention is almost solely associated with criticism and punishment, there is a general negative or unpleasant emotional state that occurs with teacher attention. Withdrawal of the teacher's attention in this situation may have little effect upon the student's misbehavior and technically such withdrawal of a negative unpleasant state would actually "reward" the student for misbehavior! In short, without a generally positive orientation, many punishment procedures are ineffective at best and may actually reinforce the student's misbehavior. As Walker and Walker (1991) have pointed out, "Chronically noncompliant students who are antisocial or defiant of adults are neither responsive to, nor impressed with adult anger." They continue to note that "more deliberate and thoughtful approaches are required for success with such students."

GETTING RID OF UNWANTED BEHAVIORS

The following are some basic procedures that have been effective in getting rid of unwanted behaviors. The first step for teachers is the selection of behaviors that they wish to change.

SELECTING BEHAVIORS TO WEAKEN OR REMOVE

Teachers often agree with parents regarding behaviors that need to change. First, it is clear that those behaviors that are dangerous to self or others are of prime concern; they include aggressive behaviors such as hitting, pushing, wielding dangerous objects (e.g., guns), and high-risk behaviors such as skating in the street, jumping from high places, or using dangerous objects inappropriately (e.g., juggling a sharp knife). Second, other behaviors, while not intrinsically dangerous in a physical sense, may be hurtful to others or simply annoying. These behaviors include such actions as aggressive outbursts, making inappropriate noises, inappropriate gestures, disrespectful talk, complaining, and annoying verbal comments and actions such as name calling. General noncompliance to authority may also be included in this category.

You have probably already made lists of all undesirable behaviors. However, it will be advantageous to review these. List those that fall into *Category A* (Physical Aggression/Dangerous Behaviors) and those that belong in *Category B* (Annoying and Noncompliant Behaviors). This will help sort out behaviors that vary in severity and make it easier to decide which techniques may be applied to change them. Hopefully, there will be few listed in Category A.

Exercise 6-13. SELECTION OF UNWANTED BEHAVIORS TO CHANGE

Category A (Physical Aggression/Dangerous Behaviors)

1. _____
2. _____
3. _____
4. _____
5. _____

Category B (Annoying/Noncompliant Behaviors)

1. _____
2. _____
3. _____
4. _____
5. _____

IGNORING SOME BEHAVIORS

Sometimes teachers feel they cannot ignore inappropriate behavior, believing that if the misbehavior is ignored the teen has "gotten away with something." However, it is now well known that many teens and especially teens with ADHD will often emit some behaviors that are certain to attract attention, "hook" the teacher, or create some desired effect and stir up some excitement such as an argument. Often such behaviors are shocking behaviors that involve some taboo (e.g., sexual gesture or curse word). The student often expects a response and when there is one, albeit negative, the response may simply reinforce the behavior; giving attention to such misbehavior may serve only to maintain it. A simple comment such as "That's a no-no" or "Stop that immediately" may inform the teen that he or she has indeed "hooked you" and, though the behavior may stop at that time, it is likely to recur soon.

Attention from a teacher is extremely powerful and may be used to reinforce many behaviors. Some teachers state that they give equal attention to appropriate and inappropriate behaviors, but this results in no change in the balance of these behaviors. Instead, a shift in the positive direction is needed, that is, withdraw attention to the annoying behavior while attending more to a desired behavior that is opposite to the annoying behavior (a more appropriate behavior). This procedure will result in a more balanced program.

Developing a Plan to Ignore Some Behaviors—Once you have categorized the undesirable behaviors, select one annoying behavior to ignore. Follow this sequence of steps:

Step One: Be prepared. This old Scouting motto is good advice. Know what to expect when a (mis)behavior is ignored. For example, if pencil tapping is selected as the annoying behavior, talk to yourself (silently) about the teen's reaction; have an internal dialogue. Say, "I know that by withdrawing my attention, John is going to become increasingly more frustrated and angry, and his pencil tapping will become more intense. I will have to continue to talk to myself so that I don't make the mistake of giving in to him."

Step Two: Say, "I know that once I choose to ignore a behavior, I'll have to continue ignoring it until it is under control. If I attend to John while he is engaged in more intense pencil tapping, I know it will be exacerbated because of his frustration and anger over being ignored; then I will simply reinforce his pencil tapping at a more intense level and also reward him for persisting in misbehavior (continuing to tap for longer periods in the absence of getting attention for it)." Continue self-talk to avoid falling into the trap of reverting to attending to the behavior. Much will depend on how well you prepare for this stage of the process and your emotional state. If you are over-stressed, drained, or too involved with personal problems, it will indeed be difficult to withstand this teen's behavior. Remember that the student is usually quite skilled and experienced at getting attention from you, and you are accustomed to giving it. Change will not come easily.

Step Three: Once you achieve success in riding out the student's behavior, provide self-reward and recognition for the way you handled that behavior. Continue self-talk to say, "Good, I did a good job of controlling myself and the situation. I am in control." This self-talk is especially important for a teacher who also has a history of ADHD and who may exhibit a tendency to react impulsively and with anger toward the student. Anytime behavior changes in an appropriate direction, it is important for that behavior to be rewarded whether it comes from the teen, parent, or teacher. Most behavioral changes are quite difficult, and ultimate success often comes in small steps. Reward each of these steps. Once the student's behavior changes and pencil tapping decreases, point out (more frequently right after the change) that the teen's behavior is now more appropriate. Reinforcement frequency may be tapered off as the behavior change becomes more stable and consistent. However, in the beginning stages of change, it is important to notice even subtle or minor improvements. "John, you've done very well at controlling some of your restless behavior—much better than in the past." Also, recognize that some of these restless behaviors are physiologically driven and thus complete control may not be possible.

TIME-OUT FOR MISBEHAVIOR

Much like ignoring, the time-out procedure removes the young teen from any potential positive reinforcement; in the case of ignoring, positive reinforcement is withheld from the student. Time-out is very much like the old "go sit in the corner" punishment. Most students reportedly hate time-out—and especially those with ADHD. They say that it's boring; many ask for other discipline rather than time-out. Also, the student with ADHD wishes to get the punishment over quickly. It should be noted here that time-out may have limited usefulness with teens. It may be used with young teens 13 or 14 years of age, as teens with ADHD are generally immature by at least two years. To use this technique beyond that point would be risky. Keep in mind that while this procedure will be reviewed, it may not be used frequently with many teens. It may, however, be redefined as a time to "chill out" or "cool down" for those teens who need to develop self-control. When reframed in such a manner, this technique could be used by anyone—even adults.

What is time-out like? If a young teen just hit a student, he might be told "No hitting; go to time-out, now!" He is then sent to a boring place—usually a hallway, a vacant room, or vacant area. The time-out place should be devoid of all reinforcements. A kitchen timer is used and set for the teen's age (i.e., one minute for each year). This and other criteria are in accordance with recommendations from Dr. Lynn Clark (1985).

While there are no specific guidelines regarding an age cut off for using time-out, it is probably best to use an alternative punishment for any teen 15 years of age and older. Less frequent use of time-out at home or in the school may begin between 13 to 15 years of age. Dr. Clark also recommends that you use no more than ten words or ten seconds to get the young teenager to time-out. Once in time-out, the teen is basically ignored until the timer rings. *This is important.* No one, other students or teachers, should pay attention to, talk to, or otherwise provide rewards for the student in time-out. You should not get hooked into attending to the behavior of a teen in time-out. Some teenagers are quite adept at getting into a hassle, particularly with a teacher, while in time-out. If time-out is used incorrectly, the misbehavior may become worse, as the teen is actually getting rewarded (by adult attention) for getting into the time-out.

Immediately when the timer rings, time-out is over and the student is asked, "Now, Jaimé, tell me—why were you sent to time-out?" If the teen says, "Because I hit another student," the teacher says, "That's right." If the teen says, "I don't know," he is given the answer and allowed to resume his activities. It is best to avoid giving much attention just after time-out and, of course, it is not recommended that the student receive anything special—or he'll get the impression that time-out really pays off! The student also should not receive a lecture after time-out, and should not be asked to promise never to exhibit that behavior again. However, it is not unusual that the teen may engage in some more appropriate behavior after time-out. When this occurs, it should not be ignored. Any time behavior changes in a more positive direction, it is best to point this out to the student. When the teen shows an improvement in behavior after time-out, *do* reinforce this change and point out that you are pleased to see this behavior. It is also useful to state the process that changed; for example, "You really have much better control over yourself now; I like the way you are getting along better with other students."

Listing Behaviors Appropriate for Time-out—Now that there is a general understanding of the time-out procedure, it is important to consider when to use time-out—and that may depend on what behavior is shown. A list of specific acting-out behaviors follows:

Hitting others, threats to hit	Throwing objects at others
Temper outbursts	Obnoxious, loud voice
Hostile teasing	Slapping
Disrespectful talk	Pinching
Angry screaming	Scratching
Grabbing others' property	Dangerous acts
Destroying property	Cursing
Kicking others	Pushing others (hard)
Hair pulling	Mocking teachers
Sexual gestures	Choking others
Loud complaining, demanding	Spitting, threats to spit
Name calling	Making faces at others
Persistent interrupting Adult conversation After a warning	Disobeying a command to stop a misbehavior

Time-out is best used for behaviors that would be classified as aggressive or acting-out behaviors. Fearful, seclusive, timid, irritable, and grumpy behaviors, for example, would not be appropriate for time-out. Note that passive behavior, such as failing to perform some chore or forgetting to do something, is not appropriate for this procedure. Not doing something is not an acting-out behavior.

Developing a Time-out Plan—It is important to understand and practice time-out before actually using it. This means that you must review and make decisions regarding some critical issues. Also, a plan should be in place to deal with any problems encountered in time-out. Now consider the following issues.

1. **Select target behavior(s).** It is important to use time-out for specific acting-out behaviors and to avoid using it for every misbehavior. Teachers who learn this procedure often use it for everything, which reduces its effectiveness, as there is a lack of balance such that punishment (time-out) may become a prime source of getting attention.

   Make a list of those behaviors that you will consider for time-out.

Exercise 6-14. BEHAVIORS FOR TIME-OUT

1. _____

2. _____

3. _____

4. _____

5. _____

Select two from your list to target for time-out (put a star next to these).

2. **Select a place for time-out.** Use any place that is boring, where the student will not receive attention from those passing by, and one where the teen has no access to rewards. In the school setting, the ideal place is probably a corner or a specified Time-Out area. Separating or segregating the student is not advisable. A special place may be set aside in the classroom and designated as a Time-Out Zone—a place for calming down and regaining control. Presented in this way, perhaps other students without ADHD might use the place when there is a need to calm down and get control.

3. **Determine how much time in time-out.** This is usually set according to the student's age (i.e., one minute for each year). Thus, a 13-year-old would receive a 13-minute time-out. When there are several teens in a school setting, a shorter specific number of minutes may be used (3 minutes, 5 minutes, 10 minutes, etc.). The total time for any time-out with younger children should generally not exceed 12 minutes; however, time-outs for teens may extend up to 15 or 20 minutes (especially when penalties are added). If a longer time-out is used, the student may be given the opportunity to work off some time with more appropriate behavior. For example, a student who was emotionally "out of control" may be able to regain control in the "chill out" zone. This may be rewarded with praise such as, "John, you did very well at gaining control of yourself—it looks like you've 'chilled out' long enough. You're free to return to your regular seat."

4. **Measure the time.** Be consistent and use a timer, preferably one that does not tick loudly. The timer or watch cannot be manipulated, rushed, or avoided. The student needs to know that he or she can come out of time-out only when time is up. This structure allows the student to know what to expect and avoids troublesome situations; responsibility is not placed on the teacher or the teen to decide when enough time is spent in time-out. If time-out is to be used, it should not focus on exaggerated attention on the student with ADHD.

5. **Withdraw attention while the teen is in time-out.** This cannot be emphasized enough. Teachers often make the mistake of lecturing or continuing a hassle with the student, which simply makes time-out ineffective. A student may complain "This isn't going to work" or continue talking loudly or complaining of pains, or even pleading to use the bathroom. All of these behaviors should be *ignored.* Any destructive behaviors during time-out may result in added punishment, such as additional minutes or a behavior penalty, and having the teen "clean up" or "pay up" for any mess or damages incurred. Alternatively, the student may need to be removed to a safer place or perhaps sent to another classroom. This problem is typically quite rare.

6. **Establish the connection after time-out.** Privately, ask the student, "Why were you sent to time-out?" or "Why did you need to chill out?" If the teen answers correctly, he or she is allowed to go back to the prior activity. If the teen answers incorrectly or doesn't know, he or she is informed of the behavior that precipitated the time-out. It is important to clarify the connection between the teen's behavior and the time-out. It is especially important to make the teen aware of the "cause–effect" sequence when there is lack of awareness and weak internal cognitive recognition about which behaviors will bring about negative consequences. The student must know what the consequences will be for certain misbehavior. The teen will learn this for the behaviors selected but only after much practice and review.

There is no need for lecturing after time-out, nor should the student be forced to "promise never to do it again." Such promises do not result in improvement and entrap the teen for any future transgressions.

When you spend an inordinate amount of time with the teen immediately after time-out, you give a message that certain behaviors can really get you upset or excited. When the teen with ADHD needs to "stir up some excitement," he or she will certainly know which buttons to push!

General Comment Regarding Time-out—It is important to note that time-out, like many other forms of punishment, is often overused by teachers, especially with young students. So much emphasis has been placed on dealing with behavior that is inappropriate, that very little time is spent focusing on which behaviors a teacher wishes to see more often. Remember, punishment never tells the student what "to do"—only what "not to do." Teachers must balance reward and punishment techniques. This does not necessarily mean an equal number of rewards and punishments. Focus on using positive reinforcements for appropriate behavior as much as or even more than using negative reinforcements for inappropriate behaviors. Skill development through reinforcement of appropriate behavior is crucial for the survival of the ADHD student.

Rehearse time-out/chill-out before you use it in the classroom. You need a kind of "dress rehearsal" to ensure there will be no surprises when time-out is actually employed with any student, and to allow each participant—teen and teacher—to review his or her role. Present time-out in the following way, saying, "For some time now, we have had hassles over name calling. This is not much fun for me or for you. So, when you 'name call' you will be sent to time-out." A general explanation should be given regarding the sequence of events in time-out. Then run through the procedure, saying "Okay, now let's suppose you have just name-called; that's a Time-Out for name calling. Go now!" The teen knows where to go and that a timer will be set for a specific number of minutes; it will be placed where he or she can hear it. When the teen comes out of time-out, you privately ask, "Why were you sent to Time-Out?" If the teen states the reason, say, "That is exactly right." If not, the teen is told the reason. This rehearsal is quite important and ensures that teacher and student are ready. The teacher may wish to rehearse this privately with a student or may use a model student to rehearse with the class. Be aware that, as Goldstein (1988) has noted, the first few times a student is placed in time-out, there may be a "Time-Out burst" where a heightened degree of aggressiveness may occur. These outbursts will usually subside, especially if the teacher adds to the duration of the time-out the number of minutes that the outburst lasts.

Time-out Procedure at Home and at School—In general, time-out will be used more frequently at home and with younger teens and children. There has been much controversy over its use in school and it has generally been difficult to set up a time-out in the school setting. Because of these difficulties, time-out has not received so much emphasis in overall behavior management programs in schools. It can also backfire, as when the student is sent outside the classroom; it is often rewarding for the teen, not punishing. Consider a young teen who is having difficulty doing a task, and becomes easily distracted to engage in some aggravating behavior with her neighbor (e.g., pinching his arm). Should this student be sent out of the room? She may actually be taken out of an unrewarding and boring task; therefore, she is rewarded for acting out and will probably repeat the behavior in the future. In normal discipline programs, when this occurs a number of times, she may be suspended and forced to leave school. What a punishment! Such a procedure of suspension from school may work for many normal teenagers who would, for varying reasons, find it unpleasant to be sent out of the class or to be sent home. It would not, however, be effective for most teens who experience behavior problems.

Typically, when time-out is used in the school, the teen simply goes to a designated place and must still follow the lesson or continue working. To reiterate, a modified time-out is a time to "calm down," "refocus," or "redirect" activities to a different situation (labeled a "Chill-out" or "Calm-down" Zone).

On school grounds there may be a different type of time-out, called *time-out for two*. Frequently, when students fight, rather than playing a detective game to discover "who started this," both students go to Time-Out. Either an average of their ages or a set number of minutes (e.g., 5 minutes) may be chosen. When the questioning to "get to the bottom of this fight" is avoided, the effectiveness of time-out is enhanced.

Remember that it is important to deliver consequences of behavior immediately following the behavior. If they are delayed, a teacher may get confused over what started the fight and the students win. Punish both by saying, "Both of you have a time-out for fighting on school grounds. Go now." The students are then sent to different areas (and certainly beyond arm's length) to serve the time-out. When they come out of the time-out, ask both why they were sent to time-out. More important, ask them, "Now, can you think of another way you could have solved your problem without fighting?" Here both students will compete for a "good answer" and this process will aid in the development of problem-solving concepts. Both students are now learning to develop cognitions that may mediate aggressive behavior in the future. When the teen knows other options and is reinforced for using them, coping skills can improve. The impulse-oriented teen with ADHD thus learns cognitive mediating techniques that essentially involve "thinking before acting" as a means of controlling impulses.

Planning for Problems with Time-out—Some students comply immediately with time-out; others resist. The easiest way to deal with resistance to time-out is to add minutes. With the young teen, simply add minutes to the time-out for each instance of resistance (i.e., failure to go). This should not exceed 5 minutes. If the resistance continues, a behavior penalty may be given (i.e., withdrawal of a privilege), or perhaps a detention.

Avoid Embarrassment—Most teens and especially teens with ADHD are quite sensitive about being perceived as different from others. Many of the signals for time-out, even for young teens, may need to be nonverbal or given privately so that the punishment is not stated in front of the class. Likewise, any rehearsal of time-out should be conducted in private and not during class for an individual student. It would, however, be important to teach *all students* that they may, from time to time, use the "Calm Zone" (i.e., Time-out Zone) to calm down when they become frustrated and upset. The teacher may use a model student for demonstration purposes. It will also be critical to examine some of the possible triggers for behaviors that might qualify for time-out. Specifically, some students may have trouble learning certain material (e.g., math), and therefore show more behavior problems during this class or during math assignments.

BEHAVIOR PENALTY

Behavior penalty or response cost involves taking a privilege away from the student a short period of time. There are some advantages to the use of behavior penalty. A behavior penalty does not require a special place; it can be administered anywhere, anytime. Misbehavior can easily be dealt with using a behavior penalty. While this technique was also described for use by parents, its employment in school may differ slightly; a review here would be helpful.

The following are general guidelines for the use of a behavior penalty:

1. Make a list of those behaviors that may be difficult to deal with using other techniques (maximum of three).

2. Inform the student which behavior will result in a behavior penalty.

3. Make a list of privileges that can be taken away for a behavior penalty.

4. Remember to review with the student the consequences for one of these misbehaviors, as well as to note the consequences for appropriate behavior. If misbehavior has occurred in some situation in the past, the student is informed which privilege will be lost should the misbehavior occur and what the reward will be should the student show alternative appropriate behavior instead. This technique, called *priming,* will increase the effectiveness of the consequences and provide some cognitive link of past consequences to behavioral control at present. Over time, there will be some internalization of what consequences will follow either misbehavior or appropriate behavior. It is also assumed that, given a choice, the student would prefer the positive consequence (reward) for appropriate behavior.

5. It is wise to give the teen some predetermined signal (preferably nonverbal) to serve as a warning and to allow him or her to develop self-control, which may subsequently be rewarded. One signal might be to hold up two fingers. This will serve as a signal to decide either: (1) to change the current misbehavior or (2) to accept the consequences. All of this is reviewed with the student prior to being in these situations and you can even have a rehearsal similar to that previously discussed for time-out.

6. Once the signal is given, say, "Students, look here" (while holding up two fingers) and give the identified student a few seconds to respond. It will be far better for this student to develop and gain control over his or her behavior.

7. If control is achieved, you may say, "John, I'm very proud of the decision you made to stop teasing (annoying, hitting, or anything else) your neighbor. I like the way you are sitting quietly with her." If you have set up a point system (as described earlier in this book), then points may be given. The teen should, however, be reminded that you will be pleased to see good behavior continue and disappointed should he or she lose the reward for any misbehavior that might surface. Remember, the last behavior prior to a reward is the one that is strengthened. If the student were to misbehave prior to getting a reward, such misbehavior would then (erroneously) be rewarded.

8. Be consistent and follow through with the procedure. If you don't, the student will see that you often say things you don't mean. It is important to provide the reward as soon as possible. Any significant delays may result in frustration and some angry, acting-out behavior.

CLASSROOM ADJUSTMENT

Walker and Walker (1991) report that teachers rated a list of 56 appropriate adaptive social–behavior skills which included following classroom rules, seeking the teacher's attention appropriately, cooperating, and volunteering as important in classroom adjustment. They also rated a list of 51 descriptive maladaptive behaviors which included complaints, lies, sulks, and talks out as unacceptable. They point out that "the maladaptive social behaviors rated as *least acceptable* were those that disrupted the classroom, challenged the teacher's control and authority, and conflicted with the teacher's values. The *most unacceptable* social behaviors on the maladaptive list tended to be low frequency but high intensity events (e.g., stealing, aggression, defiance) that teachers have great difficulty coping with and managing effectively." The highest rated least-acceptable maladaptive social behaviors in school include:

- stealing
- inattention and overactivity
- physical and verbal aggression
- noncompliance/teacher defiance
- refusal to obey classroom rules
- property destruction
- classroom disruption
- tantrums
- inappropriate sexual behavior
- lying
- cheating

These behaviors were rated as unacceptable by more than 90% of the teachers participating in the national survey. One of the most basic problems underlying these maladaptive, disruptive behaviors is noncompliance. As Walker and Walker (1991) point out, "Since noncompliance is so closely linked to other forms of maladaptive behavior, its successful remediation can also reduce or prevent other inappropriate forms of student behavior in the classroom."

The initial antecedent of noncompliance begins with a communication to the student. Distinctions should be made among *requests* usually expressed in the form of a question, *commands* that are more authoritative in nature and do not allow the option of not responding or complying, and *demands* that involve a stronger authoritative command or request and usually do not allow for refusal. Requests and commands may escalate into demands; if compliance does not follow, the situation may deteriorate into direct defiance that could be explosive, sometimes violent, and almost always damaging to the teacher–student relationship. It has been noted that noncompliance often leads to more serious forms of disruptive and aggressive behavior including crying, aggression toward others, and even self-injury. It should also be noted that the more severe the noncompliance, the more comprehensive the interventions have to be to solve them.

Walker and Walker (1991) suggest that guidelines for coping with classroom noncompliance be organized in three areas: (1) Structure the classroom so as to maximize compliance and prevent noncompliance; (2) Improve the teacher–student relationship; and (3) Manage difficult teacher–student interactions involving noncompliance. Now, let's look at each area in more detail, as suggested by Walker & Walker (1991). Much of the information in this section on noncompliance has been adapted from their work. Those interested in more details may refer directly to their work.

STRUCTURING THE CLASSROOM

Teachers should provide (a) clear expectations for academics and behavior, (b) a predictable schedule with consistent routines, (c) careful explanations of instructions and directions for assignments, and (d) frequent monitoring and feedback on student performance. Student compliance is enhanced when teachers organize and structure their class in this manner.

Steps to set up the class to maximize compliance:

1. Plan the physical arrangement of the class to accommodate different types of activities.

   a. *Independent Student Work.* Best done at the student's desk. Separate students and be distraction free.

   b. *Teacher-led/Small-group Instruction.* Rules should apply to taking turns, raising one's hand, etc.

   c. *Free Time (least structured).* Rules should address what is allowed.

2. Develop class rules to communicate expectations. Areas to consider in developing rules include:

   a. Being punctual

   b. Entering class and going to assigned area

   c. Listening to and following teacher directions, instructions, and commands

   d. Seeking teacher assistance

   e. Talking with other students

   f. Participating in group discussions

   g. Being organized for assignments and instructional activities

   h. Maintaining academic engagement

   These rules should be carefully reviewed with the class, role-played, posted, and reviewed regularly.

3. Post a daily schedule of classroom activities. Students with ADHD need to know the sequence of activities with times allotted for each, and should be informed when there is a digression. Routines may prevent many problems associated with unclear expectations.

4. Reward students for following class rules. Remember, the student with ADHD probably has a long history of problems with rule-governed behavior. Praise should be very specific, mentioning the rule followed.

IMPROVING THE TEACHER–STUDENT RELATIONSHIP

The more positive the relationship, the more likely the student will want to comply with teacher commands, instructions, and directions. The following strategies are recommended:

1. Arrange frequent opportunities for students to experience success and to develop a sense of competence.

2. Do not respond directly to student behavior that is provocative, confrontive, or passively noncompliant.

3. Praise students with noncontingent, positive attention on occasions (i.e., give praise for no apparent reason, as long as the student is not engaging in any inappropriate behavior).

4. Provide success-oriented assignments that will ensure praise for completion.

5. Praise academic and social behavior.

6. Use humor.

MANAGING DIFFICULT TEACHER–STUDENT INTERACTIONS

In general, aggressive, antisocial, and conduct-disordered students initiate more interactions with teachers perhaps because they do not listen and comprehend directions. Be vigilant to praise those approaches that are appropriate. Remember that noncompliant students have learned their behavior pattern as a response to parents and previous teachers who have failed to follow through on commands and who have failed to monitor and provide appropriate consequences for these teens. Such students experience substantial social control and, through their noncompliance, avoid unpleasant tasks. Their coercive behavior is thus motivated by the power of social domination and control.

To maximize compliance, teachers must generally establish good rapport with the student, gaining his or her trust and respect. Difficult students are often suspicious and alienate from adults. To counteract this, the following suggestions are offered:

1. Listen and determine the student's interests.

2. Initiate conversation-making comments about these interests.

3. Identify sensitive issues from reading the student's records and avoid mentioning these issues.

4. Ensure that conversations with the student are not all about commands or academics.

5. Ask the student about areas in which he or she may have special knowledge.

6. Note the student's friends and peers, and have more positive contacts with them as well.

7. Have an active interest in the student's life.

8. Express an interest in the student's success in school in a way that reflects that you care about them.

In addition to these suggestions, the following guidelines should be considered with all difficult-to-manage students.

1. Do what you say—do not bluff and threaten. Consistency is absolutely essential to effective management.

2. Determine important critical priorities for the classroom. If a student is not disturbing the class but is slouching in the seat, is it worth challenging the teen, disrupting teaching and others in the class?

3. Certain observations by the teacher can help determine when to insist on compliance. In the face of a teen's hostile body language and angry stares, to insist on strict compliance may be unwise.

4. At times, consider accepting "partial compliance." If two students begin an argument but respond to a first command to "stop," reinforce their compliance. Giving the second command, "Both of you get back to work," may not result in compliance because of their high levels of agitation. To insist on compliance at this point may make the situation worse. At such times, it may be wise to disengage and back off temporarily from this situation until the students "cool down."

5. Consider, at times, ignoring the absence of strict or immediate compliance to a command. If one student fails to start a class assignment with others in the class, there may be no need to make a comment. A general comment, such as "Think about what you need to be doing at this moment," may be sufficient for the student to get started. If the student does not begin, the teacher may softly ask, "What's the problem?" If there is no response and the student is not disrupting the class, the teacher may best ignore this reaction and leave the student alone until he or she is ready to work. There would, of course, be natural consequences for not completing the work.

6. Try never to be drawn into arguments with a student—do not get angry and do not raise your voice. Remember that noncompliant students are often masters at provoking adults into punitive, negative, and controlling responses. Essentially, the teacher needs to train the student that such provocations have no functional value or effect. Teachers who are least reactive to provocations will have fewer of them from students.

7. It is best to settle conflicts between teacher and student without help or mediation from parents, the principal, or a counselor.

SPECIAL MANAGEMENT TECHNIQUES

Several of the problem behaviors commonly associated with ADHD may actually reflect underlying physiological processes. For example, the teen with ADHD generally has a lower level of arousal in the Reticular Activating System (RAS), creating a physiologically based lower level of alertness compared with normal adolescents (refer to Biological Basis for ADHD in Chapter 1). While some of these problem behaviors may be difficult to manage without medication, several other behavioral characteristics do respond to behavioral as well as other interventions. It is also well to remember that some physiological changes occur around adolescence that result in decreases in certain characteristic ADHD behaviors. The following are suggestions for the teacher who wishes to improve some of the characteristic ADHD behaviors that occur in the school setting. Keep in mind that some of the techniques and suggestions may be more appropriate for younger teens and others better used with older teens. Some judgment must be used with regard to the teen's level of maturity since even teens with ADHD will appear to be generally more immature than other adolescents of the same age.

Before proceeding to these specific behavioral characteristics, it is important to note here that even though some of these characteristics or symptoms may be problems for the adolescent with ADHD (as well as teachers and parents), it is essential that we look at some of these characteristics as positive qualities that may actually serve the teen quite well in the future. For example, impulsiveness may be seen as decisiveness; insatiability or persistence as ambition; and distractibility as having an open mind or open awareness so important for creative thinking. Many of these problems may have existed since childhood, and may now be even more difficult to cope with. However, some of the same procedures that may be used with younger children in the early grades may also be used with teens. Teachers may select those steps that might be feasible to use for a specific teen. A number of specific problem areas will be addressed.

Steps to Control Excess Motor Activity—Many teens exhibit less motor activity but some continue to engage in excess talking or restless behaviors. Some who do not may fall asleep in class. The following suggestions address this characteristic:

1. Establish the rules and limits for these motoric activities, keeping in mind the physiological basis for the behavior.

2. Develop predetermined signals that can cue students as to when to be quiet and when to talk (e.g., finger to lips).

3. Establish a specific consequence for breaking the rule, such as loss of recess time or loss of points, tokens, tickets, etc.

4. Use students who obey the rules as models by reinforcing their quiet behavior with verbal praise. (Do not, however, compare teens.)

5. Practice using cognitive mediation by asking students who talk or who are out of their seat, "What should you be doing at this moment?"

6. Use many more positive consequences for appropriate quiet behavior, with fewer negative consequences for talking or being out of seat.

7. You may use movement or talking as a positive consequence (i.e., a privilege) for maintaining quiet or restricting movement at specified times or during certain activities. Also, other times for these behaviors may be arranged (e.g., soft talking in designated areas allowed after work is completed).

8. Use stretch breaks, exercise, or brief relaxation exercises to assist in self-control of motor movements.

9. Integrate periods of active learning with seat work. Some teachers have students stand up for review of math or historical facts (multiplication tables) and randomly call on students. This will help to maintain attention, as well as allow for some movement.

10. Allow students to become more aware of their need to move. They can ask to move to a study carrel or to even work standing up.

Steps to Control Blurting Out Answers—This characteristic is also physiologically determined and may only be controlled to a degree.

1. Review and post rules regarding raising one's hand and being called on to obtain permission (i.e., to answer a question, get assistance, go to the bathroom, etc.). Post written rules and review them often.

2. Ignore those students who blurt out answers and fail to raise their hands.

3. Praise those who do raise their hands and use them as models. Remember never to compare one teen to another; simply give the praise to the teen who does the right thing. Make the praise specific; for example, "Charles, you followed the rule and raised your hand to answer. Very good."

4. When a teen (who has blurted out before) does raise his or her hand, direct attention to him or her immediately.

5. Monitor the number of times each day that the ADHD teen raises his or her hand to answer. Reward weekly improvement over each teen's baseline levels and then over the previous week's performance. A simple count of the number of times the teen raises his or her hand to answer may be kept from week to week. The counts on the first week before the problem is addressed is used as a baseline. The intervention may start in the second week. In addition to counting the number of appropriate behaviors, give verbal praise and some backup reward when a specific goal is reached.

Steps to Control Getting "Off Task"—Distractibility may be minimized using materials of high interest and activities that are stimulating. Also, keep in mind the teen's work-load span. Students with additional LD problems will need to be closely monitored to avoid frustration associated with work assignments that may be too difficult.

1. Use preferential seating in the class so that cues/signals may be given and the student's work may be more easily monitored.

2. Positively reinforce students who are on-task. A soft pat on the shoulder (nonverbal reinforcer) may be sufficient. Be aware of those students who respond poorly to verbal praise while they are on-task. Elaborate verbal praise in some cases may actually cause those students to get off-task.

3. Reinforce for completed work; this emphasizes the importance of continuing work to completion.

4. Divide assigned work into smaller work components to help the ADHD teen. Knowing how long a teen may maintain on-task work or about how many problems/sentences the teen can do in one sitting will help you in dividing up the work. The more you know about how to structure success for the student, the better the outcome will be for you both.

5. Make it okay to not understand, to express frustration, and to ask for help. Many students get off-task when they hit a snag in the segment of the assignment they perceive as being too difficult for them, or one they simply don't understand fully. The teen must realize that he or she can communicate the difficulty to the teacher and then continue to work.

6. Utilize some of the self-monitoring procedures.

7. Use privacy boards and allow the teen to work in more isolated parts of the room or in study carrels. Also, make these available for other students as well.

8. Plan for more active involvement in learning tasks to reduce distractibility.

9. Use devices to cue the teen to stay on-task and to filter out excess distracting noise.

10. Teachers may use reminder cards taped to the notebooks. Messages might include verbal reminders: "Am I tuning out?" or "Am I listening to noises instead of the teacher?"

Steps to Control Poor Attentional Skills (Visual/Auditory)—Determine whether the teen with ADHD learns best through the visual or auditory sense modality.

1. Actively involve the student in the learning process. Call out names randomly for answers. For example, in teaching historical facts, randomly name students to answer.

2. Use high-interest material in special projects related to concepts being taught to increase the student's interest.

3. Use frequent questions to ensure that specific bits of information are learned or simply rephrase questions to foster better involvement.

4. Identify critical bits of information by actually stating "This is something to which you will need to pay attention." Often, too, a great attention-getting device is to stop talking completely and pause; on most occasions, students will stop what they are doing and turn their focus on the teacher.

5. Repeat important information and present it in different sense modalities (e.g., written [visual] and oral [auditory]). Information is processed best with redundancy and repetition. In addition to your auditory and visual presentations, have the student write the material, as well as to involve the other third sense modality, kinesthetic.

6. Print critical information in bright colors, write on the board with colored chalk, and use brightly colored paper or highlighters to help draw attention.

7. Use prompts through a teacher aide or by headphones to help the teen with ADHD get started and continue working. In class, prompt with questions, such as "Joseph, what is it that you need to be doing right now?" to provide cognitive stimulation, which should cue the student to start (or continue) work. Initially, avoid direct requests, lest the teen become dependent on your cue in order to begin work. It is far better if the idea to begin comes from the student. Once this happens, you may say, "Okay, you know what to do—now do it."

8. Provide frequent reinforcement (e.g., praise or soft touch on the shoulder) for those who need attention. Statements, such as "Joe, you listened really well and you got the answer; good for you" or "I'm really proud of the way everyone started working right after I gave the directions" or "I really appreciate the way everyone looked at me while I gave directions."

9. Use novelty to help elicit attention. Teens with ADHD often respond and act like any other teen in novel and challenging situations. In fact, novelties that may elicit mild anxiety in normal teens may be beneficial to the ADHD teen. There is, of course, a delicate balance that exists in choosing materials that are novel and stimulating and those that represent such a dramatic change that the teen would have difficulty coping. Remember, the student with ADHD will have some difficulty adapting to drastic changes and transitions.

10. Use an overhead projector. It will allow you to use graphics and to visually emphasize points of instruction. It will also allow you to reveal only those portions of the material you were discussing at the moment. This helps the student to focus on what is relevant.

11. Use specific cues to denote where and when the student's attention is required. Rief (1993) terms these "point and go signals."

Steps to Control Work Not Completed—This problem may be clearly related to some of the other basic problems of the teen with ADHD, including a poor sense of time, frustrations over the work, and various distractions. Planning and organization problems would also be implicated here. In addition, some estimate is needed on what percentage of work completed would be acceptable. This involves the issue of productivity for which there is no norm. It is useful to compare the student to the norm for the class. Specific suggestions follow:

1. Monitor the input. Determine whether the teen knows what to do by asking questions regarding class assignments or by using a homework monitoring system at home.

2. Teach the student through modeling how to self-monitor to plan and organize an assignment.

3. Teach the student how to progress toward a goal. Teach him or her to use subgoals and a time schedule, to check to see if he or she is on course and on schedule. Use positive reinforcements as each subgoal is reached to provide incentive and motivation to continue.

4. Provide periodic reminders, both visual and oral, so that the teen is aware of the consequences for incomplete work and for work completed.

Steps to Control Confusion Over Direction—This problem may also relate to problems of attention/distractibility.

1. For each task, provide simple, clear, and concise directions whenever possible.

2. When directions are unnecessarily complex involving sequential planning, break them down and present the task step-by-step, providing reinforcement for completion of each step.

3. Present directions, both in writing (visual sense modality) and orally (auditory sense modality), and then post the written directions.

4. Check to be sure the message sent was, indeed, the message received. Sometimes it is best to call on someone who usually does get directions correctly, then praise that student for his or her accurate feedback on the assignment or task. This will demonstrate that knowing what to do is important and it does pay off (student gets a positive stroke). When the correct answer is given, the teen with ADHD is then allowed to privately revise any initial misperception he or she may have had without the embarrassment of exposing his or her confusion aloud to the class.

5. You may find it beneficial to role-play and then rehearse what any student may do when he or she does not fully understand the directions for an assignment. Although this process might be obvious to most students, it may not be obvious to the teen with ADHD.

Steps to Control Disorganization—Impulsivity, careless errors, and rushing through assignments, along with forgetting, all may play a role here.

1. Model organizational behavior patterns that are critical for the teen to develop. This might include a neatly organized desk, planned lessons and activities, and an "everything-in-its-own-place" routine for materials, supplies, and books in the classroom. Even teens can model their parent's or teacher's behavior.

2. Post assignments and review them orally to aid the teen in copying the assignment.

3. Use a "study buddy" system so students can double-check homework assignments, due dates, etc., after leaving school.

4. If at all possible, enlist the active cooperation of the parents for this vast problem and use a Homework Assignment Sheet (HAS).

5. In the classroom, initial on the HAS that the young teen has written the correct assignment and has the needed books to complete it.

6. Have the parent supervise completion of the work and initial on the HAS that the work was done and that it was filed in the appropriate place in the school pack.

7. Failure to comply with a step in the sequence should result in a specific negative consequence (e.g., no privileges when materials are not brought home one day).

8. By developing the kind of organizational routine illustrated on the HAS, the teen will learn a pattern of habits that forces him or her to self-monitor his or her steps in organizational work using a checklist procedure.

9. Using this type of monitoring system on the HAS will help to encourage the student to mark a calendar with due dates for special projects.

10. Focus on improvements in neatness and organization with compliments as often as possible.

11. Follow up regularly with participating parents; they need positive feedback, too!

Steps to Control Poor Handwriting—In some cases, sloppy work may be due to the student's tendency to rush through the work.

1. Provide each student with his or her own sample of your rules for written work. This may include type of paper, placement and sequence of identifying information (i.e., name, class, date), whether to use ink or pencil, whether proofreading is

necessary, whether script or print is acceptable, as well as any other specific criteria you have for this level of instruction.

2. Use graph or computer paper to aid the young teen who continues to show fine-motor coordination problems. It may be especially helpful if the teen starts with very large graph or computer pages, then gradually reduces the size of the squares or lines (using a copying machine with the enlargement/reduction feature). This will allow you to gradually shape the size of the writing of letters or numbers as coordination improves.

3. Help the student use a cognitive mediation approach while writing. This use of self-talk forces the student to slow down and pay closer attention to the details of his or her writing; it involves commenting on every movement involved in writing. Although it is somewhat laborious at first, students who use this procedure do slow down and do generally produce neater work. Because of the verbal component (self-talk) correlated with visual and kinesthetic cues, there is more "whole brain" involvement in the graphic writing process.

4. Of course, reinforce for those papers done neatly. Also, be alert for and reinforce noticeable improvements within a paper.

5. In addition to verbal praise for better fine-motor control and handwriting, praising the student's better work will provide a model as well as reinforcement for him or her.

6. When a student has previously demonstrated better handwriting, sloppy papers may be returned to be redone.

7. Be flexible with students exhibiting dysgraphia. Note that students with severe problems, who show little variation in their poor handwriting, may function better using an alternative means to complete work, like a computer or perhaps communicating some information using tape recorders. It may be necessary for you to drastically reduce the amount of written work and tests may best be administered orally. According to Dr. Mel Levine, these techniques are called "bypass strategies" to circumvent or work around a student's dysfunctions.

8. Teens may be especially motivated to work on handwriting problems using computer technology. The *Ultraphonics Tutor*® (Version 2) is a computer-based teaching program designed to teach and reinforce written language skills in a carefully sequenced format, utilizing computer handwriting recognition. Software is available through *The ADD/ADHD Resources Catalog*.

Steps to Control Homework Problems—These problems are discussed in greater detail in Chapter 5. Cooperation between parents and teachers is essential.

1. Coordinate with parents the use of a Homework Assignment Sheet (HAS) that is checked at school and at home.

2. Assign a "study buddy" to help double-check accuracy of recording the assignments and to provide back-up information when needed.

3. Write assignments on the board and review each one orally.

4. Develop an assignment sequence in advance and make it available to parents.

5. You may need to individually modify assignments for those students who have specific learning disabilities in reading, spelling, math, or writing. If the disability is in writing, a general reduction of written work assigned is recommended and you should allow the student to use a word processor to complete some assignments.

6. Many teachers do not wish to continue to check homework assignments, especially when there are several students in the class having problems getting assignments written down. A general solution is to teach the students how to do this task with training exercises conducted on a regular basis. An excellent resource for this is the "Skills for School Success" program by Archer and Gleason (1989).

Steps to Control Social-Skill Problems—Assessment and treatment of social skills are also addressed in more detail in chapters 2, 3, and 4. Many teens with ADHD experience greater difficulty in this area because of the increased demands in peer relations that are associated with the adolescence period of development. Experts such as Linda and Nick Elksnin have noted there are differences between the social-skill problems that have resulted from "not knowing what to do" *(an acquisition defect)* versus social-skill problems that have resulted from "not doing what they know" *(a performance deficit)*. Some suggestions follow to cope with social-skill problems.

1. Post an oral review of rules for the school-related activity or situation just prior to the teen going into that situation.

2. Review the consequences for breaking those rules. Rules and consequences should be reviewed daily, especially during the beginning of the year and periodically thereafter.

3. Incorporate a "behavior report card" (see Appendix 6 for a sample form) for recess, lunch time, or on the bus as part of an overall behavior program (solely either school-based or home-school-based). This behavior report card covers both appropriate and inappropriate behavior.

4. Generally focus positively on the more appropriate alternative behavior.

5. Set up structured recreational activities where inappropriate behaviors are more likely to occur and then encourage the more appropriate behaviors.

COLLABORATING WITH PARENTS AND OTHERS

PARENT-CENTERED ACCOMMODATIONS

The teacher who has created a collaborative relationship with the parents of ADHD students can achieve a great deal. The parent can make many changes in the way he or she responds to the teen with ADHD that can influence and improve classroom behavior. There are several programs available to parents.

Develop a Home–School Behavioral Program—Behavior at school may be monitored by the student's teachers and reported back to parents to create a cooperative behavior-management program that crosses the boundary between home and school. A teacher might evaluate how well the teen completed assignments, followed instructions, obeyed class rules, and got along with others; this information might then be sent home and transferred to a Home/School Behavior Chart. This type of system allows parents and teachers to work together on problem areas and gives teachers some indirect control over the most powerful reinforcers in the teen's life. In many schools it may be difficult to monitor behavior on a daily basis. Weekly reports may suffice and such information may be collected by the school counselor since most students will have more than one teacher. This program might involve either a point system or a behavioral contract.

Practice Simulated School Behaviors—There are many situations at home that closely resemble or parallel behaviors in school: following instructions, completing homework (like classwork), getting along with siblings and friends (as with peers in school), and obeying rules. For example, if a teen has had problems getting off-task at school, the parent might work on staying on-task during homework. By working at home on these behaviors that are similar to problematic classroom behaviors, the student may more rapidly develop better on-task behavior. Learning and generalization are even further enhanced when similar procedures are used in the classroom.

Another example might be a younger teenage student who yells and talks too loudly at school. At home, parents can review the "talk in a normal voice" rule and help the youngster practice appropriate behavior. At home, the youngster might be told: "Okay, now we need to practice talking in a normal voice just like you would be asked to do at school." Also, the rule should be posted and reviewed daily in both home and school settings. In this way, parents and teachers can help the student make the association between home behavior and school behavior. When the youngster demonstrates the appropriate behavior, he or she can be reinforced with verbal praise, specific feedback on "talking in a normal voice," and a "pat on the back." In addition to the routine practice, when the student spontaneously talks appropriately, his or her behavior should be noticed and praised. The verbal praise should be very specific, such as "I'm really proud of the way you talked in a normal voice. You remembered to do it just like we practiced. I didn't even have to remind you." Many other behaviors may be modeled by the parent, reviewed, and practiced until the teen appears competent in that behavior. Such work with simulated behaviors might primarily target those youngsters in the very early teen years.

When working with these simulated behaviors, the same cue that is used by the teacher may be used by the parents. For example, if the goal is to decrease the number of times the teen interrupts others while they are talking, both teachers and parents might use the same cue or signal for control, such as the classic finger over lips or the hand raised in a "stop position." When the teen learns this cue in both situations, he or she is better able to generalize between situations, and mastery of appropriate behavior is improved. Parents may also wish to work on behaviors at home in a context or background similar to that of the classroom. For example, while training behaviors at home, the parent might play a tape of classroom noise (tapes of classroom noise available through *The ADD/ADHD Resources Catalog*) to make the home environment more like the school environment. This may further enhance generalization and transfer of the learned behavior to the classroom.

DISRUPTIVE BEHAVIOR OUTSIDE THE CLASSROOM

STUDENT-MEDIATED CONFLICT RESOLUTION

Student-mediated conflict resolution has been researched for use on school grounds. It is unfortunate but many students have learned to resolve issues by fighting. Violence has been depicted by the media and entertainment fields as instrumental in dealing with conflicts.

On-line Mediation—With "on-line mediation," student mediators (e.g., fifth grade or above) are trained and deployed on the playground. They step in immediately and give students a chance to resolve conflicts as soon as they start.

Office Mediation—"Office mediation" is more appropriate at middle school and high school levels where conflicts are generally more serious. These students may need more confidentiality and more time to resolve issues that may have been going on for a long period of time. These students may thus make an appointment with a mediator to resolve conflicts. This procedure is offered as an alternative to suspension. When resolved, these students may have to give restitution (e.g., reading to younger children or helping them with homework).

Mediation Procedures—Mediators are sent to the school grounds and may stand out dressed in brightly colored safety vests with a clipboard. These mediators can get to fights within ten seconds before they escalate into more serious acting out. The mediator queries the two students, asking, "Is there a problem here?" Common situations might involve name-calling, bumping into students, and bullying. Many students are agreeable to mediation. Each student must explain his or her side of the story and the other "must agree to listen." The process is much like that seen during labor-management disputes. The mediator asks for options and both students look at the advantages and disadvantages of each option. If an option can be agreed upon, both will sign a contract.

The use of mediators enhances the normal teacher supervision of school grounds. This system works well with just two teachers as supervisors. The mediator tries to achieve a "win–win" solution for both parties and does not find fault with either one. If both students are not agreeable to work it out, they are referred to the teacher supervisor and go through normal channels of discipline.

Mediation Training*—The training process for mediators takes about 15 hours with periodic meetings. A supportive infrastructure is important to make this system work. For example, the principal may announce comments about some great mediation, mentioning solutions and not names. He or she may cite the names of mediators on duty and remind students of the mediation role. The school may also provide a bulletin board with pictures of mediators and articles about them. Workshops may be conducted for mediators.

Results of Mediation—One school using these procedures reported more than a thousand mediations! One theory of the success of student-mediated conflict resolution is that students may be more likely to work with peers because there is not an adult "telling them what to do." Drops of 50% in aggressive behavior have been reported using student mediation. These figures remain at this new lower level in a follow-up one year later. But the program needs to be implemented as described. One school reduced the number of mediators from eight to two and found that aggressive behavior increased.

ADVANTAGES OF STUDENT MEDIATION

The advantages of student mediation are (a) a significant (50% or greater) drop in aggressive behavior, (b) it is a universal program that does not target or label anyone, (c) it provides coverage at high risk locations, such as the school grounds, and (d) it is affordable. After 15 to 20 hours of professional training, the school can sustain the program on its own. It's interesting to note that many students who volunteer as mediators have had their own problems with aggression. If the student is out on the school grounds with a clipboard, he or she is less likely to get into trouble. These students thus learn skills they may use with their own conflicts. Program and student manuals on this program are available from their respective publishers as previously noted.

---

*A good resource for student mediation and mediation training is *Ready-to-Use Conflict Resolution Activities for Secondary Students* by Ruth Perlstein and Gloria Thrall (West Nyack, NY: The Center for Applied Research in Education, 1996). Another good resource is *School: A Comprehensive Program for Teaching Conflict Resolution* by Richard Bodine, Donna Crawford, and Fred Schrumpf (Champaign, IL: Research Press, 1994).

Chapter 7

SOCIAL PROBLEMS OF TEENS WITH ADHD

Getting along with others becomes increasingly more important during the adolescent years. With a gradual movement from dependence to independence, the adolescent encounters many demands in interpersonal situations, to which he or she must adjust. Relationships with siblings, peers, parents, teachers, and others become increasingly more important. There are three basic contexts in which these relationships occur: home, school, and work/play environments.

When appropriate adjustments are not made, problem behaviors surface. These adjustments are critical and can lead to frustration, anger, and depression, along with changes in self-concept and self-esteem. Those with ADHD are known to have more difficulty with change in general, and their underlying problems may make it more difficult to make needed adjustments. Procrastination, difficulty meeting deadlines, repeatedly making the same mistakes, and inability to plan for the future are some of the problems that impair adjustment. However, it appears that major difficulty in using self-talk to guide behavior may be related to poor internalization of cognitive rules that ultimately affects the development of social skills. Many teens with ADHD including hyperactivity are often rejected by their peers; those without hyperactivity may end up being ignored or neglected.

In the teen years, there are many adjustments that are glaringly apparent. Adjustments to physical and physiological changes in the body are paramount. Critical social adjustments are needed as the teen experiences changing relationships with the opposite sex. Social relationships in general become increasingly more important as the teen develops associations with some primary group of friends. Other adjustments must be made in areas that involve work or play as the teen finds that his or her relations with co-workers or team players entail different requirements. Problem behaviors may develop in any or all of these areas of relationships and could result in the development of deviant behaviors that may change the teen's course in life.

Teachers, parents, and clinicians must have a general understanding of the nature of these social problems and have some alternate approaches in dealing with them. The recent outbreaks of violence in schools have often been traced to problems in social relationships—break up with a girlfriend, snubbing and rejection by school athletes, and ostracism from normal cliques—all potential but not always obvious contributors to the eruption of violent acting-out behaviors.

GENERAL SOCIAL RELATIONS

There are many social relationships that require special focus during the teen years and especially for those teens with ADHD. Recall that children with ADHD have general difficulty coping with social situations. These difficulties in social situations may involve one or more of the essential social skills: listening, following instructions and rules, sharing, working and playing cooperatively, problem solving, and anger control. One or more of these essential social skills may be involved in problems encountered while developing relationships with others. During this period of life, the family may be of critical importance. Parents must provide a home atmosphere that is conducive to social-skill development. One way would be to give an open invitation for the teen to bring home his or her friends.

PEER AND SIBLING RELATIONSHIPS

Teens with ADHD may encounter added problems in social relationships with their peers. Their impulsive abrupt style, difficulty maintaining interest in conversations, problems with eye contact, difficulty listening, tendency to interrupt, and their frequent desire to manipulate and dominate conversations may be a turn-off to many teens. In addition, their difficulty in playing by the rules and frequent need to enhance risk-taking during routine activities may cause others to avoid or reject them. Consequently, peer relations may be strained and sometimes reach the point where the teen with ADHD finds him- or herself without friends. This may subsequently result in the teen retreating to the home and seeking a safe, nonthreatening, secure place in his or her room. Feeling lonely and isolated, the teen may find solace at the computer, and on the Net find others who may have experienced similar rejection. In lieu of this scenario, the teen may discover material that causes others to "take notice." Coming to school with plans to "build a bomb" will certainly get some attention and recognition, but clearly not from appropriate sources.

Teens who have experienced rejection from others may find other teens who have had similar rejection and find that their common experiences form the basis for a bond. Keep in mind that the teen with ADHD has been physiologically different, sometimes from birth, and this biological difference is related to his or her behavior. Physiological differences in arousal lead to stimulation-seeking or risk-taking behaviors. Similar to addictive patterns, there is often a need to seek out increasingly greater stimulation or risk taking. Perceiving many normal teen activities as "boring," the teen with ADHD seeks to "kick up the level of stimulation" a notch. Of course, in the presence of others with similar problems, there is often a synergizing effect on each other. This results in an escalation of stimulation-seeking and risk-taking behavior beyond that which would be experienced by either one alone. This indirectly reinforces each other and creates a kind of bond between them albeit one that is based on deviant stimulation and risk-taking behavior. Thus, one can see and perhaps foresee the kind of destructive pattern of behavior and may evolve from deficient social-skill development that has been seeded during the child's early years.

While not all teens with ADHD develop this pattern, early experiences may clearly influence whether more serious aggression problems of ODD or CD will be manifested when teens with ADHD come home from school feeling rejected, frustrated, and angry; they will often displace their feelings onto siblings. Teasing, picking fights, and taking their belongings may cause siblings to either feel victimized or to retaliate with equal anger. Siblings may react immediately with anger or depression or may simply wait for the "right moment" to retaliate. Given that about one-quarter of teens with ADHD will have a sibling with ADHD and that almost half will have at least one parent with ADHD, there is an increased likelihood of frequent family turmoil, conflicts, and acting-out behaviors.

At times siblings will have mixed emotions for their brother or sister with ADHD, at times feeling sorry for him or her and at other times feeling angry and resentful. Some jealous and envious reactions may occur when siblings perceive that the teen with ADHD receives more attention, garners more time from parents, and sometimes evades punishment for seemingly punishable offenses. On occasion, the sibling without ADHD may perceive a need to "be perfect" to atone for the brother's or sister's behavior, or perhaps as a means to garner some attention. However, it is often the one exhibiting inappropriate behavior who receives the most attention, regardless of how hard one tries to be perfect.

Some studies have shown that teens who are close in age to their siblings are more likely to identify with their siblings than their parents. Also, it has been noted that teens with ADHD may have a greater impact on younger children who mimic them to obtain attention. In such cases, the older teen is viewed as a primary role model; this may especially be the case if parents have lost control.

PARENT RELATIONSHIPS

One of the primary problems in relationships with parents is the conflict that arises over noncompliance. This is, however, nothing new as there has certainly been some difficulty with compliance at earlier ages. Whether this is due to inattention to directions, memory difficulties, or blatant defiance, much conflict is generated and maintained. It is further compounded by normal adolescent rebellion and some parents' difficulties in "letting go" of directive controlling restrictions on their teen. Sometimes, not knowingly, parents accurately perceive their teen as being much younger, and use this perceived immaturity to base their continuing philosophy of direction and control, especially of the young teen.

Most experts agree that the child with ADHD lags about two years behind the normal child in overall level of maturity, and there is no reason to believe that the teen with ADHD has "caught up." Much of the conflict between parents and their teen with ADHD stems from a combination of adolescent rebellion that is often reflected in challenging authority, along with the teen's unique ADHD attributes that are often poorly understood but play a major role in conflicts. Specifically, teens with ADHD may have a lower level of frustration together with impulsivity that makes for explosive acting-out characterized by yelling, talking back, cursing, and physical acting-out in hurtful destructive ways. All of the typical adolescent characteristics are magnified by ADHD. The teen with ADHD literally "wears emotions on his or her sleeve."

Characteristic moody, irritable, defiant, and explosive behaviors are exaggerated. Sometimes it is found that such explosive behavior may have a clear neurological basis. Regardless of its origin, much anger may therefore be generated in these relationships and might either be directed outward (acting out of aggression) or may be directed inward (depression). In either case, strong emotional reactions are likely to occur and must be handled before they result in serious injury or suicide. It is not unlikely that communication problems will develop as both teens with ADHD and their parents try to distance themselves from each other.

According to Dr. Russell Barkley, many teens with ADHD and parents say mostly negative comments to each other, and, at times, communication shuts down completely. Given that many parents of teens with ADHD also have ADHD, there is often more violent interchanges and a kind of synergizing effect in arousing strong emotions within the context of their interactions. This pattern often "keeps the argument going" when there is a lull and promotes further escalation of emotional acting-out.

In addition to communication problems, teens with ADHD often develop perceptions of being treated unfairly with rules being perceived as unfair and excessively restrictive. This provides one of many areas of conflict over which numerous arguments may ensue. Due to accumulated stress, anger, and suppressed anger (frustration), parents (and more typically the mother) react from this overly stressful, angry, and depressed state resulting in more critical comments, rejection, and punishment. This will then maintain a vicious cycle that results in continual inappropriate behavioral interactions. Many parents of teens with ADHD have chronic feelings of inadequacy, depression, and self-doubt, along with a sense of hopelessness that pervades all relations with their teenager.

TEACHER RELATIONSHIPS

Teachers of teens with ADHD may encounter all of the problems that are faced by parents. They, in essence, represent authority, as do parents. Many teens with ADHD will talk about teachers they like or dislike. Often, teachers who are disliked are ones who have conflicts with their students similar to those encountered at home. Likewise, some of the same personal characteristics and their lack of understanding of ADHD may influence their relationship with teens who exhibit ADHD.

First, the teacher's knowledge and understanding of ADHD is a primary factor. If the teacher operates with a misunderstanding of ADHD, many problems may result. For example, if the teacher perceives the ADHD teen's incomplete work as "laziness"—and not due to distractibility, organizational and sustained attention factors—many critical comments, poor grades, and failure may be the consequence. Along with the development of poor self-concept, the teen with ADHD will experience low self-esteem, feelings of inadequacy, and increased avoidance of academic work with each failure.

It is also not unlikely that the teacher who takes this stance will be one who is disliked by the teen with ADHD. In general, many teens with ADHD come to class with expectations of being treated poorly because of past experiences in early years of elementary school. It is rare to find a teacher who understands their problem behavior, yet when the teen does encounter an understanding teacher this will greatly enhance his or her chances of succeeding.

Interviews with successful adults who had ADHD revealed that the most important factor implicated in their road to success in life was that one person—parent, teacher, or significant other—who understood the person's problem and helped him or her to cope with it. A second factor involves the teacher's personal characteristics. The most obvious one is "flexibility." A flexible teacher may accommodate for a teen's shorter "work span" and offer to break down assignments. The teacher who is rigid and inflexible may certainly have conflicts with the ADHD teen.

Another important characteristic is "sensitivity." The teacher who openly confronts the teen about incomplete work, test grades, or medication may create embarrassment that may enhance the ADHD teen's already heightened awareness of being different from others. While this may be a problem at any age for those with ADHD, it is clearly exacerbated for the adolescent who has a strong desire to be like other teens and to not be seen as "different."

A third teacher factor is the teacher's own style of instruction. Some of the characteristics of teaching style may prove to be problematic for the teen with ADHD. These include: (a) a hurried method of teaching, speeding through lessons and assignments; (b) a general lack of organization in presentations and lectures; (c) a strong negative orientation with a basic tendency to focus on all inappropriate behaviors while ignoring appropriate behaviors; and (d) an authoritarian approach with a strong emphasis on rules and regulations, and a rapid adherence to a narrow view of information processing that does not allow for creative problem solving.

Many very successful individuals with ADHD were quite dependent on someone who helped foster their utilization of creative thought process. It is not possible to know what creative talents lurk behind a screen of apparent academic and social incompetencies for many of today's students with ADHD. However, there is clearly a need for greater emphasis upon the ADHD teen's strengths and the further development of such strengths.

According to Thom Hartmann (1993) in his book, *Attention Deficit Disorder: A Different Perception,* Thomas A. Edison was one of the many creative individuals who "changed the world." Hartmann reports that Edison left school at age 7 with only three months of formal education. In his writings he stated, "I remember I used never to be able to get along at school. I was always at the foot of the class. I used to feel that the teachers did not sympathize with me, and that my father thought I was stupid. . . ." Edison complained about the distractions of other children: his mother took over his schooling, encouraging him to explore things he found interesting. He was basically home-schooled, developing a strong interest in reading, and learned much about a wide variety of subjects.

Edison left home at age 12 and had many short-lived jobs. When he was 17 he had four different jobs; he was fired from each because of inattentiveness. At age 15 he was employed as a railroad signal man at night; he had to clock in over the telegraph every hour. He was fired when it was discovered that his punctual check-in was telegraphed by an invention using an alarm clock that would send the Morse Code signal every hour. This invention led to the development of the first automatic telegraph. At age 21 he received $40,000 for his stock ticker, but he had held a dozen more jobs by that time. Edison used the money to set up a lab and worked on many projects at the same time.

By 1877 he had more than 40 inventions that he was working on. Edison's schedule was erratic, as he often worked through the night and when bored, quickly switched to work on something else. He admitted that his inability to stick to one task was related to his creative efforts. Edison showed many characteristics of attention deficit hyperactivity disorder, but his inventions literally transformed the twentieth century with the creation of the electric light bulb, the phonograph, celluloid film and movie projector, the alkaline storage battery, and the microphone, just a few of more than 1,000 patents registered before he died in 1931.

Recently, there has been much discussion about "resiliency," a concept that refers to a person's ability to succeed despite almost overwhelming odds. Exploration of case histories of many prominent individuals who overcame disabilities has revealed this common factor of "resiliency." While there is much to be done in remediating the person's "deficiencies," it is most important to teach to the person's strengths. Identification and cultivation of these strengths may become the critical issue in reversing some of the present-day problems. A prosocial behavioral learning approach may ultimately be of greater benefit than a total focus on remediation of problematic behavior.

According to Kimberly Gordon, Ph.D., schools can foster resiliency in their students, helping them to increase competence in the face of obstacles. Teachers may help students improve their self-esteem and develop a positive self-concept by assisting their students in setting realistic goals so that they can be successful. The manifestation of competency fosters resiliency; a sense of competency is directly related to success. Thus, through various accommodations and skill development, teachers can ensure success. Such accommodation factors as allowing sufficient time to complete tasks, using visual instructional aids, developing an active (hands-on) learning process, helping students learn to problem-solve, and a strong emphasis on positive praise, are all important ingredients in achieving success, especially for teens with ADHD.

Heterosexual Relations and Dating

Sexual behavior is both prominent and risky for all teens, but especially for teens with ADHD. Due to their general immaturity, impulsivity, and diminished foresight and judgment, they may be unable to delay gratification and may engage in sexual activity that often leads to unwanted pregnancies and/or some sexually transmitted disease (STD). These STDs include gonorrhea, syphilis, HIV infection, chlamydia, genital warts, and herpes. Most of the STD conditions can be cured with the exception of genital herpes, HIV, and AIDS. Parents must emphasize some of the major points about disease prevention. For example, many methods of birth control do not protect the teen against such diseases. Frequent reminders about taking appropriate steps to not only prevent unwanted pregnancies, but also to prevent STDs are necessary.

There are many reasons for this behavior in teens with ADHD. Combining their need for stimulation with impulsive decision-making, along with other motivations, such as "looking for love" or simply "rebellion against authority," these teens are at an even greater risk for pregnancy and/or STD, not to mention contraction of AIDS through unprotected sex.

Much of the information about sex is obtained outside of the home of teens with ADHD just as in the case with normal teens. The school setting is, however, the most convenient one to provide sex education that is often not provided at home. It is also clear that sex education must begin well before adolescence. During the pre-pubescent years, boys and girls should receive information about future changes in their bodies and what these changes represent. Menstruation should not be a surprise experience for girls, and boys need to know that nocturnal emissions or "wet dreams" are a normal part of development.

Continuing sex education during the teen years needs to focus on such issues as decision-making, responsibility, and related issues such as respect, intimacy, and love. Teens need to know about STD; however, this information alone is not sufficient to prevent the occurrence of such diseases; teens and especially teens with ADHD must be given specific information about the prevention of infections. Even though teens with ADHD may be relatively more attentive to such information, this does not guarantee that they will remember it and use appropriate protection. Repeated reviews of such information seems warranted, just as teachers might repeat assignments more than once.

Because sexual urges are heightened and "novel" in the teen years, there is likely to be much conflict around issues of dating, especially for teens with ADHD. Past conflicts over homework or playing Nintendo™ for extended periods of time may seem trivial in comparison. Not only are teens with ADHD motivated by "sexual hormones," but, due to failure experiences in school and other areas, there is a strong need to be accepted and loved as a means of feeling a sense of importance.

Low self-esteem, combined with impulsivity and this need to feel accepted, may lead to rash decisions about sexual relationships. Just as there were rules for other activities in the past, there needs to be rules for dating behavior and curfews. These rules fall into the category of those that should not be negotiated with regard to sexuality and dating, but with the exception of curfews.

Rules for dating may involve: (a) when to date (what age, how many nights, etc.); (b) who may they date (suspicion is aroused by teens who do not wish for parents to meet their dates); (c) where may they date (refers to what places may be off limits and what mode of transportation will be used); and finally, (d) what will be the consequences for violation of rules. In addition to establishing the rules around dating, it will also be important to review these rules. Frequent periodic review (especially before dates) can be helpful without going to extremes or using embarrassing comments (e.g., in the presence of the date). Some teens do need to be reminded of the rules before each date.

Of course, much of this procedure will vary as the teen gets older and certain modifications in relaxation of rules may occur with consistent demonstration of adherence to the rules. Many parents may even make a copy of the rules, since learning of the rules will occur best when presented through multiple sensory modalities.

Finally, it is essential that parents discuss with teens who have ADHD how this condition will present problems in the area of dating and around issues of sexuality. Reviews about these matters must occur long before the teen with ADHD reaches dating age.

GANG BEHAVIOR, VIOLENCE, AND THE JUVENILE JUSTICE SYSTEM

When teens with ADHD have additional co-morbid CD problems, they are more likely to show aggressive and violent behavior. Teens with ADHD who have experienced rejection from peers may affiliate with others who have similar problems. Further, active rejection by school authorities, including suspension and expulsion for disruptive behavior, may generate considerable negative feelings for teachers and school administrators that may be transferred to classmates, and provide further justification for rejection of these teens. Over time, these teens become totally disenchanted with school and ultimately drop out. As drop outs, these teens are at even higher risks for deviant and perhaps antisocial behavior, with many accompanying legal entanglements (i.e., arrests for violence, sexual crimes, and drug-related problems).

How do teens become involved with gangs? One way is through escalation of their aggressive behavior. Simply, aggressive children and teens are drawn to deviant gangs of adolescents. An alternative is that older children and teens join gangs because they lack the social ability to relate to others, not because the gang gives them a feeling of "belonging."

It is the socially marginal incompetent teen who is pressured (or attracted) to join other social deviants. Relationships in gangs may be based on common themes of rejection by representatives of society in the form of peer and authority figures. The stability of gang memberships appears consistent with the general fickleness of adolescent social relationships.

Studies suggest that membership in some gangs may actually be more stable than with nondeviant groups. Further, while some members may change groups, they usually select groups of similar nature; in essence, the group's influence and philosophy is generally maintained. Thus, it is almost inevitable that such teens will come in contact with the juvenile justice system.

THE JUVENILE JUSTICE SYSTEM

Most teens with ADHD will not experience the Juvenile Justice System. However, ADHD is one risk factor for delinquency. Other factors that appear to play a more significant role is an additional diagnosis of Conduct Disorder. Often, problems with aggression have a chronic history beginning in preschool or the elementary grades.

Several behavior-management problems with oppositional characteristics warn of a poor prognosis. Behavior problems often escalate as others react negatively to the inappropriate aggressive behavior, resulting in rejection and further distancing from others. This makes it less than likely that the adolescent will respond to any of the usual attempts at changing behavior. The teen, seen as an outcast, then may tend to associate with others who have similar problems.

Gerald Rouse, a county judge in Nebraska, has considerable experience with teens who have ADHD. He states that ADHD does not excuse the teen who breaks a law, but ADHD should be considered when making decisions about how the teen should be processed in the Juvenile Justice System. Because of their impulsive behavior and poor social skills (including eye contact, grooming, and social commentary), these teens are seen in a poor light by probation officers, judges, and others in the system.

In addition to "violating a law," teens may achieve the label of "status offender" when he or she is uncontrollable in school, stays out late at night violating curfew, or is reported to be a runaway. Information is needed by decision-makers in the Juvenile Justice System regarding the nature of ADHD, and especially about the specific combination of ADHD and co-morbid problems that the identified teen presents.

Process in the Juvenile Justice System begins when the teen makes first contact with a police officer. When a parent is at the Police Department, the teen is often not allowed to be questioned without an attorney present. If a teen's behavior has been acceptable, he or she may be released to the parents. If the teen has made "smart remarks," the teen will go through the intake process. If the teen is then released back to the parents, there will be some "conditions" that the parents will need to follow exactly. If it appears that the teen will run away, or if it seems like the teen would be a danger to self or others, he or she may be held in detention. This may last until a hearing can be held. No bail is allowed.

If it is determined at the hearing that the teen can't be released, the teen will be sent to a detention center, where medications may or may not be given. If continued education cannot be provided at the center, the teen's school will be informed and his or her school assignments, books, etc., may be sent to the detention center.

If a decision is rendered against detention, the teen may only have to do some public service work and keep up with homework, grades, and a treatment program. The Juvenile Justice System can, however, also require that the teen make restitution. A probation officer assigned to the teen's case must also know about the teen's disorder(s). The decision may be made to provide restitution and to allow for probation. It may be necessary to make restitution to the "victim," to the "public" through public service work, and to the "teen," especially cooperating in his or her treatment program. However, many teens with ADHD who go through this process are prone to impulsive behavior and poor judgment. They often frustrate supervisors and judges by their comments or "attitude," which may result in revoking of probation and more restrictive dispositions in their case.

ANALYSIS OF DELINQUENT ANTISOCIAL BEHAVIOR

Because of the frequent co-morbid association between ADHD and the aggressive and disruptive behavior disorders of Oppositional Defiant Disorder (ODD) and Conduct Disorder (CD), there is a relationship with the antisocial behaviors in the later teen and adult years. The prognosis for those teens with ADHD and CD is poor.

Since the CD component adds such significant additional risks for the teen with ADHD, it is informative to look at some of the early warning signs of CD. First, symptoms of CD that appear before 10 years of age are associated with the highest risk for later delinquent behavior during the teen years and adult antisocial behavior. Teens with ADHD who exhibit characteristics of CD in adolescence appear to be less likely to manifest severe and persistent problems in later years, compared with those whose CD characteristics began in childhood. Some of the early warning signs of CD in youth are early drinking, smoking, and sexual behavior, along with use of illegal drugs, poor performance in school, being truant, aggression toward others, destruction of property, reckless behavior, and a high degree of risk taking.

While the highest risk for the onset of ADHD and ODD is during the preschool years, the onset of CD continues throughout adolescence. Studies have reported a gradual and steady increase in the percentage of children with ADHD and CD (20%) at 4–6 years of age to almost 50% at 11–17 years of age. Less is known about the part ODD may play, but this condition has been related to both ADHD in early years and CD in later years. However, the critical factors that appear as prodromal characteristics of antisocial behavior seem to implicate ADHD and CD.

Many experts concur that the presence of both conditions makes for greater persistence and severity of later antisocial behavior. In a study by Loeber (1988), it was noted that males with high ratings on both aggression and ADHD exhibited two to three times as many criminal offenses as boys rated high only on aggression.

A similar analysis on a different sample by Ramington Loeber and Van Kanmen in 1990 reported that males rated high on both CD and ADHD in childhood, and were more likely to exhibit delinquent or criminal behavior in adolescence and adulthood than males rated high only on CD problems in childhood. Perhaps there are different forms of CD or perhaps the combination of CD and ADHD generates problematic behavior that is more serious than either alone. The latter interpretation appears more plausible.

Some of these potential delinquent and antisocial behaviors include substance abuse, rape, shoplifting, burglary, and murder. Some less severe acts might include truancy from school, running away from home, destruction of property, and some sexual misconduct. The underlying factors unifying many of these antisocial acts are: (a) rule violations, (b) risk-taking activity, and (c) aggression toward people, animals, or objects. Clearly these factors implicate ADHD with CD. In general, it is recognized that ADHD, CD, and emotional and behavior disorders are all risk factors for delinquency. Statistics indicate that as many as 90% of youths in the justice system meet the diagnostic criteria for one or more of the disorders.

It is also important to note the often-cited observation concerning the relationship between the use of Ritalin® and violent acting-out behavior. Whenever there is a story about violent acting-out behavior, the media may pick out and note that the teen was on medication. Recent school violence in Conyers, Georgia revealed that the 15-year-old shooter had used Ritalin®. Of course, the fact is that millions of children who have taken Ritalin® showed no incidence of violence. It is also known that the 15-year-old student was being treated for depression, a mood state that often accompanies ADHD. Most experts would agree that treatment must include counseling or behavioral therapy, as well as medication. Additionally, the emphasis needs to be on a proactive approach to this problem, not a reactive one. As Bob Seag commented in his Internet column on Attention Deficit Disorder, "It is not Attention Deficit that is shooting and killing our children. It is a deficit of knowledge about what makes these things happen and how we can prevent them."

ALCOHOL, DRUGS, AND OTHER ADDICTIONS

Teens with ADHD appear to be more likely to use alcohol and cigarettes, according to reports by Dr. Russell Barkley. Following a group of adolescents over a period of several years, he found that teens with ADHD were more likely to smoke and to engage in more alcohol and drug use than matched controls. These teens with ADHD also had a greater risk of HIV since they had a longer history of unprotected sex. The implication of this study is that teens with ADHD are risk takers and may behave in ways that can have serious and deleterious consequences on the teen's health now or at some future time. When teens with ADHD have co-morbid CD, there is also increased likelihood of drug abuse. Some of the primary characteristics of those teens addicted to alcohol or drugs are loss of control, preoccupation with the substance, and continued use even when there are severe and negative consequences.

Many teens do experiment with various substances, including teens with ADHD. From Barkley's study, roughly 40% of teens with ADHD reported using alcohol, while 17% used marijuana; only 4% were reported to use cocaine. Again, teens with ADHD plus CD were most likely to abuse substances like alcohol, cigarettes, and marijuana than teens with ADHD alone. Use of marijuana has been noted to increase with age: young teens' rate (about 13 years) was less than 1%; during the period of 14–16 years, the incidence was about 1.5%; at 17–20 years, it was nearly at 3%. Marijuana also appears to be a gateway drug, often leading to further drug use.

Researchers have found that two factors predict future use of drugs: (1) association with others who use drugs, and (2) aggression and hyperactivity components. Some researchers believe that those teens with ADHD who use drugs may attempt to "self-medicate" to deal with problematic behaviors of ADHD. Others may view such drug use as attempts to cope with the stress of life in a person who feels generally inadequate and who presents a low level of self-esteem. Using some drugs, the teen may experience a breakdown of inhibitory control, which may facilitate impulsive thrill-seeking behavior with drugs to the point where fatal self-injurious behavior may occur (i.e., a form of suicide).

With a history of frustration, failure, and depression, the use of some drugs to create, modify, or submerge feelings may develop some practical utility. Those teens with a history of aggression in childhood appear to be most at risk for later drug use. Much of the available evidence indicates that the use of appropriate medications for ADHD does not lead to future drug use. In fact, the risk of drug use may be reduced by appropriate treatment, including stimulant medications.

There are several areas for parents and teachers to address with regard to substance abuse:

1. Know and recognize which substances may be used and to understand what effects they may have on the body.

2. Know about possible combinations of these common drugs and especially combinations with prescribed medications for ADHD.

3. Know potential warning signs for substance abuse.

4. Know what strategies to use and how to confront the teen with ADHD who has been abusing substances. Following confrontation, an action plan must be implemented and should include restriction with curfews, no overnight stays away from home, greater structuring of the teen's time, and perhaps random drug testing (depending upon the substance used).

5. Know which treatment programs are available for such teens.

While some psychiatrists may be reluctant to prescribe medication for ADHD fearing that it may exacerbate the substance-abuse problem, others believe that treating the ADHD may allow the teens to become more involved in their substance-abuse treatment program due to better concentration and more positive feedback on their improved behavior. However, physicians may wish to concentrate on the use of certain medications. Some tricyclic antidepressants may be avoided because of some dangerous drug interaction effects. Although Ritalin® could be used, there is always the risk that it will be sold for funds to obtain other substances. Buproprion is sometimes a good alternative, but there will need to be careful monitoring of effects. Since about one-third of all teens with ADHD may abuse some drug, usually to self-medicate, many experts agree that it's essential to properly medicate those teens with ADHD and substance-abuse problems to preclude a need to misuse other substances.

These areas of concern are addressed in a handout that may be used by teachers and parents in dealing with the teen with ADHD who is involved or potentially involved with substance abuse. These handouts are found in Appendix 2 and 3, respectively.

Social-Skills Component of Self-Esteem

Teens with ADHD often present a negative self-image and low self-esteem from a history of being teased by peers and siblings, criticized by teachers and parents for inappropriate behavior, and general failure to meet unrealistic expectations and perceptions of others. Sensitive both neurologically and emotionally to their difficulties and failures, they experience much personal frustration and are generally quite aware of their numerous failures. Over time their self-perceptions become more deeply ingrained as they are seemingly more doubtful about their ability to cope with either academic or social situations.

Indeed, they are quite sensitive to the comments and actions of others, and may feel quite vulnerable, often inadequate, and at times quite depressed as they attempt to deal with the ever-increasing challenges of adolescence. It is suggested that such teens have experienced nothing to counteract the seemingly devastating effects of negative and critical events. These teens have developed a hopeless view of coping with the many academic and social situations that confront them during this period in their life, and have either avoided them or have gravitated toward deviant-behavior groups.

On the other hand, some teens with ADHD have acquired a sense of "resiliency" that may aid them in coping with future life situations. These are individuals who have experienced a sense of caring and concern from significant others that has fostered and reinforced a sense of competency, sometimes referred to as "island of competency" in a sea of confusion and negativity. Such teens have most assuredly had support from positive strokes, positive comments about strong points, and reinforcement for using strategies to cope with difficulties encountered. All contribute to the development of "resiliency" and to ultimate success in life.

Chapter 8

PREPARING FOR ADULTHOOD WITH ADHD

Transitions present major problems for teens with ADHD. Adolescence itself presents many situations that require adjustments: transition from elementary to middle school and then to high school may have been difficult. However, there is perhaps no transition that is more difficult and more important than that between adolescence and adulthood. Following high school there may either be continued education at the college level, some special vocational training, the military, or the adolescent may simply enter the workforce directly. To be successful as an adult, the teen with ADHD will need to develop and utilize success strategies, employ various aids and devices (i.e., beeper), use novel and creative techniques to maintain interest (i.e., a reminder watch), mechanisms to keep on time and on schedule (i.e., daily planner), and to remain on target (i.e., a "to do" list) to avoid the devastating effects of "chronic procrastination."

Preparation for this transition to post-high school placement usually begins in the mid-high school years; there is considerable information to gather in order that appropriate decisions may be made. There must be some occupational, educational, and vocational exploration. Meetings with the school counselor may help to coordinate information regarding interests (from tests given in high school) with the student's capabilities based on grades, scholastic achievement tests, and other information. Many teens with ADHD will have, in their student file, copies of prior psychological evaluations that were conducted when a diagnosis of ADHD was made. However, if the tests were administered several years prior, the results may be of little value regarding the cognitive abilities and achievements of the teen at this age level. Many school counselors will have reading material on various occupations and may also have the *Dictionary of Occupational Titles,* which will not only provide descriptions of various occupations with their earning potential and employment possibilities, but will also provide information on job requirements, training, and educational criteria for a particular occupation. Many schools even have computerized versions of such information. There are levels of decisions required. The first and most basic decision is the initial direction one will take. The options are (1) college; (2) vocational technical school; (3) a job; and (4) the military.

VOCATIONAL AND OCCUPATIONAL ISSUES

The student's initial selection does not need to be a final decision; however, serious thought must be given to this decision and preparation must be made to follow-through with that decision. Decisions may be changed. If one chooses the military first, this does not rule out college. Likewise, if one works for a year or two, this does not rule out going to college. Helpful in this initial decision and planning process are experiences from summer jobs, volunteer work, part-time after-school job, etc., as well as knowledge gained from reading about and talking with workers in various occupations. Hobbies and involvement in sports or music may also provide a basis for making this first basic decision. Maturity level and developmental issues certainly affect this initial decision about one's future after high school. Many high school students with ADHD are generally immature and may lag behind their non-ADHD counterparts by as much as two years. Thus, at 17 or 18 years of age, one can certainly spare two years and make another choice at 19 or 20 years of age at a time when they may be more mature and stable and are better equipped to handle a more challenging life plan.

Students should also be aware of The School to Work Opportunities Act of 1994 which emphasizes the importance of vocational education. The primary goal of this program is that every student (after completing high school) be employed or receive training that would result in employment.

School to Work Opportunities brings the workplace into the classroom, transforming workplaces into places of learning. School to Work Opportunities combines quality academic classes at school with hands-on learning and training in the workplace, and appears to be an ideal option for many teens with ADHD. For students, this program allows the teen to get actual work experiences while in school, to get potential employment contacts, and improve self-confidence. The three elements for this program are: (1) school-based learning, (2) work-based learning, and (3) connecting activities, the latter developing courses that integrate classroom and on-the-job training, matching students with employers, training, job-site instructors, and generally maintaining the interface between school and work. Graduates who have participated in this program get a High School degree or GED, as well as a "skills certificate." This program may be beneficial in reducing the drop-out rate, enhancing the employability of these teens, and expanding the skilled workforce.

Some of the other youth training programs are listed on ETA website, www.doleta.gov/programs/youthtrn.htm. In addition to the School to Work program, the list includes: apprenticeship training, Youth Fair Chance (YFC), the TTPA Summer Youth Employment Program, the JTPA Year-Round Youth Training Program, One-Stop Career Centers, and perhaps the best-known program, Job Corp. The latter will thus be described in more detail.

Job Corp is a nationwide full-time residential program that offers training, education, and support services (including housing, meals, medical care, and counseling) together with occupational exploration; world of work and social skills training; and competency-based vocational and basic education for disadvantaged youth. This program is open to those 16 to 24 years of age who may be high school drop-outs (not on probation or parole), free of serious medical/behavioral problems, and who come from disruptive environments. According to the U.S. Department of Labor Statistics, 70% are members of minority groups, 80% are high school drop-outs, and 40% are from families on public assistance. A wide variety of skills may be acquired through training in construction, auto mechanics, business and clerical skills, trades, health occupations, computer occupations, and the culinary arts. Over 40% of Job Corp students complete vocational training, and over 20% are placed in jobs or enrolled in continuing educational programs.

In the recent past there has been some apparent bias against vocational education. However, for some students plans for vocational education might best be discussed during the later years of high school or part of their Individualized Education Plan (IEP). Much of this discussion should focus on the transition from high school to vocational training and subsequently to the work place. As a service of the President's Commission in the Employment of People with Disabilities, the person with ADHD may consult the Job Accommodations Network for help in assessing the need and appropriateness of available accommodations for the employee with ADHD. Now let's look at some of the major options available.

COLLEGE

A decision regarding higher education requires a choice of either a two-year program (Associates of Arts Degree) or a regular four-year program. Many students with ADD and/or LD select the two-year program because of the following issues:

1. Students often live at home while going to a two-year community college and may therefore receive continued support and assistance from parents.

2. Classes at such schools are generally smaller.

3. Students are generally given more individual attention and assistance.

4. In addition, these two-year community colleges may provide special requested accommodations just as many four-year colleges and technical training programs do.

Four-year colleges and universities are generally larger and more impersonal, and typically have more stringent admission requirements (e.g., higher SAT scores). However, many students may be conditionally admitted into a four-year program and be required to take some remedial classes or developmental studies to make up for academic deficiencies and at the same time may give the student some taste of college life in a nondemanding course format. Before the student makes a decision to apply to a college or university, there are several important matters to consider:

1. Make sure that grades and other indicators of cognitive abilities meet prerequisite standards for this level of work. The most reliable indicators will be those grades obtained under optimal conditions of medication and perhaps behavioral intervention or coaching, or from psychological test scores indicating a high level of ability. It *must* be pointed out that superior intelligence is not required. However, a solid average or above-average grade history is essential.

2. The student must be aware of the programs of interest at the college.

3. The student should visit the college and talk with faculty, students, and perhaps even graduates to obtain the most comprehensive picture of that academic institution, in order to know if that school will meet his or her needs.

When visiting a college, the student applicant may also try to meet with the counselor at the Disabled Student's Services (DSS) office. The student needs to remember that he or she is not required to disclose any information on the admissions application about his or her disability, or even that he or she has a disability. While many college and university faculty are aware of Section 504 and accommodations made for specific disabilities, some may have little or no information. These issues are best discussed with the counselor at DSS. Parents of the teen with ADHD may also contact the Association for Higher Education and Disabilities (AHEAD) for additional information regarding various aspects of college life for individuals who are disabled. Interested parents may contact AHEAD, based in Columbus, Ohio, at its Internet address, www.netwalk.com/~ahead/ldguide.htm. Information on training, technical assistance, job listings, and guidelines for documenting a learning disability are provided.

VOCATIONAL–TECHNICAL SCHOOL

This type of training may be quite relevant to meet the increased need for graduates who have special skills in business, health sciences, industrial work, or the arts. Graduates of these programs may be able to transfer credits to a college or university should such a decision be made after completion of this program. These programs may provide excellent opportunities for teens with ADHD because: (a) the student has a strong interest in the skill training provided, (b) there is much greater emphasis on hands-on training, and (c) the programs are generally of shorter duration than traditional college programs, sometimes requiring only 9–18 months of school.

A JOB

Graduating from high school, the teen with ADHD may literally be "sick and tired of school." He or she may have had enough course preparation, homework, reading requirements, tests, and struggling to control attention and behavior in order to pass to the next grade level and to eventually graduate. This teen with ADHD may have experienced the "joy of remuneration" from summer jobs and using typical adolescent distortion develops big plans for his or her money. In today's technical world, however, there are few jobs for those who just have a high school education without any technical training. While selecting this option to go directly to a 40-hour-per-week job may not be a permanent choice, it may allow the teen with ADHD: (a) some time to mature, collect information, and make another wiser choice in the future; (b) to develop some work habits that are essential for either future education or other work activity, e.g., establishing a routine of getting up, getting breakfast, driving and being on time for work—all essential life skills that can benefit the teen in later years; and (c) to develop an appreciation of real-world basic skills needed for survival. These basic survival skills include:

1. learning to cook and clean

2. learning about money management (e.g., credit cards, checking account, paying bills, etc.)

3. learning about getting along with others at work or with others who may share living quarters

All of these skills and experiences developed while working may be sufficient to encourage the teen with ADHD to return to the school setting and to further his or her education or training, if this is at all possible based on academic and learning potential.

THE MILITARY

In the past, this option was often recommended for those students who had not decided what they wanted to do in life. Today, many students still select the military for that same reason. The military offers the student with ADHD opportunities for education and training that may not otherwise be affordable and may be carried over into later civilian life. Many students with ADHD also find the rigidity and routine of military life to be quite useful in coping with some of the difficulties they have experienced. Some of the learning experiences may be difficult, but the results may be worth it. However, a very real problem today is that the military does not accept candidates who have a history of formally diagnosed ADHD. There have even been reports of some teens who joined the military, and who later were diagnosed with ADHD, and were forcefully separated from the military.

The crux of this issue relates to the use of stimulant medication. Use of stimulants presents "management problems for the military" according to Dr. William Hathaway who has explored the details of military policy regarding ADHD. He explains that the military has a strict rule regarding use of all stimulants classified as Schedule II Controlled Substances. ADHD is considered a *Specific Academic Skill Deficit* in the 1994 Defense Department's directive entitled *Physical Standards for Enlistment, Appointment, and Induction.* Under this directive, ADHD is noted to be a condition that interferes with performance at work. However, unsuitability for military service is made on an individual basis. Specifically, there must be evidence of some impairment of ability to function such that the individual with ADHD is unable to do his or her job.

The presence of ADHD may therefore not exclude a person for military service, but it would certainly make it more difficult for that person to get assigned to specific duties or to obtain security clearance. It also seems that the more chronic the condition (i.e., the earlier the diagnosis was made), the more likely that the candidate will be ineligible for military service.

These issues may soon be moot, as there are current attempts by CH.A.D.D. to bring about changes in these policies. Those teens with ADHD wishing to have the most current information about the status of the selection procedures in the military where ADHD is concerned would be advised to consult the CH.A.D.D. Office. (See resources for contact procedures.)

FOCUS ON ABILITIES AND ACHIEVEMENTS

While key interests and the closeness of fit between personal characteristics and job features are the two primary determinants of success in any specific occupation, there is a strong need to focus on the teen's basic abilities and achievements in most all job situations. Very often, the teen with ADHD has developed some biases against personal abilities that may cloud or distort the teen's perception about whether he or she is capable of performing some specific job. The way a teen thinks about and sees him- or herself may therefore be crucial in determining whether the teen will be able to perform to capacity in the job in question. This is simply a variation of the old theme "If you think you can't do it, then you probably can't do it."

Appropriate use of positive success-oriented visualization is quite important to those who must achieve to the maximum capacity. Many superior athletes have used such visualization strategies to perform incredible feats in sporting events and in most recent applications in the Olympics. It is not unusual to find some teens with ADHD who have actually scored in the superior range of mental abilities to think that they are "not very bright" and should not attempt to engage in any challenging job or educational program. Some of our most prominent scientists, doctors, entertainers, and authors (referring only to a few groups) have been able to express their creative talents not in spite of their disability, but rather along with it. A partial list of well-known persons who were thought to have had ADHD or those living persons who have admitted to having ADHD are listed in Chapter 10. This list is certainly incomplete. There are many individuals with adult ADHD who have not been diagnosed, and many prominent or historical figures who probably had *ADHD* but could not be positively identified just from biographical records and/or interviews with those who either knew the person or who has researched the person's background.

PROBLEM BEHAVIORS EVOLVING INTO ASSETS

There are many teens with ADHD who have experienced the difficulties associated with their problematic behavior. For many of these teens, very little could be identified or construed as having a positive or desirable value when browsing through their vast repertoire of behavior. Under the control restraints of the classroom, most of these teens experienced a long history of attempts to keep their attention focused, their body still, and their behavior under control. In contrast, the older adolescent or young adult may have greater flexibility to move around, to take breaks, drink coffee, etc., so as to maintain alertness and control. Characteristics or problem behavior that would typically get the younger child in "trouble" might develop into an asset for the older teen or adult. For example, in young teens, the kind of open focus with many stimuli bombarding him or her may result in confusion and distraction. However, the same pattern in an adult, who must be aware of many things at one time, may be an asset. The pilot, for example, who must monitor many things (both visually and auditorily) simultaneously might consider this "open focus" an asset in her job. Likewise, the engineer who must keep track of information from many gauges, the surgeon who must be aware of many on-going system monitors, or even the teacher who must monitor each student's behavior on some specific skill will all benefit from this form of "open focus" attentional state.

Similarly, a person with ADHD appears to be generally sensitive, both emotionally and neurologically. Use of these clinical skills of sensitivity can aid in diagnosis and treatment for those in the mental health field. Those in creative arts may also reap benefits from their neurological sensitivity as reflected in their creations as "works of art." There is a story about Steven Spielberg when he was an adolescent in school. He was not doing well academically and yet dreamed of one day "making movies." His mother, with innate wisdom, allowed him to skip school one day so that he could go to the desert to "make a movie" with his inexpensive movie camera. His experience was not only a great motivational inspiration for him, but it also allowed him to experience and practice something that he wished to do in the future. What might we all have missed had he been denied that opportunity and instead was forced to suppress his creativity and sit in class that day! The sensitivity expressed through his creations might be considered a unique quality, yet there is something akin to this in every person with ADHD. The sensitivity, open focus, or other inborn physiologically based raw talents need to be acknowledged, developed, modulated, and directed—such talents may give rise to our next generation of creative individuals.

SELF-CONCEPT AND SELF-ESTEEM

It is important to not only consider the perception of the self, but the label and feeling states associated with it are tremendously important. Thus, one's perception of self with ADHD may be that of a "klutz," or "absent-minded professor," a "flake," "an unreliable person," and so forth. Many of these self-perceptions affect the self-concept and generate low self-esteem since these are all negative feeling states associated with the labels. Therefore, one must not only overcome these perceptions by modifying them, but also by reframing them so that they might be processed differently. Many of these perceptions will generate feelings of anger, depression, inadequacy, hopelessness, and despair.

As long as these self-perceptions with their associated feeling states exist, the person with ADHD may be weighted down with useless "excess baggage" that serve no useful function. Should these early patterns persist, the teen is put in a disadvantaged position. All attempts at adaptation to life situations will be affected by this "aura of failure and negative feeling states." It is crucial that with approaching adulthood, these perceptions and feelings must be modified not only to improve the teen's immediate personal life, but also to enhance his or her chances of success in later life.

AN ADULT WITH ADHD: MEMORIES OF TEEN YEARS

The following description of an adult who recalls early years with ADHD is a complex example of ADHD—plus a variety of other characteristics—that entailed significant problems with anger, anxiety, and depression. This pattern has evolved into a residual ADHD pattern plus evidence for Bipolar Disorder. The example is presented because, while it does represent a complex pattern that is not typical of all cases of ADHD, it depicts the concept of "resiliency." It further shows that given the structure of love and support, along with treatment and/or coaching, a person with these complex behavior patterns can adapt and survive.

While this person mentions having had some perceived difficulty socially, he does not explain that being able to talk with others, to meet and talk with strangers, and to do so in an engaging and humorous manner, was an asset that actually developed out of childhood. When analyzing his developmental history, the sensitivity in social situations was there and appears today as a well-developed attribute that may aid him in occupational as well as personal areas of his life. Now, his story.

I am a 35-year-old man and have been married three times. I have two sons, one I have not seen in years. I am very close to the other son and try to see him as much as possible. My son lives with his mother and her two children from prior relationships. I work as a marine mechanic now, but I have had many jobs before that. I am living by myself and have no current love relationship, although my third ex-wife sees me frequently and we still have a good relationship and are the best of friends.

I had a difficult childhood. I grew up with a mother who was an alcoholic and a father and stepfather who both mistreated me, often beating me and worse. I was also sexually abused. Because I was neglected, I was taken out of my home (a trailer) and had several foster parents until I was adopted around 8 years of age. I finally had a stable home.

I remember school as a difficult place to be; in fact, it was more like a "prison." I could not sit still and had trouble doing some of the work. I had trouble "paying attention" to the teachers, and when I did something wrong they often drew a lot of attention to that fact. Many kids in class would laugh at me—they thought that many things I did were funny. I was the "class clown."

I often acted angry, felt angry, and was angry. I also had a lot of trouble getting close to anybody and still do, although not so bad. I was a picky eater. I got into a lot of trouble because of my behavior. Much of this trouble occurred at school, but there was trouble in the neighborhood too with other kids. I enjoyed playing with fire; I once set a fire in one room of the house that brought the fire department there. I lost many things: money, clothing, footballs, and especially my homework and notes from school. For a long time I had very little control over my behavior and my body. I remember having many accidents in my pants. I guess I really didn't pay much attention to my needs, so when I was playing outside I really didn't notice that I had to go to the bathroom. I also had a lot of trouble controlling what I said and did. I really didn't think before doing these things—I just did them.

While my life as a child was filled with frustration, much anger, and always being in trouble, my life as a teenager was even worse. I was very angry and depressed. I continued my picky eating habits, eating mostly junk foods, chocolate, and lots of cokes. I was very slim. I continued to have trouble in school and finally dropped out before graduating. During the teen years, I had much trouble with relationships and getting approval from others. I was rebellious toward my adoptive parents and gave them a bad time. I did have a couple of close friends that I hung around with, and they are still my friends today, especially one.

During my last years in high school it was mostly a place to do things to get attention and to meet girls who were equally as exciting as me. As a teenager I cannot think of any good habits. My bad habits were smoking, drinking, cursing, skipping school, staying out late, and bad hygiene. During my spare time I played some sports, but not on a team. I did try to play the trumpet for a while but I didn't practice and finally gave it up. Throughout my childhood and teenage years I really liked to fish. I even got pretty good at it and continue to fish to this day whenever I can. As a teen I did have sleep problems; it was hard for me to go to sleep and then it was hard to wake up. I smoked cigarettes and marijuana. I also had more frequent times when I was depressed. From about the time when I was 17 years old I drank heavily. I had motor vehicle violations associated with alcohol (i.e., DUIs). My hobbies during these years consisted of fishing (the major one) and playing football and pinball, and, of course, girls.

I started dating when I was 13 years old. I had at least two girlfriends at a time and I had sex whenever possible. I think what got me into the most trouble was drinking. On looking back on my past behavior and how it has affected me today, the main thing that comes to mind is that it has shown me how not to act. As long as I don't drink or use drugs I can have a good job and I am rarely late because of hangovers or staying out too late. This was, however, not the case during my teenage years, as I often drank, did have trouble getting up and going to a job, and as a result I often got fired.

I have held many jobs, from cook to dishwasher, to plumbing helper to pulling parts from wrecked autos. On some jobs I was fired, on others I just quit. I could get jobs pretty easily, keeping them was the problem. I have learned that I must first respect myself before I can respect others. I have learned that it is important to take care of yourself mentally and physically. I have also learned to enjoy my leisure time only when I am caught up with my life's responsibilities. But, I guess one of the main things I have discovered is to not give up no matter what. I also know that it's important to think before I do things.

Many people have tried to help me during different periods in my life, but I think that the most important one was myself. It was when I started to make decisions that were good for me that my life changed. I still slip up and make mistakes, but I have a good job, some good friends, and people around me to give support and guidance. I also have love and acceptance and even though I had difficulty in my relationships with "father figures" in my early childhood, I now enjoy the responsibility and pleasure of fatherhood. I look forward to seeing my son grow up, perhaps without as many challenges as I had.

Many stories abound concerning adults who have had ADHD, continue to have symptoms, but have utilized these characteristics to aid them in their jobs or careers. In a recent interview with Mark Lowry, published in *Attention*™ magazine, he commented that he continues to have symptoms of ADHD but notes, "I'm very lucky—because I can do many things. I have an internet newsletter, I write songs, I write stories, I sing in a quartet, I do solo concerts, so I don't do anything long enough to get bored with it. People around me would consider me hyper. . . ." These comments are quite relevant as they reflect the many options and flexibility that adults have to actually use some ADHD characteristics to their advantage in their job or career. When asked, "Do you think having the disorder (ADHD) has helped your career?" Mark responded, "Most definitely. I couldn't do all that I do if I wasn't hyper—whatever it is that makes me *me*—has helped me do all that I've done. I think I might be satisfied with mediocrity if I didn't have ADHD. That's why I always say that people with ADHD are blessed; we're not cursed! I have never looked at my life as a struggle. I look at it as a journey of interesting things." Those interested in learning more about Mark Lowry may visit his website at www.marklowry.com. All can appreciate the candor of his comments and hopefully all can be inspired by them.

Chapter 9

NETWORK OF SUPPORT

The teen with ADHD must have considerable support and structure to cope with the many possible challenging behaviors that are characteristic of ADHD throughout the life span. Adolescence is perhaps the most difficult of all periods where many crucial adjustments, accommodations, and additional coping strategies are most needed. Adolescence is the most difficult transition period for all teens, but especially those with ADHD. It may therefore be important for those involved with the teenager with ADHD to learn how to best help the teen during this difficult and demanding period.

HOW TEACHERS MAY HELP

Next to parents, teachers may potentially become one of the best advocates for a teen with ADHD. Teachers need to first understand the nature of ADHD and its many characteristics. A handout for teachers is available in Appendix 2. In addition to a general understanding of the problems, teachers should learn those techniques that have worked best with teens who have ADHD to maximize their learning potential and to minimize the effect of any possible behavioral problems. It is crucial to teach to the student's strengths while bypassing or remediating deficiencies. It is also important to deal with any behavioral and emotional difficulties that affect the student's ability to function in school. This does not mean that the teacher needs to be a counselor as well as an academic instructor; it simply means that the teacher must deal with those behavioral/emotional issues that occur in school. In part, the teacher may function as one member of a team that approaches these problems. The teacher is essentially a "front-line observer" of the teen's behavior. Much valuable information may be given to parents and other professionals who are involved with the teen. It is important for the teacher to remember that when academic performance is maximized and behavioral/emotional problems are minimized, the teen's overall self-concept is improved and self-esteem is enhanced. Perhaps most important of all with regard to self-esteem is to adopt and maintain a positive orientation in all behavioral interventions. Focusing on developing appropriate behaviors with extensive use of positive reinforcement, and especially positive praise, will be essential. These factors are inextricably related to success in school and ultimately to success in life.

How Parents May Help

While teachers are on the "front-line" at school, parents are on the "front-line" at home. One of the most important tasks parents have is to understand how ADHD relates to the teen's driving behavior, and how to develop and supervise it appropriately. While there are many important areas of behavior to monitor, this area may be critical for the teen as well as others.

It is difficult to accurately categorize "driving behavior" for teens with ADHD. Perhaps it could be classified as a mechanical skill or maybe even a form of social-skill behavior since so many teen activities appear to center around or involve driving. Dating, sex, drug and alcohol use, independence, narcissistic urges, power, and control are just a few of the behavioral categories and issues associated with driving. It is, in short, closely identified with the developmental period of adolescence, and this is no exception for teens with ADHD.

However, there are some factors that make driving different for teens with ADHD as compared with teenagers in general. Teens with ADHD have four times as many accidents, are more likely to receive citations for speeding, seven times as likely to be involved in two or more crashes, and over four times more likely to be at fault. These statistics come from a study by Barkley (1996).

Based on these statistics, parents of teens with ADHD are at greater risk, compared with parents of teens without ADHD, for (1) serious injury or death of a child in an accident, (2) more property damage, (3) more legal/liability, and (4) higher insurance rates.

Educating these teens with ADHD about good driving and rules of the road has not been effective. It has been proposed that driving be considered in the context of the overall treatment plan. Thus, one motivating factor for driving privileges could be associated with the medication regime. However, driving could also be used as a powerful motivator to improve academics and to ensure appropriate parent–teen communication. The teen with ADHD should be present for meetings with the parent's insurance agent. Having the agent explain the factors that will reduce or keep rates low may be more meaningful than if the same information came from the parent.

Some suggestions have been provided in "Helping Your Teen Develop Safe Driving Habits" by Marlene Snyder, Ph.D., and Rae Hemphill (CH.A.D.D. chapter coordinator). The following information is adapted from their article in *Attention*™ magazine. As with any other behavior, a prime recommendation is to be a good model and exhibit good driving behavior. Remember that teens will be influenced more by what you "do" than by what you "say":

- Supervise your teen's driving.

- Schedule short (30 minutes or less) driving sessions, emphasizing what the teen does not know about driving.

- After learning the basic skills, expose the teen to driving in different weather conditions. Prohibit driving with other teens in the car (for now).

- No unsupervised late night driving.

- Seat belts must be worn at all times.

- Of course, the rule is no drinking and driving.

- Research safety data and choose a safe car for the teen to drive. Note that teens who own their cars have more citations and accidents.

- Review and role-play what to do in an emergency or accident. Also cover the packet of pages in the glove compartment for vehicle registration, insurance card with agent contact number, emergency phone numbers, and coins for phone calls. There should also be a letter reviewing procedures after an accident, and a letter (from the doctor) regarding what medications the teen takes and that the medications are safe to use while driving.

- Have a (behavior) contract with the teen for driving safety. Driving privileges may be restricted or removed as needed depending upon the teen's driving performance (i.e., citations and/or accidents), or for other violations in use (e.g., late for curfew or driving beyond time allotted).

- Pass along payment of fines, repairs, or insurance increases when these are indicated by agreement. Suspend driving privileges until these expenses are met. All agreements and contracts must be clarified in writing before the teen with ADHD begins to drive. As a parent, you will need to monitor your teen's driving in most cases until the teen either leaves home or demonstrates appropriate driving habits over a minimum period of one year. Then only periodic checks are suggested. The duration, frequency, and how closely driving is monitored will depend largely on the teen's driving record. Considering the known risks and potential outcomes, to protect the teen as well as others, this seems to be a small price to pay.

Of course, parents must be involved in all aspects of the teen's adjustment during this crucial period of adolescence. Parents must know how to weather the stormy interpersonal interactions between the teen with ADHD and themselves as well as other family members. Parents will be in a crucial position of not only helping the identified teen cope with ADHD behavioral challenges, but also to help others (e.g., siblings, relatives, friends, teachers, and school administrators). Parents must be involved in the following:

1. Dissemination of information about ADHD to others to help them understand the vagaries of behavior characteristics of ADHD. For example, it is most important to distinguish between noncompliance and incompetence. In the former there is deliberate avoidance of a task knowing full well what to do; in the latter case, the teen simply has an inability to do the task. Either not knowing what to do or being distracted from doing what is known would be classified as incompetence.

2. Parents must know and be able to model the most appropriate and effective ways of coping with ADHD behavior. This includes (but is not limited to) communication skills, problem solving, and especially negotiation and conflict resolution within the family.

3. Parents must be able to promote effective ways of coping with ADHD behaviors in others.

4. Parents must be knowledgeable and persistent advocates for the ADHD teen to facilitate implementation of accommodations in the school and perhaps in other situations as needed.

5. Parents must be thoroughly familiar with the most effective behavioral interventions for teens.

In order to facilitate the above tasks, a handout for parents may be found in Appendix 3. The job for parents is immense and sometimes foreboding but always challenging. It is clear that parents have the most difficult job—but their payoff is also the most rewarding when successes are achieved.

How Siblings May Help

This title focuses on how the teen's brothers or sisters may help. In many cases there is distance in such relations or prior experiences may have been limited to many fights and other negative behavior interactions. When parents communicate the nature of the teen's behavior characteristics (to siblings who are able to process such information), then helpful behavior by siblings may be reinforced by parents. Siblings may experience a wide range of emotions in their encounters with the teen with ADHD. Some may be sympathetic, but at the same time, feel much anger when this teen gets into their things or hassles with their friends. Some resentment by the sibling may be associated with the "attention" that the identified teen with ADHD receives or with differential treatment given following transgressions. In some families, siblings may strive for perfection to compensate for the family's "imperfect" child. Perhaps the most difficult thing for siblings to deal with is the apparent insensitivity that many teens with ADHD show over conflicts with their siblings. However, many of these teens may also have other co-morbid conditions that involve disregard for others' rights, property, and feelings. Problems are further exacerbated when one or more siblings have ADHD. Of course, conflicts may arise exponentially when one or both parents have ADHD. Siblings may help best by:

1. Understanding the nature of ADHD

2. Agreeing to rules of interaction with the ADHD teen set down by parents

3. Giving feedback on their feelings when the teen's inappropriate behavior affects them

4. Agreeing to keep things that they wish to be private in safe places not obvious to their sibling with ADHD

5. Modeling more appropriate behavior without flagrant comparisons with the identified teen

6. Serving as a resource (for older teens) to assist with some cognitive or perhaps vocational adjustment

How Relatives May Help

Many persons in the extended family may help the teen with ADHD in several ways. First, adult relatives may serve in the capacity of alternative parent figures. Knowing about ADHD and how to respond to the teen with ADHD may provide additional learning trials for the reinforcement of some appropriate behavior and also provide some consistency in the teen's relations with others. The greater the number of learning trials and the more situations in which they occur will translate into faster learning and more generalized learning. It is therefore worth the extra effort to talk with and to involve relatives in the teen's extended program.

A special case of this situation may involve families with divorced parents. In essence, the identified teen with ADHD will have different adjustments to make within each family. Much will depend upon how amicable relations are between these two households. Communication problems may be a major issue. However, in many families, some unresolved issues may be tabled to provide the teen with ADHD the best chance to survive the challenges of the adolescent years. Often, agreements may be reached to ensure that there is consistency in treatment across both households. Again, this will maximize the teen's learning of coping strategies and enhance generalization across many situations. It is especially important for both mother and father to agree on and be consistent with the handling of rules—both negotiable and nonnegotiable, but especially rules in the latter category.

How Friends May Help

Teenage peers are extremely important and there is no exception regarding the teen with ADHD. Just as with others involved in the teen's life, it is important that friends understand the nature of these problems. Perhaps the handout for teens found in Appendix 1 would be helpful for their friends. In some cases, a good friend (especially a girlfriend or boyfriend) may have a very positive effect on academic work, particularly if the friend is a good student. On the other hand, sometimes teens with ADHD behaviors that have been chronic and severe may associate with friends who may facilitate an escalation of inappropriate behavior. In such instances, parents may (a) encourage the teen to develop a wide variety of friendships and (b) provide information to the friend (who may also have ADHD or other behavioral problems) and to his or her parents or school counselor.

While some may consider such outcomes intrusive, if another teen with ADHD can be helped, these actions may be worthwhile. Good friends may help with such issues as note taking, study sessions, and even provide feedback on certain behaviors that the teen with ADHD may be working on to change. For example, the ADHD teen might tell his friend, "You know, I'm sometimes bossy and forceful in trying to get others to do what I want. It would help me if you could give me some kind of signal when you see me coming on too strong with others. That can help me to be more aware of this and to change it before it gets out of hand." Some nonverbal cue may then be arranged so that if the identified teen initiates such an approach, his friend will cue him so that he has the opportunity to change this behavior.

How school administrators may help

Even today, there are many school administrators who are either unfamiliar with the nature of ADHD behaviors or who have adopted a policy that essentially states that "these behaviors may be real, but that ADHD does not exist." Although there are a few authorities who continue to make such claims about "the myth of ADHD" and that such problems merely reflect one's lack of knowledge in handling such behavior, most experts in the field agree that ADHD behaviors are real and that the disorder does exist. Mounting scientific evidence from neuroanatomical and neurophysiological studies now make it difficult to hold onto oppositional or alternative views of ADHD and the behavioral characteristics involved. Furthermore, there is increasing legal constraints that directly influence most all schools, but especially those that receive any federal subsistence.

Accommodations have become increasingly more important to teens with ADHD; cooperative efforts from the top decision-makers in the school system will facilitate the student's adjustment and future success. Although based on a good understanding of the nature of ADHD, some decisions are too often economically determined. In short, it is sometimes costly to provide all accommodations and interventions requested. School administrators are therefore caught in conflictual situations of having to meet demands for accommodations and at the same time do this within budgetary restrictions. Thus, some resistance may be encountered upon first request of special services or accommodations. Parents must persist to obtain some agreements. While there has been but few legal actions taken to date regarding implementation of special provisions, little is known about what legal measures may be needed or even effective in the future.

How AFTER-SCHOOL PROGRAMS MAY HELP

Some of the major problems shown by teens with ADHD and other co-morbid disorders is that they often get into trouble during after-school hours. In many cases, these teens are not able to be supervised adequately by parents when both are employed and may not return home until 5 P.M. or 6 P.M. This situation often leaves the teen unsupervised for 2 or 3 hours before the parents come home. One young teen was known to be home with an older brother. He was perhaps bored, and may have been encouraged to "call in a bomb threat" to his school. This took place just following the incident of the Colorado school massacre. While this was viewed as a prank by the teen, it was taken seriously by the school officials and police who averted the teen and placed him in juvenile detention. Due to the zero-tolerance policy, this youngster was brought through a series of steps that (a) kept him away from his family and (b) resulted in placement in an alternative school. The young teen certainly did not foresee these complications that could possibly have been avoided with adequate supervision after school.

According to one family life specialist, Dr. Sarah Anderson, there is a need for some type of "after-school care" programs for teens similar to programs for young children. National estimates of the number of children and adolescents who care for themselves alone at some time during the day is at 15 million. However, because parents may be reluctant to admit to such conditions, accurate statistics are difficult to obtain. After-school programs for teens are most commonly located on school grounds. However, community centers, day home providers, and private homes have been open to this kind of program.

Dr. Anderson describes many instructional programs that could be carried out during the after-school hours (e.g., social skills, safety skills, or academic skills). While little attention appears directed toward teens, this may be an excellent time to develop some technical skills (e.g., computer knowledge, sports skills, or even some basic skills in music). The goal(s) of such a program would be to provide: (a) educational or technical instruction that can serve to enhance the teen's sense of competency; (b) to provide hands-on activities that are fun and stimulating while also providing a context for the teen to experience good positive feelings; and (c) the opportunity to have contact with and perhaps form a positive bond with a person who may be a supportive advocate for the teen throughout life. Although such a program is publicly known to exist only in Texas, there is an apparent need for a broader nationwide program.

Chapter 10

Resources for Teens with ADHD

There is an increasing number of resources not only for parents, teachers, and counselors, but also for teens with ADHD. Books, tapes, videos, computer software, group activities, and hobbies can serve to aid the teen with ADHD. These resources may be broken down into several categories.

Books, Magazines, Tapes, and Videos

Some of these resources address general issues about ADHD while others focus on a specific problem area. Books may even be subdivided. There are books or tapes that are available from either "Talking Book" or "Recordings for the Blind" that may be used with the teen who has additional reading problems or when a second mode of information processing (auditory) may be desired. Many of the literature classics, which may be assigned reading, could even be available on tape in the school or public library. Many libraries also have a Kurzweil Personal Reader, which may either read aloud a book placed on its scanner or record it on audiotape. Tapes may be made of a single page, a chapter, or the entire book.

A partial listing of books that focus on ADHD may be found in Table 10-1 on the following page.

Table 10-1. **BOOKS FOR TEENS WITH ADHD**

Title	Author
➡ *Making the Grade: An Adolescent's Struggle with ADD*	Roberta N. Parker
➡ *How Rude! The Teenager's Guide to Good Manners, Proper Behavior, and Not Grossing People Out*	Alex J. Parker, Ph.D.
➡ *Help 4 ADD @ High School*	Kathleen Nadeau, Ph.D.
➡ *I Would If I Could: A Teenager's Guide to Hyperactivity*	Michael Gordon, Ph.D.
➡ *Keeping a Head in School: A Student's Book About Learning Abilities and Learning Disorders*	Mel Levine, M.D.
➡ *Adolescents and ADD: Gaining the Advantage*	Patricia O. Quinn, M.D.
➡ *Put Yourself in Their Shoes: Understanding Teenagers with Attention Deficit Hyperactivity Disorder*	Harvey C. Parker, Ph.D.
➡ *Social Skill Strategies (Revised) Book A*	Nancy Gejewski
➡ *Social Skill Strategies (Revised) Book B*	Patty Mayo
➡ *ADHD—A Teenager's Guide*	James J. Crist, Ph.D.
➡ *A Teenager's Guide to ADD*	Anthony J. Amen, Sharon R. Johnson, & Daniel G. Amen, M.D.

Magazines may also be helpful for many teens with ADHD. Some may feature easy-to-read articles on topics that are of high interest to the teen with ADHD. Two of these are listed in Table 10-2.

Table 10-2. MAGAZINES/NEWSLETTERS

Magazines/Newsletters	Editors
ADDvance (Teens)	Kathleen Nadeau, Ph.D. and Patricia O. Quinn, M.D.
Brakes: The Interactive Newsletter for Kids with ADD (Ages 7–14)	Judith M. Stern, M.A. and Patricia O. Quinn, M.D.

Two important books for those teens planning to attend college include Dr. Jennifer Bramer's book *Succeeding in College with ADD*, which discusses the advantages of various programs and services that can help the student with ADHD succeed in college, and the *K&W Guide to Colleges for the Learning Disabled* (4th edition) by Mary Beth Kravets and Emy Wax. This is an excellent resource that lists institutions offering programs and services for disabled students.

Tapes are useful in several ways:

1. There are tapes that discuss the nature of ADHD and its treatment, such as the tape entitled "ADHD: A Teenager's Guide" by James Crist, Ph.D. On this tape, in a question-and-answer format, teens discuss many relevant issues about ADHD and its treatment. These teens present as spontaneous and caring individuals, not "crazy" or weird. There is a companion book by the same title.

2. Tapes may be used for relaxation exercises. A special relaxation tape for teens is available through *The ADD/ADHD Resources Catalog.*

3. Tapes may be used to facilitate learning. Tapes of lectures can be quite helpful in lieu of note taking, especially when there is a writing problem. Tapes of reviews of factual information, spelling words, or definitions can provide alternate modes of learning.

4. A continuous beep tape, with random beeps, is available to assist students in staying on-task. The program, developed by Dr. Harvey Parker, is entitled "Listen, Look, and Think" and is also available through *The ADD/ADHD Resources Catalog.*

Videos can clearly depict ADHD behaviors. There is one 20-minute videotape called "ADHD in Adolescence: Our Point of View" by Dr. Schubiner (produced by Children's Hospital of Michigan, Department of Educational Services, 1995) that is ideally suited for teen support groups or forums addressing ADHD behavior (also available from the ADD/ADHD Resources catalog).

COMPUTERS AND OTHER TECHNOLOGIES

The use of computers with ADHD has both general and specific applications. First, the general use of computers provides positive incentive motivation for many teens with ADHD, who dislike either reading or writing in the conventional mode in school. Perhaps it is the positive association with stimulating computer graphics in many computer games that may enhance academic applications; but for whatever the reason, teens generally appear to like doing their work on or with computers.

Second, there are some specific training programs available. Computer software has been available to address several aspects of ADHD characteristics:

1. There is the training of basic attentional skills. In the Attend-O™ series, Volume 2 focuses on basic and complex attentional skill training and development. Clinical studies at the ADD Clinic in Biloxi have demonstrated that attentional skills may follow the typical learning curve when this computer training is conducted at home, at school, or in the clinic. Additional programs in this series are being developed to focus on the training and enhancement of "behavioral inhibition skills."

2. There is software that focuses on conflict resolution and anger management.

3. These is currently under development (personal communication with Richard Goldsworthy) software that addresses social-skill development through the use of an interactive CD format.

Other technologies might include the use of computer interfaced neuro-feedback devices. Although still somewhat controversial, these technologies have evolved to the point of being able to provide a personal neuro-feedback device that may be used at home to support training in the clinic and to facilitate the acquisition of learned neurophysiological control. While not recommended at this point in development, such technologies are worth monitoring for possible use in the future.

INNER-PERSONAL SUPPORT

Assistance for the teen with ADHD may come from within (e.g., learned skills, information, etc.) or from outside of the individual (e.g., school, peers, coaches, supervisors, as well as parents). The inner-personal support may be classified as:

1. **Self-monitoring**—The learned ability to monitor self-performance.

2. **Self-talk**—The use of either supportive self-statements to increase or maintain motivation (e.g., affirmations) or to self-direct an activity to prevent careless errors (i.e., slow down procedure).

3. **Learned skills**—There are many possible skill deficits for the teen with ADHD. These skills have been exhaustively described in a previous chapter; a list of a few that may be helpful to the teen with ADHD include: social skills, study skills, memorization skills, note-taking skills, and many others.

4. **Past successes**—There is nothing quite like success to beget more success. Previous success experiences provide associated positive good feelings, positive value in self-concept and self-esteem, as well as general incentive motivation to consider more challenging situations and tasks.

INTER-PERSONAL SUPPORT

A network of supportive persons is just about the most important factor in the successful adjustment of the teen with ADHD. There is, of course, the obvious influence of parents and teachers, but there are also others who can potentially play very important roles in the teen's success.

PEER GROUP ACTIVITIES

The quality of experiences with peer groups is a major factor to consider. Teens with ADHD will encounter those on the positive side who can assist with feedback and modeling of appropriate behavior, and those on the negative side who can synergistically escalate inappropriate or risk-taking behavior. The greater the number of *positive* group associations and relationships, the greater the *positive* influence on academic and personal behavior.

Structured peer group activities can be specifically geared to have a positive influence. First, there are special teen groups or forums offered. To be informative and helpful in dealing with ADHD characteristics, many of these groups have been associated with CH.A.D.D.—some with local chapters and some through the national organization's annual conference. Many of these have been organized by Dr. Arthur Robin; some have featured the 20-minute video on "ADHD in Adolescence" by Dr. Schubiner. Such meetings are typically led by older teens and young adults who have ADHD and who can communicate with and lead discussion groups. At times, featured adult speakers are brought in to talk "briefly" about a specific topic of interest requested by teens. It has been noted, however, that positive peer models can have a much greater influence on the teen with ADHD than adults. Other adolescents are generally seen as more credible figures by adolescents with ADHD and may be influenced by these positive peer models to make changes in any negative attitudes toward ADHD.

ADVISORS AND COACHES

One of the most effective procedures has involved the use of ADHD coaches with adolescents and young adults. Both high school and college students have benefited from such advisors. These persons have been trained to provide ADHD coaching. The actual coaching is not therapy, but can be quite beneficial for many teens who do not have more serious problems. Coaches may advise students, but mainly "keep the student on track," moving in a positive direction toward established goals. Redundancy and review of strategies, techniques, and cues for effective academic and personal life functions are all targeted areas for coaches.

APPRENTICESHIP TRAINING

For the teen with ADHD who elects to go directly to work following high school, an apprenticeship is an excellent introduction to the world of work. Essentially, the teen would get "hands-on" training in specific skills. Many teens can even begin such programs while still in high school and are typically enrolled in a non-college track that allows part-time work and school attendance for the remainder of each day. This arrangement introduces the student to the world of work in a gradual way, allowing the teen to get supervised "hands-on" training. When work follows the academic component, the student may actually improve his or her academic performance because (a) class time is not a full day, (b) instruction is generally of high interest and relevant to work activity, and (c) class work is followed by preferred work activity (i.e., the academic component gets reinforced by the work component). When the student completes academic requirements, he or she may then become involved with job activities full-time. While there were generally more apprenticeship opportunities in the past, society's need for workers with specific technological skills may increase the need and availability of such arrangements in the future.

SPORTS AND RECREATION

Some activities in this category may aid the teen with ADHD, such as the recreational activities of running or swimming that can improve attentional skills. Exercise has been shown to be beneficial for ADHD characteristics; some of these activities may be developed within a group or team concept (e.g., the track or swim teams). Some sporting activities might best be avoided while others can be helpful and should be sought out. Playing the outfield in baseball may be a poor choice and could be very unrewarding. With long intervals between fly balls, there is increased opportunity for distraction. Getting involved counting the lights in the ballpark or reading the signs may cause the player to miss simple fly balls and bring about the ire of follow teammates—experiences that could be quite negative. Playing a game where there is near constant movement (e.g., soccer) may actually maintain attention better. However, the prerequisite for a positive experience in any sporting activity is adequate physical talent and coordination. While some teens with ADHD have only fine-motor coordination problems, others do have difficulty with large-muscle movement and may not do well in most any organized sport.

Many teens with ADHD may find other forms of recreational activity are better suited for them. Many, for instance, may develop significant relationships and perhaps even acquire some skills that will either supplement their monies earned or may become a primary source of income. One such activity is music. It is, no doubt, stimulating and may enhance arousal level, but it may also allow the teen with ADHD creative outlets for his or her talents. It may become an area where the teen excels and further develops skills that can bring about a lifetime of rewards and pleasurable experiences. Another such activity is fishing. This is certainly true of our son, Mark, who not only still enjoys bass fishing, but has also developed some mechanical skills for marine engine repair that "keep him close to the water." Mark has become an expert at fishing, often catching fish when others do not. He has learned the complexities of bass fishing that take into consideration many factors such as location or habitat, water temperature, types of lures and rigs to use, and feeding habits of the fish; his hobby is literally a gold mine of information that could easily be established and offered in the form of a bass-fishing guide.

BIOGRAPHIC NOTES ON ADULTS WITH ADHD

Conditions like ADHD and LD are classified as disabilities, and individuals who have these conditions are viewed as somehow different. Yet many of these persons may have an underlying potential for greater achievement than one would expect. Associated qualities such as impulsiveness, an open focus of attention that is subject to distraction, risk-taking and a need for greater challenges, insatiability, and a unique individualized mode of thinking may not be rewarded when these qualities deviate from the norm. However, impulsiveness could be viewed as a form of decisiveness, insatiability could be manifested as ambition, and distractibility could be seen as a form of creativity or open mindedness.

Some very significant historical figures have shown these characteristics, although one may only infer that they may have had ADHD and/or LD since there can be no means of getting the proper background information, behavior ratings, or to even test them. However, the anecdotal and historical background information in their biographies strongly suggest that these conditions (i.e., ADHD and/or LD) did exist. In looking at some of the historically important and creative persons who manifested such ADHD characteristics, it is clear that there are few differences between some of the behaviors typically associated with giftedness and those found in ADHD.

A partial list of historically significant figures who have been noted to have had ADHD or LD follows, with relevant comments:

➡ **Ben Franklin**—Disorganized and argumentative; brimmed with endless ideas and imaginative projects.

➡ **Albert Einstein**—Described as a poor student, distractible, socially awkward and messy, yet infinitely creative.

➡ **Winston Churchill**—Noted to be a bad student who couldn't concentrate, yet he achieved political prominence.

➡ Some other famous personalities include: **Bruce Jenner,** Olympic athlete; **Woodrow Wilson,** U.S. President; **Leonardo da Vinci,** artist; **Thomas Edison,** inventor; **Agatha Christie,** author; **Greg Louganis,** Olympic athlete; **Cher,** singer, actress, author; and **Tom Cruise,** actor.

This list is based on information obtained from the ERIC Clearinghouse on *Disabilities and Gifted Education and Articles Focus on Ability* (1990) and *Life in Overdrive* (1994). Others noted to have had ADHD or LD are:

John F. Kennedy	**Danny Glover**
Robert Kennedy	**Henry Ford**
Magic Johnson	**Ludwig van Beethoven**
Sylvester Stallone	**Louis Pasteur**
Robin Williams	**Alexander Graham Bell**

The above list is a partial listing from the Child Development Institute's "Famous People With Attention Deficit and Learning Disorders" (1998). The entire list of all famous and noted individuals who have had or currently have ADHD would indeed be very long. It is, however, clear that those qualities of ADHD do not prevent manifestations of greatness and success. These qualities may, in fact, provide obstacles and challenges for such individuals. Given support, coaching, and therapy to maximize potential and manage any interfering behavioral and/or educational obstacles, we know that these individuals with ADHD can be successful. However, without such guidance and opportunities, many of these individuals may not make significant contributions to society—some may even contribute to the detriment of it. There is a definite payoff when teens with ADHD can be helped on the road to success and the realization of their potential.

APPENDICES

Appendix 1

QUESTIONS ABOUT ADHD:
INFORMATION AND COPING STRATEGIES FOR TEENS

Have you been diagnosed as having ADHD or do you wonder if you may have ADHD? Here is basic information, along with helpful tips to deal with ADHD. Now, let's talk about ADHD.

What is ADHD? ADHD stands for Attention Deficit Hyperactivity Disorder. It is related to some difficulties in how the brain functions, but it is not brain damage. Roughly about 2% of teens might have ADHD.

ADHD has three basic characteristics:

1. **Inattention**—Some might say that you have trouble paying attention, especially your teachers. You might get distracted by noises, you might even daydream a lot. These things do interfere with getting work completed, and you may even feel bored or sleepy in class more so than other teens. Getting organized may also be a problem, and you may lose many things such as clothes, jewelry, as well as your notes and homework. Research shows that many more boys than girls have ADHD (sometimes 4 times as many); girls with ADHD mostly daydream and have trouble paying attention, while boys are more restless.

2. **Hyperactivity** is the second basic characteristic of ADHD. When you were younger, you may have been overactive and had trouble sitting still for a long period of time. Now you may be less active overall, but may still be restless, like tapping your pencil or your feet; or perhaps teachers have commented that you "talk too much." You may, however, still have trouble sitting still for long periods and feel an urge to move around.

3. **Impulsivity.** Basically, you may "act before you think." For instance, you may interrupt others or blurt out something for which you later feel embarrassed, or you might do something inappropriate without thinking of the consequences. You may also be accident prone, especially in doing things that others might consider risky.

Be aware, though, that not all teens with ADHD have all of these signs or do all of these things all of the time. In fact, all teens engage in some of these behaviors some of the time. The key is how often and when these problems occur. If these behaviors interfere with your completing work, getting good grades, or getting along with others, then you need to deal with them. Know also that some of these characteristics that cause problems now in the teen years might become assets later on. For instance, being distracted easily may cause you a problem in your high school math class, but being able to pay attention to many things at once may be a distinct asset for an adult who works as an Air Traffic Controller.

How can I tell if I have ADHD? ADHD must be diagnosed by a qualified professional such as a physician, psychologist, clinical social worker, or licensed professional counselor. A teacher is not qualified to make a diagnosis but may contribute very important observations and ratings on questionnaires about ADHD that will be very helpful in diagnosis. Much family background information and medical history need to be obtained—primarily from your parents or guardians. It is not easy to diagnose ADHD since many other conditions and problems produce symptoms very much like those seen with ADHD. For example, moods such as depression or anxiety may produce symptoms that mimic ADHD; they may also occur in addition to ADHD.

One major characteristic that is associated primarily with ADHD is inconsistency. This means that you might do well some days and not so well on other days. This inconsistency appears to reflect variations in your nervous system. Specifically, your nervous system may function much like a roller coaster with ups and downs, and perhaps this would also be the way you would describe yourself behaviorally.

Another characteristic for most teens with ADHD is that problems seem to occur more frequently in the school setting, and especially in the context of groups of other students. Symptoms appear less often when you are with only one other person. It may also seem easier to work on things that really interest you, like computing sports averages or a challenging, stimulating computer game. Few teens with ADHD may have trouble in their favorite subject and few teens with ADHD have trouble playing computer games such as Nintendo™. In contrast, it may be difficult to focus on math problems that are viewed as boring.

What causes ADHD? At this point it is known that ADHD is related to some differences in the nervous system. Certain areas of the brain seem to be more involved, and certain brain chemicals or neurotransmitters appear to be lacking. ADHD also seems to be inherited in most cases. In other cases, it may be related to use of drugs or alcohol or even smoking during pregnancy. It is, however, not contagious, and it is not brought about by what you eat.

What problems are associated with ADHD? Difficulties may occur in several areas. In school there is, of course, increased risk of failure and drop-out. This may be magnified when there is an associated Learning Disability (for example, specific problems in math, reading, spelling, or writing). There is also increased risk for using alcohol or drugs (e.g., marijuana), but the majority of those who have problems with these substances have another condition besides ADHD that is more serious (i.e., Conduct Disorder).

Many teens with ADHD do have trouble in social relationships, having problems with irritability and temper outbursts. Over time such problems may worsen and result in continued or more significant difficulty in higher educational settings, or on a job, affecting both productivity and social interpersonal relations. With increasing problems and accumulated failure, one's self-concept may be poor and self-esteem may hit an all-time low. Depression is therefore not uncommon during adolescence and especially in teens with ADHD. Each teen with ADHD must be aware of these feelings and of changes in behavior and activities. Lack of pleasure in activities, changes in eating and sleeping habits, withdrawing from people, sleeping too much, or having constant thoughts about suicide are all significant warning signals. There is a very serious concern when specific plans are made to carry out one's suicide.

Can ADHD be treated? It is important for the teen with ADHD to know that effective treatment can be offered. Sometimes this might involve medication(s). In most all cases, there is a need for some form of behavioral intervention. One form might be a program that is carried out with the cooperation of parents and teachers. Another might involve learning some skills that might even "take the place of pills." Such skills might help counteract some of the characteristic problems of ADHD. Other skills might focus on developing some skill that is basically deficient (e.g., to learn and develop better attentional skills or better self-control skills).

What about medications? Medications may also be very helpful when they are indicated. Many teens may be painfully aware of the problems associated with taking medication. However, there are some that can be taken only once per day only at home. Roughly 75% or more of the students who take the basic medication are helped. These basic meds include Ritalin®, Dexedrine®, Cylert®, and Adderal®. All may improve attention and have beneficial effects in other areas (for example, self-control, better social interaction, and even better handwriting). Other medications include antidepressants such as Tofranil®, Prozac®, Wellbutrin®, and Pamelor®. In addition, medications such as Catapres® and Tegretal® may also be used.

Like most medications, these may have some side effects, but most all have been shown to be safe and quite effective for thousands of teens. With the basic medications there may be some problems with sleep or eating, and at times irritability and stomach upsets. With antidepressants, there may be dry mouth, some drowsiness, headaches, constipation, and some blurring of vision. Most all side effects are mild and only temporary; otherwise, your doctor may either alter the dose or change the medication.

Response to a medication is not predictable; but most all teens show a positive response. When this medication regime is combined with behavioral interventions or coaching, some very significant positive changes can occur. Although it is difficult to say how long the teen might need to take medications, it is important to try this approach if your doctor finds it is indicated.

With some basic medications there will be very quick feedback on whether it works. Within about one hour these medications are in your system. With others it may take a few weeks to determine whether they are truly effective. Although the basic medications may be assimilated into bodily systems quickly, this is not true of some other medications. A more gradual dose increase in these other meds may be needed over time. Consequently, it is best that your doctor supervise medication adjustment closely to determine when an effective dose has been reached, and to determine when a medication needs to be changed or completely discontinued.

What can the school do to help? ADHD is now considered a disability under Federal law if it significantly impairs a person's ability to learn. Therefore, you may be eligible for some special services that may help you succeed in school. Likewise, there are some recommendations that can be made to accommodate you in one or more areas that relate to your disability. For example, if you have trouble finishing tests on time because your writing is poor and labored, extra time may be given to finish tests. With special assistance and accommodations in school—along with coaching on getting organized, improving study habits, improving social relations, and appropriate medications as needed—you may effectively cope with ADHD symptoms and realize your potential.

SOME GENERAL COPING STRATEGIES FOR TEENS WITH ADHD*

⟶ When necessary, ask your teacher, parent, or boss to repeat or explain instructions, rather than guess.

⟶ Break large assignments or job tasks into small, simple tasks. Set a deadline for each task and reward yourself as you complete each one.

---

*Strategies adapted from: Weinstein, C., "Cognitive Remediation Strategies," *Journal of Psychotherapy Practice and Research*, 3(1):44–57, 1994.

➡ Each day, make a list of what you need to do. Plan the best order for doing each task. Then make a schedule for doing them and estimate the time required to complete each one. Use a calendar or daily planner to keep yourself on track.

➡ Work in a well-lighted, quiet area. Do one thing at a time. Give yourself short breaks. (Some teens may, however, need some stimulation, such as music, for optimal work conditions.)

➡ Write things you need to remember in a notebook with dividers. Write different kinds of information—like assignments, appointments, and phone numbers—in different sections. Keep your daily planner and a pen with you all of the time.

➡ Post notes to yourself to help remind yourself of things you need to do. Tape notes on the bathroom mirror, on the refrigerator, in your school locker, on the dashboard of your car—wherever you're likely to need the reminder.

➡ Store similar things together. For example, keep all your Nintendo™ disks in one place, and CDs or cassette tapes in another. Keep important papers in one place and bills in another.

➡ Create a routine. Get yourself ready for school or work at the same time, in the same way, every day.

➡ Exercise, eat a balanced diet, and get enough sleep.

COPING WITH SCHOOL FOR TEENS WITH ADHD

➡ Inform your teachers at the start of a new school year that you have ADHD and ask for their help.

➡ Use a Homework Assignment Book to keep track of assignments, tests, and projects. Check off these when completed.

➡ Use a folder for homework with one side pocket for "work to be done" and the opposite for "work completed to be turned in."

➡ Prepare your bookbag the night before, putting completed work in a routine place.

➡ If you have a choice, take a seat a distance from distractions, such as the hallway, window, or known class clowns. If seats are assigned, talk with your teacher about preferential seating.

➡ Taking notes will help to maintain attention, but you may need to consult the teacher or a peer's notes if you miss something. It's okay to ask the teacher to slow down when needed.

➡ Tape lectures if you have difficulty paying attention to the teacher.

➠ Try different strategies to cope with situations and use the best.

➠ Inform close friends that you have ADHD so they can support and provide cues or reminders to help you get things done.

➠ Take time for exercise and other forms of stress management.

➠ Keep a "to do" list and have a check-off procedure for things completed.

➠ Use "I" statements to express your feelings (e.g., "I get angry when . . ." instead of "You make me angry").

➠ While ADHD does not appear to be outgrown, your adjustment and adaptation to it can result in success in school as well as in later life.

➠ It's important to remember that many people with ADHD tend to be very creative and gregarious people with much energy.

➠ It is essential that you, as a teen with ADHD, know you can be successful in many endeavors that are well suited for persons with ADHD. Developing good coping strategies will pay off.

Appendix 2

UNDERSTANDING AND MANAGING ADHD IN TEENS: A HANDOUT FOR TEACHERS

What is ADHD? ADHD is a neurobiological condition that may impair the teen's academic, social, and personal life. The teen who continually disrupts a class and has difficulty completing assignments and may also daydream and stare out a window instead of focusing on your instruction would be a likely candidate for a diagnosis of ADHD. This teen may be restless, talkative, and show continued difficulty with impulse control, often blurting out answers or responding with poor judgment or at inappropriate times.

Understand that ADHD is a disorder based in the nervous system; ADHD misbehavior does not reflect intentional acting out. In addition to a general understanding of the nature of the disorder, it is important that you understand what treatments are available and who may coordinate them. Having a good knowledge of behavioral techniques may certainly facilitate their use, and will help you be an integral participant in helping the teenage student with ADHD.

Identifying teens with ADHD. Most teens with ADHD will probably already have been diagnosed with ADHD, except for those who exhibit a primary inattentive type. While many teenage students with ADHD do not show extreme overactivity that they may have shown in the past, they may exhibit restlessness—fidgeting in their chair, swinging their leg, tapping their foot, or tapping a pencil. The hyperactivity component in the teen with ADHD may also be shown by excessive talking (i.e., vocal motor activity). Impulsivity may still be obvious as the teen with ADHD may blurt out comments in class and might also make inappropriate critical comments that may hurt others' feelings. Poor judgment as to content or poor timing may be reflected in such comments that the teen may later regret. Basically, these teens with ADHD don't think of the consequences of their behavior.

Overall, the teen with ADHD seems immature (some appear younger by 2 years). Teens with ADHD continue to have trouble focusing and sustaining their attention to tasks. Consequently, they may go from one assignment to another without finishing any of them. Many times these teens with ADHD will get distracted either by internal thoughts or by external visual or auditory factors. Associated problems include poor organization and study skills, poor management of time, and problems taking notes and tests. Many teens with ADHD will also tend to engage in risk-taking activities, some of which may be quite dangerous. Problems with driving (e.g., speeding or accidents), sexual acting out (pregnancy and STD), and drug use are all possible. Those teens with ADHD plus Conduct Disorder (CD) may also engage in risky criminal activity (e.g., robbery, rape, etc.).

Although you are not expected to diagnose ADHD and related conditions, you would do well to keep a log of behavioral incidents. During the process of assessment or during treatment monitoring, you might provide helpful diagnostic or prognostic information. Teachers should remember that diagnosis of ADHD and the many related conditions is complex. There are many conditions that may initially appear to be ADHD, but upon clinical evaluation may reflect other problems such as pure depression, anxiety, physical/sexual/emotional abuse, neurological disorders, specific Learning Disability, CD with drug abuse, or a severely dysfunctional family.

When a student presents problem behavior, you should consult with the principal and/or school counselor who may shed some light on the teen's situation. If not, consultation with the teen's parent would be indicated. During such a meeting it will be important for you to show the behavioral log to the parent—to focus on what behaviors have been problematic and have interfered with the teen's academic performance. During the assessment/monitoring phase, you are often asked to complete standardized rating forms as well as to provide narrative comments about problems. The behavior log will then be invaluable in providing objective observations.

Managing ADHD problems. There are three basic areas of treatment: (1) educational accommodations/interventions, (2) behavioral accommodations/interventions, and (3) medications. You might become involved in all three basic areas to help the adolescent adjust to ADHD or to circumvent problems (i.e., bypass strategies). Some behavioral interventions may be conducted solely in school, while others will involve some cooperative effort between parents and teachers. Working together with parents will provide greater consistency in attempts to help the teen change target problematic behavior using a home–school program. You will then have access to and use of some of the more significant home-based privileges in the teen's life (e.g., telephone use, driving privileges, etc.).

Medications: What teachers need to know. Teachers must not expect that medication(s) will address all of the teen's problems. Ratings on the impact of medications on academic as well as behavioral changes will normally be requested, as well as any comments about undesirable behavior changes or "side effects." Again, the behavior log may be useful in recording such information. Teens who are overmedicated may not present any behavioral problems, but they also may not process much information (i.e., learn). Monitoring medication effects is critical.

Classroom strategies. Many of these suggestions are general ones that will help all students, not just those with ADHD. These interventions may be supplemental to any accommodations that are delineated by the assessment team. In some cases the accommodations will simply need to be updated from a prior assessment conducted at a younger age.

The single best recommendation is to provide consistent structure in the classroom where class rules and expectations are clearly communicated to the teen by posting (visual) and by conducting periodic oral review (auditory). Just as important is for you (and hopefully the entire school) to have a generally positive orientation. When assignments are too complex (for any student), you should break them down and reinforce completion of each part. Give feedback on time allotments for various tasks, and during each task tell students how much time is left. Also, give extra time for written tests, give oral tests when there are writing problems, and have a quiet place in the class for a distraction-free space.

The use of a "study buddy" approach can help keep students on track and may provide "a readily accessible coach" when needed. It is essential to teach to the student's strengths while attempting to deal with deficits. Give both visual and oral directions for tasks. Also, help students with transitions between classes or activities by announcing to prepare students for upcoming activities. When addressing the student with ADHD, say the name—pause—then continue with the question or instruction.

Most teens with ADHD find school boring, so try to (a) use humor, (b) change voice inflections, (c) use different modalities with the same material, (d) use high-interest materials, and (e) vary brightly colored paper on which assignments are handed out. There are many other variations that may be selected—you are encouraged to use creativity in selecting materials/activities and to keep in mind the nature of ADHD: These teens with ADHD, like their younger counterparts, still need stimulation and perhaps to an even greater extent. Provide this stimulation within the context of a routine. A checklist type of behavioral record may be used to communicate with parents regarding the teen's (a) coming to class on time, (b) being prepared, and (c) completing work. Homework assignments need to be checked until the student develops a routine of doing it. This process will be facilitated when significant privileges are made contingent on writing correct homework assignments.

You must not only be able to enhance academic productivity of teens with ADHD; you must also manage any interfering behaviors. More appropriate behavior may be encouraged by positive reinforcement (e.g., praise) for all appropriate behavior. Remember that many teens with ADHD carry with them a long history of negative comments, poor self-concept, and low self-esteem. They can use all of the positive comments possible. In addition, behavior contracts and point systems are also effective; the former with older adolescents in general, the latter with younger adolescents. Concentrate on only a few (e.g., one to three) behaviors at a time—you can't deal with everything at once. A response-cost procedure (where points are lost for undesirable behavior) also works quite well with ADHD teens. Likewise, do not overburden the child with too many rules. Keep rules clear, concise, and few in number.

Since many teens have possibly heard "Time-Out" from their preschool years, it's best to reframe this concept. Time-out may be promoted as a place to "calm down," "chill out," or "get control." Teach the teen that everyone from time to time may simply need to get away, to withdraw, so they may regroup and come back to deal with a situation more effectively. In general, this concept may still be most effective with the youngest of teens with ADHD. In any case, this reframed procedure can be taught to be a self-imposed self-control technique.

A final comment is that when you and parents work together by setting common (similar) rules for class and home, and when similar procedures and cues are used, the teen with ADHD should respond and learn more rapidly. It is always best to foster self-control and behavior change that results from internal cognitive decisions made by the teen in response to a cue provided by you or the parent. For instance, a good general cue is to hold up two fingers; from prior instruction this signals (nonverbally) that the teen has two choices: (a) continue the misbehavior and get the prearranged negative consequence, or (b) change the behavior to a more desirable one and receive a positive consequence. Such a technique enhances independent thinking and develops responsibility, making the teen less dependent upon the adult to direct his or her behavior. Quick feedback on the teen's decision would also be essential.

Recognizing signs of depression/suicide. Among teens ages 15 to 24, suicide is the third leading cause of death. Teens with ADHD are, in general, at risk for depression and suicide. Depression over losses (e.g., parents [through death or divorce], loss of girl- or boyfriend), accumulated stress over failures, inability to meet unrealistic expectations, and poor self-concept and low self-esteem (with feelings of worthlessness and hopelessness about the future) are all factors that contribute to depression, and at times to suicide. If you deal with a teen in such a condition, it is essential to be aware of the signs of serious and perhaps imminent danger.

The following is a list of warning signs for depression and associated suicide:

1. Explicit or casual statements reflecting a wish to die

2. Significant weight loss and loss of energy

3. Reported changes in eating or sleeping patterns (e.g., lack of appetite/excessive sleeping)

4. Apathy—withdrawal from activities that were once enjoyable

5. Dramatic change in grades

6. Isolation—withdrawal from friends and family, spending more time alone

7. Putting affairs in order—when the teen gives away prized possessions, this requires immediate attention

8. Increased risk-taking behavior—may involve alcohol or drugs, or more frequent dangerous behavior (e.g., speeding)

9. Personality changes—from normally quiet to excessively loud, or the opposite

10. Recent loss—death of someone close or break up in a love relationship

11. Running away from home—perhaps a "cry for help"

12. Preoccupation with death—writings or artwork that depict themes of death

13. Focus on weapons—talking about having or buying a gun or knife

14. Prior suicide attempts—initially a "cry for help"—with each attempt there is increased likelihood of success; of course, the teen may succeed on any attempt by accident

Recognizing signs of substance abuse. Teens with ADHD do have an increased risk of substance abuse. However, it has been found that ADHD combined with CD is associated with the highest risk. In any case, some teens who experiment with drugs are not addicted and may not show clear signs of abuse. Much depends on the substance used and the stage of usage. There may be physical changes, behavioral/emotional changes, and environmental evidence for potential substance abuse problems.

Physical Signs

➠ Poor coordination

➠ Slurred speech

➠ Bloodshot eyes and dilated pupils

➠ Lapses in memory

➠ Poor hygiene/grooming

➠ Even greater difficulty with attention/concentration

➠ Chronic nasal problems

➠ Change in eating habits

Behavioral Signs

➠ Sleep problems

➠ Dishonest behavior (lying/stealing)

➠ Change in friends (evasive about new ones) laughter

➠ In Stability of mood

➠ Borrowing/stealing money from parents/friends

➠ Isolation from family/secretiveness

➠ Inappropriate affect—silly

➠ Lack of interest in activities/hobbies

- Staying out late
- Increases in inappropriate anger/
  secretiveness

- Progressively poorer grades
- Increased absenteeism/tardiness

Environmental Changes

- Drug-related paraphernalia found
  (e.g., clips, rolling papers, eyedrops,
  small butane torch)
- Possession of pills, small glass vials,
  needles, unused seeds or leaves
- Odor of drugs or substances to
  "cover up" drug odors

- Drug-related clothing/magazines
- Preoccupation with drugs (jokes/talk)
- Defensive when discussing drugs

While schools may differ in their policy regarding the discovery of substance abuse, evidence, and the problematic behavior associated with it, the critical factor will be to call a meeting with the teen's parents and to discuss the evidence obtained in the school setting and to determine whether there is collaborative evidence in the home. Further investigation and action would therefore be warranted.

Appendix 3

UNDERSTANDING AND MANAGING ADHD IN TEENS: A HANDOUT FOR PARENTS

What is ADHD? Attention Deficit Hyperactivity Disorder (ADHD) is a neurobiological condition that may impair the teen's academic, social, and personal life. The teen who continually disrupts a class, blurts out answers, has difficulty organizing and completing assignments, may also daydream and stare out a window instead of focusing on the teacher's questions or instruction, would be a likely candidate for evaluation of ADHD. The teen may continue to be restless, talkative, and show pervasive difficulty with impulse-control, often responding to situations with poor judgment or poor timing.

Teens with ADHD have primary problems in school, and often similar difficulties at home. Understand that the nature of ADHD is based within the nervous system and usually does not involve intentional misbehavior or acting out. When parents have a good understanding of ADHD and behavioral principles that help to manage the ADHD behavior, there can be good outcomes. In addition to behavioral interventions, medications are often needed during the adolescent years and sometimes beyond.

Identifying teens with ADHD. Most teens with ADHD probably already have been diagnosed with ADHD (except for those who exhibit a primary inattentive type). During adolescence, most of those with ADHD have shown a decrease in significant overactivity. Instead, they may now show fidgeting, tapping their foot, or perhaps excessive talking. Impulsivity can still occur as the teen may make critical comments that reflect poor judgment or poor timing. Afterward, there may be regret over these behaviors. It may be difficult for the teen with ADHD to think of the consequences of behavior. Overall, the teen appears immature and more like a person about two years younger.

Teens with ADHD continue to have basic problems focusing and sustaining attention. Consequently, they may fail to complete chores or homework, often getting distracted by either internal (thoughts) or external visual or auditory factors. Many teens with ADHD tend to engage in risk-taking behavior, some of which may be quite dangerous. Often, such behaviors may reflect a need for stimulation. Dangerous hobbies, extreme music forms, and perhaps a need to "stir up some excitement" can all be characteristic with all but the inattentive type of ADHD. Many experts consider this subtype so different as to be of a different origin. Problems driving (i.e., accidents), sexual acting out (pregnancy and Sexually Transmitted Disease), and drug use all fall into the category of risk-taking behavior reflecting a need for self-stimulation. It is, however, primarily those teens with ADHD plus Conduct Disorder who go beyond that and engage in risky criminal activity (e.g., robbery, rape, etc.). Most teens with ADHD do not engage in such serious behavior.

In order to properly treat teens with ADHD, there must be proper assessment. Talk with others to confirm evidence of these aforementioned behaviors in other situations. Perhaps the most important setting to check out is the school. Teacher observations in different classes/school situations may provide useful information for the physician or psychologist who will evaluate the teen. The teen's physician may provide a general medical exam and perhaps a referral for neurological consultation if needed.

Diagnosis of ADHD and the many related conditions is complex. There are many conditions that initially appear to be ADHD but upon clinical evaluation may reflect other problems such as pure depression, anxiety, physical/sexual emotional abuse, neurological disorders, specific Learning Disability, Conduct Disorder with drug abuse, or severe dysfunction in the family. The teen's behavior may be explained by any one of these problems or by a combination of them.

ADHD in school. Two Federal laws cover the education of children and teens with ADHD—the Individuals with Disabilities Education Act (IDEA) and Section 504 of the Rehabilitation Act of 1973. This legal information is complex and thus difficult to abstract or summarize. The information is also not offered to obviate the need for personal legal consultation. However, the information may be helpful in making informal decisions in conjunction with personal legal consultation when needed.

The teen's school is responsible to provide an educational diagnosis. A multidisciplinary team will discuss and evaluate the teen's behavior. You will need to bring relevant materials such as behavior notes, report cards, prior evaluations, medical reports, etc., that are often accumulated. You may be asked to fill out questionnaires and rating forms pertaining to ADHD and other conditions. A two-tiered approach is followed: (1) determine the presence of ADHD and (2) determine what, if any, adverse affect it may have on the teen's academic performance.

Following the evaluation, modifications may be made in the classroom and regarding schoolwork based on the teen's special needs (i.e., accommodations). Students may also be placed in specific programs involving study skills, organization skills, and classroom management. There may be pull-out programs for social skills and other resources (e.g., special reading programs), various behavioral interventions are also available for possible implementation. There are many ways that you and the teen's teachers can cooperate in coordinated home–school behavioral programs. If your teen is on medication, it will be necessary to have teachers periodically monitor progress and/or problems (e.g., side effects).

It is best for you and the teachers to discuss and coordinate a basic set of rules that might be applicable to both home and school settings. In all cases, learning and acquisition of rules will be faster if there is redundancy and consistency across settings; this would minimize the number of unique rules in either home or school setting.

What parents must know about medications. You must know the purpose and general use of prescribed medications. Knowledge of the desired or expected effects of the drug, side effects, and possible complications is also important. You must know what to expect from the medication and when to expect it (i.e., time course for effectiveness of the medication). You must be good observers of your teen. All changes, overt or more subtle, must be noted, and in many cases formally recorded. These observations may be very useful for the prescribing physician.

You also need to know about adjustment on medications, possible changes, rebound effects, and other issues about medications. You should also be instructed in the primary purpose of the medications and should realize that medication is not going to solve all the problems. Know that "pills do not teach skills." Many teens with ADHD are deficient with regard to specific skill areas that may affect their academic and social life. These deficiencies must be remediated through educational and therapeutic behavioral programs. You must remember that the best long-range outcome results from behavioral programs and skill training, in conjunction with needed medications.

Strategies for dealing with ADHD in the home. Adolescents are able to develop some skills that will aid them in either compensating for ADHD problems or adjusting to them. It is essential that you focus on the teen's assets to enhance self-esteem and to provide the structure and guidance to deal with increasingly difficult life challenges. The following are basic strategies you may use to cope with ADHD.

➠ Negotiable and nonnegotiable rules need to be established with clearly stated consequences for rule violations. State these rules in a positive (not negative) manner, and provide general praise for all acceptable good behavior.

➠ Structure consequences to enhance incentive motivation and engage the teen in decisions about consequences. Whether provided in a contract or point system, consequences are more meaningful when teens participate in such decisions. Continue to systematically work on improving only one to three behaviors at a time.

➠ While time-out may be used with younger teens, it is best to reframe it as a "cool down" procedure. Behavior penalty is, however, still quite effective, whereby the teen basically has a privilege and can only lose it by the accumulated loss of a prearranged number of points.

➠ You need to be a homework consultant, but you should not do the teen's assignments. Set up a designated place (not the kitchen table) where homework can be done in the same place and same time each night. Use of a home–school communication system may "keep the teen honest" until homework becomes "habit forming."

➠ Help the teen as much as possible (or provide a coach) to organize long-term assignments, projects, agreements, etc. An organization sheet on the door, wall, or bulletin board may be helpful. Likewise, effective use may be made of Homework Assignment Books or a daily planner.

➠ Avoid responding to the teen with sarcasm, ridicule, or anger. Remember that many of the teen's behaviors are determined by his or her nervous system, and not reflective of deliberate misbehavior. It is far better to effectively use cues and mild reprimands to redirect behavior. Also always focus on the positive—either (a) good behavior or (b) an improvement in behavior. Behavior can be shaped in this way, but it is a gradual process and patience is required!

➠ Be your teen's best advocate. Teens will begin to assume some responsibility for taking care of their needs, but many need good models regarding how to do this. Be a good model for your teen in every way. Show the teen how to prioritize and structure time.

Recognizing signs of depression/suicide. Among students ages 15 to 24, suicide is the third leading cause of death. Teens with ADHD are, in general, at risk for depression and suicide. Depression over losses (e.g., parents through death or divorce and loss of girl- and/or boyfriend), accumulated stress over failure, inability to meet unrealistic expectations, and poor self-concept and low self-esteem with feelings of worthlessness and hopelessness about the future are all factors that contribute to depression, and at times to suicide.

The following is a list of warning signs for depression and associated suicide:

1. Explicit or casual statements reflecting a wish to die

2. Significant weight loss and loss of energy

3. Reported changes in eating or sleeping patterns (e.g., lack of appetite/excessive sleeping)

4. Apathy—withdrawal from activities that were once enjoyable

5. Dramatic change in grades

6. Isolation—withdrawal from friends and family, spending more time alone

7. Putting affairs in order—when the teen gives away prized possessions, this requires immediate attention

8. Increased risk-taking behavior—may involve alcohol or drugs, or more frequent dangerous behavior (e.g., speeding)

9. Personality changes—from normally quiet to excessively loud, or the opposite

10. Recent loss—death of someone close or break up in a love relationship

11. Running away from home—perhaps a "cry for help"

12. Preoccupation with death—writings or artwork that depict themes of death

13. Focus on weapons—talking about having or buying a gun or knife

14. Prior suicide attempts—initially a "cry for help"—with each attempt there is increased likelihood of success; of course, the teen may succeed on any attempt by accident

Recognizing signs of substance abuse. Teens with ADHD do have an increased risk of substance abuse. However, it has been found that ADHD combined with Conduct Disorder is associated with the highest risk. In any case, teens who experiment with drugs are not addicted and some may not show clear signs of abuse. Much depends on the substance used and the stage of usage. There may be physical changes, behavioral/emotional changes, and environmental evidence.

Physical Signs

➧ Poor coordination

➧ Slurred speech

➧ Bloodshot eyes/dilated pupils

➧ Lapses in memory

➧ Poor hygiene/grooming

➧ Even greater difficulty with attention/concentration

➧ Chronic nasal problems

➧ Change in eating habits

Behavioral Signs

➧ Sleep problems

➧ Dishonest behavior (lying/stealing)

➧ Change in friends (evasive about new ones)

➧ Instability of mood

➧ Staying out late

- Increases in inappropriate anger
- Borrowing/stealing money from parents/friends
- Isolation from family/secretiveness
- Inappropriate affect—silly laughter
- Lack of interest in activities/hobbies
- Progressively poorer grades
- Increased absenteeism/tardiness

Environmental Changes

- Drug-related paraphernalia found (e.g., clips, rolling papers, eyedrops, small butane torch)
- Possession of pills, small glass vials, needles, unused seeds or leaves
- Odor of drugs or substances to "cover up" odors
- Drug-related clothing/magazines
- Preoccupation with drugs (jokes/talk)
- Defensive in discussing drugs

Appendix 4

LEGAL RIGHTS FOR ADHD TEENS*

FEDERAL LAWS AFFECTING CHILDREN WITH ADHD

Both the *Individuals with Disabilities Education Act (IDEA)* and *Section 504 of the Rehabilitation Act of 1973* provide coverage for children with ADHD. When the disability adversely affects educational performance, eligibility for special education should be approached through the processes of IDEA. When the disability does not affect education performance but does substantially limit one or more major life activities, eligibility should be approached through Section 504.

The following are highlights of each law as it affects the education of children with ADHD.

INDIVIDUALS WITH DISABILITIES EDUCATION ACT, PART B

➠ Requires that state and local districts make a free appropriate public education (FAPE) available to all eligible children with disabilities.

➠ Requires that the rights and protections of Part B of IDEA are extended to children with ADHD and their parents.

➠ Requires that an evaluation be done, without undue delay, to determine if the child has one or more of 13 specified disabling conditions and requires special education and related services.

➠ Requires that children with ADHD be classified as eligible for services under the "other health impaired" category in instances where ADHD is a chronic or acute health problem that results in limited alertness that adversely affects a child's educational performance. Children with ADHD can also be served under the categories of "learning disabilities" or "seriously emotionally disturbed" if the evaluation finds these conditions are also present.

➠ Does not allow local districts to refuse to evaluate the possible need for special education and related services of a child with prior medical diagnosis of ADHD solely by reason of that medical diagnosis. On the other hand, a medical diagnosis of ADHD does not automatically make a child eligible for services under Part B (IDEA).

➠ Requires that a full and individual evaluation of the child's educational needs must be conducted in accordance with requirements in Part B (IDEA). A multidisciplinary team must perform the evaluation, with at least one teacher or other specialist with knowledge in the area of ADHD on the team.

➠ Requires that a due-process hearing take place, at the request of the parents, if there is a disagreement between the local district and the parent over the request for evaluation, the evaluation, or the determinations for services.

---

* Information on this handout has been adapted from several sources; most material has been provided by CHADD.

SECTION 504 OF THE REHABILITATION ACT OF 1973

➠ Prohibits discrimination on the basis of disability by recipients of federal funds.

➠ Provides appropriate education for children who do not fall within the disability categories specified in Part B (IDEA). Examples of potential conditions not typically covered under Part B (IDEA) are: communicable diseases (HIV, tuberculosis), medical conditions (asthma, allergies, diabetes, heart disease), temporary medical conditions due to illness or accident, and drug/alcohol addiction.

➠ Requires that a free appropriate public education be provided to each qualified child who is disabled but does not require special education and related services under Part B (IDEA). A free appropriate public education (FAPE) under Section 504 includes: regular or special education and related aids and services that are designed to meet the individual student's needs and are based on adherence to the regulatory requirements on education setting, evaluation, placement, and procedural safeguards.

➠ Guarantees parents the right to contest the outcome of an evaluation if a local district determines that a child is not disabled under Section 504.

➠ Requires the local district to make an individualized determination of the child's educational needs for regular or special education or related aids and services if the child is found eligible under Section 504.

➠ Requires the implementation of an individualized education program (IEP). One means of meeting the free appropriate public education requirements of Section 504 is to follow the IEP guidelines as set forth in the regulations for Part B (IDEA).

➠ Requires that the child's education must be provided in the regular education classroom unless it is demonstrated that education in the regular environment with the use of supplementary aids and services cannot be achieved satisfactorily.

➠ Requires that necessary adjustments be made in the regular classroom for children who qualify under Section 504.

COMPARISON OF IDEA AND SECTION 504 PLAN

IDEA	Section 504 Plan
Most of those with disabilities receive Special Education here.	Some are served under Section 504.
Find more severe disabilities here.	Find less severe disabilities here.
The law that governs all Special Education Services and provides federal funding to support Special Education-related services.	There is a civil rights statute that provides no funding, but covers all programs/activities that receive federal financial assistance. Requires that schools not discriminate against those with disabilities.
Must meet criteria in one of the eligibility categories—emotional disturbance, LD, MR, TBI, autism, vision/hearing impairments, physical disabilities, and other health impairments. In 1991, a policy was issued stating that ADHD could be covered under *Other Health Impairment* if criteria were met (i.e., diagnosed with ADHD and if ADHD affected educational performance requiring Special Education). On March 12, 1999, the U.S. Dept. of Education issued final regulations that explicitly incorporated ADHD as a disability under *Other Health Impairment.*

Children are protected only if they need Special Education in order to cope with their disability. However, by the 1999 regulations, Special Education can include special instruction with the regular class. | Child is eligible if a physical or mental condition limits a major life activity (i.e., learning). Section 504 protects children who may need services even if they do not require Special Education. |
| A multidisciplinary evaluation is essential to determining eligibility and further requires that reevaluation be conducted every 3 years. Specifications for non-discriminatory test procedures are made, and evaluations by private practitioners must be considered and sometimes paid for by one's school district. | Testing is also required here but there are fewer regulations about test procedures. Further, no procedures relating to frequency of tests or to the use of private evaluations are specified. Also, parents do not need to consent to testing. An evaluation/reevaluation is needed prior to any change being made in the 504 plan. |
| School districts must attempt to identify and evaluate those with potential disabilities and provide services when needed. The student does not need to be in a public school. | The school might only identify those with disabilities who are within the school district and are not receiving a public education. |

(Cont'd)

IDEA	Section 504 Plan
Requires schools to provide a FAPE to those identified with a disability.	Requires schools to provide a FAPE to those identified with a disability.
Once eligibility is determined, the student is entitled to have an Individualized Education Plan (IEP) which has annual goals and short-term objectives. The IEP must be reviewed at least annually. IEPs are applicable in regular and Special Education classes.	Once eligible under Section 504, the school district must develop a 504 Plan. No provisions are made for periodic reviews of the plan, nor specifications made regarding the parent's part in developing the plan. The 504 Plan is not limited to regular classes; Special Education services may be received.
Services should be provided in the least-restrictive environment.	Services should be provided in the least-restrictive environment.
Specifies that student be in the class appropriate for him/her if the disability were not present, and as close to home as possible.	No comparable regulations on this point.
Parents have the right: to consent to initial evaluation and services in Special Education; to be notified of IEP meetings and to participate; to discuss student's placement; to notice when school board takes or fails to take action in placement; to request a due-process hearing; to have an independent hearing officer; to present testimony; to exclude evidence not given five days before hearing; to counsel and recordings of the written decision. Hearing officer is appointed by the state education agency.	Parents may review records, have an impartial hearing with participation of parents and counsel, and a review procedure. The school district may appoint an impartial hearing officer. No provision made for bringing parents into decision-making.
Should parents request a due-process hearing, the student stays in the current placement until legal proceedings are concluded (called "stay-put" or "frozen placement" provision).	Does not have a "stay-put" provision.
With the 1999 IDEA regulations, single or multiple suspensions in excess of 10 days are considered changes in placement—can invoke "stay-put" if parent requests due-process hearing challenging the suspension.	

(Cont'd)

IDEA	Section 504 Plan
School districts may transfer a student for up to 45 days when drugs or weapons are found at school or at a school function if child is likely to hurt him-/herself. School district may go to Court to get Court Order for emergency placement if student is dangerous.	
Parent can request a due-process hearing if unhappy with action/inaction by the school district. When complaints are filed, the State Education Agency or U.S. Department of Education will conduct an investigation.	Parent can file request for a due-process hearing with the school district. Also, may file with the U.S. Department of Education Office for Civil Rights for Section 504 violations.

Appendix 5

12-STEP PROGRAM FOR PARENTS AND TEACHERS OF ADHD TEENS

1. Clearly state what you do want or expect of the teen—not what you don't want.

2. Be a good role model. Show the kind of behavior you wish for the teen to establish.

3. Give more immediate consequences for behavior—mild punishments (e.g., behavior penalty) when needed for inappropriate behavior, but many more positive consequences, using rewards with high reinforcement properties for appropriate behaviors.

4. Always focus on improvements—expect small and sometimes subtle changes.

5. When complimenting with social praise (or pats on the back), be specific about the behavior you like instead of just saying "good"; avoid negative comments and, of course, any physical punishments.

6. Give warnings to allow the teen to change a problem behavior, and thereby receive a positive instead of negative consequence.

7. Use a proactive approach—plan on how to deal with a problem behavior rather than waiting to react to it.

8. Keep in mind that many behaviors associated with ADHD have a biological basis in the nervous system—changes and sometimes even control will be difficult. Parents and teachers will thus need to disengage when nothing seems to work.

9. Withdraw your attention from those annoying behaviors (i.e., ignore) whenever possible. Make some rewards and privileges contingent upon specified appropriate alternate behavior.

10. Make sure that communications with the teen are clearly stated requests, not strong directives.

11. When family conflicts arise, be sure to rely on negotiation and problem-solving skills for resolution.

12. As Dr. Barkley* has noted, parents especially (but also teachers) may practice forgiveness of (a) the teen for transgression, (b) others who may have misunderstood the teen's behavior, and (c) themselves for mistakes in dealing with the teen.

---

*From Dr. Barkley's "Eight Principles to Guide ADHD Children" in the *ADHD Report,* Volume 1 (#2), April 1993. Published by Guilford Publications. Used with permission.

Appendix 6

FORMS AND RECORDKEEPING:
THE TEEN YEARS OF ADHD

ADHD SCHOOL SYMPTOM HISTORY GRID

Name of student _____ Today's Date _____

Form completed by _____

Current School _____ Grade _____

Please review each of the items listed below. Place an "x" in the boxes, which represent the grades in school when that item was a problem for the student named above. Leave the box blank if the item was not a problem in that grade.

Sample

Making careless mistakes was a problem for Bill from second through fifth grades. Mrs. Jones placed x's in the appropriate boxes.

	P	K	1	2	3	4	5	6	7	8	9	10	11	12
Makes careless mistakes				X	X	X	X							

	P	K	1	2	3	4	5	6	7	8	9	10	11	12
1. Makes careless mistakes														
2. Fidgets, is restless														
3. Doesn't pay attention														
4. Leaves seat in class														
5. Doesn't listen when spoken to directly														
6. Doesn't follow instructions														
7. Doesn't finish in-class assignments														
8. Doesn't finish homework														
9. Has difficulty with organization														
10. Talks too much														
11. Socializes too much in class														
12. Daydreams in school														
13. Blurts thing out, interrupts														
14. Is impatient, can't wait turn														
15. Is easily distracted														
16. Doesn't bring materials to class														
17. Doesn't bring papers/notes home														
18. Has sloppy handwriting														
19. Has low test scores														
20. Asks for help when needed														
21. Is argumentative in class														
22. Gets in fights in school														
23. Cheats														
24. Steals														

ADHD BEHAVIOR CHECKLIST
PARENT RATING TEEN'S PRESENT BEHAVIOR

Name of Person Being Rated _____

Date _____

Name of Rater _____

Circle the number that best describes your adolescent's behavior over the past 6 months.

		Never or rarely	Sometimes	Often	Very often
1.	Fails to give close attention to details or makes careless mistakes in work.	0	1	2	3
2.	Fidgets with hands or feet or squirms in seat.	0	1	2	3
3.	Has difficulty sustaining attention in tasks or fun activities.	0	1	2	3
4.	Leaves seat in classroom or on other situations in which seating is expected.	0	1	2	3
5.	Doesn't listen when spoken to directly.	0	1	2	3
6.	Feels restless or moves about excessively.	0	1	2	3
7.	Doesn't follow through and fails to finish work.	0	1	2	3
8.	Has difficulty engaging in leisure activities to doing fun things quietly.	0	1	2	3
9.	Has difficulty organizing tasks and activities.	0	1	2	3
10.	Feels "on the go" or "driven by a motor."	0	1	2	3
11.	Avoids, dislikes, or is reluctant to engage in work that requires sustained mental effort.	0	1	2	3
12.	Talks excessively.	0	1	2	3
13.	Loses things necessary for tasks or activities.	0	1	2	3
14.	Blurts out answers before questions have been completed.	0	1	2	3
15.	Is easily distracted.	0	1	2	3
16.	Has difficulty awaiting turn.	0	1	2	3
17.	Is forgetful in daily activities.	0	1	2	3
18.	Interrupts or intrudes on others.	0	1	2	3

Note. From Murphy & Barkley (1995). Copyright 1995 by The Guilford Press. Reprinted in *Managing Teens With ADHD* by Grad L. Flick

NORMATIVE DATA ON THE DSM-IV ADHD BEHAVIOR CHECKLIST

Age	N	Inattention				Hyperactivity - impulsivity				Total Score			
		Mean (SD)	90th %ile	93th %ile	98th %ile	Mean (SD)	90th %ile	93th %ile	98th %ile	Mean (SD)	90th %ile	93th %ile	98th %ile
Parent normative data for males (DuPaul, Anastopoulos, Power, Reid, Ikeda, & McGoey, in press) - summation scores													
11-13 yr.	149	6.70 (6.27)	18.0	18.5	24.0	4.79 (5.54)	14.0	16.0	21.0	11.50 (11.32)	31.0	34.0	47.0
14-18 yr.	133	5.70 (5.36)	13.6	15.6	23.0	3.68 (4.32)	10.0	11.0	16.3	9.38 (8.96)	23.4	27.0	36.3
Parent normative data for females - summation scores													
11-13 yr.	173	4.61 (6.27)	12.8	16.0	21.0	2.88 (5.54)	9.0	10.0	12.0	7.49 (11.32)	20.0	21.6	28.5
14-18 yr.	225	4.07 (4.57)	12.2	14.0	16.5	3.29 (3.82)	10.0	11.0	16.0	7.36 (7.74)	22.0	24.0	32.5

Normative data for older adolescents and young adults (ages 17-29) on DSM-IV ADHD Behavior Checklist (Murphy & Barkley,1996a)

	Mean	SD	+1.5 SD cutoff
Number of symptoms			
Inattention	1.3	1.8	4.0
Hyperactivity - impulsivity	2.1	2.0	5.1
Total ADHD score	3.3	3.5	8.6
Summation of symptom ratings			
Inattention	6.3	4.7	13.4
Hyperactivity - impulsivity	8.5	4.7	15.6
Total ADHD score	14.7	8.7	27.8

Note. SD, standard deviation.

ISSUES CHECKLIST

	Adolescent			Adolescent
	Mother	*with*		Mother
	Father			Father

Name: _____ Date: _____

Below is a list of things that sometimes get talked about at home. We would like you to look carefully at each topic on the left-hand side of the page and decide whether the *two of you together* have talked about that topic at *all* during the last two weeks.

If the two of you together have discussed it during the last 2 weeks, circle *Yes* to the right of the topic.

If the two of you together have *not* discussed it during the last 2 weeks, circle *No* to the right of the topic.

Now, we would like you to go back over the list of topics. For those topics for which you circled *Yes*, please answer the two questions on the right-hand side of the page.

1. How many times during last 2 weeks did topic come up?
2. How hot are the discussions?

Go down this column for all pages.   *Go down this column for all pages.*

Topic			How many times?	How hot are the discussions?				
				Calm		A little angry		Angry
1. Telephone calls	Yes	No		1	2	3	4	5
2. Time for going to bed	Yes	No		1	2	3	4	5
3. Cleaning up bedroom	Yes	No		1	2	3	4	5
4. Doing homework	Yes	No		1	2	3	4	5
5. Putting away clothes	Yes	No		1	2	3	4	5
6. Using the television	Yes	No		1	2	3	4	5
7. Cleanliness (washing, showers, brushing teeth)	Yes	No		1	2	3	4	5
8. Which clothes to wear	Yes	No		1	2	3	4	5
9. How neat clothing looks	Yes	No		1	2	3	4	5
10. Making too much noise at home	Yes	No		1	2	3	4	5
11. Table manners	Yes	No		1	2	3	4	5
12. Fighting with brothers and sisters	Yes	No		1	2	3	4	5
13. Cursing	Yes	No		1	2	3	4	5
14. How much money is spent	Yes	No		1	2	3	4	5
15. Picking books or movies	Yes	No		1	2	3	4	5
16. Allowance	Yes	No		1	2	3	4	5
17. Going places without parents (shopping, movies, etc.)	Yes	No		1	2	3	4	5

(Cont'd)

Topic			How many times?	How hot are the discussions?				
				Calm		A little angry		Angry
18. Playing stereo or radio too loudly	Yes	No		1	2	3	4	5
19. Turning off lights in house	Yes	No		1	2	3	4	5
20. Drugs	Yes	No		1	2	3	4	5
21. Taking care of records, games, toys, and things	Yes	No		1	2	3	4	5
22. Drinking beer or other liquor	Yes	No		1	2	3	4	5
23. Buying records, games, toys, and things	Yes	No		1	2	3	4	5
24. Going on dates	Yes	No		1	2	3	4	5
25. Who should be friends	Yes	No		1	2	3	4	5
26. Selecting new clothing	Yes	No		1	2	3	4	5
27. Sex	Yes	No		1	2	3	4	5
28. Coming home on time	Yes	No		1	2	3	4	5
29. Getting to school on time	Yes	No		1	2	3	4	5
30. Getting low grades in school	Yes	No		1	2	3	4	5
31. Getting in trouble in school								
32. Lying	Yes	No		1	2	3	4	5
33. Helping out around the house	Yes	No		1	2	3	4	5
34. Talking back to parents	Yes	No		1	2	3	4	5
35. Getting up in the morning	Yes	No		1	2	3	4	5
36. Bothering parents when they want to be left alone	Yes	No		1	2	3	4	5
37. Bothering teenager when he/she wants to be left alone	Yes	No		1	2	3	4	5
38. Putting feet on furniture	Yes	No		1	2	3	4	5
39. Messing up the house	Yes	No		1	2	3	4	5
40. What time to have meals	Yes	No		1	2	3	4	5
41. How to spend free time	Yes	No		1	2	3	4	5
42. Smoking	Yes	No		1	2	3	4	5
43. Earn money away from the house	Yes	No		1	2	3	4	5
44. What teenager eats	Yes	No		1	2	3	4	5

Check to see that you circled Yes or No for every topic. Then tell the interviewer you are finished.

Tell the interviewer you are finished.

CONFLICT BEHAVIOR QUESTIONNAIRE: PARENT VERSION

You are the child's ____ mother ____ father (check one). You are filling this questionnaire out regarding your ____ son ____ daughter (check one) who is _____ years old. Think back over the last 2 weeks at home. The statements below have to do with you and your child. Read the statement, and then decide if you believe the statement is true. If it is true, then circle *true*, and if you believe the statement is not true, circle *false*. You must circle either *true* or *false*, but never both for the same item. Please answer all items. Answer for yourself, without talking it over with your spouse. Your answers will not be shown to your child.

true	false	1. My child sulks after an argument.
true	false	2. My child is easy to get along with. [a,b]
true	false	3. My child and I sometimes end our arguments calmly.
true	false	4. My child is receptive to criticism. [a,b]
true	false	5. My child curses at me. [a]
true	false	6. We joke around often. [a]
true	false	7. My child, for the most part, accepts punishments.
true	false	8. My child enjoys being with me. [a]
true	false	9. At least once a week, we get angry with each other.
true	false	10. My child is well behaved in our discussions. [a,b]
true	false	11. My child lets me know when s/he is pleased with something I have done.
true	false	12. We do a lot of things together. [a]
true	false	13. My child almost never complains.
true	false	14. For the most part, my child likes to talk to me. [b]
true	false	15. We almost never seem to agree. [a,b]
true	false	16. My child usually listens to what I tell him/her. [a,b]
true	false	17. My child never talks when I discuss things with him/her.
true	false	18. I enjoy the talks we have. [a]
true	false	19. Often when I talk to my child, s/he laughs at me.
true	false	20. My child will approach me when something is on his/her mind. [a]
true	false	21. At least three times a week, we get angry at each other. [a,b]
true	false	22. My child screams a lot. [a]
true	false	23. Several hours after an argument, my child is still mad at me. [a]
true	false	24. After an argument which turns out badly, one or both of us apologizes. [a]
true	false	25. My child doesn't pay attention when I have discussions with him/her. [a]
true	false	26. My child says that I have no consideration of his/her feelings. [a,b]
true	false	27. We argue at the dinner table at least half the time we eat together. [a]
true	false	28. My child embarrasses me in front of my friends.
true	false	29. My child does not usually abide by decisions that the two of us reach.
true	false	30. We listen to each other even when we argue.
true	false	31. When we discuss things, my child gets restless.
true	false	32. My child usually starts our arguments.
true	false	33. My child and I compromise during arguments. [a,b]

(Cont'd)

true	false	34. I enjoy spending time with my child.
true	false	35. My child mistreats me in front of his/her friends.
true	false	36. At least once a day we get angry at each other. [a]
true	false	37. My child leaves the house after an argument.
true	false	38. My child runs to his/her bedroom after an argument. [a,b]
true	false	39. We argue until one of us is too tired to go on.
true	false	40. My child often seeks me out. [a]
true	false	41. My child often doesn't do what I ask. [a,b]
true	false	42. The talks we have are frustrating. [a,b]
true	false	43. My child often seems angry at me. [a,b]
true	false	44. My child often cries when I question him/her. [a]
true	false	45. We have enjoyable talks at least once a week.
true	false	46. When angry, my child becomes aggressive.
true	false	47. My child acts impatient when I talk. [a,b]
true	false	48. My child and I speak to each other only when we have to. [a]
true	false	49. My child often criticizes me.
true	false	50. My child says I don't love him/her. [a]
true	false	51. In general, I don't think we get along very well. [a,b]
true	false	52. My child holds a grudge.
true	false	53. My child contradicts everything I say. [a]
true	false	54. We argue at the dinner table almost every time we eat. [a]
true	false	55. My child almost never understands my side of an argument. [a,b]
true	false	56. My child lies to me often. [a]
true	false	57. We never have fun together. [a]
true	false	58. During a heated discussion, my child tries to hit me. [a]
true	false	59. My child slams the door after a big argument.
true	false	60. My child and I have big arguments about little things. [a,b]
true	false	61. My child is defensive when I talk to him/her. [a,b]
true	false	62. My child thinks my opinions don't count. [b]
true	false	63. We have enjoyable talks at least once a day. [a]
true	false	64. My child does things to purposely annoy me.
true	false	65. My child provokes me into an argument at least twice a week. [a]
true	false	66. We argue a lot about rules. [b]
true	false	67. My child rarely follows with his/her end of the bargain, after we have reached an agreement. [a]
true	false	68. My child tells me s/he thinks I am unfair. [a,b]
true	false	69. My child compares me to other parents.
true	false	70. My child talks under his/her breath during a discussion.
true	false	71. My child blows up for no reason. [a]
true	false	72. My child often isolates himself/herself in his/her room after an argument with me.
true	false	73. If I speak calmly, my child doesn't do what I ask. [a]
true	false	74. My child doesn't look up to me when I try to talk to him/her. [a]
true	false	75. When my child is upset about something, s/he clams up.

Note: The CBQ is reproduced with permission of Dr. Ronald J. Prinz

[a] Items included in the 44-item revised version

[b] Items included in the 20-item revised version

CONFLICT BEHAVIOR QUESTIONNAIRE—SCORING

The CBQ is introduced to the family by going over the instructions written on the questionnaire and asking if family members have any questions about the form. Although the CBQ was originally labeled "The Interaction Behavior Questionnaire" on the form given to families to disguise its purpose, this practice has created sufficient confusion among investigators using the instrument that we now label the questionnaire with its proper name.

SCORING INSTRUCTIONS: LONG VERSION CBQS

Two scores are obtained for each family member.

Parent version:

1. Parent's report of adolescent's behavior (53 items):

   a. Add one point for each of the following items answered *true:* 1, 5, 17, 19, 22, 23, 25, 26, 28, 29, 31, 32, 35, 37, 38, 41, 43, 44, 46, 47, 49, 50, 52, 53, 55, 56, 58, 59, 61, 62, 64, 65, 67, 68, 69, 70, 71, 72, 73, 74, 75.

   b. Add one point for each of the following answered *false:* 2, 4, 7, 8, 10, 11, 13, 14, 16, 20, 34, 40.

2. Parent's report of dyadic behavior (22 items):

   a. Add one point for each *true:* 9, 15, 21, 27, 36, 39, 42, 48, 51, 54, 57, 60, 66.

   b. Add one point for each *false:* 3, 6, 12, 18, 24, 30, 33, 45, 63.

Adolescent version:

1. Adolescent's report of parent's behavior (51 items):

   a. Add one point for each of the following items answered *true:* 1, 2, 4, 5, 7, 8, 11, 14, 17, 19, 20, 22, 28, 31, 32, 34, 35, 37, 38, 40, 41, 43, 44, 50, 55, 56, 58, 59, 61, 62, 64, 65, 67, 68, 72, 73.

ADD/ADHD DIAGNOSTIC CHECKLIST
AND TREATMENT ORGANIZER

CHILD'S NAME _____ AGE _____ BIRTH DATE _____ GRADE _____

CLINICIAN _____ DATE _____

I. DIAGNOSTIC PHASE

A. Assessment—Psychological

	Relevant	Date Started	Date Completed	Defer to
1. Background Information and Developmental History (Parent/Guardian)				
2. Behavioral Observation				
3. Rating Scales—Parent				
4. Rating Scales—Teacher				
5. Assess Ability/Achievements				
6. Assess Executive Control				
7. Assess Visual-Motor				
8. Assess Memory				
9. Assess Attentional Skills				
10. Assess Self Concept/Self-Esteem				
11. Assess Social Skills				
12. Assess Visual-Spatial Skills				
13. Assess Language				
14. Assess Behavioral/Emotional				
15. Assess Inclusion Potential				

B. Assessment—Medical

1. Medical History				
2. Medical Exam				
3. Neurological Exam (optional)				

C. Assessment—Other (optional)

1. Vision				
2. Hearing				
3. Speech and Language				

(Cont'd)

D. Differential Diagnosis

	Relevant	Date Started	Date Completed	Defer to
1. Meets DSM-IV Criteria for:				
(a) 314.01 ADHD—Combined Type				
(b) 314.00 ADHD—Predominantly Inattentive Type				
(c) 314.01 ADHD—Predominantly Hyperactive—Impulsive Type				
2. Co-Morbid/Mimic Syndromes Considered				
Learning Disability				
Mental Retardation				
Oppositional Defiant Disorder				
Conduct Disorder				
Dysthymic Disorder (Depression)				
Anxiety Disorder				
Bipolar Disorder				
Obsessive Compulsive Disorder				
Head Injury				
Other Psychological Condition				
Medical Condition Considered				

II. TREATMENT PHASE

A. Medical Intervention

	Relevant	Date Started	Date Completed	Defer to
1. Medical Test Needed				
2. Pre-Treatment/Baseline Teacher Ratings Obtained				
3. Medication Trial on				
(a)				
(b)				
(c)				

(Cont'd)

B. Classroom Accommodations

	Relevant	Date Started	Date Completed	Defer to
1. School Consultation with Teachers				
2. IEP Discussed/Implemented				
3. Special Education Resources for				
(a)				
(b)				
4. Special Education Placement in				
5. Inclusion Strategies:				
Proximity Control				
Preferential Seating				
Tape Recorder				
Overhead Projector				
Self-Monitoring				
Special Materials				
Special Signals				
Study Carrels				
Display Clear Rules				
Review Clear Rules				
Homework Assignments Written Down/Reviewed				
Day Schedule Posted/Reviewed				
Alternate Work Activity				
Multi-sensory Instruction				
Reduction Homework/Assignments				
Use of Peer Tutors				
Extended Time for Tests				
Oral Examinations				
Use of Computer				
Monitor Homework Assignment Sheet/Check Backpack				
Premack Principle (Schedule Hard Work Before Easy Work)				

(Cont'd)

B. Classroom Accommodations *(cont'd)*

	Relevant	Date Started	Date Completed	Defer to
Adjust Schedule for Peak Performance				
Use of Electronic Assist Devices				
Establish Set Routine with Variation Within Routine				
Designated Quiet Zone in Class				
Use of Self-Instruction Procedure				

C. Behavioral Intervention

	Relevant	Date Started	Date Completed	Defer to
1. In Class				
(a) Verbal Praise/Positive Approach				
(b) Ignoring				
(c) Response Cost Procedure to Develop: _____				
(d) Time-out for _____				
(e) Time-in for _____				
(f) Inclusive Classroom Behavioral Program				
(g) Point/Token System				
2. Home-School Program				
(a) Periodic Communication Established				
(b) Check on Consistency in Both Settings				
(c) Teacher/Parent Roles Defined				
3. Parent/Teacher Training				
(a) Parents/Teachers have at least one full day of behavioral training				
(b) Parent/Teacher knowledge of ADD/ADHD and behavioral techniques assessed				
(c) Appropriate educational resources available to Parent/Teacher on ADD/ADHD and behavioral techniques				
(d) Mechanism in place for communication about problems in behavioral program				
4. Parent Behavioral Program				
(a) General Positive Orientation				

(Cont'd)

C. Behavioral Intervention *(cont'd)*

		Relevant	Date Started	Date Completed	Defer to
(b)	Alternative Behaviors Listed				
(c)	Balanced Program Established				
(d)	Point/Token System				
(e)	Response Cost				
(f)	Time-out/Time-in				
(g)	Positive Practice				
(h)	Grounding				
(i)	Simulated School Behaviors				
	Impulse Control				
	Listening Skills				
	Following Directions				
	Work Completion				
	Sustaining Attention				
	Social Skills				

D. Supplementary Remedial Program

		Relevant	Date Started	Date Completed	Defer to
1.	Tutoring				
(a)	One-on-One				
(b)	Computerized				
2.	*Skills for School Success* Program				
3.	*Homework Helpers* Program				
4.	Speech/Language Therapy				
5.	Motor Coordination Therapy				
(a)	Gross Motor				
(b)	Fine Motor/Handwriting				
6.	Attentional Skills Training				
(a)	Home				
(b)	School				

(Cont'd)

E. Legal Resources

Parents/Guardians have understanding of:	Relevant	Date Started	Date Completed	Defer to
1. Section 504 Rehabilitation Act				
2. Individuals with Disabilities Act (IDEA)				
3. Advocacy Needed for _____				

F. Clinic/Therapy Programs

		Relevant	Date Started	Date Completed	Defer to
1. Parent Centered Programs					
(a)	General Discussion of the A-B-C of Behavioral Programs				
(b)	Antecedents				
	Review /Development of Rules				
	Expectations Discussed				
	Communication Style Addressed				
	Meta-Communication Considered				
(c)	Behaviors Discussed				
	Inappropriate Behaviors Listed				
	Alternative Behaviors Listed				
	Can Ignoring Be Used?				
(d)	Consequences				
	Types of Consequences Discussed				
	Instrumental Behavior Analysis				
	Shaping Discussed				
	Concept of Balanced Behavior Program				
(e)	Managing Behaviors				
	Time-out Discussed				
	Time-in Discussed				
	Behavior Penalty Discussed				
	Grounding Applications				
	Point/Token System				

(Cont'd)

F. Clinic/Therapy Programs *(cont'd)*	Relevant	Date Started	Date Completed	Defer to
2. Child-Centered Programs				
(a) Skill Development				
Attention Training				
Impulse Control Training				
Social Skill Training				
Self-Concept/Self-esteem Focus				
Organizational and Study Skills				
Anger Control Training				
Problem Solving Training				
Handwriting Program				
(b) Cognitive Mediation				
Self-instruction				
Self-monitoring				
Positive Self-talk				
Problem Solving Exercises				
(c) Counseling				
Understanding of ADD/ADHD				
Understanding Medications				
Understanding and Focusing on Strengths				
Social Group Interaction Structured				

III. FAMILY FUNCTIONING

A. Relationships with Parents

	Relevant	Date Started	Date Completed	Defer to
1. Child provided structured activities based on strengths and abilities				
2. Some time (preferably 1 hour) set aside for "pure fun" activity				
3. Parents are consistent and model appropriate behavior				
4. Rules/chores written down and reviewed				

(Cont'd)

B. Relationship with Siblings

	Relevant	Date Started	Date Completed	Defer to
1. Encourage cooperation and sharing				
2. Discourage discrimination (i.e., scapegoating) and name-calling				
3. Sibling(s) understand nature of ADD/ADHD				
4. Balance time for ADD and non-ADD sibling(s)				

C. Parent Survival Techniques

1. Knowledge and Acceptance of ADD/ADHD				
2. Use Relaxation/Stress Reduction				
3. Maintain a Routine				
4. Stay Positive				
5. Maintain Clear Communication				
6. Join a Support Group				
7. Continue Education About ADD				
8. Be Aware of Adult ADD Characteristics				
9. Use Affirmations				
10. Use Broken Record Technique				

D. Other Factors

1. Diet				
2. Sleep				
3. Assist Devices				
4. Homework Habit Development				
5. Use Simulated School Behaviors in Home Behavioral Program				

(Cont'd)

E. Additional Considerations

	Relevant	Date Started	Date Completed	Defer to
1. Parent Behavior Management Workshops				
2. Educational Consultation/Tutoring				
3. Speech and Language Therapy				
4. Occupational Therapy/Motor Coordination				
5. Psychiatric Consultation				
6. Home Computer Training				

IV. PLANNING AND REVIEW

A. Who will coordinate it? _____

B. How often? _____

C. Who will be involved? _____

D. Future Considerations (list)

_____

_____

_____

_____

V. COMMENTS

_____

_____

_____

_____

_____

_____

_____

_____

_____

_____

_____

SURVEY OF "SKILLS FOR SCHOOL SUCCESS"
Parent/Teacher Form

CHILD'S NAME _____ BIRTH DATE _____ AGE _____

GRADE _____ SCHOOL _____ HOMEROOM TEACHER _____

NAME OF RESPONDENT _____ DATE _____

___PARENT ___TEACHER ___OTHER _____ Information obtained by this survey will be used to determine your child's strengths and weaknesses with reference to the "Skills For School Success Program." Please reply to the following statements, giving your perceptions about this child's school behavior, work and study habits. Please reply for each statement.	**RESPONSE KEY:** N/A = Does not apply 1 = YES 2 = MOSTLY YES 3 = SOMETIMES 4 = MOSTLY NO 5 = NO					

About CLASS BEHAVIOR, this child:	N/A	1	2	3	4	5
Uses time wisely to prepare for class (e.g., getting pencils, papers and materials ready).						
Spends the time in class listening to the teacher and completing assignments.						
At the end of a class period, spends time getting ready for the next subject.						
If required to change classes, does so quietly and goes directly to the next class.						
Writes the homework assignments down in Homework Assignment Book.						

RESPONSE KEY: 1 = YES   2 = MOSTLY YES   3 = SOMETIMES   4 = MOSTLY NO   5 = NO

About ORGANIZATIONAL BEHAVIOR, this child:	N/A	1	2	3	4	5
Brings all needed supplies to school.						
Keeps all papers and work in a divided binder with pockets, and uses a plastic pouch for pencils, erasers, etc.						
Has a Homework Assignment Book to record all assignments.						
Keeps a routine schedule of study time and other activities.						
Has a calendar for long-range projects and assignments.						
Hands in work "on time."						
Keeps desk neat and organized.						

RESPONSE KEY: 1 = YES   2 = MOSTLY YES   3 = SOMETIMES   4 = MOSTLY NO   5 = NO

About LEARNING AND STUDY STRATEGIES, this child:	N/A	1	2	3	4	5
Makes sure of the directions for each assignment.						
Studies a little bit each night several days before a test.						

LEARNING AND STUDY STRATEGIES *(continued)*	N/A	1	2	3	4	5
Checks over work after completing an assignment.						
Looks over the content of an assignment before doing it.						
Asks self-questions during process of reading assigned material.						
Uses visual (seeing), auditory (hearing), or touch (feeling/sensation) as a help to learn things.						
Notes the kind of test to study for (e.g., true-false, essay, multiple-choice, fill-in-the-blanks).						
Practices taking tests by making up questions.						
Records notes by seeing and hearing the information presented in class.						

RESPONSE KEY: 1 = YES   2 = MOSTLY YES   3 = SOMETIMES   4 = MOSTLY NO   5 = NO

About NOTE TAKING, this child:	N/A	1	2	3	4	5
Writes notes about materials presented.						
Reviews notes to pick out important points.						
Compares notes with others when there are questions about accuracy.						
Has learned to use various symbols and abbreviations in notes.						
Tries to relate information in the text to note taking.						
Reviews notes in advance of tests.						

RESPONSE KEY: 1 = YES   2 = MOSTLY YES   3 = SOMETIMES   4 = MOSTLY NO   5 = NO

About TEST TAKING, this child:	N/A	1	2	3	4	5
Re-reads test instructions to be sure to know what to do.						
Keeps old tests for review.						
Reviews recent tests to correct errors and learn from mistakes.						
Knows how to approach different kinds of tests.						
Recognizes the components of a test which may be worth more points toward the test grade.						
Uses old (corrected) tests to prepare for the final exam.						
Seems satisfied with the kinds of grades earned on tests.						
Knows which kind of tests s/he can do well on and which kind s/he does poorly on.						
Can do equally well on a written test as compared to one given orally.						
Handwriting speed is adequate during test-taking and especially on tests requiring long answers.						

RESPONSE KEY: 1 = YES   2 = MOSTLY YES   3 = SOMETIMES   4 = MOSTLY NO   5 = NO

About USING REFERENCE MATERIAL, this child:	N/A	1	2	3	4	5
Looks at the Table of Contents before reading a book.						
Uses the Index and Glossary.						
Is familiar with pie, bar, and line graphs.						

USING REFERENCE MATERIAL *(continued)*	N/A	1	2	3	4	5
Has practiced reading tables to obtain information.						
Can compare tables and graphs to determine similarities and differences.						
Can locate words quickly in a dictionary.						
Has used an encyclopedia to obtain information.						

RESPONSE KEY: 1 = YES   2 = MOSTLY YES   3 = SOMETIMES   4 = MOSTLY NO   5 = NO

About INFORMATION PROCESSING, this child:	N/A	1	2	3	4	5
Can read and identify main ideas in stories.						
Understands what is read and can relate the information to others.						
Sees how material is organized (chapter, title, and paragraph headings).						
When encountering unknown words, writes them down or looks them up and notes the definition in the book.						
Reads best and retains the information when relaxed but alert.						

RESPONSE KEY: 1 = YES   2 = MOSTLY YES   3 = SOMETIMES   4 = MOSTLY NO   5 = NO

About INFORMATION RETENTION, this child:	N/A	1	2	3	4	5
Knows other methods to remember information other than re-reading it over and over.						
Knows memory strategies to help remember things.						
Can remember a general theme as well as details in a story.						
Can remember things best after review by seeing, hearing, and writing informational facts.						
Remembers information best when given a signal or cue as a reminder that something is important and will probably be on a test.						

RESPONSE KEY: 1 = YES   2 = MOSTLY YES   3 = SOMETIMES   4 = MOSTLY NO   5 = NO

About HOMEWORK, this child:	N/A	1	2	3	4	5
Uses a Homework Assignment Book.						
Checks off things that will be needed at home for assignments.						
Has a routine place and time for homework.						
Does most difficult homework first; then, the easier, more liked things.						
Files completed homework and checks it off the list.						
Checks over homework for mistakes.						

RESPONSE KEY: 1 = YES   2 = MOSTLY YES   3 = SOMETIMES   4 = MOSTLY NO   5 = NO

About RELATIONSHIP WITH TEACHERS, this child:	N/A	1	2	3	4	5
Believes the teacher understands his or her problems.						
Is aware of the teacher's expectations of him or her.						
Knows the class rules.						

RELATIONSHIP WITH TEACHERS *(continued)*	N/A	1	2	3	4	5
Feels free to ask questions.						
Can always go to the teacher for help with some assignment or subject.						

OTHER OBSERVATIONS OR COMMENTS: _____

_____

_____

_____

_____

_____

_____

_____

_____

_____

_____

_____

_____

_____

_____

_____

_____

_____

_____

_____

_____

_____

_____

S-ADHD-RS MEDICATION MONITORING PROFILE

Week(s) _5_ After Medication

Name _John_ Date_____ Grade _4_

Physician _Dr. Mach_ Teacher _Ms. Brown_

Behaviors Associated with ADHD

	ADHD Symptoms			Social Symptoms				Academics			Classroom Behavior				
Score	AT	IP	HY	PI	SC	SS	Ob	RD	MA	WL	CA	AO	NC	OS	VI
6	.	.	.	.	.	.	.	.	.	.	.	.	.	.	.
5	.	.	.	.	.	.	.	.	.	.	.	.	.	.	.
4	.	.	.	.	.	.	.	.	.	.	.	.	.	.	.
3	.														
2															
1	.	.	.	.	.	.	.	.	.	.	.	.	.	.	.
N	.	.	.	.	.	.	.	.	.	.	.	.	.	.	.

AT = Attention
IP = Impulsivity
HY = Hyperactivity

PI = Peer Interaction
SC = Self Concept
SS = Social Skills
OB = Outbursts

RD = Reading
MA = Math
WL = Written Language

CA = Complete Assignments
AO = Ability to Organize
NC = Non Compliant
OS = Out of Seat
VI = Verbal Interpretations

Medication Side Effects

Score	AI	IS	HA	SA	TI	IR	DP
6	.	.	.	.	.	.	.
5	.	.	.	.	.	.	.
4	.	.	.	.	.	.	.
3	.	.	.	.	.	.	.
2	.	.	.	.	.	.	.
1				.		.	

AL = Appetite Loss
IS = Insomnia
HA = Headaches
SA = Stomach Ache
TI = Tics
IR = Irritability
DP = Depression

S-ADHD-RS MEDICATION MONITORING FORM

Name ___John___ School _____
Teacher ___Ms. Brown___ Grade ___4___ Age ___9 yr 10 mo.___
Physician ___Dr. Mach___ Date _____
Completed by ___Ms. Brown___ Parent _____ Teacher ___✓___
How long has this child been on medication? ___1 month___
Has there been a change in prescription or dosage? ___Yes___

Typically, children improve their behavior when placed on medication; however, not all behaviors respond favorably.

Behaviors
Rate the following current behaviors using the scale below:

1 = No longer a problem   4 = No improvement
2 = Lots of improvement   5 = Behavior is worse
3 = Good improvement   6 = Major deterioration
                           N = Never a problem

ADHD Symptoms
Attention ___2___
Impulsivity ___3___
Hyperactivity ___3___ Total ___8___

Social Symptoms
Peer Interaction ___3___
Self Concept ___2___
Social Skills ___2___
Outbursts ___2___ Total ___9___

Academic
Reading ___3___
Math ___2___
Written Language ___3___ Total ___8___

Classroom Behavior
Complete Assignments ___2___
Ability to Organize ___3___
Noncompliant ___3___
Out of Seat ___3___
Verbal Interruptions ___2___ Total ___13___

Side Effects (if any) Rate intensity: 1=none; 2=low; 3=mild; 4=moderate; 5=high; 6=very high

Appetite Loss ___1___
Insomnia ___1___
Headaches ___1___
Stomach Ache ___2___
Tics ___1___
Irritability ___2___
Depression ___2___

Would you recommend that medication be continued? ___YES___
Has the student made substantial gains since medication? ___YES___
Comments:

TEACHER RATING FORM

ACTeRS

Rina K. Ullmann, M. Ed.
Esther K. Sleator, M.D.
Robert L. Sprague, Ph.D.

2nd Edition

Below are descriptions of behavior. Please read each item and compare the child's behavior with that of his or her classmates. Circle the number that most closely corresponds with your evaluation. Transfer the total raw score for each of the four sections to the profile sheet to determine normative percentile scores.

Child's Name: Chris Student
Rater: Mrs. Truitt
ID#: 60952
Date: 9-11-97

ATTENTION

	Almost Never				Almost Always
	1	2	3	4	5
1. Works well independently	1	(2)	3	4	5
2. Persists with task for reasonable amount of time	(1)	2	3	4	5
3. Completes assigned task satisfactorily with little additional assistance	1	(2)	3	4	5
4. Follows simple directions accurately	1	2	(3)	4	5
5. Follows a sequence of instructions	1	(2)	3	4	5
6. Functions well in the classroom	1	(2)	3	4	5

ADD ITEMS 1-6 AND PLACE TOTAL HERE **12**

HYPERACTIVITY

	Almost Never				Almost Always
	1	2	3	4	5
7. Extremely overactive (out of seat, "on the go")	1	2	3	(4)	5
8. Overreacts	1	(2)	3	4	5
9. Fidgety (hands always busy)	1	2	(3)	4	5
10. Impulsive (acts or talks without thinking)	1	(2)	3	4	5
11. Restless (squirms in seat)	1	2	3	(4)	5

ADD ITEMS 7-11 AND PLACE TOTAL HERE **15**

SOCIAL SKILLS

	Almost Never				Almost Always
	1	2	3	4	5
12. Behaves positively with peers/classmates	1	2	(3)	4	5
13. Verbal communication clear and "connected"	1	2	3	(4)	5
14. Nonverbal communication accurate	1	2	3	(4)	5
15. Follows group norms and social rules	1	(2)	3	4	5
16. Cites general rule when criticizing ("We aren't supposed to do that")	1	2	3	(4)	5
17. Skillful at making new friends	1	(2)	3	4	5
18. Approaches situations confidently	1	2	3	4	(5)

ADD ITEMS 12-18 AND PLACE TOTAL HERE **24**

OPPOSITIONAL

	Almost Never				Almost Always
	1	2	3	4	5
19. Tries to get others into trouble	1	(2)	3	4	5
20. Starts fights over nothing	(1)	2	3	4	5
21. Makes malicious fun of people	1	(2)	3	4	5
22. Defies authority	1	(2)	3	4	5
23. Picks on others	1	(2)	3	4	5
24. Mean and cruel to other children	1	(2)	3	4	5

ADD ITEMS 19-24 AND PLACE TOTAL HERE **11**

MetriTech, Inc.

Copyright © 1986, 1991 by MetriTech, Inc.
4106 Fieldstone Road, Champaign, Illinois 61821
(217) 398-4868 • FAX (217) 398-5798
No portion of this form may be copied in any way without written permission.

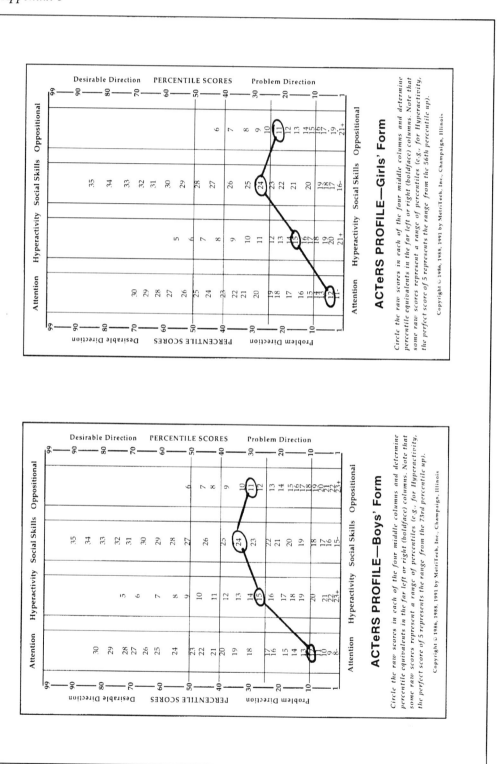

PARENT RATING FORM

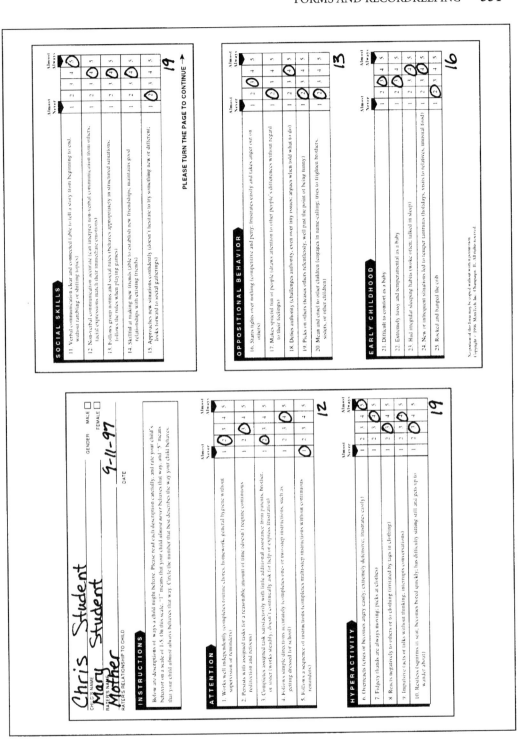

PARENT PROFILE FORMS

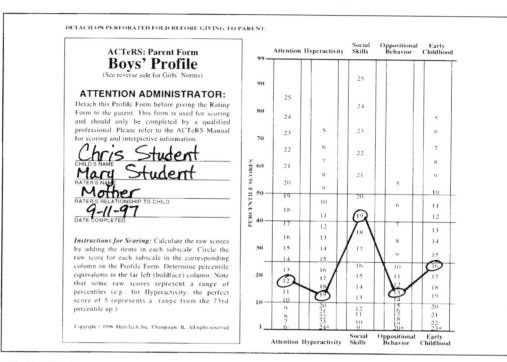

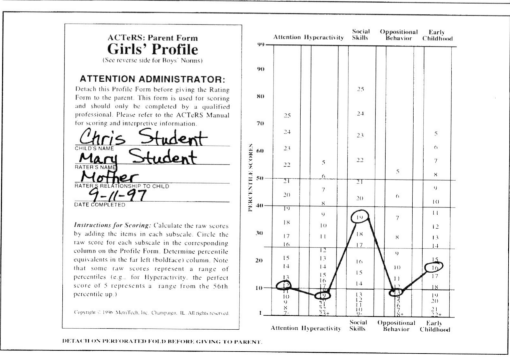

ACADEMIC PERFORMANCE RATING SCALE

STUDENT _____   DATE _____

AGE _____   GRADE _____   TEACHER _____

For each of the below items, please estimate the above student's performance over the **PAST WEEK.** For each item, please circle **one** choice only.

1. Estimate the percentage of written **math** work *completed* (regardless of accuracy) relative to classmates.	0-49%	50-69%	70-79%	80-89%	90-100%
	1	2	3	4	5
2. Estimate the percentage of written **language arts** work *completed* (regardless of accuracy) relative to classmates.	0-49%	50-69%	70-79%	80-89%	90-100%
	1	2	3	4	5
3. Estimate the *accuracy* of completed written **math** work (i.e., percent correct of work done).	0-64%	65-69%	70-79%	80-89%	90-100%
	1	2	3	4	5
4. Estimate the *accuracy* of completed **written language** arts work (i.e., percent correct of work done).	0-64%	65-69%	70-79%	80-89%	90-100%
	1	2	3	4	5
5. How consistent has the quality of this child's academic work been over the past week?	Consistently poor	More poor than successful	Variable	More successful than poor	Consistently successful
	1	2	3	4	5
6. How frequently does the student accurately follow teacher instructions and/or class discussion during *large-group* (e.g., whole class) instruction?	Never	Rarely	Sometimes	Often	Very Often
	1	2	3	4	5
7. How frequently does the student accurately follow teacher instruction and/or class discussion during *small-group* (e.g., reading group) instruction?	Never	Rarely	Sometimes	Often	Very Often
	1	2	3	4	5
8. How quickly does this child learn new material (i.e., pick up novel concepts)?	Never	Rarely	Sometimes	Often	Very Often
	1	2	3	4	5

(Cont'd)

					Above	
9.	What is the quality or neatness of this child's handwriting?	Poor 1	Fair 2	Average 3	Average 4	Excellent 5
10.	What is the quality of this child's reading skills?	Poor 1	Fair 2	Average 3	Above Average 4	Excellent 5
11.	What is the quality of this child's speaking skills?	Poor 1	Fair 2	Average 3	Above Average 4	Excellent 5
12.	How often does the child complete written work in a careless, hasty fashion?	Never 1	Rarely 2	Sometimes 3	Often 4	Very Often 5
13.	How frequently does the child take more time to complete work than his/her classmates?	Never 1	Rarely 2	Sometimes 3	Often 4	Very Often 5
14.	How often is the child able to pay attention without you prompting him/her?	Never 1	Rarely 2	Sometimes 3	Often 4	Very Often 5
15.	How frequently does this child require your assistance to accurately complete his/her academic work?	Never 1	Rarely 2	Sometimes 3	Often 4	Very Often 5
16.	How often does the child begin written work prior to understanding the directions?	Never 1	Rarely 2	Sometimes 3	Often 4	Very Often 5
17.	How frequently does this child have difficulty recalling material from a previous day's lessons?	Never 1	Rarely 2	Sometimes 3	Often 4	Very Often 5
18.	How often does the child appear to be staring excessively or "spaced out"?	Never 1	Rarely 2	Sometimes 3	Often 4	Very Often 5
19.	How often does the child appear withdrawn or tend to lack an emotional response in a social situation?	Never 1	Rarely 2	Sometimes 3	Often 4	Very Often 5

NOTE. From "Teacher Ratings of Academic Skills: The Development of the Academic Performance Rating Scale" by George J. DuPaul, Mark D. Rapport, and Lucy M. Perriello, 1991, *School Psychology Review, 20,* 284-300. Reprinted with permission.

BEHAVIOR REPORT CARD

NAME _____ DATE _____

Dear Rater:

Please assess the child's behavior on the following items using the following scale:

Excellent = 4, Good = 3, Fair = 2, Poor = 0 or N/A (Not applicable).

Observation # _____

BEHAVIOR ITEMS	1	2	3	4
1. Keeps hands to self (does not push, shove, pinch, or touch others inappropriately).				
2. Avoids fighting (does not hit, kick, or bite others).				
3. Avoids provoking fights (does not trip others or take things).				
4. Behavior appropriate to situation				
5. Plays cooperatively/gets along				
Time-outs				
Fines				
Rater's Initials				
Rating period code: Free time (FT); Lunchroom (LR); Recess (R); other (O)				

Appendix 7

DSM–IV CRITERIA: ADHD

DIAGNOSTIC CRITERIA FOR ATTENTION DEFICIT HYPERACTIVITY DISORDER

A. Either (1) or (2):

   (1) Six (or more) of the following symptoms of **inattention** have persisted for at least 6 months to a degree that is maladaptive and inconsistent with developmental level:

INATTENTION

    (a)   often fails to give close attention to details or makes careless mistakes in schoolwork, work, or other activities

    (b)   often has difficulty sustaining attention in tasks or play activities

    (c)   often does not seem to listen when spoken to directly

    (d)   often does not follow through on instructions and fails to finish schoolwork, chores, or duties in the workplace (not due to oppositional behavior or failure to understand instructions)

    (e)   often has difficulty organizing tasks and activities

    (f)   often avoids, dislikes, or is reluctant to engage in tasks that require sustained mental effort (such as schoolwork or homework)

    (g)   often loses things necessary for tasks or activities (e.g., toys, school assignments, pencils, books, or tools)

    (h)   is often easily distracted by extraneous stimuli

    (i)   is often forgetful in daily activities

   (2) Six (or more) of the following symptoms of **hyperactivity–impulsivity** have persisted for at least 6 months to a degree that is maladaptive and inconsistent with developmental level:

HYPERACTIVITY

    (a)   often fidgets with hands or feet or squirms in seat

    (b)   often leaves seat in classroom or in other situations in which remaining seated is expected

    (c)   often runs about or climbs excessively in situations in which it is inappropriate (in adolescents or adults, may be limited to subjective feelings of restlessness)

    (d)   often has difficulty playing or engaging in leisure activities quietly

    (e)   is often "on the go" or often acts as if "driven by a motor"

    (f)   often talks excessively

IMPULSIVITY

    (g)   often blurts out answers before questions have been completed

    (h)   often has difficulty awaiting turn

    (i)   often interrupts or intrudes on others (e.g., butts into conversations or games)

B. Some hyperactive–impulsive or inattentive symptoms that caused impairment were present before age 7 years.

C. Some impairment from the symptoms is present in two or more settings (e.g., at school [or work] and at home).

D. There must be clear evidence of clinically significant impairment in social, academic, or occupational functioning.

E. The symptoms did not occur exclusively during the course of a Pervasive Developmental Disorder, Schizophrenia, or other Psychotic Disorder and are not better accounted for by another mental disorder (e.g., Mood Disorder, Anxiety Disorder, Dissociative Disorder, or a Personality Disorder).

Code based on type:

314.01 *Attention Deficit Hyperactivity Disorder, Combined Type:* if both Criteria A1 and A2 are met for the past 6 months.

314.00 *Attention Deficit Hyperactivity Disorder, Predominantly Hyperactive–Inattention Type:* if Criterion A1 is met, but Criterion A2 is not met for the past 6 months.

314.01 *Attention Deficit Hyperactivity Disorder, Predominantly Hyperactive–Impulsive Type:* if Criterion A2 is met, but Criterion A1 is not met for the past 6 months.

Coding notes: For individuals (especially adolescents and adults) who currently have symptoms that no longer meet full criteria, "In Partial Remission" should be specified.

DIAGNOSTIC CRITERIA FOR 313.81 OPPOSITIONAL DEFIANT DISORDER

A. A pattern of negativistic, hostile, and defiant behavior lasting at least 6 months, during which four (or more) of the following are present:

(1) often loses temper

(2) often argues with adults

(3) often actively defies or refuses to comply with adults' requests or rules

(4) often deliberately annoys people

(5) often blames others for his or her mistakes or misbehavior

(6) is often touchy or easily annoyed by others

(7) is often angry and resentful

(8) is often spiteful or vindictive

Note: Consider a criterion met only if the behavior occurs more frequently than is typically observed in individuals of comparable age and developmental level.

B. The disturbance in behavior causes clinically significant impairment in social, academic, or occupational functioning.

C. The behaviors do not occur exclusively during the course of a Psychotic or Mood Disorder.

D. Criteria are not met for Conduct Disorder, and, if the individual is age 18 years or older, criteria are not met for Antisocial Personality Disorder.

DIAGNOSTIC CRITERIA FOR 312.8 CONDUCT DISORDER

A. A repetitive and persistent pattern of behavior in which the basic rights of others or major age-appropriate societal norms or rules are violated, as manifested by the presence of three (or more) of the following criteria in the past 12 months, with at least one criterion present in the past 6 months.

AGGRESSION TO PEOPLE AND ANIMALS

(1) often bullies, threatens, or intimidates others

(2) often initiates physical fights

(3) has used a weapon that can cause serious physical harm to others (e.g., a bat, brick, broken bottle, knife, gun)

(4) has been physically cruel to people

(5) has been physically cruel to animals

(6) has stolen while confronting a victim (e.g., mugging, purse snatching, extortion, armed robbery)

(7) has forced someone into sexual activity

DESTRUCTION OF PROPERTY

(8) has deliberately engaged in fire setting with the intention of causing serious damage

(9) has deliberately destroyed others' property (other than by fire setting)

Deceitfulness or Theft

(10) has broken into someone else's house, building, or car

(11) often lies to obtain goods or favors or to avoid obligations (i.e., "cons" others)

(12) has stolen items of nontrivial value without confronting a victim (e.g., shoplifting, but without breaking and entering; forgery)

Serious Violations of Rules

(13) often stays out at night despite parental prohibitions, beginning before age 13 years

(14) has run away from home overnight at least twice while living in parental or parental surrogate home (or once without returning for a lengthy period)

(15) is often truant from school, beginning before age 13 years

B. The disturbance in behavior causes clinically significant impairment in social, academic, or occupational functioning.

C. If the individual is age 18 years or older, criteria are not met for Antisocial Personality Disorder.

Specify type based on age at onset:

Childhood-Onset Type: onset of at least one criterion characteristic of Conduct Disorder prior to age 10 years

Adolescent-Onset Type: absence of any criteria characteristic of Conduct Disorder prior to age 10 years

Specify severity:

Mild: few if any conduct problems in excess of those required to make the diagnosis and conduct problems cause only minor harm to others

Moderate: number of conduct problems and effect on others intermediate between "mild" and "severe"

Severe: many conduct problems in excess of those required to make the diagnosis or conduct problems cause considerable harm to others

Appendix 8

PARENT–TEACHER CHECKLIST

CHARACTERISTICS OF <u>ADHD</u> IN TEENS

1. Gives the impression of not hearing instructions.
2. Seems to be distracted easily.
3. Makes impulsive careless errors.
4. Has difficulty waiting his or her turn in groups.
5. May appear restless or talkative.
6. Has difficulty following through with requests.
7. May continue to blurt out in class.
8. Inconsistent in academic performance.
9. Has difficulty organizing things.
10. Has difficulty estimating and managing time.

CHARACTERISTICS OF <u>ODD</u> IN TEENS

1. Frequently loses temper.
2. Argumentative with adults (parents/teachers).
3. Shows frequent noncompliance to requests from adults.
4. Seems to deliberately annoy others.
5. Blames others for mistakes or misbehaviors.
6. Easily annoyed by others.
7. Appears angry and resentful.
8. May be spiteful or vindictive.
9. Excessively moody.
10. Often in dysfunctional family with a history of harsh, inconsistent, or neglectful parenting.

CHARACTERISTICS OF <u>CD</u> IN TEENS

1. Shows aggression toward people and animals that causes harm.
2. Is destructive with property.

3. Has been deceitful or has stolen things.

4. Has shown frequent serious violation of rules.

5. Has little concern for others' feelings and rights.

6. Shows little or no remorse over inappropriate behavior.

7. May project an image of toughness attempting to cover up feelings of inadequacy and low self-esteem.

8. Has frequent driving accidents or may be described as accident prone.

9. High risk-taking manifested in sexual behavior, smoking, substance abuse, and engagement in other risky dangerous activities.

10. May have chronic history of school suspensions and/or expulsion, along with poorly developed abilities and achievements.

CHARACTERISTICS OF <u>LD</u> IN TEENS

1. Difficulty with spoken language manifested by developmental delays or discrepancies between listening and speaking skills.

2. Difficulty with reading comprehension.

3. Difficulty with written language skills and evidence of reversals beyond age 6.

4. Difficulty with arithmetic manifested by problems performing calculations or in comprehending basic concepts.

5. Difficulty with reasoning skills manifested by problems organizing and interpreting cognitive thought patterns, along with poor short- and long-term memory.

6. Inconsistency in test performance as well as in grades.

7. Perceptual impairments manifested by visual–spatial problems, visual–perceptual distortion, or sequencing difficulty.

8. Difficulty in fine-motor coordination, awkwardness, or a previous delay in the development of definitive hand preference.

9. General difficulty in organizational skills that affect all facets of learning.

10. Absence of any factors that might account for specific academic problems (e.g., cultural, neurological, audiological, visual, or educational).

Appendix 9

WARNING SIGNS OF VIOLENT BEHAVIOR

When ADHD is combined with Conduct Disorder or even more serious forms of psychopathology, there is an increased risk of acting-out behavior. While it is not possible to predict with certainty when "violent" behavior may erupt, there are some warning signs that have been based on information provided by the U.S. Department of Education. The following list of indicators may forewarn of future violent behavior:

1. the student who withdraws from other students—the "loner"
2. students who have been victims of violence at home or at school will be at risk
3. the student who is "persecuted" by being picked on, left out, teased, or bullied
4. any student who expresses violence in writings or drawings is at risk
5. any student who displays frequent and intense anger in response to minor problems
6. any student with a history of intense prejudice toward other races, ethnic groups, religion, language, gender, sexual orientation, or physical appearance
7. any student who has a history of drug and/or alcohol abuse
8. any student who has easy access to firearms (or who seems preoccupied with firearms)
9. students who make or have made specific threats of violence
10. students with diagnosed problems involving impulse-control, anger, depression, low-frustration tolerance, low self-esteem, social skill problems, and severe academic difficulty

While there are no known critical items, it must be assumed that the greater the number of items considered to be of concern, the greater the risk of violent acting-out behavior. However, identification of items that are of concern for a specific individual will allow teachers and parents time to initiate some types of interventions that may prevent the student from acting-out in the future. While some students may be unable to change actual traumatic events that have occurred in the past, at least reframing them (i.e., viewing them from a different perspective) may change their prognostic influence on behavioral outcomes.

Appendix 10

A PERSONAL GUIDE FOR TEENS WITH ADHD

The following guide is offered as a brief introduction to some principles that will certainly aid most all teens.

Information from *The Seven Habits of Highly Effective People* by Steven Covey has been shown to be beneficial for adults with ADHD. Likewise, similar information from *The Seven Habits of Highly Effective Teens* by Sean Covey may also provide a practical guide for teens with ADHD. The basic tenet of this guide focuses on the development of "habits." The seven habits are described as the seven characteristics that happy and successful teens may have in common. They are as follows:

1. Be proactive—take responsibility for your life.
2. Begin with the end in mind—define your mission and goals in life.
3. Put first things first—prioritize and do the most important things first.
4. Think win–win—have an "everybody can win" attitude.
5. Seek first to understand, then to be understood—listen to people sincerely.
6. Synergize—work to achieve more.
7. Sharpen the saw—renew yourself regularly.

The above habits build upon one another. Habits 1–3 deal with "self mastery"; habits 4–6 deal with relationships and teamwork; habit 7 feeds on all the others. Mr. Covey notes that perceptions (labeled paradigms) refer to the way you see things (i.e., if you believe you're dumb, you will feel and act dumb; if you believe someone else is dumb, you'll look for evidence to support this belief).

Perceptions can either help or hinder you. When you see things in a different light, it's like getting a new pair of glasses—everything becomes clear again. Negative perceptions impose limitation on you; positive perceptions can bring out the best in you. One way to change these perceptions is to spend time with someone who believes in you and builds you up. This could be a teacher, parent, friend, grandparent, or a coach.

Seeing things differently from another point of view can make a difference in your attitude toward others. Often we have distorted perceptions that are sometimes incomplete or inaccurate; changing our perceptions (or paradigms) can make a difference in how we act around and toward others. Some of a teen's most important perceptions include: friends, material things, the opposite sex, school, parents, sports/hobbies, heroes, enemies, self, and work. These perceptions can "mess you up" if your life is centered on them. Some realistic guidelines about each area of perceptions may help.

- *Friend Centered*—Make as many friends as you can but don't build your life around them.
- *Material Things*—Think of the old saying, "He who dies with the most toys wins." Confidence needs to come from within, not from "stuff."
- *Heterosexual Relations*—Centering your life on someone else doesn't show that you love them, only that you're dependent on them.

➠ *School Centered*—The real purpose of school is to learn, not just to get good grades. Also, it's possible to do well in school and have a balance with other things in life.

➠ *Parent Centered*—Care about what your parents think. Respect for their opinions is important, but be responsible for your life and please yourself first.

➠ *Other Centered*—This focus doesn't provide the stability that's needed in life.

➠ *Principle Centered*—This one does work. Use principles that govern the real world. If you live by them, you'll excel. If you break them, you'll fail.

True principles include honesty, service, love, hard work, respect, gratitude, moderation, fairness, integrity, loyalty, and responsibility. When you decide to make *principles* your life center (or paradigm), say "for every problem, search for the principle that will solve it."

Sean Covey cites the movie starring Bill Murray ("What About Bob?") where he is told to take "baby steps" to deal with his anxiety and panic in the real world. Some of the suggestions based on this concept may be very helpful for teens as well as parents and teachers. These "baby steps" are things that you can do immediately to apply some of the principles that may help you achieve even more important goals.

1. When you look in the mirror, say something positive about yourself.

2. Give others positive comments (e.g., "Hey, that was a cool idea").

3. Act opposite of some constricting perception of yourself (e.g., if you think yourself as shy, go up and introduce yourself to several people).

4. Think of someone who has acted differently from the way they usually act and consider some things that may have brought about that change.

5. When you have nothing to do, what occupies your thoughts? What occupies your time and your energy?

6. Begin today to treat others as you would want them to treat you. Don't bad mouth someone unless you want them to bad mouth you.

7. When you're in a quiet place all alone, think about what really matters to you.

8. Listen carefully to the words of the music you enjoy. Are they consistent with the principles you believe in?

9. When you do your chores or work, go the extra mile and do more than what is expected.

10. When you're in a difficult situation and don't know what to do, ask yourself, "What principle should I apply (i.e., honesty, love, loyalty, hard work, or patience)?" Follow that principle and don't look back.

These are some of the important first steps to get you started. It would be beneficial to all teens with ADHD to read the entire book, *The Seven Habits of Highly Effective Teens.* This step-by-step guide is written in an entertaining style with many cartoons, interesting quotes, and fascinating stories of actual teenagers around the world. There is also an audio-taped version that may be even more acceptable to teens with ADHD while still providing all of the basic information that such teens may find beneficial. Both book and audio versions are available from Simon & Schuster. In addition to the four-tape audio program, there is an accompanying workbook.

Appendix 11

PSYCHOLOGICAL REPORT

PSYCHOLOGICAL REPORT

NAME: <u>C.P.S.</u>   DATE TESTED: <u>7/3/96</u>

BIRTHDATE: <u>1/17/82</u>   EXAMINER: <u>G. L. Flick, Ph.D.</u>

AGE: <u>14 years 6 months</u>   GRADE: <u>8th</u>

TESTS ADMINISTERED

Wechsler Intelligence Scale for Children–III (WISC–III)

Wide Range Achievement Test–3 (WRAT–3)

Beery Developmental Test of Visual–Motor Integration

Gordon Diagnostic System

The Brown Scales

The ADHD Test

Conners Parent Rating Scale

Behavioral Assessment System for Children (BASC)

Parent Rating Scale/Adolescent

Millon Adolescent Clinical Inventory

ADHD History Grid

Conflict Behavior Questionnaire

Issues Checklist

Human Figure Drawings

Kinetic Family Drawing

Sentence Completion Test

Behavioral Observation Checklist

Pediatric ADD/ADHD Information Sheet

Pediatric Questionnaire

Clinical Interviews

REFERRAL AND BACKGROUND INFORMATION

According to C.P.'s mother, this youngster "does not want to go to school or do homework." His mother also related that he refuses to do chores around the house and "breaks everything he puts his hands on." When queried about this last item, his mother noted he "takes things apart to see how it works and then cannot put them back together."

A developmental history was provided by C.P.'s mother. She indicated that C.P.'s problems started with writing difficulties in the early grades. He reportedly did okay in reading, but by the third grade could not copy. He also complained of headaches at that time. His mother reported that he was never a behavioral problem and appears to process information well through the auditory sense modality. She noted that he did go through a special handwriting program and was diagnosed as learning disabled in written expression. At two years of age she reported that he did have an accident when he fell off a trampoline and "busted a kidney." She could not remember whether he also had hit his head. C.P. had reportedly taken Ritalin®, but this gave him more headaches and made him "sick to his stomach." His mother noted that "I've always had to drag him out of the bed in the morning." Ritalin® was prescribed when he was in second to third grade. He also took medication for migraine, but his mother could not remember what it was. She did note that when he was about 8 to 9 years of age, he would often "vomit in class."

C.P.'s mother could recall no specific problems during her pregnancy and yet the delivery was "terrible." She reported to be in labor 48 hours. Although no instruments were used, she noted that the "doctor reached in and turned his head." She recalled that he did have bruises on his face and head. However, there were no significant problems after birth. He was reportedly very active when he was young, but his activity decreased around the third to fourth grades when he was about 10 years of age. Motor developmental milestones were generally within normal limits. Likewise, speech and language development was within normal limits as his mother noted that he first babbled at about 6 to 7 months, said his first words at about 8 months, and used groups of words meaningfully at about one year of age. She notes that early on C.P. tended to be destructive and he reacted to punishment with "fighting," especially with his mother. C.P.'s mother also noted that he was somewhat clumsy or poorly coordinated. She noted that he would always fall down "when he played ball." She also commented that he was "never good at sports."

In school, C.P.'s best subjects were reportedly science and reading, but his mother notes that he has a very hard time with writing and resists doing it. His mother further notes that he learns differently from what they teach. "The teachers think he is dumb. He can tell them all the answers because he listens very well; he just has a hard time writing them." She also noted that he could not look at a chalkboard and write down what he has seen. His schoolteachers report that he is "lazy." C.P. has become quite resistant to doing his homework and tends to avoid his mother when she cues him to do it. She also notes that C.P. has complained of being sick to get out of going to school.

C.P.'s mother noted that she, herself, had had some difficulty in school. She reported that she would have to cover up her words so that she could read one word at a time. She did not finish school but quit at about the eighth or ninth grade; she also failed to complete her high school degree. C.P.'s father reportedly went to college and had no academic difficulty, other than trouble with handwriting. There were no reported medical or psychiatric problems on either side of the family. C.P.'s mother noted that she had difficulty with math and reading, and also had a bad handwriting when she was younger.

BEHAVIORAL OBSERVATIONS

C.P. was seen on 7/3/96. He appeared for this evaluation neatly dressed in a polo shirt, baggy pants, and a baseball cap. C.P. is rather tall for his age and is quite muscular in build. He was a bit apprehensive upon initial contact but showed good cooperation and good eye contact throughout the testing session. No unusual mood state was exhibited; his mood was fairly stable. C.P. did take his hat off and put it back on several times during the session. Attention and concentration were deemed to be good, and his activity level fairly normal. He did engage in some fidgeting, but he was persistent to complete tasks and did not show any excess impulsivity. His motivation to perform appeared to be fair. Occasionally he became distracted but appeared bored on several occasions, looking around the room and asking how long would he be in testing. C.P. did initiate some conversation with the examiner, and his verbalizations appeared to reflect logical sequential thinking, which was relevant to the topic. Comprehension appeared to be good, and he was generally alert and oriented to the tasks. There was little change in affect as C.P. smiled only occasionally. He did show good rapport with the examiner. On one occasion, he did state that he wished to leave (after about 30 minutes of paper-and-pencil testing), indicating that his neck hurt. He was able to complete the test session.

ASSESSMENT OF ABILITIES AND ACHIEVEMENTS

On the WISC–III, C.P. obtained a Full Scale IQ of 110, a Verbal IQ of 118, and a Performance IQ of 100. He is basically functioning within the upper limits of the high-average range of intellectual ability. C.P. had the greatest difficulty on those tasks involving visual–spatial and visual–motor integrative skills. He also experienced difficulty on those tasks requiring greater attention and concentration.

On the Wide Range Achievement Test–3, C.P. obtained the following test scores in basic skill areas of reading, spelling, and arithmetic:

WRAT–3	SS	PERCENTILE	GRADE LEVEL
READING	120	91	POST H.S.
SPELLING	102	55	8th
ARITHMETIC	89	23	6th

On the Beery Developmental Test of Visual–Motor Integration, C.P.'s overall score was several years below his chronological age. He obtained a VMI age equivalent of 11 years 3 months (25th percentile).

ASSESSMENT OF ATTENTIONAL BEHAVIOR

On the Gordon Diagnostic Assessment of Attention, C.P. is currently functioning within the normal range with regard to his capacity for delay and inhibition. On the Vigilance Task his performance, again, was entirely within normal limits, reflecting adequate sustained attention on this computerized task. On the Distractibility Task his performance was within the borderline range, reflecting mild problems with regard to vigilance and alertness on this complex attentional task. However, on both the Vigilance and Distractibility tasks, he showed a normal level of impulsivity.

On the ADHD test, C.P.'s overall ADHD quotient of 96 falls at the 39th percentile and is within the average range with regard to the probability of ADHD. In order of increasing significance, his impulsivity subscale was at the 99th percentile, hyperactivity at the 50th percentile, and inattention at the 75th percentile.

PARENT RATING SCALES

On the BASC Adolescent Version, the overall assessment was valid. C.P.'s mother noted that this teen's problems with attention are significant; the Attention Problem Scale is the one with the highest elevations. This is followed by somatization and conduct problems.

SELF-REPORT SCALES

On the Brown Scales, C.P.'s overall score of 86 was clearly within the clinical range for attention deficit problems. His highest score was in cluster 5, Working Memory, reflecting significant problems in this area. Also elevated was his score on cluster 3, Effort, and this also is fairly consistent with his reported writing difficulties. Difficulties on cluster 1, Activation, involving organizing and activating for work reflects his difficulty in getting started and organized because of being scattered or perhaps from worry.

BEHAVIORAL AND EMOTIONAL ASSESSMENT

Overall, this teen exhibits a characteristically irritable, negativistic, and unpredictable behavior pattern. He seemingly complains of being misunderstood and unappreciated, and is easily offended and provoked into impulsive, obstructive, or angry reactions. This touchiness appears to reflect an oversensitivity often seen in reaction to others' comments and criticisms. Inclined to expect criticism from his parents, he may act defensively and angrily, thereby precipitating his anticipated and feared rejection.

This teen's complaining, moody, and pessimistic attitude appears to be associated with frequent outbursts and unruly behavior. Unresolved conflicts between issues of dependence, resentment, and guilt appear to surface erratically and may add to the stress of his life. Some of the difficulties he experiences at home may be reacted to with oppositional behavior. In addition to the tensions these actions may produce, there is also anxiety over feeling vulnerable at home. With frequent family conflicts and confrontations, C.P. is liable to act out in an annoyed, sarcastic, and resentful manner, often looking to blame others for his discomfort. He is apparently quite sensitive to rejection and, having experienced many disappointments in the past, he has an apparent lack of confidence in others. He appears especially sensitive to his teacher's lack of understanding and lack of compassion with regard to the difficulties that he has experienced. It is apparent that C.P. has experienced considerable anxiety and tension, and this has had some effect upon bodily functions. Complaints of headaches, stomachaches, vomiting—all appear to be stress-related problems connected to some of the difficulties he has experienced. In order to avoid these build-ups of stress, he attempts to avoid some of the academic problems that have precipitated those symptoms.

SUMMARY AND RECOMMENDATIONS

C.P. is a 14-year-old white male who has become increasingly avoidant of most all academic work and has reached the point where he is currently failing in school. This teen has experienced an accumulation of difficulties over the years and presents chronic problems with handwriting. He is, however, generally bright, especially in the area of verbal skills. Nonverbal visual–motor and visual–spatial skills appear to be less well-developed. While C.P. has experienced little difficulty with reading, he has had major problems with those academic areas requiring writing. Specifically, he has had difficulty with math and with spelling. His nonverbal learning disability appears to be biologically based as both mother and father have reported problems with handwriting; his mother is also reported having had a learning disability. Attentional problems have been longstanding and have primarily affected his ability to engage in sustained effort on tasks and his working memory. Both C.P. and his mother are consistent in their rating of his attentional problems. While C.P. would qualify for a diagnosis of ADHD—primarily inattentive type—his inability to stay on task and to complete tasks appears more directly related to his writing problem or dysgraphia. The stress he has experienced over being unable to perform adequately in writing is rather significant. Anxiety, tension, and even some mild depression are indicated.

The following recommendations are offered in this case:

1. A medication consult is indicated. A long-acting or sustained medication is recommended. Any change in medication, however, may not be made with regard to his reported headaches. It is felt that the headaches may be more attributable to some of the demands that are made upon C.P. to complete work that is difficult for him because of his writing problems. Any further adjustment in medication might await implementation of school accommodations to be recommended.

2. It is suggested that the following accommodations be made with regard to C.P.'s academic placement: (a) Provide more time for tests; (b) administer more oral tests than written tests, written tests may be restricted to short answer, true–false or multiple choice; (c) adjustment in assignments so that he may have shorter assignments or may complete assignments on the computer; (d) use tape recorder or computer to aid in recording assignments or in completing work; (e) provide an initialized daily homework assignment sheet; (f) repeat and simplify instructions as necessary for in-class and homework assignments; (g) use behavioral management techniques, such as frequent positive reinforcement and especially sending good notes home periodically; and (h) use a more detailed checklist of the accommodations as provided along with this report.

3. School consultation to help teachers and other school personnel implement some of the accommodations as recommended.

4. Parent behavioral counseling to provide more consistent and effective discipline by both C.P.'s mother and father. It is clear that his mother has had more conflicts and difficulties in managing his behavior, but there are also discrepancies between how each will handle C.P.'s behavior. Consultation regarding effective behavioral techniques, as well as effective communication procedures, would be recommended.

NEUROPSYCHOLOGICAL/PSYCHOLOGICAL
TEST SCORE SUMMARY SHEET

NAME: C.P.S.

BIRTHDATE: 1/17/82

AGE: 14 years 6 months

DATE TESTED: 7/3/96

PARENTS: Mr. & Mrs. S.

EXAMINER: G. L. Flick, Ph.D.

WISC-III	S.S.	RANGE
Verbal	118	High Average
Performance	100	Average
Full Scale	110	High Average

VERBAL SCALES		PERFORMANCE SCALES	
Information	13	Picture Completion	10
Similarities	14	Picture Arrangement	15
Arithmetic	9	Block Design	8
Vocabulary	15	Object Assembly	10
Comprehension	14	Coding	7
SUM SS	**65**	**SUM SS**	**50**

WRAT-3	SS	%	GRADE
Reading	120	91	Post H.S.
Spelling	102	55	8
Arithmetic	89	23	6

GORDON DIAGNOSTIC SYSTEM (GDS)*		
Delay	Efficiency Ratio	0.93 (N)
Vigilance Task	Correct Responses	45 (N)
	Commission Errors	0 (N)
Distractibility Task	Correct Responses	25 (B)
	Omission Errors	2 (N)

* N = Normal Range, B = Borderline

Beery VMI: Age Equivalent <u>11-3</u>   % <u>25</u>   Scaled Score   <u>8</u>
PPVT-R: SS <u>117</u>   % <u>87</u>   Age Equivalent <u>22</u>

BROWN SCALES

Total Raw Score	86

Scales	T-Scores
Activating to Tasks	76
Sustaining Attention	59
Sustaining Effort	83
Managing Affect	63
Working Memory	88
TOTAL SCORE	**76**

CONNERS PARENT RATING SCALE

	Mother	**Father**
Conduct Problems	70	60
Learning Problems	75	66
Psychosomatic	76	50
Anxiety	40	40
Hyperactivity Index	55	46

BASC SCALES (Parent) M/F

Caution Index	**Raw Score**		**Comment**
F	2		Caution
Response pattern	69		Acceptable
Consistency	13		Acceptable

Scales	**T-Score**	**%**	**Sig. Level**
Hyperactivity	49	50	NS
Aggression	55	74	NS
Conduct Problems	66	92	NS
Anxiety	53	69	NS
Depression	45	34	NS
Somatization	76	98	0.05
Atypical			

ADHD TEST (Mother)	SS	%
Hyperactivity	10	50
Impulsivity	6	99
Inattention	12	75
ADHD QUOTIENT	96	39

MILLON ADOLESCENT CLINICAL INVENTORY

High Point Scores (Categories)		BR
Modifying Indices	WNL	—
Personality Patterns	Oppositional	69
	Submissive	69
	Dramatizing	69
	Conforming	67
Expressed Concerns	Sexual Discomfort	54
	Social Insensitivity	51
	Family Discord	50
Clinical Syndrome	Anxious Feelings	61
	Delinquent Predisposition	43
	Depressive Affect	32

ADHD History Grid (all rated from 3rd grade on)

Paying Attention
Completing Classwork
Sloppy Handwriting

Conflict Behavior Questionnaire

M = 5	F = 2	CP/M = 3	CP/F = 1

Issues Checklist

Number of Issues	M = 5	F = 2	CP = 1

Appendix 12

ACCOMMODATIONS FOR SECONDARY EDUCATION

STUDENT _____ DATE _____

SCHOOL _____ GRADE _____

We have listed below many of the school-based interventions that have proven effective with youngsters with ADHD and related problems. We have checked off the accommodations we believe are most relevant to the student named above. We would appreciate your considering these suggestions in planning for this student.

HOMEWORK ACCOMMODATIONS

____ Shortening homework assignments

____ Supplying daily assignment book and reminding student to use it

____ Sending home a week/month's assignments in advance

____ Giving credit for late assignments

____ Grading on content, not appearance or spelling

____ Providing a second set of textbooks to keep at home

____ Making an organizational check of assignment sheet/materials in school

____ Assigning study buddy for each class

____ Assigning peer tutor who reminds student to write down assignment

____ Providing teacher consultant to assist with tracking homework

TEST-TAKING ACCOMMODATIONS

____ Direct training in SQ4R method for test preparation

____ Permit extra time during tests

____ Let student take test in nondistracting environment

____ Arrange for oral testing

____ Let student demonstrate competence through an alternative modality

____ Permit short breaks during tests

____ Use short, frequent quizzes instead of longer tests

____ Provide computer/word processor access during essay exams

____ Adjust grading criteria

374

___ Permit student to retake tests

___ Allow open book examinations

___ Allow take-home examinations

___ Allow approved notes as prompts for recall during test

READING COMPREHENSION

___ Providing books on tape

___ Providing student with written outline of the chapters

___ Cueing the student to remain on task during reading

___ Highlighting main ideas in the text

___ Substituting easier texts on the same topic

___ Teaching SQ4R method for reading

___ Providing reading specialist to tutor student

LESSON PRESENTATION/NOTE TAKING

___ Seat student near teacher

___ Assign student to a low-distraction work area

___ Slow down rate of presentation of lecture

___ Pause frequently during lecture to give student chance to take notes

___ Repeat information often

___ Summarize information often

___ Verbally emphasize key points for note taking

___ Write key points on board

___ Make sure lecture is audible and visuals are visible

___ Give permission to tape-record lecture

___ Allow laptop computer for note taking

___ Give student copy of teacher outline/overheads

___ Have another student take notes for student

___ Allow student to attend class twice/audit before taking for credit

___ Give student feedback on his or her notes

___ Provide direct instruction in note taking

___ Stand near student when giving instructions

___ Break lecture into short segments

___ Ask student to repeat your instructions

___ Call on student often

GENERAL ORGANIZATION

___ Schedule last period study hall

___ Schedule A.M. checkin to organize for day

___ Schedule P.M. checkout to organize for homework

___ Give time to organize locker during school

___ Assist in organizing binder/notebook/backpack

___ Train in time management

___ Prompt students to use calendar, planner

___ Permit student to bring backpack to each class

MOTIVATIONAL TECHNIQUES

___ Increase frequency of feedback in the following classes _____

___ Send weekly progress note home

___ Institute behavioral contracting

___ Schedule regular meetings with student, parents, teachers, administrators

___ Schedule in-school suspension

___ Provide special activities in school (computers, internet, hobbies)

ADDITIONAL SUPPORT

___ Peer tutoring

___ Learning resource center (regular or special education)

___ Librarian assistance

___ Teacher consultant services

___ Meetings with teachers before or after school

___ Hand scheduling of courses

___ Case manager assigned to oversee plan

PARENT INVOLVEMENT

___ Parent conferences. Frequency _____

___ Parental involvement in selecting teachers for next year

INPUT TO MEDICAL/THERAPEUTIC SUPPORT

___ Provide narrative log of significant events

___ Complete teacher ratings as follows _____

___ Look for following medication side effects _____

___ Administer medication as prescribed

___ Remind student to go to office to take medication

___ Check to see if medication is wearing off too soon

Thank you for your assistance.

NOTE. From *ADHD in Adolescents: Diagnosis and Treatment* by Arthur L. Robin. Copyright 1998 by The Guilford Press. Used with permission.

Appendix 13—MEDICATION CHART TO TREAT ADHD

Drug	Form	Dosing	Common Side Effects	Duration of Behavioral Effects	Pros	Precautions
RITALIN® Methylphenidate	Tablets 5 mg 10 mg 20 mg	Start with a morning dose of 5 mg/day and increase up to 0.3–0.7 mg/kg of body weight. 2.5–60 mg/day*	Insomnia, decreased appetite, weight loss, headache, irritability, stomachache	3–5 hrs	Works quickly (within 30–60 minutes); effective in over 70% of patients; good safety record	Not recommended in patients with marked anxiety, motor tics, or with family history of Tourette's Syndrome
RITALIN-SR® Methylphenidate	Tablet 20 mg	Start with a morning dose of 20 mg. Increase by 20 mg as indicated. Often helps to use short-acting form in morning for quicker action as effect of SR form on behavior may be slower. Dose range up to 60 mg/day	Insomnia, decreased appetite, weight loss, headache, irritability, stomachache	7 hrs	Particularly useful for adolescents with ADHD to avoid noontime dose; good safety record	Slow onset of action (1–2 hours); use cautiously in patients with marked anxiety, motor tics, or with family history of Tourette's Syndrome
DEXEDRINE® Dextroamphetamine	Tablet 5 mg Spansules 5 mg 10 mg 15 mg	Start with a morning dose of 2.5–5 mg increase weekly by 5 mg as indicated. Tablet form often requires two or three doses each day. Daily dose range 2.5–40 mg/day	Insomnia, decreased appetite, weight loss, headache, irritability, stomachache	3–5 hrs (tablet) 7–10 hrs (spansule)	Works quickly (within 30–60 minutes); may avoid noontime dose with spansule; good safety record	Use cautiously in patients with marked anxiety, motor tics, or with family history of Tourette's Syndrome
ADDERAL® Mixed salts of a single-entity amphetamine product	Tablets 10 mg 20 mg	Start with a morning dose of 2.5 mg for 3–5 year olds. For 6 years and older start with 5 mg once or twice daily	Insomnia, decreased appetite, weight loss, headache, irritability, stomachache	3–6 hrs	Works quickly (within 30–60 minutes); action may last somewhat longer than other standard stimulants	Use cautiously in patients with marked anxiety, motor tics, or with family history of Tourette's Syndrome
CYLERT® Pemoline	Tablets (Long Acting) 18.75 mg 37.5 mg 75 mg chewable 37.5 mg	Start with a morning dose of 18.75–37.5 mg and increase up to 112.5 mg as needed in a single morning dose. Daily dose range 18.75–112.5 mg/day. Do not skip daily dosing	Insomnia, agitation, headache, stomachache; infrequently—abnormal liver function tests have been reported	12–24 hrs	Given only once a day	May take 2–4 weeks for clinical response; regular blood tests needed to check liver function. Because of this not recommended as first line medication for treatment of ADHD

Medication	Form/Dose	Dosage	Side Effects	Duration	Comments	Notes
TOFRANIL® Imipramine Hydrochloride	Tablets 10 mg 25 mg 50 mg	Start with a dose of 10 mg in evening if weight <50 lbs. and increase 10 mg every 3–5 days as indicated. Start with dose of 25 mg in evening if weight is >50 lbs. and increase 25 mg every 3–5 days as indicated. Given in single or divided doses, morning and evening. Daily dose range 25–200 mg/day. Do not skip days	Dry mouth, decreased appetite, headache, stomachache, dizziness, constipation, mild tachycardia	12–24 hrs	Helpful for ADHD patients with co-morbid depression or anxiety; lasts throughout day	May take 2–4 weeks for clinical response; to detect pre-existing cardiac conduction defect, a baseline ECG may be recommended. Discontinue gradually
NORPRAMIN® Desipramine Hydrochloride	Tablets 10 mg 25 mg 50 mg 75 mg 100 mg 150 mg	Start with a dose of 10 mg in evening if weight <50 lbs. and increase 10 mg every 3–5 days as indicated. Start with a dose of 25 mg in evening if weight is >50 lbs. and increase 25 mg every 3–5 days as indicated. Given in single or divided doses, morning and evening. Daily dose range 25–150 mg/day. Do not skip days	Dry mouth, fatigue, sedation, weight gain or loss, headache, dizziness, constipation, mild tachycardia, tremor	12–24 hrs	Helpful for ADHD patients with co-morbid depression or anxiety; lasts throughout the day	May take 2–4 weeks for clinical response; to detect pre-existing cardiac conduction defect, a baseline ECG may be recommended. Discontinue gradually
CATAPRES® Clonidine Hydrochloride	Tablets 0.1 mg 0.2 mg 0.3 mg Patches TTS-1 TTS-2 TTS-3	Start with a dose of .025–.05 mg/day in evening and increase by similar dose every 3–7 days as indicated. Given in divided doses 2–4 times per day. Daily dose range 0.1–.3 mg/day. Do not skip days	Sleepiness, hypotension, headache, dizziness, stomachache, nausea, dry mouth, localized skin reactions with patch	3–6 hrs (tablets) 5 days (skin patch)	Helpful for ADHD patients with co-morbid tic disorders or severe hyperactivity and/or aggression	Sudden discontinuation could result in rebound hypertension; to avoid daytime tiredness starting dose given at bedtime and increased slowly

*Daily dose range
**Published with permission from Specialty Press (1995) and distributed by ADD Warehouse (1-800-233-9273)

How can medication help? There is emerging evidence to suggest that individuals with attention deficit disorders may have some form of dysfunction occurring in regions of the brain associated with the control and regulation of attention, arousal, and activity. The medications charted above fall into three classes: stimulants (Ritalin, Dexedrine, Adderal, Cylert), antidepressants (Tofranil, Desipramine), and antihypertensives (Catapres). These medications have all been shown to be effective in increasing attention and reducing impulsivity and hyperactivity. However, each individual responds in their own unique way to medication depending upon the person's physical make-up, severity of symptoms, and other possible problems accompanying the ADD. Therefore, careful monitoring should be done by a physician in collaboration with the teacher, therapist, parents, and patient.

Medications to treat attention deficit disorders and related conditions should only be prescribed by a physician. Information presented here is not intended to replace the advice of a physician.

Appendix 14

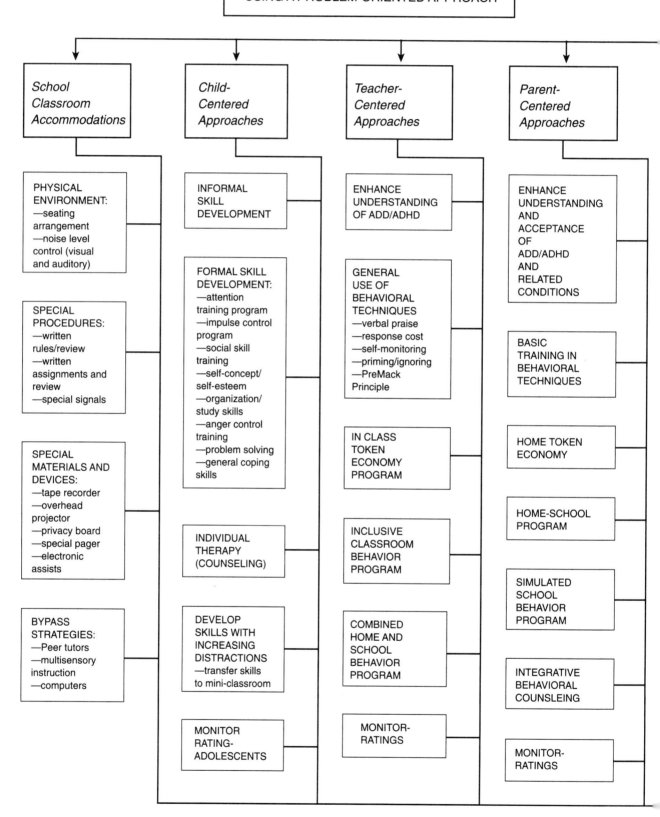

TREATMENT OPTIONS FOR ADD/ADHD USING A PROBLEM-ORIENTED APPROACH

School Classroom Accommodations

PHYSICAL ENVIRONMENT:
—seating arrangement
—noise level control (visual and auditory)

SPECIAL PROCEDURES:
—written rules/review
—written assignments and review
—special signals

SPECIAL MATERIALS AND DEVICES:
—tape recorder
—overhead projector
—privacy board
—special pager
—electronic assists

BYPASS STRATEGIES:
—Peer tutors
—multisensory instruction
—computers

Child-Centered Approaches

INFORMAL SKILL DEVELOPMENT

FORMAL SKILL DEVELOPMENT:
—attention training program
—impulse control program
—social skill training
—self-concept/ self-esteem
—organization/ study skills
—anger control training
—problem solving
—general coping skills

INDIVIDUAL THERAPY (COUNSELING)

DEVELOP SKILLS WITH INCREASING DISTRACTIONS
—transfer skills to mini-classroom

MONITOR RATING-ADOLESCENTS

Teacher-Centered Approaches

ENHANCE UNDERSTANDING OF ADD/ADHD

GENERAL USE OF BEHAVIORAL TECHNIQUES
—verbal praise
—response cost
—self-monitoring
—priming/ignoring
—PreMack Principle

IN CLASS TOKEN ECONOMY PROGRAM

INCLUSIVE CLASSROOM BEHAVIOR PROGRAM

COMBINED HOME AND SCHOOL BEHAVIOR PROGRAM

MONITOR-RATINGS

Parent-Centered Approaches

ENHANCE UNDERSTANDING AND ACCEPTANCE OF ADD/ADHD AND RELATED CONDITIONS

BASIC TRAINING IN BEHAVIORAL TECHNIQUES

HOME TOKEN ECONOMY

HOME-SCHOOL PROGRAM

SIMULATED SCHOOL BEHAVIOR PROGRAM

INTEGRATIVE BEHAVIORAL COUNSLEING

MONITOR-RATINGS

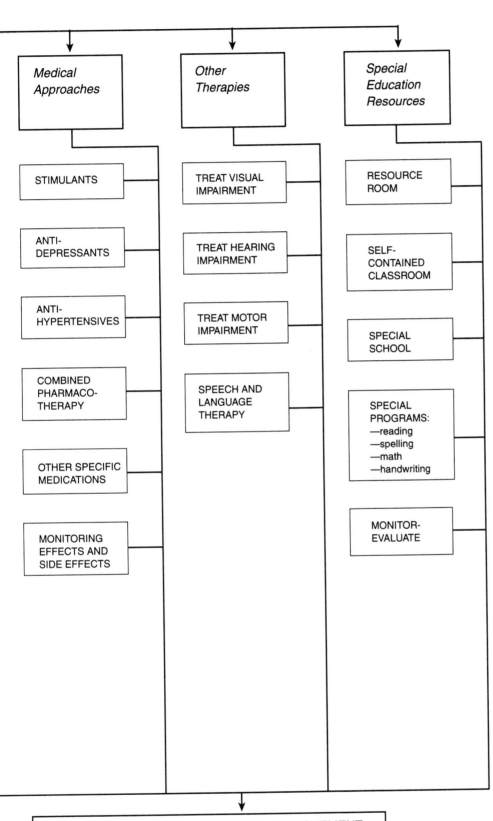

Medical Approaches	Other Therapies	Special Education Resources
STIMULANTS	TREAT VISUAL IMPAIRMENT	RESOURCE ROOM
ANTI-DEPRESSANTS	TREAT HEARING IMPAIRMENT	SELF-CONTAINED CLASSROOM
ANTI-HYPERTENSIVES	TREAT MOTOR IMPAIRMENT	SPECIAL SCHOOL
COMBINED PHARMACO-THERAPY	SPEECH AND LANGUAGE THERAPY	SPECIAL PROGRAMS: —reading —spelling —math —handwriting
OTHER SPECIFIC MEDICATIONS		MONITOR-EVALUATE
MONITORING EFFECTS AND SIDE EFFECTS		

RE-EVALUATE CHILD'S NEEDS WITH IMPROVEMENT AND/OR AS ADDITIONAL PROBLEMS MAY DEVELOP

Appendix 15

CLINICIAN'S GUIDE

OVERVIEW OF CLINICAL PROCEDURES

1. Obtain background information and present problems from parents.
2. Give rating scales/questionnaires to parents.
3. Intake interview with adolescent/parents.
4. Administer core assessments.
5. Send teacher ratings.
6. Collate data (ratings, testing, behavior observations).
7. Provide feedback/recommendations.
8. Establish treatment plan.
9. Write report.

PROTOCOL FOR ADHD INTAKE INTERVIEW

The clinician may obtain the most accurate information by directing questions to the adolescent first, and then obtain supporting data from the parent, guardian, sibling, or friend.

PRESENTING COMPLAINTS

1. What is the reason that you are here today? What problems do you have at home or at school?
2. Does anyone else in the family have similar problems? Did either of your parents have similar problems when they were your age?
3. When did you first start to have these problems?
4. Has anything seemed to make these problems better or worse?

SCHOOL

1. Have you had any difficulty in school with either grades or your behavior?
2. What are your best subjects? Your worst?
3. Is there anything in school that makes things better? Or worse?
4. Do you get homework? How much time do you spend on it? Do you generally complete your assignments? Do you get all your assignments written down?
5. How do you get along with other students? Do you have friends? Do you have conflicts or fights? Do you feel comfortable with other students? What do they say about you?

HOME/FAMILY

1. Who's in your family? Brothers, Sisters, Grandparents—who lives with you? What does your mother/father do? How much education does each one in the family have? What do your siblings say about you? Your parents? Other relatives?

2. What do you and your family do for fun? What do you most enjoy doing? Who do you like to be with?

3. What kind of hobbies do you enjoy? Do you have some special skills (e.g., sports, computer, etc.)?

4. Who are your friends? Do you prefer to invite them over or to go to their house? What do you enjoy doing with your friends?

PERSONAL LIFE

1. Do you have a job? How do you get along with your boss? Your co-workers? Have you had any problems on your job?

2. What do you do in your leisure time? How do you relax? Do you prefer to spend free time alone or with others?

3. If you make money or get an allowance, what do you generally do with the money? What kind of things do you buy? Do you ever save money?

4. Are you driving a car (if age appropriate)? Have you had any accidents? Speeding tickets? Parking tickets?

MEDICAL/PSYCHIATRIC INFORMATION

1. What kinds of medical problems have any of your blood relatives had or have?

2. What kind of emotional problems have any of your blood relatives had or have?

3. Has anyone in your family (i.e., blood relatives) had a problem with alcohol or drugs? Anyone get DUIs?

4. Has any blood relative in your family ever been arrested for anything other than minor traffic offenses?

5. Have you ever had any trouble with the law?

6. Has anyone in your family, including yourself, had any academic or behavioral problems in school? Any trouble with reading? Writing? Arithmetic? Spelling?

7. Has any blood relative had trouble with their temper? Has anyone (person/animal) been hurt by that person?

8. Has any blood relative had a problem of being so frightened that they had trouble going out of the house? Has anyone been described as a worrier? Anyone have panic attacks?

9. Has anyone in your family (including yourself) had any injury to their head? Were they rendered unconscious? How long? Did they have any trouble recovering from the accident?

10. Have you had any history of ear infections with high fevers? Any infections with high fevers? How high were the fevers?

11. Has anyone in the family (including yourself) had any type of epileptic seizure or convulsions? When was this discovered?

12. Has anyone in the family (including yourself) attempted suicide? How many attempts? Has anyone in your family committed suicide?

KEY QUESTIONS FOR ASSESSING
COMORBIDITY/DIFFERENTIAL DIAGNOSIS

NAME OF ADOLESCENT _____ DATE _____

NAME OF RESPONDENT _____

Please respond to each of the following questions by circling YES or NO.

OPPOSITIONAL DEFIANT DISORDER

1. Which of the following negativistic, hostile, and defiant behaviors is your adolescent currently exhibiting, and has he or she been exhibiting them for at least 6 months? (Circle YES if the behavior occurs now and has occurred for at least 6 months.)

a. Often loses temper	YES	NO
b. Often argues with adults	YES	NO
c. Often actively defies or refuses to comply with adults' requests or rules	YES	NO
d. Often deliberately annoys people	YES	NO
e. Often blames others for his or her mistakes or misbehavior	YES	NO
f. Is often touchy or easily annoyed by others	YES	NO
g. Is often angry and resentful	YES	NO
h. Is often spiteful or vindictive	YES	NO

CONDUCT DISORDER

2. Which of the following behaviors is your adolescent currently exhibiting, and has your adolescent been exhibiting for the past 6–12 months? (Circle YES if behavior is currently exhibited and has occurred over the past 6–12 months.)

AGGRESSION TO PEOPLE AND ANIMALS

a. Often bullies, threatens, or intimidates others	YES	NO
b. Often initiates physical fights	YES	NO
c. Has used a weapon that can cause serious physical harm to others (e.g., a bat, brick, broken bottle, knife, gun)	YES	NO

d. Has been physically cruel to people	YES	NO
e. Has been physically cruel to animals	YES	NO
f. Has stolen while confronting a victim (e.g., mugging, purse snatching, extortion, armed robbery)	YES	NO
g. Has forced someone into sexual activity	YES	NO

DESTRUCTION OF PROPERTY

h. Has deliberately engaged in fire-setting with the intention of causing serious damage	YES	NO
i. Has deliberately destroyed others' property (other than by fire-setting)	YES	NO

DECEITFULNESS OR THEFT

j. Has broken into someone else's house, building, or car	YES	NO
k. Often lies to obtain goods or favors or to avoid obligations (i.e., "cons" others)	YES	NO

MOOD DISORDERS

3. In the past month, has your adolescent felt or acted depressed, most of the day, every day, for any period of time?	YES	NO
4. If YES, did the depressed mood last at least 2 weeks?	YES	NO
5. Did the depressed mood interfere with daily functioning in school, at home, with peers, or in recreation?	YES	NO
6. Have there been any other periods of depressed mood earlier in your adolescent's life, lasting most of the day, every day, for at least 2 weeks?	YES	NO
7. Has your adolescent been depressed, most of the time, for the past year?	YES	NO
8. Has your adolescent become depressed, for several days, in response to any acutely upsetting event (e.g., breakup with boyfriend/girlfriend, failing a test, argument with you)?	YES	NO
9. Has there been any period, within the past month, when your adolescent felt or acted abnormally irritable (e.g., screaming, shouting, yelling, etc., with extreme intensity)?	YES	NO

10.	Did this period of irritability last for more than a few hours, even for days or weeks?	YES	NO
11.	Has there ever been any other period, earlier in your adolescent's life, when he or she was abnormally irritable for long periods of time?	YES	NO
12.	Has there been any period, within the past month, when your adolescent felt or acted very elated, manic, or in a high mood (not connected with drugs)?	YES	NO
13.	Did this period of elation or mania last more than a few hours, even for days or weeks?	YES	NO
14.	Has there ever been any other period, earlier in your adolescent's life, when he or she was abnormally elated, manic, or in a high mood (not connected with drugs) for long periods?	YES	NO

ANXIETY DISORDERS

15.	Has your adolescent ever had a panic attack, in which he or she suddenly felt very frightened, anxious, or extremely uncomfortable?	YES	NO
16.	Has your adolescent ever been afraid of going out of the house alone, being in a crowd, standing in line, traveling on buses, trains, or riding in cars?	YES	NO
17.	Has your adolescent ever been afraid of doing things in front of other people, like speaking, eating, or writing, or of interacting with other people?	YES	NO
18.	Has your adolescent ever been afraid of going to school (e.g., truly afraid, not trying to avoid school)?	YES	NO
19.	Has your adolescent ever been very afraid of things like flying, heights, seeing blood, thunder, lightning, closed places, animals, or insects?	YES	NO
20.	Has your adolescent ever been bothered by thoughts that didn't make any sense and kept coming back even when he or she tried not to have them?	YES	NO
21.	Has your adolescent ever had things that he or she had to do over and over again and couldn't resist (e.g., compulsive acts such as washing hands, checking something, touching things in a certain order, walking a certain way)?	YES	NO

22. Has your adolescent ever been in a very dangerous/ traumatic situation, or witnessed firsthand a very dangerous/traumatic situation? (violence, physical/ sexual abuse, accident, near-death situation, etc.)   YES   NO

23. If YES to 22, has your adolescent ever had these things come back over and over again in nightmares, flashbacks, or obsessive thoughts?   YES   NO

24. In the past 6 months, has your adolescent been generally worried, anxious, and nervous for at least half of the time (not in response to just one event)?   YES   NO

TIC/MOVEMENT DISORDERS

25. Has your adolescent ever had any tics (involuntary, rapid, recurrent movements such as eye blinking, twitches, or head turning, etc.)?   YES   NO

26. Does your adolescent ever say words or make other sounds, besides burping or hiccups, that are not intended, that keep repeating, and that he or she can't stop?   YES   NO

27. Has your adolescent ever had any unusual habits, movements, etc.?   YES   NO

EATING/SLEEP DISORDERS

28. Has your adolescent ever had a period of being under-weight? For girls, during this time, did she stop menstruating or have irregular periods?   YES   NO

29. Has your adolescent ever been afraid of getting fat or believed that he or she is fat when in reality he or she is not?   YES   NO

30. Has your adolescent ever engaged in out-of-control eating (e.g., eating a lot in a short time and feeling out of control about it)?   YES   NO

31. Has your adolescent ever gotten rid of unwanted food and calories through vomiting, using laxatives, excessive exercise, or fasting?   YES   NO

32. Does your adolescent have any difficulty with sleep (getting to sleep, staying asleep, waking up)?   YES   NO

PSYCHOTIC SYMPTOMS

33. Has your adolescent ever reported seeing, hearing, smelling, or feeling things that were not based in reality?   YES   NO

34. Has your adolescent ever reported having any of the following possibly delusional beliefs:

    a. People were taking special notice of him or her   YES   NO

    b. Receiving special messages from TV, radio, newspaper, etc.   YES   NO

    c. Feeling important and having special powers that others don't have   YES   NO

    d. Something strange happening to his or her body despite doctor finding nothing   YES   NO

    e. Feeling he or she committed a crime and should be punished   YES   NO

    f. Something external to the teenager is controlling his or her thoughts and actions against his or her will (beyond normal complaints that parents are too controlling)   YES   NO

    g. Thoughts that are not his or her own are being put into his or her head   YES   NO

    h. Thoughts are being broadcast so others can hear them   YES   NO

DRUGS/ALCOHOL

35. Does your adolescent have any problems with alcohol or drugs?   YES   NO

RESOURCES

REFERENCES

Abikoff, H.B. & Hechtman, L. (1996). "Multimodal Therapy and Stimulants in the Treatment of Children with Attention Deficit Hyperactivity Disorder." In E.D. Hibbs & P.S. Jensen (Eds.), *Psychosocial Treatments for Child and Adolescent Disorders: Empirically-Based Strategies for Clinical Practice* (341–369). Washington, DC: American Psychological Association.

Abikoff, H.B. & Klein, R.G. (1992). "Attention-Deficit Hyperactivity Disorder and Conduct Disorder: Comorbidity and Implications for Treatment." *Journal of Consulting and Clinical Psychology,* 60, 881–892.

Achenback, T.M. (1986). *Manual for the Child Behavior Checklist—Direct Observation Form.* Burlington: University of Vermont, Department of Psychiatry.

Alexander-Roberts, C. (1995). *ADHD and Teens: A Parent's Guide to Making It Through the Tough Years.* Dallas, TX: Taylor.

Amen, D.G. & Amen, A.J. (1995). *A Teenager's Guide to ADD: Understanding and Treating Attention Deficit Disorder Through the Teenage Years* (audio cassette tapes). Fairfield, CA: MindWorks Press.

Amen, A.J., Johnson, S. & Amen, D.G. (1996). *A Teenager's Guide to ADD: Understanding and Treating Attention Deficit Disorder Through the Teenage Years.* Fairfield, CA: MindWorks Press.

American Academy of Pediatrics (1996). *Diagnostic and Statistical Manual for Primary Care (DSM–PC), Child and Adolescent Version.* Elk Grove, IL: AAP.

American Psychiatric Association: *Diagnostic and Statistical Manual of Mental Disorders,* Fourth Edition. Washington, DC, American Psychiatric Association, 1994.

Anastopoulos, A.D., Barkley, R.A. & Sheldon, T.L. (1996). "Family Based Treatment: Psychosocial Intervention for Children and Adolescents with Attention Deficit Hyperactivity Disorder." In E.D. Hibbs & P.S. Jensen (Eds.), *Psychosocial Treatments for Child and Adolescent Disorders: Empirically-Based Strategies for Clinical Practice* (267–284). Washington, DC: American Psychological Association.

Anesko, K.M. & Levine, F.M. (1987). *Winning the Homework War.* New York: ARCO/Simon & Schuster.

Archer, A. & Gleason, M. (1989). *Skills for School's Success (Grades 3–6).* North Billerica, MA: Curriculum.

Arcia, E. & Conners, C.K. (1998). "Gender Differences in ADHD." *Journal of Developmental and Behavioral Pediatrics,* 19, 77–83.

Atkeson, B.M. & Forehand, R. (1979). "Home-Based Reinforcement Programs Designed to Modify Classroom Behavior: A Review of Methodological Evaluation." *Psychological Bulletin,* 86, 1298–1308.

Aylward, G.P. (1994). *Practitioner's Guide to Developmental and Psychological Testing.* New York: Plenum Medical Book Company.

Baren, M. (1996). "Advanced Pharmacotherapy for the Treatment of Children and Adolescents with ADD." Presentation at the 8th Annual Conference, CH.A.D.D., Chicago.

Barkley, R.A. (1987). *Defiant Children: A Clinician's Manual for Parent Training.* New York: Guilford Press.

_____. (1990). *Attention-Deficit Hyperactivity Disorder: A Handbook for Diagnosis and Treatment.* New York: Guilford Press.

_____. (1991). "The Ecological Validity of Laboratory and Analogue Assessment Methods of ADHD Symptoms." *Journal of Abnormal Child Psychology,* 19, 149–178.

_____. (1994). "Can Neuropsychological Tests Help Diagnose ADD/ADHD?" *ADHD Report,* 2, 1.

_____. (1994). "Impaired Delayed Responding: A Unified Theory of Attention-Deficit Hyperactivity Disorder." In D.K. Routh (Ed.), *Disruptive Behavior Disorders in Childhood* (11–57). New York: Plenum Press.

_____. (1995). *Taking Charge of ADHD: The Complete Authoritative Guide for Parents.* New York: Guilford Press.

_____. (1997). *Defiant Children: A Clinician's Manual for Assessment and Parent Training* (2nd Ed.). New York: Guilford Press.

_____. (1998). *Attention-Deficit Hyperactivity Disorder: A Handbook for Diagnosis and Treatment* (2nd Ed.). New York: Guilford Press.

_____. (1998). "The Prevalence of ADHD: Is it Just a U.S. Disorder?" *ADHD Report,* 6, 1–6.

Barkley, R.A., Anastopoulos, A.D., Guevremond, D.G. & Fletcher, K.E. (1991). "Adolescents with ADHD: Patterns of Behavioral Adjustment, Academic Functioning, and Treatment Utilization." *Journal of the American Academy of Child and Adolescent Psychiatry,* 30, 752–761.

Barkley, R.A., Fischer, M., Edelbrock, C.S. & Smallish, L. (1990). "The Adolescent Outcome of Hyperactive Children Diagnosed by Research Criteria: An Eight-Year Prospective Follow-up Study." *Journal of the American Academy of Child and Adolescent Psychiatry,* 29, 547–557.

Barkley, R.A., Edwards, G.H. & Robin, A.L. (in press). *Defiant Teens: A Clinician's Manual for Assessment and Family Training.* New York: Guilford Press.

_____. (1991). "The Adolescent Outcome of Hyperactive Children Diagnosed by Research Criteria: III. Mother–Child Interactions, Family Conflicts, and Maternal Psychopathology." *Journal of Child Psychology and Psychiatry,* 32, 233–255.

Barkley, R.A., Guevremont, D.G., Anastopoulos, A.D., DuPaul, G.J. & Shelton, T.L. (1993). "Driving-Related Risks and Outcomes of Attention Deficit-Hyperactivity Disorder in Adolescents and Young Adults: A 3- to 5-year Follow-up Survey." *Pediatrics,* 92, 212–218.

Barkley, R.A., Guevremont, D.G., Anastopoulos, A.D. & Fletcher, K.E. (1992). "A Comparison of Three Family Therapy Programs for Treating Family Conflict in Adolescents with Attention-Deficit Hyperactivity Disorder." *Journal of Consulting and Clinical Psychology,* 60, 450–462.

Bellak, L. (1985). "ADD Psychosis as a Separate Entity." *Schizophrenia Bulletin,* 11, 523–527.

Biederman, J., Faraone, S.V., Kennan, K., et. al. (1992). "Further Evidence for Family-Genetic Risk Factors in Attention-Deficit/Hyperactivity Disorder Veterans of Co-morbidity and Probands and Relatives in Psychiatrically and Pediatrically Preferred Samples." *Archives of General Psychiatry,* 49, 728, 728–738.

Biederman, J., Faraone, S.V., Mick, E., Wozniak, H., Chen, L., Oullete, C., Marrs, A., Moore, P., Garcia, J., Mennin, D. & Lelon, E. (1996). "Attention-Deficit Hyperactivity Disorder and Juvenile Mania: An Overlooked Comorbidity?" *Journal of the American Academy of Child and Adolescent Psychiatry,* 35, 997–1008.

Biederman, J., Faraone, S.V., Milberger, S., Curtis, S., Chen, L., Marrs, A., Oullette, B.A., Moore, P. & Spencer, T. (1996). "Predictors of Persistence and Remission of ADHD Into Adolescence: Results from a Four-year Prospective Follow-Up Study." *Journal of the American Academy of Child and Adolescent Psychiatry,* 35, 343–351.

Biederman, J., Faraone, S.V., Milberger, S., Guite, J., Mick, E., Chen, L., Mennin, D., Marrs, A., Oullette, C., Moore, P., Spencer, T., Nomran, D., Wilens, T., Kraus, I. & Perrin, J. (1996). "A Prospective 4-year Follow-up Study of Attention-Deficit Hyperactivity and Related Disorders." *Archives of General Psychiatry,* 53, 437–446.

Bodine, R.J., Crawford, D.K. & Schrumpf, F. (1994). *Creating the Peaceable School: A Comprehensive Program for Teaching Conflict Resolution* (text/student manual). Champaign, IL: Research Press.

Bowen, J., Fenton, T. & Rappaport, L. (1990). "Stimulant Medication and Attention-Deficit Hyperactivity Disorder: The Child's Perspective." *American Journal of Diseases of Childhood,* 145, 291–295.

Bowring, M. & Kovacs, M. (1992). "Difficulties in Diagnosing Manic Disorders Among Children and Adolescents." *Journal of American Academy of Child and Adolescent Psychiatry,* 31, 611–614.

Bracy, B.L. (1983–1993). *Soft Tools.* Indianapolis: Neuroscience Publishers.

Bramer, J.S. (1996). *Succeeding in College with Attention Deficit Disorders: Issues and Strategies for Students, Counselors, and Educators.* Plantation, FL: Specialty Press, Inc.

Brown, R.T. & Sexson, S.B. (1988). "A Controlled Trail of Methylphenidate in Black Adolescents: Attention, Behavioral, and Physiological Effects." *Clinical Pediatrics,* 27, 74–81.

Campbell, S.B. (1990). *Behavior Problems in Preschool Children: Clinical and Developmental Issues.* New York: Guilford Press.

Carey, W.B. & McDevitt, S.C. (1995). *Coping with Children's Temperament: A Guide for Practitioners.* New York: Basic Books.

Carlson, C.L., Pelham, W.E., Milich, R. & Dixon, J. (1992). "Single and Combined Effects of Methylphenidate and Behavior Therapy of the Classroom Performance of Children with Attention-Deficit/Hyperactivity Disorder." *Journal of Abnormal Child Psychology, 20,* 213–232.

Carlson, G.A. (1990). "Annotation: Child and Adolescent Mania—Diagnostic Considerations." *Journal of Child Psychology and Psychiatry, 37,* 331–341.

Chamberlain, P. (1996). "Intensified Foster Care: Multi-Level Treatment for Adolescents with Conduct Disorders in Out-of-Home Care." In E.D. Hibbs & P.S. Jensen (Eds.), *Psychosocial Treatments for Child and Adolescent Disorders: Empirically-Based Strategies for Clinical Practice* (475–496). Washington, DC: American Psychological Association.

Chelune, G.J., Ferguson, W., Koon, R. & Dickey, T.O. (1986). "Frontal Lobe Disinhibition in Attention-Deficit Disorder." *Child Psychiatry and Human Development, 16,* 221–234.

Clark, Lynn S. (1985). *S.O.S.! Help for Parents.* Bowling Green, OH: Parents Press.

Cohen, M.D. (1999). *Summary of IDEA Section 504* (Revised). Plantation, FL: CH.A.D.D.

Colby, C.L. (1991). "The Neuroanatomy and Neurophysiology of Attention." *Journal of Child Neurology, 6,* 90–118.

Conger, J.J. (1977). *Adolescence and Youth: Psychological Development in a Changing World.* New York: Harper.

Conners, C.K. (1995). *Conners Continuous Performance Test version 3.0 User's Manual.* North Tonawanda, NY: Multi-Health Systems.

Coons, H.W., Klorman, R. & Borgstedt, A.D. (1987). "Effects of Methylphenidate on Adolescents with a Childhood History of Attention Deficit Disorder: II. Information Processing." *Journal of the American Academy of Child and Adolescent Psychiatry, 26,* 368–374.

Davis, L., Sirotowitz, S. & Parker, H.G. (1996). *Study Strategies Made Easy.* Plantation, FL: Specialty Press.

DuPaul, G.J. & Stoner, G. (1994). *ADHD in the Schools: Assessment and Intervention Strategies.* New York: Guilford Press.

Evans, S.W. & Pelham, W.E. (1991). "Psychostimulant Effects on Academic and Behavioral Measures for ADHD Junior High Students in a Lecture Format Classroom." *Journal of Abnormal Child Psychology, 19,* 537–552.

Evans, S.W., Pelham, W.E. & Grudberg, M.V. (1995). "The Efficacy of Notetaking to Improve Behavior and Comprehension of Adolescents with Attention Deficit Hyperactivity Disorder." *Exceptionality, 5,* 1–17.

Faraone, S.V., Biederman, J., Keenan, K. & Tsuang, M.T. (1991). "A Separation of DSM-III Attention-Deficit Disorder and Conduct Disorder: Evidence from a Family-Genetic Study of American Child Psychiatric Patients." *Psychological Medicine,* 21(1), 109–121.

Findley, L.J., Barth, J.T., Powers, M.E., et. al. (1986). "Cognitive Impairment in Patients with Obstructive Sleep Apnea and Associated Hypoxemia." *Chest,* 90, 686–690.

Fine, A. & Goldman, L. (1994). "Innovative Techniques in the Treatment of ADHD: An Analysis of the Impact of EEG Biofeedback Training in a Cognitive Computer Generated Training." Paper presented at the American Psychological Association Annual Meeting, Los Angeles.

Fischer, M., Barkley, R.A., Edelbrock, C.S. & Smallish, L. (1990). "The Adolescent Outcome of Hyperactive Children Diagnosed by Research Criteria: II. Academic, Attentional, and Neuropsychological Status." *Journal of Consulting and Clinical Psychology,* 58, 580–588.

Flick, G.L. (1969). "Attention to Colorful Stimuli as a Function of Stimulus Parameters and the Level of Adaptation in Normal and Mentally Retarded Children." Unpublished doctoral dissertation. University of Miami, Coral Gables, FL.

_____. (1996). *Power Parenting for Children with ADD/ADHD: A Practical Parents' Guide for Managing Difficult Behaviors.* West Nyack, NY: The Center for Applied Research in Education.

_____. (1998). Workshop presentation on "Managing Difficult Children for Teachers." University of Southern Mississippi (Gulf Park), Long Beach.

_____. (1998). *ADD/ADHD Behavior-Change Resource Kit.* West Nyack, NY: The Center for Applied Research in Education.

_____. (1999). *Attend-O™ Volume 1: Test of Attentional Deficits (TOAD)—Manual.* Biloxi, MS: Seacoast Publications.

Ford, M.J., Poe, V. & Cox, J. (1993). "Attending Behaviors of ADHD Children in Math and Reading Using Various Types of Software." *Journal of Computing in Childhood Education,* 4(2), 183–196.

Forehand, R., Wierson, M., Frame, C., Kempton, T. & Armistead, L. (1991). "Juvenile Delinquency and Persistence: Do Attention Problems Contribute to Conduct Problems?" *Journal of Behavior Therapy and Experimental Psychiatry,* 22, 261–264.

Fowler, M. (1992). *CH.A.D.D. Educator's Manual.* Fairfax, VA: CASET Associates.

Gastfriend, D.R., Biederman, J. & Jellinek, M.S. (1985). "Desipramine in the Treatment of Attention Deficit Disorder in Adolescence." *Psychopharmacology Bulletin,* 21, 144–145.

Gephart, H.T. (1997). "A Managed Care Approach to ADHD." *Contemporary Pediatrics,* 14, 123–139.

Giles, J. (1998). *The ADDept Curriculum.* Santa Barbara, CA: CES Publications.

Goldstein, A.P. (1988). *The Prepare Curriculum: Teaching Pro-social Competencies.* Champaign, IL: Research Press.

Goldstein, S. & Goldstein M. (1990). *Managing Attention Disorders in Children.* New York: John Wiley & Sons.

Goldsworthy, R. (1998). "Technology: What Are the Possibilities?" Presentation at CH.A.D.D. 10th Annual Conference, New York.

Gordon, M. (1987). "How Is a Computerized Attention Test Used in the Diagnosis of Attention Deficit Disorder?" In J. Loney (Ed.), *The Young Hyperactive Child: Answers to Questions About Diagnosis, Prognosis, and Treatment,* 53–64. New York: Haworth Press.

Gordon, M. & Keiser, S. (1998). *Accommodations in Higher Education Under the Americans with Disabilities Act (ADA).* New York: Guilford Press.

Gordon, M., Thomason, D., Cooper, S. & Ivers, C.L. (1991). "Nonmedical Treatment of ADHD/Hyperactivity: The Attention Training System." *Journal of School Psychology,* 29, 151–159.

Greenberg, L.M. (1992). *Specificity and Sensitivity of the Test of Variables of Attention (VOVA).* Minneapolis: University of Minnesota.

Hagerman, R.J., Kempter, M. & Hudson, M. (1985). "Learning Disabilities and Attentional Problems in Boys with Fragile-X Syndrome." *American Journal of Diseases of Children,* 139, 674–678.

Hanf, C. (1969). "A Two-Stage Program for Modifying Maternal Controlling During Mother/Child Interaction." Paper presented at the meeting of the Western Psychological Association, Vancouver, British Columbia.

Hathaway, W.L. (1997). "ADHD and the Military." *ADHD Report,* 5, 1–6.

Hechtman, L.T. (1992). "Long-term Outcome in Attention-Deficit Hyperactivity Disorder." *Child and Adolescent Psychiatric Clinics of North America,* 1, 553–565.

_____. (1994). "Genetic and Neurobiological Aspects of Attention-Deficit/Hyperactive Disorder: A Review." *Journal of Psychiatry and Neuro Science,* 19 (3), 193–201.

Hechtman, L.T., Weiss, G. & Perlman, T. (1984). "Young Adult Outcome of Hyperactive Children Who Received Long-term Stimulant Treatment." *Journal of the American Academy of Child and Adolescent Psychiatry,* 23, 261–269.

Heilman, K.M., Voeller, K.K.S. & Nadeau, S.E. (1991). "A Possible Pathophysiologic Substrate of Attention-Deficit/Hyperactivity Disorder." *Journal of Child Neurology,* 6th, S76–S81.

Henggeler, S.W. & Borduin, C.M. (1990). *Family Therapy and Beyond: A Multi-Systematic Approach to Treating the Behavior Problems of Children and Adolescents.* Pacific Grove, CA: Brooks/Cole.

Henggeler, S.W., Schoenwald, S.K., Borduin, C.M., Rowland, M.D. & Cunningham, P.B. (1998). *Multisystemic Treatment of Antisocial Behavior in Children and Adolescents.* New York: Guilford Press.

Hibbs, E.D. & Jensen, P.S. (Eds.), (1996). *Psychosocial Treatments for Child and Adolescent Disorders: Empirically-Based Strategies for Clinical Practice.* Washington, DC: American Psychological Association.

Kazdin, A.E. (1996). "Problem Solving and Parent Management in Treating Aggressive and Antisocial Behavior." In E.D. Hibbs & P.S. Jensen (Eds.), *Psychosocial Treatments for Child and Adolescent Disorders: Empirically-Based Strategies for Clinical Practice* (377–408). Washington, DC: American Psychological Association.

Kendall, P.C. & Treadwell, K.R.H. (1996). "Cognitive-Behavioral Treatment for Childhood Anxiety Disorders." In E.D. Hibbs & P.S. Jensen (Eds.), *Psychosocial Treatments for Child and Adolescent Disorders: Empirically-Based Strategies for Clinical Practice* (23–42). Washington, DC: American Psychological Association.

Klorman, R., Coons, H.W. & Borgstedt, A.D. (1987). "Effects of Methylphenidate on Adolescents with a Childhood History of Attention Deficit Disorder. I. Clinical Findings." *Journal of the American Academy of Child and Adolescent Psychiatry,* 26, 363–367.

Koepke, T. (1986). "Construct Validation of the Parent–Adolescent Relationship Inventory: A Multidimensional Measure of Parent–Adolescent Interaction." Unpublished doctoral dissertation. Wayne State University, Detroit, MI.

Kotwal, D., Montgomery, D. & Burns, W. (1994). "Computer Assisted Cognitive Training for ADHD: A Case Study." Presented at the Annual Convention of the APA.

Leventhal, B. (1996). "ADHD: An Update of Psycho-pharmacotherapy." Presented at the CH.A.D.D. 8th Annual Conference, Chicago.

Levine, M. (1994). *Educational Care.* Cambridge, MA: Educators Publishing Service.

Markel, G. & Greenbaum, J. (1996). *Performance Breakthroughs for Adolescents with Learning Disabilities of ADD.* Champaign, IL: Research Press.

Miller, K.J. (1996). "Medication in Attention-Deficit/Hyperactivity Disorders." Presentation at the CH.A.D.D. 8th Annual Conference, Chicago.

Mirsky, A.F. (1987). "Behavioral and Psychophysiological Markers of Disordered Attention." *Environmental Health Perspectives,* 74, 191–199.

Moffitt, T.E. & Silva, P.A. (1988). "Self-Reported Delinquency, Neuropsychological Deficit, and History of Attention Deficit Disorder." *Journal of Abnormal Child Psychology,* 16, 553–569.

Nadeua, K. (1996). *Adventures in Fast Forward.* New York: Magination Press.

Novaco, R.W. (1975). *Anger Control: A Development and Evaluation of an Experimental Treatment.* Lexington, MA: Lexington Press.

O'Dell, S. (1974). "Training Parents in Behavior Modification: A Review." *Psychological Bulletin,* 81, 418–433.

Parker, G. (1990). "The Parental Bonding Instrument: A Decade of Research." *Social Psychiatry and Psychiatric Epidemiology,* 25, 281–282.

Parker, G., Tupling, H. & Brown, L.B. (1979). "A Parental Bonding Instrument." *British Journal of Medical Psychology,* 52, 1–10.

Parker, H.C. (1999). *Put Yourself in Their Shoes: Understanding Attention Deficit Hyperactivity Disorder.* Plantation, FL: Specialty Press.

Patterson, G.R. (1982). *Coercive Family Process.* Eugene, OR: Castalia.

Pelham, W.E., Bender, M.E., Caddell, J., Booth, S. & Moorer, S.H. (1985). "Methylphenidate in Children with Attention-Deficit Disorder." *Archives of General Psychiatry,* 42, 948–952.

Pelham, W.E. & Murphy, H.A. (1986). "Attention-Deficit and Conduct Disorders." In M. Hersen (Ed.), *Pharmacological and Behavioral Treatment: An Integrative Approach* (pp 108–148). New York: Wiley.

Phelan, T. (1998). "Lessons from the Trenches: Managing the Teen with ADD." *Attention,* 4, 44–47.

Podd, M.H., Mills, M.W. & Seelig, D.P. (1989). *A Manual for NeuroXercise™!* Published and distributed by Dr. Podd.

Rapoport, J. (1996). "Neurobiological Research Updates on Attention-Deficit Disorders." Presented at the CH.A.D.D. 8th Annual Conference, Chicago.

Rappley, M. (1996). "The Use of Methylphenidate in Michigan." *ADHD Report,* 4(3), 8–10.

Rappley, M.D., Gardiner, J.C., Jetton, J.R. & Houang, R.T. (1995). "The Use of Methylphenidate in Michigan." *Archives of Pediatric and Adolescent Medicine,* 149, 675–679.

Reif, S. (1993). *Simply Phonics—Quick and Easy.* Birmingham, AL: EBSCO Curriculum Materials.

Roberts, M.L. & Landau, S. (1985). "Using Curriculum-Based Data for Assessing Children with Attention-Deficits." *Journal of Psychoeducational Assessment.* Monograph series, Special ADHD Issue, 74–87.

Robin, A. (1990). "Training Families with ADHD Adolescents." In R. Barkley (Ed.), *Attention Deficit Hyperactivity Disorder.* New York: Guilford Press (pp 462–497).

Robin, A. & Vandermay, S. (1996). "Validation of a Measure for Adolescent Self-Report of Attention Deficit Disorder Symptoms." *Journal of Developmental and Behavioral Pediatrics,* 17, 211–215.

Robin, A.L. (1976). "Behavioral Instruction in the College Classroom." *Review of Educational Research,* 46, 313–354.

————. (1998). *ADHD in Adolescents: Diagnosis and Treatment.* New York: Guilford Press.

Robin, A.L. & Foster, S.L. (1989). *Negotiating Parent–Adolescent Conflict: A Behavioral-Family Systems Approach.* New York: Guilford Press.

Robin, A.L., Koepke, T. & Moye, A. (1990). "Multidimensional Assessment of Parent–Adolescent Relations." *Psychological Assessment: A Journal of Consulting and Clinical Psychology,* 2, 451–459.

Rosvold, H.E., Mirsky, A.F., Sarason, I., Bransome, E.D. & Beck, L.H. (1956). "A Continuous Performance Test of Brain Damage." *Journal of Consulting Psychology,* 20, 343–350.

Rourke, B.P. (1994). "Neuropsychological Assessment of Children with Learning Disabilities: Measurement Issues." From G.R. Lyon (Ed.), *Frames of Reference for the Assessment of Learning Disabilities: New Views on Measurement Issues* (475–514). Baltimore: Paul H. Brookes.

Safer, D.J. (1996). "Medication Usage Trends for ADD. In Children and Adults with Attention Deficit Disorder." *ADD and Adolescence: Strategies for Success from CH.A.D.D.* (16–18). Plantation, FL: CH.A.D.D.

Safer, D.J. & Allen, R.P. (1975). "Stimulant Drug Treatment of Hyperactive Adolescents." *Diseases of the Nervous System,* 36, 454–457.

_____. (1976). *Hyperactive Children.* Baltimore: University Park Press.

Sandford, J.A. (1995). "Improving Cognitive Behavioral Psychotherapy Treatment of ADHD and ADD Disorders with the Captain's Log™: Cognitive Training System." *Newsletter of the Society for Cognitive Rehabilitation* (Fall–Winter Issue).

Sandford, J.A. & Browne, R.J. (1988). *Captain's Log™ Cognitive System.* Richmond, VA: Brain Train, Inc.

Satterfield, J.H. & Dawson, M.E. (1971). "Electrodermal Carlics of Hyperactivity in Children." *Psychophysiology,* 8, 191–197.

Schubiner, H. (1995). *ADHD in Adolescence: Our Point of View* (videotape). Detroit: Children's Hospital of Michigan Department of Educational Services.

_____. (1996). "ADHD/Cocaine Dependence: Stimulant Trial." Grant proposal submitted to the National Institute on Drug Abuse, Washington, DC.

Shaywitz, B.A., Cohen, D.J. & Bowers, M.B. (1977). "CSF Monoamine Metabolites in Children with Minimal Brain Dysfunction: Evidence for Alteration of Brain Dopamine." *Journal of Pediatrics,* 1, 67–71.

Shaywitz, S.E. & Shaywitz, B.A. (1991). "Attention-Deficit Disorder: Diagnosis and Role of Ritalin® in Management." In L.L. Greenhill & B.B. Osman (Eds.), *Ritalin®: Theory in Patient Management* (45–67). New York: Marianne Liebert.

Snyder, M. & Hemphill, R. (1999). "Parents of Teen Drivers with ADHD: Proceed With Caution." *Attention,* Volume 5(4).

Sohlberg, M.M. & Mateer, C.A. (1987). "Effectiveness of an Attention Training Program." *Journal of Clinical and Experimental Neuropsychology,* 9, 117–130.

_____. (1989). *Introduction to Cognitive Rehabilitation: Theory and Practice.* New York: Guilford Press.

Spencer, P. (1996). "Current Concepts in Pharmacotherapy and Issues on Co-Morbidity in the Treatment of ADD in Children and Adolescents." Panel presentation at CH.A.D.D. 8th Annual Conference, Chicago.

Spires, H.A. & Stone, D.P. (1989). "The Directed Notetaking Activity: A Self-Questioning Approach." *Journal of Reading,* 33, 36–39.

Steinberg, L., Fletcher, A. & Darling, N. (1994). "Parental Monitoring and Peer Influences on Adolescent Substance Abuse." *Pediatrics,* 93, 1060–1064.

Steinberg, L., Lamborn, S.D., Darling, N., Mounts, N.S. & Dornbusch, S.M. (1994). "Over-Time Changes in Adjustment and Competence Among Adolescents from Authoritative, Authoritarian, Indulgent, and Neglectful Families." *Child Development,* 65, 754–770.

Stern, S.B. (in press). "Anger Management in Parent–Adolescent Conflict." *The American Journal of Family Therapy.*

Stoudemire, A. (1994). *Clinical Psychiatry for Medical Students* (2nd Ed.). Philadelphia: J.B. Lippincott.

Swanson, J.M., Wigal, S., Greenhill, L., Browne, R., Waslik, B., Lerner, M., Williams, L., Flynn, D., Agler, D., Crowley, K., Fineberg, E., Baren, M. & Cantwell, D.P. (1998). "Analog Classroom Assessment of Adderal in Children with ADHD." *Journal of the American Academy of Child and Adolescent Psychiatry, 37,* 519–526.

Varley, C.K. (1983). "Effects of Methylphenidate in Adolescents with Attention Deficit Disorder." *Journal of the American Academy of Child Psychiatry, 22,* 351–354.

Vincent-Roehling, P. & Robin, A.L. (1986). "Development and Validation of the Family Beliefs Inventory: A Measure of Unrealistic Beliefs Among Parents and Adolescents." *Journal of Consulting and Clinical Psychology, 54,* 693–697.

Vuchinich, S., Wood, B. & Angelelli, J. (1996). "Coalitions and Family Problem Solving in the Psychosocial Treatment of Preadolescents." In E.D. Hibbs & P.S. Jensen (Eds.), *Psychosocial Treatments for Child and Adolescent Disorders: Empirically-Based Strategies for Clinical Practice* (497–518). Washington, DC: American Psychological Association.

Walker, H.M. & Walker, J.E. (1991). *Coping With Noncompliance in the Classroom: A Positive Approach for Teachers.* Austin, TX: Pro-Ed.

Webb, D. (1987). "Discriminant and Concurrent Validity of the Structural Scales of the Parent Adolescent Relationship Questionnaire." Unpublished doctoral dissertation, University of South Carolina, Columbia.

Weinberg, W.A. & Emslie, G.J. (1991). "Attention-Deficit/Hyperactivity Disorder: The Differential Diagnosis" (Supplement). *Journal of Child Neurology, 6,* S21–S34.

West, S., McElroy, S., Strakowski, S., Keck, P. & McConville, B. (1995). "Attention Deficit Hyperactivity Disorder in Adolescent Mania." *American Journal of Psychiatry, 152,* 271–274.

Wielkiewicz, R.M. (1990). "Interpreting Low Scores on the WISC–R Third Factor: It's More Than Distractibility." *Psychological Assessment: A Journal of Consulting and Clinical Psychology, 2,* 91–97.

Wilens, T. (1996). "Chart Concepts in Pharmacotherapy and Issues in Co-Morbidity in the Treatment of ADD in Children and Adolescents." Panel presentation at CH.A.D.D. 8th Annual Conference, Chicago.

Williams, D.J. (1989). "A Process-Specific Training Program in the Treatment of Attention-Deficits in Children." Unpublished doctoral dissertation, University of Washington.

Williams, J.M. (1992). *Software for Psychological Testing in Education.* Walkersville, MD: Cool-Spring Software.

Wilson, J.M. & Marcotte, A.C. (1996). "Psychosocial Adjustment and Educational Outcome in Adolescents with a Childhood Diagnosis of Attention Deficit Disorder." *Journal of the American Academy of Child and Adolescent Psychiatry, 35,* 579–587.

Wozniak, J., Biederman, J., Kiely, K., Ablon, J.S., Faraone, S.V., Mundy, E. & Mennin, D. (1995). "Mania-like Symptoms Suggestive of Childhood-onset Bipolar Disorder in Clinically Referred Children." *Journal of the American Academy of Child and Adolescent Psychiatry,* 34, 867–876.

Zametkin, A.J., et. al. (1990). "Cerebral Glucose Metabolism in Adults with Hyperactivity of Childhood Onset." *New England Journal of Medicine,* 323, 1361–1366.

Zeigler Dendy, C.A. (1995). *Teenagers with ADD: A Parents' Guide.* Bethesda, MD: Woodbine House.

Zentall, S.S. (1985). "A Context for Hyperactivity." In K.D. Gadow & I. Bialer (Eds.), *Advances in Learning and Behavioral Disabilities* (Vol. 4, 273–343). Greenwich, CT: JAI Press.

Zimetkin, A.J. & Rapoport, J.L. (1987). "Neurobiology of Attention Deficit Disorder with Hyperactivity: Where Have We Come in 50 Years?" *Journal of the American Academy of Child and Adolescent Psychiatry,* 26, 676–686.

RECOMMENDED RESOURCES FOR TEENS

Bramer, J.S. (1996). *Succeeding in College with Attention Deficit Disorders: Issues and Strategies for Students, Counselors, & Educators.* Plantation, FL: Specialty Press.

Covey, S. (1998). *The 7 Habits of Highly Effective Teens.* New York: Fireside.

Crist, J. (1996). *ADHD: A Teenager's Guide.* King of Prussia, PA: Center for Applied Psychology.

Cummings, R. & Fisher, G. (1993). *The Survival Guide for Teenagers with LD** (*Learning Differences). Minneapolis: Free Spirit Press.

Davis, L., Sirotowitz, S. & Parker, H. (1997). *Study Strategies Made Easy: A Practical Plan for School Success.* Plantation, FL: Specialty Press.

Dendy, C.A. (1994). *Teenagers with ADD: A Parent's Guide.* Rockville, MD: Woodbine House.

Gordon, M. (1993). *I Would If I Could: A Teenager's Guide to ADHD/Hyperactivity.* DeWitt, NY: GSI Publications.

Janoner, C. (1997). *Zipper, The Kid with ADHD.* Bethesda, MD: Woodbine House.

Kelly, K. & Ramundo, P. (1993). *You Mean I'm Not Lazy, Stupid, or Crazy? A Self-Help Book for Adults with Attention Deficit Disorder.* Cincinnati, OH: Tyrell and Jerem Press.

Levine, M.D. (1990). *Keeping Ahead in School.* Cambridge, MA: Educators Publishing Service.

McCutcheon, R. (1998). *Get Off My Brain: A Survival Guide for Lazy Students.* Minneapolis: Free Spirit Press.

Nadeau, K. (1998). *Help4ADD@ High School.* Bethesda, MD: Advantage Press.

Nadeau, K. & Biggs, S.H. (1993). *Schools' Strategies for ADD Teens.* Annandale, VA: Chesapeake Psychological Publications.

Nadeau, K.G. (1994). *Survival Guide for College Students with ADD or LD.* Washington, DC: Magination Press.

Parker, A.J. (1997). *How Rude! The Teenager's Guide to Good Manners, Proper Behavior, and Not Grossing People Out.* Minneapolis: Free Spirit Press.

Parker, R.N. & Parker, H.C. (1992*). Making the Grade: An Adolescent's Struggle with Attention Deficit Disorders.* Plantation, FL: Specialty Press.

Quinn, P. (1994). *ADD and the College Student: A Guide for High School and College Students with Attention Deficit Disorder.* Washington, DC: Magination Press.

_____. (1994). *ADD and The College Student.* Washington, DC: Magination Press.

_____. (1995). *Adolescents and ADD: Gaining the Advantage.* Washington, DC: Magination Press.

VIDEOS FOR TEENAGERS

Bramer, J.S. & Fellman, W. (1997). *Success in College and Career with Attention Deficit Disorders.* Plantation, FL: Specialty Press.

Davis, L., Sirotowitz, S. & Parker, H. (1997). *Study Strategies Made Easy: A Practical Plan for School Success.* Plantation, FL: Specialty Press.

RECOMMENDED RESOURCES FOR PARENTS

Alexander-Roberts, C. (1994). *The ADHD Parenting Handbook.* Dallas, TX: Taylor Publishing.

_____. (1995). *ADHD and Teens: A Parent's Guide to Making It Through the Tough Years.* Dallas, TX: Taylor Publishing.

Anderson, W., Chitwood, S. & Hayden, D. (1990). *Negotiating the Special Education Maze: A Guide for Parents and Teachers.* Rockville, MD: Woodbine House.

Barkley, R. (1990). *Attention Deficit Hyperactivity Disorder: A Handbook for Diagnosis and Treatment.* New York: Guilford Press.

_____. (1995). *Taking Charge of ADHD: The Complete Authoritative Guide for Parents.* New York: Guilford Press.

Christenson, S.L. & Conoley, J.C. (Eds.) (1992). *Home–School Collaboration.* Silver Spring, MD: National Association of School Psychologists.

Colemann, W. (1993). *Attention Deficit Disorders, Hyperactivity and Associated Disorders: A Handbook for Parents & Professionals,* 6th Ed. Madison, WI: Calliope Books.

Conner, C. (1989). *Feeding the Brain: How Foods Affect Children.* New York: Plenum.

Copeland, E. & Love, V. (1995) *Attention, Please!* Plantation, FL: Specialty Press.

Cutler, B. (1993). *You, Your Child and Special Education: A Guide to Making the System Work.* Baltimore: Paul H. Brookes.

Dendy, C.A. (1995). *Teenagers with ADD: A Parents' Guide.* Rockville, MD: Woodbine House.

Fellman, W.R. (1997). *The Other Me: Poetic Thoughts on ADD for Adults, Kids, and Parents.* Plantation, FL: Specialty Press.

Flick, G.L. (1996). *Power Parenting for Children with ADD/ADHD: A Practical Parent's Guide for Managing Difficult Behaviors.* West Nyack, NY: The Center for Applied Research in Education.

_____. (1998). *ADD/ADHD Behavior-Change Resource Kit.* West Nyack, NY: The Center for Applied Research in Education.

Fowler, M. (1990). *Maybe You Know My Kid: A Parent's Guide to Identifying, Understanding and Helping Your Child With Attention-Deficit Hyperactivity Disorder.* New York: Birch Lane Press.

Friedman, R. & Dogal, G. (1992). *Management of Children and Adolescents with Attention Deficit Hyperactivity Disorder.* Dallas, TX: Pro-Ed.

Goldberg, R. (1991). *Sit Down and Pay Attention: Coping with ADD Throughout the Life Cycles.* Washington, DC: The PIA Press.

Goldstein, S. & Goldstein, M. (1992). *Hyperactivity: Why Won't My Child Pay Attention.* New York: Wiley-Interscience.

Goldstein, S. & Mathers, N. (1998). *Overcoming Underachievement: An Action Guide to Helping Your Child Succeed in School.* New York: John Wiley & Sons.

Gordon, M. (1991). *ADHD/Hyperactivity: A Consumer's Guide.* DeWitt, NY: GSI Publications.

Greenberg, G. & Herm, W. (1991). *Attention Deficit Hyperactivity Disorder: Questions and Answers for Parents.* Champaign, IL: Research Press.

Hallowell, E.H. (1996). *When You Worry About the Child You Love: Emotional and Learning Problems in Children.* New York: Simon and Schuster.

Hallowell, E. & Ratey, J. (1994). *Driven to Distraction: Recognizing and Coping with Attention Deficit Disorder from Childhood Through Adulthood.* New York: Pantheon.

Hartmann, T. (1993). *Attention Deficit Disorder: A Different Perception.* Navato, CA: Underwood-Miller.

Hechtman, L. & Weiss, G. (1986). *Hyperactive Children Grown Up.* New York: Guilford Press.

Ingersoll, B. & Goldstein, S. (1993). *Attention Deficit Disorders and Learning Disabilities; Realities, Myths, and Controversial Treatments.* New York: Doubleday.

Kelly, K. & Ramundo, P. (1993). *You Mean I'm Not Lazy, Stupid, or Crazy? A Self-Help Book for Adults with Attention Deficit Disorder.* Cincinnati, OH: Tyrell and Jerem Press.

Koplewicz, H.S. (1996). *It's Nobody's Fault: New Hope and Help for Difficult Children and Their Parents.* New York: Random House.

Latham, P.S. (1994). *Succeeding in the Workplace: Attention Deficit Disorder & Learning Disabilities in the Workplace.* Washington, D.C.: JKL Communications.

Latham, P. & Latham, P. (1998). *ADD and The Law,* Second Edition. Washington, DC: JKL, Communications.

Levine, M. (1990). *Keeping a Head in School.* Cambridge, MA: Educator Publishing Service.

Maxey, D. (1993). *A Different Way of Dealing with ADHD: 365 Daily Meditations for Encouragement.* Roanoke, VA: AAAD Support Groups.

_____. (1993). *How to Own and Operate an Attention Deficit Kid.* Roanoke, VA: AAAD Support Groups.

Parker, H.C. (1994). *The ADD Hyperactivity Workbook for Parents, Teachers, and Kids,* Second Edition. Plantation, FL: Specialty Press.

_____. (1999). *Put Yourself in Their Shoes: Understanding Teenagers with Attention Deficit Disorder.* Plantation, FL: Specialty Press.

Phelan, T. (1993). *Surviving Your Adolescents.* Glen Elyn, IL: Child Management.

Quinn, T. (1998). *Grandma's Pet Wildebeast Ate My Homework.* Wildwood, MO: Dunvegan Publishing.

Robin, A.L. & Weiss, S.K. (1997). *Managing Oppositional Youth: Effective, Practical Strategies for Managing the Behavior of Hard to Manage Kids and Teens!* Plantation, FL: Specialty Press.

Shur, M. & Oparah, D.C. with Anderson, B. (1997). *How to Raise and Teach a Thinking Child: Helping Young Children Think About What They Do and Why.* Plantation, FL: Specialty Press.

Silver, L. (1993). *Dr. Larry Silver's Advice to Parents on Attention Deficit Disorder.* Washington, DC: American Psychiatric Press.

Weiss, G. & Hechtmann, L.T. (1993). *Hyperactive Children Grown Up,* Second Edition. New York: Guilford Press.

Wender, P.H. (1987). *The Hyperactive Child, Adolescent, and Adult.* New York: Oxford Press.

Zeigler Dendy, C.A. (1995). *Teenagers with ADD: A Parent's Guide.* Bethesda, MD: Woodbine House, Inc.

RECOMMENDED RESOURCES FOR TEACHERS

Barkley, R. (1994). *ADHD in the Classroom: Strategies for Teachers* (video). New York: Guilford Press.

Copeland, E. & Love, V. (1990). *Attention Without Tension.* Atlanta, GA: 3 C's of Childhood.

Davis, L. & Sirotowitz, S. with Parker, H.C. (1996). *Study Strategies Made Easy.* Plantation, FL: Specialty Press.

DuPaul, G.G. & Stoner, G. (1994). *ADHD in the Schools: Assessment and Intervention Strategies.* New York: Guilford Press.

Flick, G.L. (1998). *ADD/ADHD Behavior-Change Resource Kit.* West Nyack, NY: The Center for Applied Research in Education.

_____. (1999). *Managing Difficult Behaviors in the Classroom: A Pocket Guide for Teachers.* Biloxi, MS: Seacoast Publications.

Fowler, M.C. (1992). *CH.A.D.D. Educator's Manual.* Plantation, FL: CH.A.D.D.

Goldstein, S. & Goldstein, M. (1987). *A Teacher's Guide: Attention Deficit Hyperactivity Disorder in Children.* Salt Lake City: Neurology Learning and Behavior Center.

_____. (1990). *Educating Inattentive Children* (video). Salt Lake City: Neurology Learning and Behavior Center.

McGinnis, E. & Goldstein, A.P. (1997). *Skillstreaming the Adolescent: New Strategies and Perspectives for Teaching Prosocial Skills.* Champaign, IL: Research Press.

Nadeau, K.G., Dixon, E.B. & Biggs, S.H. (1995). *Schools' Strategies for ADD Teens.* Annandale, MD: Chesapeake Psychological Publications.

Parker, H. (1992). *ADAPT: Attention Deficit Accommodation Plan for Teaching.* Plantation, FL: Specialty Press.

_____. (1992). *The ADD Hyperactivity Handbook for Schools.* Plantation, FL: Impact Publications.

Pierangelo, R. & Jacoby, R. (1996). *Parent's Complete Special Education Guide: Tips, Techniques, & Materials for Helping Your Child Succeed in School and Life.* West Nyack, NY: The Center for Applied Research in Education.

Rhode, R., Jenson, W.R. & Reavis, H.K. (1992). *The Tough Kid Book: Practical Classroom Management Strategies.* Longmont, CO: Sopris West.

Rief, S. (1993). *ADHD Inclusive Instruction and Collaborative Practice* (video). New York: National Professional Resources.

_____. (1993). *How to Reach and Teach ADD/ADHD Children.* West Nyack, NY: The Center for Applied Research in Education.

_____. (1997). *The ADD/ADHD Checklist: An Easy Reference for Parents and Teachers.* West Nyack, NY: The Center for Applied Research in Education.

Rief, S. & Heimburge, J. (1996). *How to Reach and Teach All Students in the Inclusive Classroom.* West Nyack, NY: The Center for Applied Research in Education.

Shapiro, E.S. & Cole, C.L. (1994). *Behavior Change in the Classroom: Self-Management Interventions.* New York: Guilford Press.

RECOMMENDED PROFESSIONAL RESOURCES

Benoit, M., Parker, H.C., Penrod, J.C., Restin, A. & Schmidt, C. (1995). *Why Can't Bobby Pay Attention? Current Issues and Answers in Attention-Deficit/Hyperactivity Disorder* (video). Plantation, FL: Specialty Press.

Biederman, J., Spencer, T. & Wilens, T. (1997). *Medical Management of Attention-Deficit/Hyperactivity Disorder* (video) (Parts I and II). Plantation, FL: Specialty Press.

Conners, C.K. (1996). *Attention-Deficit/Hyperactivity Disorder: Assessment and Treatment for Children and Adolescents.* New York: Multihealth Systems.

Copeland, E.D. (1991). *Medications for Attention Disorders.* Atlanta, GA: SPI Press.

Copps, S.C. (1996). *The Attending Physician.* Plantation, FL: Specialty Press.

Davis, L. & Sirotowitz, S. (1997). *Study Strategies Made Easy Video: A Practical Plan for Schools' Success.* Plantation, FL: Specialty Press.

Fisher, B.C. (1998). *Attention Deficit Disorder Misdiagnosis: Approaching ADD From a Brain–Behavior Neuropsychological Perspective for Assessment and Treatment.* Boca Raton, FL: CRC Press, L.L.C.

Flick, G.L. (1998). *ADD/ADHD Behavior-Change Resource Kit.* West Nyack, NY: The Center for Applied Research in Education.

Goldstein, S. (1996). *Managing Attention and Learning Disorders in Late Adolescence and Adulthood: A Guide for Practitioners.* New York: John Wiley & Sons.

Gordon, M. & Keiser, S. (1998). *Accommodations in Higher Education Under the Americans with Disabilities Act (ADA): A No-Nonsense Guide for Clinicians, Educators, Lawyers, and Administrators.* New York: Guilford Press.

Robin, A. (1998). *ADHD in Adolescents.* New York: Guilford Press.

ADDITIONAL RESOURCES

LEGAL RESOURCES

Hanlon, G.M. (1996). *3 R's of Special Education: Rights . . . Resources . . . Results.* Fair Haven, NJ: Advantage Media.

———. (1996). *A New IDEA for Special Education: Understanding the System and the New Law.* Fair Haven, NJ: Advantage Media.

Horovitz, I., King, T. & Meyer, E. (1993). "Legally Mandated Options Available to Children with ADHD within Public Education." *Clinical Pediatrics,* Vol. 32(11), 702–704.

Kincaid, J.M. & Simon, J.A. (1999). *Legal Insights in Higher Education for Students with Learning Disabilities and Attention Deficit/Hyperactivity Disorder.* Plantation, FL: Specialty Press.

VIDEOS FOR PARENTS AND TEACHERS

Barkley, R. (1992). *ADHD—What Can We Do?* New York: Guilford Press.

_____. (1992). *ADHD—What Do We Know?* New York: Guilford Press.

_____. (1994). *ADHD in the Classroom: Strategies for Teachers.* New York: Guilford Press.

_____. (1997). *Understanding Defiant Behavior.* New York: Guilford Press.

_____. (1997). *Managing Defiant Behavior.* New York: Guilford Press.

Berg, B. (1996). *Self Control Video Skits* (for teens). Dayton, OH: Cognitive Therapeutic.

Biederman, J., Spencer. T. & Wilens, T. (1997*). Medical Management of Attention Deficit Hyperactivity Disorder—Parts I and II.* Plantation, FL: Specialty Press.

Brooks, R. (1997). *Look What You've Done! Learning Disabilities and Self-Esteem: Stories of Hope and Resilience.* Washington, DC: WETA.

Goldstein, S. & Goldstein, M. (1989). *Why Won't My Child Pay Attention?* Salt Lake City: Neurology Learning and Behavior Center.

_____. (1990). *Educating Inattentive Children.* Salt Lake City: Neurology Learning and Behavior Center.

Lavoie, R. (1990). *How Difficult Can This Be? The F.A.T. City Workshop.* Washington, DC: WETA.

McGinnis, E. & Goldstein, A.P. (1997). *Skills Streaming Video for Students. People Skills: Doing 'em Right* (Adolescent Level). Champaign, IL: Research Press.

Phelan, T. & Bloomberg, J. (1994). *Medication for Attention Deficit Disorder: All You Need to Know.* Glen Ellyn, IL: Child Management.

Reif, S. (1993). *ADHD Inclusive Instruction and Collaborative Practices.* New York: National Professional Resources.

_____. (1997). *How to Help Your Child Succeed in School.* San Diego, CA: Educational Resource Specialists (1-800-682-3528).

_____. (1999). *Successful Classrooms: Effective Teaching Strategies for Raising Achievement in Reading and Writing.* San Diego, CA: Education Resource Specialists.

_____. (1999). *Successful Schools: How to Raise Achievement and Support "At Risk" Students.* San Diego, CA: Educational Resource Specialists.

Robin, A. (1993). *ADHD in Adolescence: The Next Step—A Video Guide for Clinical Description, Diagnosis, and Treatment of Adolescents with ADHD.* Worcester, MA: Madison Avenue Marketing.

Robin, A.L. & Weiss, S.K. (1997). *Managing Oppositional Youth. Effective, Practical Strategies for Managing the Behavior of Hard to Manage Kids and Teens!* Plantation, FL: Specialty Press.

ADD Resource Catalogs

The ADD Clinic
ADD/ADHD Resource Catalog
983 Howard Avenue
Biloxi, MS 39531
1-800-962-2673, FAX: 228-435-2674
www.the-ADD-Clinic.com

ADD Warehouse
300 Northwest 70th Avenue
Suite 102
Plantation, FL 33317
1-800-233-9273, FAX: 954-792-8545
www.addwarehouse.com

Prentice Hall/Center for Applied Research in Education
PH Resources for Educators
P.O. Box 362916
Des Moines, IA 50381-2916
FAX: 1-800-835-5327

National Professional Resources, Inc.
Dept. C95, 25 South Regent Street
Port Chester, NY 10573
914-937-8879; FAX: 914-937-9327

Council for Exceptional Children
1920 Association Drive
Reston, VA 20191-1589
1-800-328-0272
E-mail: ericec@cec.sped.org

Recordings for the Blind and Dyslexic
20 Roszel Road
Princeton, NJ 08540
1-800-221-4792 (for books on tape)

Newsletters (those with * are for kids)

ADD Forum (CompuServe)
500 Arlington Blvd.
P.O. Box 20212
Columbus, OH 43220
1-800-524-3388 (Representative 464)

The ADHD Report
Russell Barkley, Editor
Guilford Publications
72 Spring Street
New York, NY 10012
212-431-9800

ADDult News
c/o Mary Jane Johnson
ADDult Support Network
2620 Ivy Place
Toledo, OH 43613

Advance, a publication of ADDAG
8091 S. Ireland Way
Aurora, CO 80016

*BRAKES: The Interactive Newsletter for Kids with ADHD
Magination Press
19 Union Square West
New York, NY 10003
1-800-825-3089

Electronic Bulletin Boards
(a) America Online
(b) Prodigy
(c) Disabilities Forum
(d) ADD Bulletin Board

Attention (magazine)
CH.A.D.D. National Headquarters
8181 Professional Plaza, Suite 201
Landover, MD 20785
301-306-7070, FAX: 301-306-7090
http://www.chadd.org

Attention Please, **Newsletter for Children
with Attention Deficit Disorder**
2106 3rd Ave., N.
Seattle, WA 98109-2305
206-935-8303

Kids Getting You Down?
Learning Development Services
3754 Clairemont Drive
San Diego, CA 92117
619-276-6912

The Rebus Institute Report
1499 Bayshore Blvd., Suite 146
Burlingame, CA 94010

COMPUTER SOFTWARE RESOURCES

ABLEDATA
National Rehabilitation Information Center
Catholic University of America
4407 Eighth St., NE
Washington, DC 20017
202-635-5822

INTERNET RESOURCES

ADD and ADHD Infoline:
http://www.alcasoft.com/add
Information and resources put together by a family's personal experience with ADD.

ADD Resources for Adults & Teens:
http://www.surfsouth.com
General information on ADD for adults and teens.

ADD Webnet (AOL):
http://members.aol.com/addwebney/index.html
A central directory of links that connect you to sites of individuals or groups that provide information, offer support, or share insights on ADD.

ADHD News.Com:
http://www.adhdnews.com
An ADHD Newsstand—provides free newsletters—"Added Attractions."

One ADD Place:
http://www.oneaddplace.com
A "virtual neighborhood" that consolidates information and resources.

ORGANIZATIONS/SUPPORT GROUPS

Attention Deficit Disorder Association (ADDA)
P.O. Box 972
Mentor, OH 44060
888-265-8711

Attention Deficit Disorder Advocacy Group (ADDAG)
8091 South Ireland Way
Aurora, CO 80016
303-400-1619

ADDult Information Exchange Network (ADDIEN)
P.O. Box 1701
Ann Arbor, MI 48106

ADDult Support Network (for ADD Adults)
Mary Jane Johnson
2620 Ivy Place
Toledo, OH 43613

Attention Deficit Information Network (AD-IN)
475 Hillside Avenue
Needham, MA 02494
781-455-9895

Professional Group for ADD and Related Disorders (PGARD)
28 Fairview Road
Scarsdale, NY 10583
914-723-0118
914-253-6818

Children & Adults with Attention Deficit Disorders (CH.A.D.D.)
CH.A.D.D. Chapters
8181 Professional Plaza, Suite 201
Landover, MD 20785
301-306-7070, FAX: 301-306-7090
http://www.chadd.org

The Council for Exceptional Children (CEC)
1920 Association Drive
Reston, VA 20191-1589
703-620-3660

Learning Disabilities Association (LDA)
4156 Library Road
Pittsburgh, PA 15234
412-341-1515

National Network of Learning Disabled Adults (NNCDA)
808 West 82nd St., F-2
Scottsdale, AZ 85257

ADVOCACY RESOURCES

Learning Disabilities Association of America (LDA), 412-341-1515 (Pennsylvania) (State LDA Office and Local LDA Chapter)

Orton Dyslexia Society, 1-800-222-3123 (Maryland)

National Center for Learning Disabilities, 212-545-7510 (New York)

CH.A.D.D. (Children & Adults with Attention Deficit Disorders) National Office, 301-306-7070 (MD) (Ask for local chapters)

TAPP/PTI Office (Technical Assistance for Parent Programs Project/Parent Training & Information Projects). Check with your state or local LDA Office or call the Federation for Children with Special Needs, 617-482-2915 (Massachusetts).

National Association of Protection & Advocacy Systems (legal information & support), 202-408-9514 (Pennsylvania)

HEATH (National Clearinghouse on Post-secondary education for Individuals with Disabilities) 1-800-544-3284 (Washington, DC)

NICHCY (National Information Center for Children and Youth with Disabilities) 1-800-695-0285 (Washington, DC)

ERIC Clearinghouse for Handicapped and Gifted Children, Council for Exceptional Children, 703-264-9474 (Virginia); 1-800-328-0272

Office for Civil Rights (Contact your state LDA or TAPP/PTI Office)

Local Special Education Attorney

Local School Psychologist, Personnel, and Superintendent

INDEX

Association for Higher Education and
  Disabilities (AHEAD), 280
Attend-O™ Attention Training Games, 93
  Behavioral Inhibition Training, 98-101
  description of, 94
  theory behind, 95-96
Attend-O™ Volume 1. *See Test of Attentional
  Deficits (TOAD)*
Attend-O™ Volume 2, 34
Attention. *See also* Distractibility; Inattention
  assessment of skills, 30-34
  measuring, 24-25
    neuropsychological assessment and, 27
  medical conditions associated with impair-
    ment of, 49
  sustained, 95
    game to improve, 94
  teachers increasing sustained, 89
  training for improved, 93-98
    attentional games, 93, 94
    criteria for programs, 97-98
    program applications, 96-97
    theory-based, 95-96
Attention Deficit Disorder, ADHD and, 48
Attention Deficit Disorders Evaluation Scale
  Secondary-Age Student (ADDES-S), 42
Attention Deficit/Hyperactivity Disorder Test, 24
Attention Process Training (APT), 96
Attention (Response Cost) Trainer, 114-16
Attention Trainer™, 116
Audio-visual materials, using, 161
Auroix maclobemide, 84-85
Automobile accidents/citations. *See also* Driving
  issues
Automobile accidents/citations, ADHD and, 2

B

Background information
  evaluating, 19-20
  gathering for diagnosis, 43-45
Background music, 227
  in classroom, 158
Background noise. *See also* Classroom, monitoring noise in
  reducing, 111, 112-13
BASC. *See* Behavioral Assessment System for
  Children (BASC)
Basic skills, 47

Behavior Disorders Identification Scale
  (BDIS), 43
Behavior Inhibition concept, 23
Behavior penalty plan, 210-11, 212
  in classroom, 245-46
*Behavioral Assessment System for Children, The
  (BASC) Self-Report of Personality,* 23
  monitoring stimulants and, 76
Behavioral Assessment System for Children
  (BASC), 41
  monitoring medication and, 76
Behavioral characteristics, overlaps of ADHD
  and other syndromes, 48
Behavioral contract, 208, *208-9,* 210
Behavioral-emotional assessment, 35-38
Behavioral impulsivity, 3. *See also* Impulsivity
Behavioral Inhibition concept, 25
Behavioral Inhibition Training (BIT), 98-101
Behavioral interventions, 206. *See also*
  Antecedents; Behaviors; Consequences
  A-B-C program, 194-95
  antecedents, 192
  behavior and, 203-4
  behavior defined for, 192-93
  behavior penalty plans, 210-12
  behavioral contract, 208-10
  behavioral momentum, 224
  consequences and, 205
  controlling blurting out answers, 252
  controlling confusion over direction, 255-56
  controlling disorganization, 256
  controlling excess motor activity, 251-52
  controlling for attention all skills, 253-55
  controlling getting "off task," 253
  controlling homework problems, 257-58
  controlling incomplete work, 255
  controlling poor handwriting, 256-57
  controlling social-skills problems, 258
  defining consequences for, 193-94
  grounding, 212-13
  at home, 191
  ignoring behaviors and, 206-7
  instrumental behavior plans, 208
  medication and, 70, 77
  over correction with positive practice and
    restitution, 213
  point systems, 214-17, 214-23
  positive orientation, 226
  positive response program, 225-26

Minnesota Percepto Diagnostic Test, 29-30

Mistakes, learning from, 233

MMPI-A. See Minnesota Multiphasic Personality Inventory-Adolescent (MMPI-A)

Mnemonic devices, 114

Model of attentional processes, 8

Molecular genetic studies, 7

Mood Disorders, key questions for assessing co-morbidity/differential diagnosis, 385-86

Mood disturbances, as overlapping symptom of ADHD and other syndromes, 48

Mood stabilizers, 84

MotivAider™, 111

Motivation
    achievements as, 299
    adolescent development and, 16
    electronic devices for, 111-12
    poor, 16

Motor activity, controlling excess, 251-52

Motor skills. *See also* Visual-motor skills
    assessment of, 30
    fine, 5

MSCS. *See* Multidimensional Self-Concept Scale (MSCS)

Multidimensional Self-Concept Scale (MSCS), 34

Multiple impact therapies, 64

Multisystemic Therapy, 92

Music. *See* Background music

N

Narcissism, 123

Narcolepsy, 50-51

Negotiable rules, 133

Negotiating. See Conflict resolution/problem solving

Neuro-feedback devices, 298

Neuroanatomical studies, 7-9

Neurochemical studies, 9-11

Neuroleptics, 84

Neuropsychological assessments. See Assessments, neuropsychological

Neuropsychological studies, 9

NeurXercise™, 101

Noise. *See* Background noise; Classroom, monitoring noise in; White noise generators

Noisebuster Extreme®, 113

Nonadrenergic system, 9-10

Noncompliance
    in the classroom, 246-47

managing at home, 119

with medications recommendations, 80

vs. inattention, 106

Nonnegotiable rules, 133

Norpramin®, 80-82

Nortriptyline. *See* Pamelor®

Note-taking strategies, 168

O

Observations, of adolescent behavior, 22

Obsessive compulsive disorder (OCD), 59-60

Obsessive thinking, persistent, 6

Ocularmotor symptoms, 8

Office mediation, 260

Oil of Evening Primrose, 69

On-line mediation, 260

Open trial, 70

Oppositional Defiant Disorder (ODD), 58-59. *See also* Aggressive behavior; Conduct Disorder (CD); Violent behavior
    ADHD and, 1
    analysis of, 272-73
    characteristics of in adolescents, 360
    diagnostic criteria for, 357-58
    emotional impulsivity and, 121
    key questions for assessing co-morbidity/differential diagnosis, 384

Orange juice
    Ritalin and, 79
    stimulants and, 74

Organizational skills
    developing for academic success, 165-68
    lacking, 4
        adolescent development and, 16
        managing at home, 120
    training, 102-3

Organizational structure, teaching, 158, 233

Overhead projectors
    using classroom, 158, 227

Overprotection, parenting with, 130

P

Pamelor®, 80-82

Parenting strategies, 131, 316
    creating healthy family structure and orientation, 131-35
    reinforcing school behaviors with, 163-64